Freedom Over the Airwaves

Jacques Semelin

English translation of

La liberté au bout des ondes: Du coup de Prague à la chute du mur de Berlin

Nouveau Monde Éditions, 2009

Freedom
OVER THE
Airwaves

From the Czech Coup to the
Fall of the Berlin Wall

Jacques Semelin

translated by
Elizabeth Carey-Libbrecht

Foreword by Adam Roberts
Afterword by Howard Barrell

2017

Published in the United States of America in 2017 by the
International Center on Nonviolent Conflict
Under the imprint of ICNC Press
1775 Pennsylvania Ave NW, Ste 1200, Washington, DC 20006
www.nonviolent-conflict.org
© 2017 by International Center on Nonviolent Conflict. All rights reserved

Library of Congress Cataloging-in-Publication Data
A Cataloging-in-Publication Data record for this book
is available from the Library of Congress.
ISBN: 978-1-943271-07-8

Translated from French by Elizabeth Carey-Libbrecht
Publication coordination by Amber French
Cover design by David Reinbold
Printed and bound in the United States of America

English translation of *La liberté au bout des ondes: Du coup de Prague à la chute du mur de Berlin*, published by arrangement with Nouveau Monde Éditions

TABLE OF CONTENTS

Foreword by Adam Roberts	vii
Author's Preface: From the conquest of words to the conquest of images	xi
Acknowledgments	xxiii
Introduction: Communication as resistance	1

PART ONE: Radio bridges

I. War on the West-East airwaves: Media interference in practice	9
II. East-West reception: Between attraction and withdrawal	41

PART TWO: Tragedies behind closed doors

I. Reclaiming the public sphere: The first attempts (1953-1968)	69
II. The public sphere as a battlefield: Budapest, 1956 and Prague, 1968	103

PART THREE: Resisting via the West

I. The immobile battle: Gdansk, 1980	139
II. Escape: From television to the border, Berlin, 1989	179
Conclusion: The fall of the three walls	225
Afterword by Howard Barrell	233
Bibliography	263
Index	271

*"These regimes lived by the word
and perished by the word"*

—Timothy Garton Ash

FOREWORD

by Adam Roberts

From the printing press to the smartphone, communications media have continuously transformed politics and society. Yet they have not done so in any uniform or linear fashion. Sometimes the prevailing technologies have served the purposes of states and large corporations, yet at other times they have helped to create conditions for revolt and revolution. At times they have stirred up violence, at other times they have assisted non-violent movements and peaceful change. Such complex and varied roles have often been the subject of shallow analysis and simplistic generalization. Not so in the present work.

First I cannot forbear from mentioning my family and personal interest in the subject of Jacques Semelin's book. My father, Michael Roberts—teacher, writer, poet and polymath—worked in the European Service of the BBC from 1941 to 1945. In 1943-4 he held the new post of clandestine press editor, in which capacity he introduced broadcasts specifically for the editors of the clandestine press in occupied Europe; and in 1944 he headed the European Service's Czech section. So I may well have a genetic predisposition to study the connections between broadcasting and resistance. And I should add my personal declaration, that as a student of civil resistance for over half a century, I have indeed always been fascinated by the important and ever-changing roles of the media. In addition, I have also for several decades been impressed by Jacques Semelin's unique scholarly contributions to the study of civil resistance.

Freedom over the Airwaves is a highly readable, and also profound, essay on the roles of media in influencing political and social developments in the Soviet empire in the Cold War years. It concentrates on Western broadcasting to the countries of Eastern Europe, and on how this assisted movements of civil (i.e. nonviolent) resistance there. The focus is particularly, but not exclusively, on three countries: Czechoslovakia, Poland and East Germany. In all three cases, Western radio and television, even though heavily jammed, had a significant influence. The best witnesses, namely the men and women within these countries who were involved in one way or another in the end of communist rule there, testified to it.

So you might think, or even fear, that this book is a love-poem to the alphabet soup of anti-communist broadcasters of the Cold War years? Not a bit of it. Semelin is tough in his analysis of the various approaches taken by VOA, BBC, RIAS, RFE, Radio Liberty, and Vatican Radio. He points to the obvious bias of Voice of America, which was quick to condemn communist sins but could not bring itself to mention human rights violations in Chile or other US-favored countries. He is blunt about the CIA role in Radio Liberty. He notes how only in 1956–7 did Radio Free Europe finally reach some clarity that it should support gradual change, not violent insurrection. He emphasizes how the managers and staff often had little knowledge of the countries to which they were broadcasting. He is critical of the weak French performance, but he also notes that West German radio and TV stations had a subtle approach to broadcasting to their compatriots in the East.

What Semelin shows convincingly is that all this involved something vastly more complex than the vision of the truth being broadcast in the West and received by grateful listeners in the East. Firstly, there was always the risk of the broadcasters, whether or not drawn from émigré populations, being out of touch with changed conditions in the target country. Secondly, not all the intended recipients were grateful: for example, and in contrast to their colleagues in Gdansk, workers in Stettin were nervous about contact with Western media. And thirdly, there was also an East–West–East process going on, as information provided by such bodies as Charter 77 in Czechoslovakia and Solidarity in Poland reached Western broadcasters and then was beamed back in. More generally, audience feedback encouraged the stations to broaden their output, and even to represent different points of view. There were also other processes going on. Semelin mentions the interesting phenomenon of leading communists in communist countries tuning in to Western radio stations. This tallies with my own experience. I well remember in 1971, on my first visit to Poland, being quietly informed by a member of the Central Committee of the Polish United Workers' Party that all his fellow CC members listened daily to the news on Radio Free Europe. That was something that can hardly have been in the CIA's original script.

As Semelin says, the impact of Western radio in the Cold War years is hard to measure, and cannot be reduced to the assumed size of the audience. He does a wonderful job of suggesting the many ways in which it did influence events. Above all, it helped to ensure that totalitarian leaders were not, in Raymond Aron's apt phrase, 'left alone with their peoples'.

This book's central purpose is to explore the many links between these information media and civil resistance. This is not a completely new subject. Civil resistance movements have often depended on new media. A clear early example is the way in which, in the 1960s, the US civil rights movement made clever use of TV reporting of police outrages against demonstrators in southern cities. Another astute use of media was the French government's response when, in April 1961, four retired French generals seized power in a *coup d'état* in Algiers in an attempt to keep Algeria French. President de Gaulle memorably used broadcast media to appeal to the troops over the heads of their senior officers. The French soldiers serving in Algeria, most of whom were conscripts, listened to de Gaulle on the new technology of the day—the transistor radio—and refused cooperation with the coup's leaders. This case of civil resistance by soldiers was sometimes called 'la victoire des transistors'.

Jacques Semelin provides a detailed account of, and theoretical framework for understanding, the role the media played in successful civil resistance in Eastern Europe. As he shows, Western radio stations made several distinct contributions to civil resistance, and more generally to the larger processes of political change there. But they did not do so alone. He emphasizes the key roles played by domestic media *within* the countries concerned—whether it was the astonishing performance of Czechoslovak Radio in the first week of the Soviet-led invasion in August 1968, or the use of internal communications systems in the Lenin Shipyard in Gdansk. That these things could happen at all in supposedly totalitarian states was an indicator of something deeper that was going on in Eastern Europe and the Soviet Union—the slow disintegration of communism. The decline of faith in Communist Party rule had been particularly marked in Eastern Europe, even in East Germany. That—alongside the Helsinki process and the rise of Gorbachev to power in the Soviet Union—provides a good part of the explanation of why in 1989 civil resistance could have such remarkable success, in ushering out communist rulers in most of Eastern Europe.

In the years since the end of the Cold War, and particularly since 1997, when this book was first published in France, there has been a great deal more experience of the role of the media vis-à-vis campaigns of civil resistance. Already in August 1991 the resistance to the last-ditch communist *coup d'état* in Moscow (an episode outside the geographical and temporal scope of this particular work by Semelin) had shown that civil resistance had spread further since the revolutions of 1989. The demonstrations in Serbia in 2000 that finally unseated President Milosevic, the 'Rose revolution' in Georgia in 2003, and the 'Orange revolution' in Ukraine the following year, all confirmed this conclusion. Often, as in Belgrade, local broadcasting stations, which had supported the regime, were the targets of demonstrators. Increasingly in these cases, mobile phones and the internet enabled opposition groups to organize effectively. Then, in 2011, came the Arab Spring, in which information flows of all kinds were key factors in a chain of revolutions that encompassed Tunisia, Yemen and a great many other countries in the region. But in many countries the Arab Spring was followed by disasters, including lawlessness, civil wars, terrorism, and reversion to authoritarian rule.

In a remarkable Afterword that is included in this book, Howard Barrell discusses the many developments since the end of the Cold War. He does so in an exemplary manner, and in the spirit of Jacques Semelin. He notes the emergence in Myanmar/Burma of a technique of systematically smuggling out video footage to be broadcast back into the country. However, drawing on his own extensive experience with African National Congress of South Africa in the 1980s, he is rightly critical of the simple view, widely canvassed during the Arab Spring, that the building of political networks can be all-digital. He astutely observes that the most valuable of the media studies of the Arab Spring are the ones that are most restrained in their conclusions. He faces up to the failure of many Arab Spring movements, with the exception of that in Tunisia, to follow up deposition of a hated dictator with the creation of a new political order. His conclusion about all these events, and about Semelin's book, is one I share:

> When, however, we return in years to come to examine the uprisings of 2011 in Arab lands we will likely be asking the same basic questions of those who were involved in them as one tends to ask of any group of would-be revolutionaries: How did those involved read their circumstances in their attempt to exercise agency? How accurate was their reading? And how plausible were the strategy and tactics with which they sought to exercise agency? Few if any group of action takers have read their moment and their circumstances with more wisdom and skill than those who led the democratization of Eastern Europe from the streets and shipyards in the late 1980s. And few, if any, have achieved such considerable revolutionary success at such low cost. Their genius was particularly evident in Poland and Czechoslovakia. Although, in years to come, technologies, their possibilities and constraints will again have changed, the road to understanding radical democratization and the role of media in achieving it is likely still to lead through Gdansk, Prague, Budapest and Berlin—and I doubt there will yet be a map better than the one provided by Jacques Semelin.

—*Adam Roberts*
Oxford, July 2016

AUTHOR'S PREFACE:
From the conquest of words to the conquest of images

Twenty years have already passed since the unbelievable was achieved: on the night of November 9 to 10, 1989 the "wall of shame" separating the two Germanys, and thus the two Europes, suddenly collapsed in a climate not of fear and war, but of joy and celebration! Do today's young generations have any idea just how unpredictably powerful that extraordinary event was? Visiting Prague, Sofia, Bucharest or Tallinn is easy today; in the 1980s it was far less so. Anyone traveling to Eastern Europe—from the West—had the impression of entering another world, one in which an entirely different mindset prevailed: the other side of the Wall. We Westerners had mentally integrated the strategic partitioning of the continent: the Wall was firmly entrenched in our minds. Yet right here, in Paris, the Czech writer Milan Kundera tried to tell us that Prague, like the rest of central Europe, was a kidnapped West.[1] From the experts in strategy we heard that this division of Europe was going to last for decades. As it was the keystone of international security, destabilizing it could trigger a new world war, so that change could but be slow and gradual, step by step, through cultural and economic cooperation.

In 1989 history belied all these superficial foresights in one fell swoop. History? It had already struck hard in this part of the world in 1980. Whereas in those days time had seemed to have come to a standstill in most of the region, a mass movement erupted in Poland: an unexpected, acute provocation of the advocates of "real socialism" launched in Gdansk by striking Baltic shipyard and dock workers of the Solidarity movement (Solidarnösc). Their main, extremely audacious goal was the creation of an independent trade union in a communist state, that is, a country supposedly governed by the "workers' party." Was the Soviet "big brother" once again going to stamp out this breath of freedom, as it had already done by repressing the Hungarian uprising in 1956 and the "Prague Spring" in 1968? No, the unbelievable actually happened. Instead of that catastrophic scenario, on August 31, 1980 the Gdansk workers and their leader Lech Walesa secured an unprecedented victory in Eastern Europe: the creation of a trade union that was independent of the communist state; a free union that went by the same name as their movement, Solidarnösc. Most importantly, this event, relayed by media across the world, was the birth—or rebirth—of a hope for change in the East, finally accomplished less than 10 years later. The events of 1989, which spread throughout Central Europe, can be understood only if we bear in mind this political earthquake in 1980 in Poland.

Yet at one stage the communist authorities seemed to have won back control. On December 13, 1981, Polish General Jaruzelski instituted martial law in the country and thousands of Solidarnösc members were jailed. Once again, all hopes of change were shattered. On a visit to Poland in 1985, I was able to witness just how disillusioned people were regarding the tense situation in their country. This was clearly apparent in a secret interview with Bronislaw Geremek, where he expressed his concern about the future should the Polish authorities refuse to show any tangible signs of opening up to change.[2]

During that visit one fact did nevertheless strike me: to obtain information on their own country, and thus to defy the propaganda of the official media, almost all opponents of the regime regularly listened to Western radio stations. Working at the time on various examples of civil resistance in Nazi-dominated Europe, and on the way in which the BBC had echoed—even amplified—it,[3] I immediately saw an historical continuum. In communist Poland, people three generations later were still in the habit of tuning into the Polish service of the BBC, as they had under Nazi occupation! Of course the conditions in which they did so had changed profoundly, for in 1985 the risk was no longer what it had been in 1939. Notwithstanding the differences in the historical situations, the fact of listening to Western radio was inspired by the same wish to obtain news deemed to be truthful, from foreign sources. During that trip I learned that two other radio stations, the Voice of America and Radio Free Europe, were equally popular. In the evenings, in the intimacy of their homes, people switched from station to station to get an idea of the day's news. The exercise was sometimes disappointing, when the sound was poor, as some of these radio stations' programs were jammed. Yet many persisted in their efforts to capture what they perceived to be the voices of the "free world." At a time when their spirits tended to flag, this way of tapping into the West seemed to give them some hope, even though they were aware that the foreign stations also broadcast a form of propaganda. As few researchers had analyzed this phenomenon, I decided to explore it. At that stage it was still a vague project, one among many others. Only after the events of 1989 did I become more aware, with hindsight, of the importance of the role of communication and the use of the media throughout the history of attempted resistance in the "communist bloc."

I would like to take the opportunity afforded by the publication of the French edition of this book in paperback, to re-examine this research itinerary. The subject is, I believe, fundamental to an understanding of the emancipation of the peoples of central Europe from the Soviet yoke, despite the importance of other factors.

When I undertook this work, the study of modes of opposition in Nazi-controlled and then Soviet Europe was of interest to me for two reasons: first, the historical interest that had taken me to Poland to investigate the amazing clandestine education movement which emerged in that country in 1939-40 (to preserve the values of Polish culture, seriously threatened by the Nazi occupiers); and, second, my interest as a citizen, which made me feel very close to Solidarnösc. I'm sure that it was this dual approach to completely different historical periods that enabled me to discover and then to work on the essential issue of relations between communication and resistance in what political science calls "non-democratic regimes." So how did I shift from one period to the other?

I decided to begin my study in the early days of the Cold War, from the late 1940s, when the United States and the USSR started to wage war over the air. The subject may seem relatively insignificant compared to the concomitant arms race and the balance of nuclear terror. Yet if we agree, as Georges-Henri Soutou pointed out, that this fifty years' Cold War was above all ideological, then the study of the transnational vehicles of confrontation between the competing ideologies is clearly essential.[4] At the end of the 1960s, we find a certain balance of power in this respect, but not from the point of view of audiences: it was one thing to broadcast towards the enemy's camp, and quite another to be listened to in that camp! In the West hardly anyone listened to programs from the communist bloc, whereas many in the East did their best to capture Western broadcasts, even though they were jammed. The experts were unable to carry out surveys in Central Europe and the Baltic states, yet they knew that that was where most of the audiences of Western radio were. This was an early sign of the decline of the communist ideology within the Soviet Bloc. That is why the first part of this book tells the largely unknown story of the West's radio offensive against the East, including the action of the two US stations created in the early 1950s by the CIA: Radio Free Europe, which broadcast to Central and Eastern Europe, and Radio Liberty which broadcast to the USSR. In 1962, Raymond Aron had already picked up the importance of this battle of international communication as a means of preventing "totalitarian regimes from being alone with their peoples."[5] At that stage, France was virtually absent from the scene.

For me, the most interesting aspect was however the relationship between dissidents in the East and Western radio stations. Although I was more familiar with the history of attempted opposition in Central Europe, I wanted to include the contribution of Soviet dissidents as precursors to the rise of protest in Eastern Europe. I was curious to see just how important Western radio stations were for Soviet dissidents, starting with the most famous ones. The subject was not as noble as an in-depth study of their most important texts, but it seemed to me important to understand how these texts had become known both in the East and in the West, other than via independent self-publishing (*samizdat*).

To my surprise, I found that references to Western radio stations were actually frequent in these dissidents' memoirs. Writer Aleksandr Solzhenitzyn, academic Andrei Sakharov and activist Vladimir Bukovsky all highlighted the role of these foreign stations in their own struggles, even though they sometimes cursed what they had said, failed to say, or distorted. Listening to foreign programs was part of their daily lives. The stations' broadcasts were usually scrambled and all too often the quality of their programs was poor, yet they offered vital moral support for those needing a breath of fresh air in a stifling social environment. It was perhaps Bukovski who wrote the most moving testimony about these radio stations. He explained that, in the camp in which he was interned, he managed to build a radio receiver that could pick up short-waves: "It was a superb radio—it picked up everything: the BBC, Voice of America, Radio Liberty, Deutsche Welle, and even Radio Monte Carlo. [...] The radio was kept in one of the schoolrooms where school equipment as stored, disguised as a piece of physics apparatus. The school steward, a prisoner, used to let me into that room secretly every evening, and there I would plunge into a completely different life. I was back with my friends, deploring their arrests, accompanying them to Red Square to protest against the occupation of Czechoslovakia, writing protest letters." Further on he added: "in the evenings, just before lights out, when I returned to the compound after listening to these broadcasts, and strolled along the barbed-wire fence, brightly illuminated by the search lights, I was filled with a wonderful sense of freedom, ease and power."[6]

In the dissident's world, radio was not perceived simply as a technical means of accessing national or international news; listening to foreign programs was a personal psychological investment and a sign of complicity with another world. Solzhenitzyn reported how, during one of his countless meetings with Aleksandr Tvardovsky, editor-in-chief of *Novy mir* (which had published his first book, and with which he had constantly been in conflict), Tvardovsky suddenly leapt towards the wireless "just as eagerly and impatiently as I had rushed to my set, punctually to the minute, for so many years past. This uncontrolled impulse, more than anything, made me feel closer to him, much closer, than ever before." And both concluded that the BBC was "a radio you can take seriously—absolutely without bias."[7]

We can't understand a dissident's relationship with the West without taking into consideration this personal contact with foreign radio stations. The mere fact of listening to them projected the dissident onto the international scene, yet before he actually entered that scene it had come to him, on the air. In the dynamics of his uncertain engagement, he hoped to appear there himself, to make himself heard and thus to get the whole world to recognize the audacity and novelty of his struggle.

This approach to the outside world, to what we now call "international public opinion," took a great deal of courage at the time. Traditionally, in the Soviet world protest was not public; it was addressed directly to the authorities concerned. Those who failed to abide by this rule were automatically accused of disloyalty towards the state. For instance, academic Andrei Sakharov started his militant engagement in February 1967 with a confidential letter to Brejnev, a plea in favor of political prisoners. And for years Solzhenitzyn refused to grant interviews to Western journalists because, he wrote, "not wishing to lie, and not daring to rebel, I preferred silence."[8]

The dissident act, on the other hand, implied a process of rupture, a dangerous departure from the prevailing ideological and social norms whose legitimacy it defied. Through a public deed that challenged the powers-that-be, which immediately placed him or her outside the bounds of the system's norms, the dissident "floated" in society without any real point of anchorage. Yet, in spite of the risk of greater marginalization, a feeling of security was derived from recognition by the West. This external acknowledgement came via Western radio stations, which were often the first to inform their listeners in the East of acts of opposition within the communist bloc. They were therefore at the heart of a play of mirrors, where the dissident tried to identify his or her own image in order to forge a new identity as an opponent of the regime.

This evolution is striking in the case of Sakharov. In April 1968 he took the decisive step towards the opposition by allowing his famous text "Progress, Coexistence, and Intellectual Freedom"[9] to be circulated by *samizdat*. This meant that sooner or later the document would end up in the West, and indeed, only a few weeks later, on July 10, he heard on a Western radio station that precisely that had occurred. "[I] heard my name," he wrote. "The announcer reported that on July 6, the Dutch newspaper *Het Parool* had published an article by A.D. Sakharov, a member of the Soviet Academy of Sciences who, according to Western experts, had worked on the Soviet hydrogen bomb. [...] The die was cast. That evening I had the most profound feeling of satisfaction."[10] The academic was immediately subjected to his colleagues' and superiors' reprobation, yet had the feeling of serenity that stems from seeing something through to the end. The fact that his document had been reported on in the West was also a way for him to change his identity; it was as if he had "gone over to the West" without leaving the East. He was thus able to reach an international audience, and his article, published on July 21 by the *New York Times* and circulated in 18 million copies, in thirty languages, had a considerable impact.

It was also by listening to Western radio that Solzhenitzyn became aware of the international resonance of his public letter of protest against censorship, addressed to the Writers' Congress on May 16, 1967—a decisive step on his path towards open opposition to the regime. Its international impact was considerable: "For a whole fortnight," he wrote, "[...] radio stations around the world were busy quoting, expounding, reading verbatim and (sometimes very shortsightedly) commenting on my letter. [...] I began to feel that I had, surprisingly, not merely defeated but utterly routed my enemies!"[11] These two actions, of Solzhenitzyn and Sakharov, were characteristic of the opposition that developed in the USSR in the late 1960s, based on the principle of open protest and an appeal to public opinion. Dissident texts were already using the term *Glasnost* to express the wish for transparency based on the use of "publicity," in the sense of the expression of civil rights.

Based on this research on some Soviet dissidents and additional data collected in parallel, on the role of Western media in Poland and the former German Democratic Republic, I formulated a more general and ambitious question: what was the role of the media in the main crises of the communist bloc which, from the 1950s, destabilized Moscow's domination of Central Europe? My initial explorations left no doubt as to the importance of the subject. In 1953, when workers of East Berlin went on strike, they wanted the event to be covered by a US radio station. In 1956, when the Hungarians rebelled against Soviet rule, the insurgents started to besiege the national radio station while the US's Radio Free Europe, broadcasting from Munich, poured oil on the flames to incite them to take up arms. In 1968, it was Czech journalists who, broadcasting clandestinely in Prague occupied by Soviet tanks, seemed to keep the bare-handed resistance of the population at bay. In 1980, at the time of the Gdansk strikes, television became omnipresent. Through the images that leaked out of Poland, people in the West had the impression of sharing the daily lives of the Gdansk workers defying the Polish authorities and their Soviet big brother. Finally, in 1989, the "velvet revolutions" spreading across Central Europe seemed to signify the triumph of television. Journalist and academic Timothy Garton Ash aptly coined the term "telerevolutions."[12]

Initially the answer to my general question was therefore obvious: throughout all these crises, certain media played a tactical, if not strategic, role in opposing the enemy's violence. The asymmetry of this power struggle could be summed up as: media against tanks! But is that not over-simplified? How can its relevance be verified? Apart from the actions of Western media, would it not be necessary to examine the role of local media in these crises as well, as the first sign of the re-conquest of freedom?—starting with the press? Were the media content to "follow" the events or had they in some cases become actors? The questions abounded. This was clearly a fascinating research subject, and after several years of investigation it led me to write this book. Although others have already recounted the main events of this tormented history of Europe under Moscow's yoke, punctuated by the East Germans', Hungarians', Czechs' and Poles' attempts to win back their freedom, I have endeavored here to shed a different light on that period.

What is the main "discovery" of this research? I show that, during those years of gloom and bloodshed, while the peoples of Eastern Europe seemed to be set in an unchanging present, and acts of open rebellion were rare, a truly inventive way of protesting and communicating was maturing. The Eastern Europeans had long since stopped believing in the Bolshevik ideology of seizing state power through the "violence of the masses." Polish, Hungarian and Czech dissidents of the 1970s and 1980s sought a form of engagement diametrically opposed to the "revolutionary communism" that—through terror and massacres—had founded the Soviet Union. They were thus gradually to develop a "resistance know-how" that took past failures into account. Through the conquest of speech and then of the streets, it was to culminate in 1989 in the destabilization of the system from within.

This final scenario of the "velvet revolutions" took many by surprise. Apart from the violent episode in Romania in December, mass demonstrations in Leipzig, Berlin and then Prague were the expression of a Gandhi-style nonviolent civil resistance in the very heart of post-totalitarian regimes. If we are to fully understand why opponents of these regimes opted for a more subtle, symbolic struggle via the media, rather than physical confrontation, in a period when communist ideology was falling into decay, we need to look at the tragic history of struggles in Central Europe. A precise analysis of the development, by trial and error, one could say, of relations between communication and resistance is crucial for an in-depth interpretation of the denouement in 1989. In this respect, I identified three basic stages in this slow process of maturation. As they are set out in the introduction to the first edition of this book, I won't discuss them here.

Those who believe that armed struggle alone makes history surely have no clue of the effective mobilization of these peoples, supposedly stunned by decades of propaganda, yet who had the courage to peacefully defy heavily armed regimes. I have to admit, however, that despite my knowledge of the history of dissidence and resistance in Eastern Europe, my awareness of the role of Western radio, and my familiarity with the thinking of US political scientist and Harvard theoretician on nonviolent action, Gene Sharp, I was no better than anyone else at predicting the extent of the impending events. From 1988, I had been doing the spadework on this question of the media in Eastern Europe, as I had intuitively recognized their strategic importance in a possible opening up of communist Europe. My interest was attested by the first article that I published on the subject, in the journal *Etudes*, in … May 1989! There I emphasized the fact that the upsurge of Western broadcasting media in the East, in spite of the strategic partitioning of the European continent, was clearly a challenge for the communist regimes.[13] In Moscow the new head of the Soviet Union, Mikhail Gorbachev, was fully aware of that as he endeavored, in a sense, to accompany an inevitable evolution with *Glasnost* (a word already used by dissidents twenty years earlier). But I had no idea that this new policy in Moscow was going to trigger snowballing protest movements throughout Soviet-dominated Europe. Gorbachev was moreover probably no less surprised, as were all the other world leaders. It was thus "the 1989 event" that, with hindsight, provided me with the key to its understanding, thus enabling me to structure the various elements of information that I had collected over the preceding years, and to build the framework of analysis summarized above. The course of this research confirms the relevance of Hannah Arendt's observation that the event illuminates its own past but cannot be inferred from it.

This book concludes with what I have called "the fall of the three walls": the psychological wall of fear; the strategic wall of the East-West partitioning; and the physical wall in the city of Berlin. There could be a follow-up now, for the two essential ingredients of the 1989 upheavals—civil resistance and use of the media—were present once again a decade later in Serbia, in the movement that triggered Milosevic's fall, and then in the "color revolutions": Georgia's Rose Revolution, Ukraine's Orange Revolution, and Kyrgyzstan's Tulip Revolution. Each of these examples is of course different and must be analyzed in its specific context. There is nevertheless one noteworthy element: the students of the Otpor movement, the spearhead of protests in Serbia in the late nineties, had taken on board the recommendations of none other than Gene Sharp when embarking on a nonviolent struggle. These recommendations were summarized in *From Dictatorship to Democracy: a Conceptual Framework for Liberation* (translated into Serbo-Croatian).[14] As advocates of civil disobedience they managed to create a mass movement which, on October 4, 2000, tolled the knell of the Milosevic regime. This success boosted all those in Georgia or Ukraine who also wanted to instigate profound political change. The Otpor students cannot however be considered as the only artisans of this political success. Other Serbian actors likewise played an instrumental role, as did foreigners and above all Americans—an issue that has generated much controversy.[15] In both Georgia and Ukraine we witnessed the reappearance of the same methods of nonviolent mobilization and confrontation experimented in Serbia. The role of the media in the course of these struggles was equally important: Radio B92 in Belgrade and television in Kiev. There is therefore ample material for a comparative study on these "color revolutions," using the framework of analysis proposed here. Hopefully a book will be published in the near future that, as a follow-up to the present one, affords an historical perspective on these changes.[16]

"Velvet revolutions," "color revolutions": the scenarios of these collective mobilizations matched a universal pattern: the asymmetrical struggle of the weak against the strong. They were cases of bare-handed resistance to authoritarian or post-totalitarian regimes. In his famous essay *The Power of the Powerless*,[17] Vaclav Havel, from the depths of his dissident's solitude in 1978, intuitively understood the moral and political strength that inspires this form of resistance. As paradoxical as it may seem, this text, circulated secretly at the time, is reminiscent of Gandhi's thinking in several respects—even though the Mahatma had fought a very different opponent in an entirely different cultural context. As he received the Indira Gandhi prize in 1995, Vaclav Havel made this connection himself: "I believe that a reflection of [Mahatma Gandhi's] life's work might even be seen in the attempt my friends and I made, in Charter 77, to create a nonviolent opposition to the totalitarian regime in our country."[18]

Since September 11, 2001, people nevertheless seem to believe that the main contemporary expression of the "battle of the weak against the strong" is terrorist action. But the fall of the Berlin Wall has been a reminder not only of the possibility, but also of the destabilizing force, of another figure of asymmetrical struggle: civil resistance which combines collective action with a subversive use of the means of communication. The heritage of these forms of civil resistance is richer than is generally believed. The voluminous collective volume edited by Timothy Garton Ash and Adam Roberts bears witness to this, with its wide variety of case studies that were discussed in a major international conference at Oxford University.[19]

Finally, I wish to emphasize the connection between civil resistance and the construction of what communication specialists call the public sphere. The thinking of philosopher Jürgen Habermas is useful in this respect.[20] Any willful opposition within a non-pluralist regime is confronted with the prohibition on physical occupation of the public sphere (for instance the streets) to openly and publicly express disagreement. Hence, the emergence of a critical public sphere, in Habermas' sense, can for a while serve as a substitute for expression in a public space in which it is dangerous to appear. The main means for creating this public sphere are precisely the media, for their ubiquity makes it possible to delocalize the transmission of information and its modes of reception. There is no need to march through the streets to be a stakeholder in this alternative public sphere; one can stay at home and listen to a banned radio station or use one's personal computer to share critical opinions of the regime online. We know for instance that Chinese dissidents—both within China and without—try to use Internet technology as much as possible, despite Peking's measures to control it. The official media consequently have to compete with the possible extension of this critical public sphere that can also resort to more conventional media (the underground printed press).

If such a critical public sphere manages to spread, thus reflecting an increasingly broad wish for change within a given society, it becomes more and more probable that individuals and groups will take the risk of physically expressing themselves in public. This will lead them to revert to more traditional forms of public demonstration. Critical expression will be conveyed no longer solely through the dissemination of ideas and images defying all forms of censorship, but also through the presence in the streets and public squares of bodies free of fear and proud to emancipate themselves together, openly. In general, this takes a long time, sometimes generations. It is the process that led to the scenario of 1989, via the prior, uncertain and gradual conquest of freedom ... over the airwaves.[21]

Notes

1. Milan Kundera, "The Tragedy of Central Europe" in *The New York Review*, April 26, 1984.

2. Interview published in *Le Monde* on August 31, 1985.

3. In particular, I have in mind the lesser known talks of General de Gaulle broadcast over the BBC in the period 1940 to 1942, calling the French to publicly voice and demonstrate their attachment to patriotic values in the unoccupied southern zone of France. See Aurélie Luneau, *Radio Londres : les voix de la liberté (1940-1944)*, Paris, Perrin, 2005; Jacques Semelin, *Sans armes face à Hitler. La résistance civile en Europe (1939-1943)*, Paris, Payot, PPB, 1998, p. 110-111.

4. Georges-Henri Soutou, *La guerre de cinquante ans. Les relations Est-Ouest, 1943-1990*, Paris, Fayard, 2001.

5. Raymond Aron, *Peace and War: a Theory of International Relations*, New Brunswick, New Jersey, Transaction Publishers, 2003, p. 165.

6. Vladimir Bukovski, *To Build a Castle: My Life As a Dissenter*, London, André Deutsch Limited, 1978, p. 269-270.

7. Aleksandr Solzhenitzyn, *The Oak and The Calf*, London, Collins and Harvill Press, 1980, p. 228-229.

8. *Ibid*, p. 52.

9. See Andrei Sakharov, *Sakharov Speaks*, New York, Vintage Books, 1974.

10. ID, *Memoires*, London, Hutchinson, 1990, p. 286.

11. Solzhenitzyn, *The Oak and the Calf*, op. cit., p. 165.

12. See Timothy Garton Ash, *The Uses of Adversity*, Cambridge, Granta Books, 1989.

13. Jacques Semelin, "La communication Est-Ouest. De la radio sur ondes courtes à la télévision par satellite?" in *Etudes*, May 1989.

14. Gene Sharp, *From Dictatorship to Democracy: A Conceptual Framework for Liberation*, Boston, The Albert Einstein Institute, 2003 (translated into 22 languages).

15. See Boris Petric, "A propos des révolutions de couleur et du *soft power* américain" in *Hérodote*, n° 129, 2008, p. 7-20.

16. The first outline of this approach was first described by Régis Genté. See Régis Genté, "Des révolutions médiatiques," in *Hérodote*, op. cit., p. 37-68.

17. Vaclav Havel, "The power of the Powerless," in *The Power of The Powerless: Citizens Against the State in Central-Eastern Europe*, London, Hutchinson, 1985, p. 23-96.

18. http://old.hrad.cz/president/Havel/speeches/1994/0802_uk.html

19. Timothy Garton Ash & Adam Roberts, *Civil Resistance and Power Politics*, Oxford, Oxford University Press, 2009.

20. Jürgen Habermas, *L'Espace public*, Paris, Payot, 1993.

21. For this new edition the book's bibliography has been enriched and updated considerably. This necessary work was possible thanks to the help of Danielle Leny, information officer at the Sciences Po library, to whom I am deeply grateful.

ACKNOWLEDGMENTS

First of all, I wish to express my deep gratitude to the members of the International Center on Nonviolent Conflict (ICNC, Washington D.C.), especially Peter Ackerman, Jack Duvall, Hardy Merriman, and Nicola Barrach. Indeed, it was the generous support of ICNC which made the English translation of this book possible. I like to also thank Liz Libbrecht, who marvelously and accurately translated this book. And finally my warm regards go to Amber French, ICNC Manager of Editorial Initiatives, whose French-English skills and determination to one day see this book come to fruition have been extremely helpful to achieve the final result.

The bibliography of this edition has been expanded considerably and updated, thanks to the efficient and painstaking help of Danielle Leny at the Sciences Po library in Paris. My thanks also go to Amber French for her additional work to adapt the bibliography for an English-speaking readership.

I would also like to thank the historians, sociologists, journalists and experts from the former Soviet Bloc countries who not only an-swered my numerous questions, but also agreed to offer their comments and suggestions on some parts of the book: Jacques Amalric, Nicole Bary, Karel Bartosek, Bernard Dréano, Jaroslav Jiru, Pierre Kende, Marcin Frybes, François Gault, Pierre Hassner, Anne Le Huerou, Miroslav Novak, Krzysztof Pomian, Jean-Yves Potel, Thomas Schreiber, Michel Tatu, and Cécile Vayssié.

This work would furthermore not have been possible without the crucial material provided by several research centers and archives in Europe, particularly:

- the Marc Bloch Center and the Institute for Contemporary History in Berlin, the 1956 Institute in Budapest, and the Bibliothèque de Documentation internationale contemporaine in Nanterre;
- the audience councils of the B.B.C., the R.F.E./R.L. and the R.F.I., the Deutsches Rundfunkarchiv in Frankfurt, the archives of Radio France and the French Inathèque.

My appreciation goes to Howard Barrell for his review and comments on the English manuscript, as well as his edifying and expansive Afterword. Finally, I am indebted to Adam Roberts, whose Foreword has reinvigorated this book's significance for today's readers, and whose comments on the translation in its final stages were abundantly helpful.

INTRODUCTION:
Communication as resistance

The fall of the Berlin Wall, on November 9, 1989, has remained an enigma. How was it that this momentous event happened, engulfed not in the flames of war as many experts had predicted, but in the jubilation of festive crowds gathered in Berlin, their joy exploding before the television cameras of the world? It has since become commonplace to credit primarily Mikhail Gorbachev and his *Glasnost* policy. Then, as the story goes, US military pressure on the USSR, through Ronald Reagan's program known as "Star Wars," precipitated the breakdown of the Soviet system. The role played by the people of Central Europe is thus downplayed, even forgotten. Other explanations—economic, sociological, or demographic—are put forward. As in the case of the French Revolution, various lines of interpretation compete to explain the fall of the Berlin Wall and the ensuing collapse of the Soviet regime. Without denying the weight that external factors—from Moscow or Washington—may have had on the destinies of the populations of Central Europe, this book seeks to reassess those peoples' own role in the downfall of regimes once thought to be eternal. After all, 1989 marked their triumph, their capacity to resist Soviet domination as best they could for over four decades.

Yet this "resistance" should not be overestimated. As a form of organized opposition, it was a minor phenomenon: first because in the immediate postwar era many did believe in the virtues of communism; and second because almost everyone was coerced into some form of "collaboration" or other with the system, if only to earn a living. Save a few dramatic episodes, best exemplified by the 1956 Budapest uprising, this resistance was not synonymous with armed struggle. Modes of protest were diffuse and largely unstructured. They looked more like passive resistance, closer to the forms of civil resistance that I have described in the context of Nazi domination in Europe.[1] Fascinating studies are yet to be undertaken on the comparative meaning, nature, and forms of resistance in the respective contexts of Nazi Europe and Soviet Europe. In both cases, attempts at resistance within countries under occupation certainly did share a reliance on national identity, but there were also fundamental differences.

Having studied both contexts, I was so struck by one phenomenon that I chose to research it for a number of years, making it the main theme of this book: the vital role of communication, more concretely the media, in the development of resistance within the Soviet Bloc, from the Cold War era to its final collapse. Timothy Garton Ash, the outstanding commentator on Central Europe, couched it in the following terms: *"these regimes lived by the word and perished by the word."*[2] The vital role of communication in building the process of resistance can be understood only in relation to the very nature of the totalitarian project. If the essence of totalitarianism rests on the organic link between terror and ideology, as Hannah Arendt asserted, it follows that the essence of anti-totalitarian resistance lies, *a contrario*, in a twin liberation from fear and propaganda: freeing oneself from paralyzing fear, and freeing oneself from blinding propaganda. The writings of the most famous dissidents—Aleksandr Solzhenitzyn, Václav Havel or Adam Michnik—were inspired by this one theme: stop collaborating with the lie. The first step in dissidence is therefore to reclaim the spirit. The move from dissidence to resistance then involves sharing this refusal, which means convincing and organizing. To resist, we must recognize each other as a resisters, build modes of communication, then touch public opinion to widen the audience.

Some will object that this dynamic can be found within all opposition, under all dictatorships. This would overlook the fact that the communist dictatorship is unique in its initial intent to create a "New Man." The party-state must exert absolute control over the media, not only to impose censorship (a feature shared with any dictatorial regime), but also to ensure that all individuals think what the party wants them to think. Any form of free speech therefore takes on strategic value within such a system. Whether in the form of poems, great philosophical discourses or a few sentences scribbled on a placard, to paraphrase Polish poet Janusz Szpotanski, words thus become dynamite. While it is true that words and symbols also had an impact in the context of Nazi Europe—the BBC broadcasts served to boost the morale of the population and provide instructions to the resistance—one major difference was found in the era of Soviet Europe. The period now known as the "Cold War" lent greater importance to words than to weapons. Because the threat of an even more horrific war than the one just ended was looming, the ideological confrontation became all the more ruthless. This context of "non-war," the balance of terror, feeds the power of words: always better to fire off ideological rather than nuclear missiles. On the domestic front, a simple manifesto by dissenting writers could destabilize a regime.

For all these reasons, the main theme of this book is how speech was reclaimed under regimes where it was once confiscated, annihilated, warped. The book walks though the main historical landmarks of a collective epic—from Berlin to Budapest, Warsaw or Prague, through London, New York, Munich or Paris—that saw individuals, groups and at times whole populations free themselves from fear and reclaim a voice—their own. This liberation came through use of the media—from both the West and the East—to make these voices heard, and recognized.

The book is comprised of three parts, each covering one of three phases in this liberation process. The first opens in the early days of the Cold War, when Eastern Europeans lived under the yoke of Stalinist terror. Free speech at that time originated primarily from outside, mostly through international radio stations that practiced what we would call today a form of media interference. In the West we have remained largely unaware of how important these broadcasts from the BBC, Voice of America, and later Radio Free Europe, actually were. Even though their content was also characterized by propaganda, and they were often jammed, they proved invaluable to those who, in the Eastern block, sought to escape totalitarian ideology. These radio stations threw an invisible bridge from the West to the East, constituting what I call here the *West-East* communication channel. From these early days, for those who lived in the Eastern Bloc, freedom was already on the airwaves.

Stalin's death in 1953 ushered in a second phase, with the first attempts at emancipating speech within the system itself. In some countries public debate and even public protest actions were seen reemerging. A new form of identity-based, national communication started appearing. The 1956 Hungarian insurrection and the Prague Spring of 1968 were its more portentous and most tragic moments. For while there was indeed a rekindling of internal communications, the reconnection of an East-East line of communication striving to free itself from Soviet tutelage, this took place in a "fishbowl," so to speak, with no outside support. These unusual episodes were in a sense tragedies behind closed doors, as the West displayed nothing more than the guiltiest passivity in the face of Moscow's attempts to clamp down.

The third and final stage witnessed the emergence in the 1970s of dissidents on the international scene. In this new era, the Western world started shifting views on "real socialism." As a result, those seeking to bring free speech to the Eastern Bloc could now start to rely on new allies in the West. Dissidents learned at the same time to make indirect use of Western radio broadcasts with reception in the Eastern Bloc countries, as a way to address their fellow citizens. And thus was born a new means of communication in the Eastern Bloc, via the West. This East-West-and-back-to-East communication channel became a full-fledged resistance strategy in Poland, coming into its own during the days of the Solidarity movement. It was ultimately successful in 1989, as it overtook the last remaining strongholds of the Soviet system, starting with East Germany which was reunited with West Germany through a "televisual bridge."

This study of the relationship between communication and resistance introduces a new understanding of the events that led to the fall of the Soviet system. This book examines the major crises of Central Europe as part of their own historical continuum. As we start putting each crisis in relation to the others, we find that beyond cultural and national differences among the countries of Eastern Europe, resistance know-how was built up in a little over three generations: a know-how that tied together means of opposition with means of communication. Non-provocative methods of action, that we could call "nonviolent," came to supersede uncontrolled forms of violence, and even the mere temptation of armed struggle. From 1968 to 1989, one could witness the empowerment of civil resistance movements in Central Europe, a phenomenon that must be put in relation to the emergence or rebuilding of "civil society" (in the sense that Dominique Colas has proposed, for example[3]). Repression of these resistance movements, failing the justification of combating violence, looked all the more illegitimate, which in turn allowed these movements to gain access to wider audiences and international support.

The clear refusal to engage in physical confrontation led opponents to defy their communist rulers on the symbolic front, over a domain where they were increasingly vulnerable because of their failure to make people believe in values in which they, themselves, no longer seemed to believe. That is why communication became such a pivotal issue in resistance processes, especially through access to the media.

As with my previous work on civil resistance in Nazi Europe, the hope is that this book may make some contribution to political science and history. As regards the former, it proposes to shed some light on the debate, still very much alive, on the issue of totalitarianism. The word "totalitarianism" has been so used and abused for ideological purposes that the whole concept must now be critically examined: did totalitarianism ever truly exist? As a project for society and individuals it certainly did, especially under Stalinism. This is what I mean when, on a few rare occasions, I use "totalitarian" as an adjective. But as an accomplishment, fully-fledged system, the debate is open. This is what this whole story here proves: the totalitarian project will fail in its aims because it always comes up against the resistance of some individuals who prove unwilling to swallow the propaganda, even as they are partly influenced by it. Together with Pierre Hassner, I would say that communist dictatorships fall in a fuzzy area between authoritarianism and totalitarianism.[4] I hope to show how, even within communist dictatorships, and often very early on, spaces for free communications were established among individuals, first in concealment, then increasingly in public. Of course, the countries of Central Europe were quite distinct from those of Eastern Europe and the Soviet Union. But are we still faced with a totalitarian system when, according to many testimonies, one could listen unhampered to Western radio broadcasts as early as the late 1970s, even in the USSR?

This is one page of history that this book wants to tell. We have known for a long time that the media play a central role in all major social and political upheavals (remember the role of the press during the French Revolution[5]). However, there are as yet no written accounts of resistance within the Soviet Bloc through use of the media. That would be a complex task requiring many studies, and this book is primarily an essay. The aim is obviously not to write a history of the Polish, Czech or Hungarian media, but to show how the media were both witnesses and actors in the difficult emancipation of Central Europe, and how social representations of the media evolved, based for instance on technology (moving from radio to television), the identity of the occupied countries, change in East-West relations, etc.

When conducting field research in Prague, Warsaw, Budapest or Leipzig, I searched for anything relevant to the relationship between communication and resistance. I focused on deepening the analysis of certain fascinating episodes, for instance, how the Czechs, through a system of clandestine radio stations, were able to defy the Red Army in August 1968. This story, Václav Havel said in one of his political essays, should one day be the subject of a dedicated study. I set out on a quest to find the many acts of "micro- resistance," as Michel de Certeau would call them, even small anecdotes that are sometimes the telltale signs of another paradigm. For instance, the story of a Hungarian student who, while Budapest was burning in 1956, built a radio broadcast station on his own because, as he said, he had to "tell the whole world the truth about the events in my country."

Experts on the Eastern Bloc countries already know about the events recounted here; my hope is that I may help them to see these events under a different light. However, my main aim is to bring to life for a larger public the epic moments of these battles for freedom, of this victory for free speech in the land that Milan Kundera dubbed the "Kidnapped West." Although they are part of our European history, too little is known about these events, even today.

This is why this book is also written as a *story*. Once we have established, in the first part, the backdrop of East-West radio bridges spanning the entire period, the second and third parts present a series of tableaus where, from crisis to crisis, the actors of history find their position along the narrative thread. Thus, we set out on a story line, starting from voices regained, to fledgling attempts to take off over the Wall, finally reaching beyond all walls that seek to enclose.

I hope that in these pages the reader will perceive something of the atmosphere that prevailed at the time, along with the drama or joy experienced by men and women in those countries, of which Europeans in the West had so little knowledge.

Notes

1. Jacques Semelin, *Unarmed against Hitler*, Praeger Publishers, Westport, 1994.
2. Timothy Garton Ash, *The Uses of Adversity*, Cambridge, Granta Books, 1989.
3. Dominique Colas, *Civil Society and Fanaticism: Conjoined Histories*, Stanford University Press, Stanford (Calif.), 1997.
4. Pierre Hassner, "Totalitarismes," in Pierre Hassner, *La Violence et la Paix*, Paris, éditions Esprit, 1995.
5. See, for instance, Jean-Noël Jeanneney on the subject in *Une histoire des médias*, Paris, Le Seuil, 1996.

PART ONE

Radio bridges

I

War on the West-East airwaves: Media interference in practice

During the Cold War it was usual to refer to "East-West" conflict. Today, while the Soviet Bloc has come to an end, "East-West" remains the stock phrase. But should we not question the order in which these two words appear? Why not "West-East"? Is it a matter of phonetics, as "East-West" sounds better than "West-East"?—unless this preference conceals a deeper choice of semantics. Putting East first in the pair may suggest that policy in the Soviet camp largely determined the nature of East-West relations. Such a perspective offers obvious historical consistency: it was in fact the East that chose to isolate itself from the world to "build socialism" and launch an attack on a "corrupt and decadent" capitalist world, compelling the West to react. Two words and a hyphen: a summary of over 40 years of rivalry between the two blocs!

This is as good a way as any other to narrate History. Yet East-West relations can also be interpreted through an inversion of the terms, by showing how much the West influenced the changing nature of the East on the military, economic, political and cultural fronts. From the creation of the Marshall Plan in the 1950s to rebuild the economies of Western Europe, to the "Star Wars" program of the 1980s to drain the USSR on the military front, there was no lack of Western (mostly US) initiatives against the East—mostly of an offensive rather than reactive nature. In this respect, there remains one field where the importance of Western action has not been seriously recognized and analyzed: that of communications. Yet its significance was considerable. Because it answered the hopes of those who did not want to be cut off from the Western world, the *West-East War of the Airwaves* was by nature strategic.

Despite the division of Europe, the media were therefore called on to establish a minimal cultural link. How was this done? Taking the Western press to the East was almost impossible at the time. Only international broadcasting, with capabilities that had already been tried and tested during World War II, could reach those living within the Soviet Bloc. The audibility of these broadcasts on short-wave and medium frequency was obviously poor, but potential listeners in the East had little choice in the matter. The development of television broadcasting, in the 1960s, did allow them to watch Western programming of a completely different kind, but this possibility was limited to those living near the border of a Western country. Except in East Germany, where West German television broadcasts could technically cover almost the whole territory,[1] television coverage was of course limited. Examples of Western television broadcasts reaching the East must at any rate be clearly separated from the case of international radios. In the case of television, we are dealing with "spill-over coverage" (the airwaves know no borders), as television programs were never intentionally broadcast to people living in the Soviet Bloc. With regard to international radio broadcasts, however, there was a clear *intentionality*: a desire to enter the territorial space of another state to allow its population to receive the signal of a foreign station. This clearly constitutes what we today call *foreign interference*.

Yet, at the time, few Western leaders understood the strategic importance of this type of international communication. Most showed little interest, and provided only scant resources to these radio stations, considered as outdated propaganda tools inherited from the Second World War.[2] As a result, there was no coherent effort from the West on this front, even as the Cold War was waged on the ideological battlefield. The professionals who worked at the radio stations were well aware of this situation. Their actions were questioned many a time at the whim of changing administrations and budget squeezes, the case of France being the most symptomatic in this regard. A quick overview of the history of the main actors in the West-East war of the airwaves is therefore relevant, given the dearth of research in this area. Three types of radio stations can be defined:

- Representation radio stations, such as Voice of America (VOA) or the British Broadcasting Corporation (BBC);
- Substitution radio stations, such as Radio Free Europe (RFE) or Radio Liberty (RL);
- Religious radio stations, primarily Vatican Radio.

1. Representation radio stations: VOA, BBC and the others

As the extended voice of their sponsor state, representation radio stations allow the expatriates of a nation, scattered across the world, to stay in touch with the home country. They seek to maintain a permanent national link across distances and borders. That is why these stations broadcast regular programs in the national language of the home country. Another objective is, however, also to address a much wider audience, as they seek to be a vector of cultural outreach, a kind of broadcasting mirror, for the sponsoring state. Representation radio stations must therefore keep within specific terms of reference established by the administrative authority (generally the Foreign Affairs Department): legitimize the foreign policy of the sponsoring state, promote the nation's economy, and spread its culture and language. A cross between journalism and diplomacy, this type of radio station is an instrument of what some today call "public diplomacy"[3]—a rather elegant phrase that refers to modern forms of international propaganda. Ultimately, it aims at furthering the interests and values of the state it represents, within the public opinion of foreign countries.

Yet as representation radio stations aim to reach the whole world, as it were, they fail to adapt to the specific features of national audiences. Their claim to reach a global audience is a constant threat to their ability to speak anything to anybody, as they do not take into account who they are trying to reach. The only way to get through to potential foreign audiences is of course to broadcast in their own language. The importance of this type of station will then be measured by the number of programs it offers in different languages. But that wider reach serves only to amend a principle of communication still defined from the *source*, and not the *target*. As such, the communications logic of a representation radio station is based on a *dynamic of attraction*. Its set objective is to contribute to the outreach of the broadcasting country.

Accordingly, representation radio stations do not—at least in theory—serve the function of broadcasting alternative information to countries where the media are heavily censored. Even though they still happen to serve that purpose regularly, it is over and above their general mandate, and not because of any democratic zeal. These radio stations obey their own self-interest: when they seek to attract a specific audience, their aim is primarily to broaden their international audience.

VOA (Voice of America)

The most powerful radio station of its kind in the Western world, Voice of America (VOA), was created in 1942 at the insistence of famous playwright Robert Sherwood, who was able to convince then President

Roosevelt to launch an international information service to support the US war effort. He believed the most convincing propaganda was to tell the truth to the world, something he thought was inherent in the very nature of the American people!

The station started broadcasting on February 24, 1942, and soon offered programming in most European languages, including Albanian, Bulgarian, Czech and Slovak, Hungarian, Polish, Romanian, Serbo-Croatian, Slovenian, Lithuanian, Estonian, and Latvian.[4] In July 1944 it reached its highest level of activity: 119 hours of daily programming in 50 languages. Soon after WWII and under a new administration less keen on keeping a foreign information service, VOA started to decline rapidly. By the end of 1945 its staff was cut by half, while programming fell to under 65 hours a day, in 24 languages.

In 1946, as relations with the Soviet Union swiftly deteriorated, the question of the radio station's revival was brought to the fore as a way of promoting US policy in the world, especially in Europe. Following the recommendation of a few diplomats, including Averell Harriman, VOA started broadcasting in Russian on February 17, 1947. When President Truman launched his Campaign of Truth in April 1950 and called on the media to promote the truth about America and help combat communist distortions, VOA was granted substantial funding and started blooming again. While in June 1950 it still broadcast under 30 hours daily in 23 languages, a year later its activity had increased to almost 50 hours in 45 languages, including Albanian, Latvian, Lithuanian, Estonian, Slovenian, Armenian, Azerbaijani, Georgian, Tatar, and Turkmen.[5] Its propaganda themes depicted Americans as good people concerned about freedom in the world, and as peacemakers. The station's jazz programming helped to build its renown, including in France.[6]

McCarthyism, paradoxically, put the brakes on the radio station's expansion. In 1953 there were suspicions that "Soviet agents" had infiltrated it. These groundless accusations prompted a string of resignations and a brutal cut to the station's budget, which was slashed from $22 million, to $15 million in 1954. Under the watchful eye of Congress, VOA broadcast the most strident anticommunist programs during that period. These were not toned down until after Khrushchev's visit to the US, in 1959. Based on the recommendation of a report by William A. Jackson (who had served as deputy director of the CIA), President Eisenhower created the U.S. Information Agency (USIA) in 1953, which oversaw VOA. As a consequence of the Jackson Report, which questioned the effectiveness of broadcasting toward the Soviet Union, a number of foreign-language stations were closed, including those in Tatar, Azerbaijani, and Turkmen.[7]

Voice of America was often perturbed by crises, because of the constant meddling of the federal government in its editorial policy. While some of VOA's officers sought a more independent course, they were no match for the insistence of the powers-that-be. The members of Congress who had to approve the annual budget were often divided. Some, mainly Republicans, wanted more funds; others, especially Democrats, wanted to cut back. In 1976 the VOA Charter sought to put an end to political interference, to no avail. The Charter did nevertheless provide a legal framework for VOA's work, which could no longer be considered an instrument of the US government but the real voice of America around the world.

In the 1970s, the decade of détente, US international broadcasting underwent a period of stagnation, even decline. During that period, VOA broadcast 860 hours of programming a week, in 35 languages. As the United States lost much prestige (a consequence of the Vietnam debacle, and Watergate), VOA went through an identity crisis. It became unsure as to what its message should be. As a tool of anticommunist propaganda, it seemed unable to adapt to the new rapprochement between the United States and the Soviet Union. Officials forced decisions on the radio station that journalists did not understand, such as requesting an end to the reading of *The Gulag Archipelago* on the air in 1973, or shutting down a frequency used for Russian programming, which the Soviets had long complained interfered with their domestic broadcasts. In 1979 the State Department went so far as to blame VOA for having spoken of the Katyn massacre perpetrated by the Red Army against Polish officers in 1940.[8] Caught in the crossfire, the editorial staff reacted indignantly to conflicting demands: on the one hand, dissident groups clamoring for stronger anti-Sovietism and, on the other, the State Department calling for a more conciliatory approach.[9]

The Human Rights theme developed by the Carter administration brought renewed legitimacy to VOA's actions, although its focus in this area seemed highly selective. The station was keen to condemn the plight of dissidents in Eastern Bloc countries, through constant reminders of the commitments in the 1975 Helsinki Accords, but it conveniently overlooked human rights violations in Chile, Iran, or the Philippines, countries that received US backing. In this regard, VOA remained faithful to its fundamental mission: to support American interests in the world.

With Ronald Reagan as a new President, the Soviet intervention in Afghanistan and the crisis in Poland, VOA gained new momentum. In 1981, it broadcast 905 hours a week, in 39 languages. The Reagan administration allocated a $21.3 million budget to "Project Democracy," to combat "global communism" and to support all those who fought for democratic ideas in the world, in accordance with US views. This vast program was presented as a vital complement to US military efforts seeking to force the Soviets to give up the arms race.

BBC (British Broadcasting Corporation)
In 1932, the BBC created its "External Service" (called "Empire Service" at the time), which earned it considerable prestige during the Second World War.[10] On September 7, 1939, the British broadcaster started broadcasting in Polish, followed from 1939 to 1941 by all of the other languages of Central and Eastern Europe. By 1945, the BBC was broadcasting in 36 languages around the world but not yet in Russian. Why broadcast in Russian, since the Soviet Union was then part of the Allied forces? In the winter of 1945-1946 it nevertheless started to seriously contemplate such plans, based on a recommendation from the British embassy in Moscow, which reported an increasing number of attacks against Great Britain in the Soviet press and radio. The service in Russian was launched on March 24, 1946, with three broadcasts a day, for a total of 75 minutes. Russian programming followed the same structure as the BBC's other international broadcasts: an international news bulletin and newscast about Great Britain (the same for every country), followed by commentary on some of the day's events. In the early days, Russian audiences had mixed reactions to the London-based radio broadcasts. The embassy reported, for instance, that the first listeners were unhappy with the use of Russian speakers flaunting a highly unpopular accent, similar to the Oxford accent in English.[11] Like other international radio stations, the BBC was finding it difficult to recruit freshly landed Russian immigrants.

In 1949 the BBC's Overseas Service was still the world's leading broadcaster, with a total of 687 hours a week, versus 464 for the Soviet Union and 214 for the United States. But in 1950, with major budget cutbacks by the British government, many of the Western European and Scandinavian-language sections were slashed. In 1951 and 1952, the rise of VOA put the BBC in second place. Its sections in Eastern European languages were however saved, some even growing slightly (except for the Albanian section, which closed in 1967). The BBC's famous *English by Radio* broadcasts were gradually introduced in language programming targeted at Soviet Bloc countries: in October 1956 in the Russian section, in June and October 1958 in the Czech and Hungarian stations, and in February 1959 in the Polish section.

Officials at the BBC strove to avoid the trappings of anticommunist propaganda, of the type used by VOA. They maintained a stance of objectivity that became the hallmark of the British station during the war. It was based on four principles:

- avoid getting into a polemic with radio broadcasters in unfriendly territory: this would play into the hands of the opponent, on a terrain he has chosen;
- present information and opinions in a language devoid of emotional content, in an objective and accurate fashion: journalists should not expose their personal bias;
- ensure that international news is covered with a measure of balance, so that listeners don't assume news stories from their own country are always the most important;
- do not turn the BBC into the mouthpiece of the British government: on domestic or foreign issues, its mission is to present the diversity of viewpoints from the main actors and experts.

This ideal view was sometimes contradicted by concrete assessment of the content, whose quality varied from one language section to the next. Because each section had to translate the same news bulletin, written in English in the main newsroom, major errors could be made in the translation. In 1975, for example, an evaluation report by Alexander Lieven, head of European Service, stressed that: "accuracy was generally high, but that there were horrendous errors in translation from time to time, caused by ignorance, sloppiness, or occasionally, an apparent desire to develop a different interpretation in the translated item."[12]

Britain's political and military commitments on the world stage also had an obvious influence on how the BBC's strict line of neutrality could be maintained with regard to British power. The broadcaster's independence was strained, for example, during the Anglo-French expedition on the Suez Canal in 1956, as it was during the Falklands War of 1982. Broadcasts aimed at the East were also the object of specific criticisms. A number of articles by British Sovietologists in *The Spectator* in 1957-1958 questioned the policy orientations of the Russian program. They challenged its overly diplomatic language aimed, in their opinion, at lifting signal jamming. They felt the BBC, under cover of objectivity, was too complacent toward Soviet authorities and not vigilant enough when it came to flaws in the system.[13]

Among all major international radio broadcasters, the 1960s were characterized by the development of programming aimed at Africa. The continent was experiencing a time of upheaval, bustling with national decolonization movements. On May 1st, 1965, the English service, known as the "Overseas Service," was renamed the BBC's "World Service." The election of Edward Heath in 1970 allowed the BBC to secure major funding to overhaul its network of transmission towers, most of which dated from the days of WWII. But the 1973 oil crisis brought new budgetary restrictions. For the BBC, as for VOA, the climate of détente between East and West led to a plateauing of its "External Service" (723 hours of weekly programming in 1970, 719 hours in 1980). Some even said the BBC should recede from its political role in the East, in favor of more active promotion of British businesses and culture. But the Val Duncan Report replied to those set on turning the BBC into a "traveling salesman" that "the main value of the External Services is not [to] help people sell tractors or nuclear reactors..." but to combat ideologies before they ultimately become military threats.[14]

In 1979 the BBC again entered a difficult period as the government set out to make deep new cuts in its operating budget. A media campaign, largely orchestrated by parliamentarians, was successful in rolling back most of the government's initial plans. After the Russian invasion of Afghanistan, followed by the crisis in Poland, the Foreign Office provided the BBC with additional resources to broadcast in these countries. In the 1980s moderate growth was back (765 weekly hours in 1988). That same year the decision was made to bring all language stations under the main "World Service" banner. British radio, which at the time broadcast in 43 languages, succeeded in remaining the standard in international radio. As one of its former experts once quipped: "as Chile exports copper, and Australia wool, so Britain exports honest information."[15]

From "Poste Colonial" to RFI (Radio France Internationale)
France's foreign radio efforts pale in comparison to other similar services. Before WWII, however, the country did own a first-rate broadcasting infrastructure that rivaled that of Great Britain. French broadcasts from its *Poste Colonial* started even earlier than the BBC's "Empire Service."[16] On the eve of Hitler's invasion, the French radio station, now called "*Paris Mondial*" had been broadcasting in 21 languages, including Polish, since October 1938. The German invasion broke that momentum. By war's end, French radio was a mere shadow of itself. Efforts at rebuilding an ambitious foreign broadcasting service (*Émissions vers l'Étranger*, or EVE) fell under the budgetary restrictions of the "axe commission," a decision that Raymond Aron deplored at the time, saying the

government was depriving itself of the most affordable form of propaganda.[17] Even while government officials claimed the need to challenge Soviet propaganda, and launched a "communist witch hunt," including within the radio station itself, the international broadcasting service was neglected, isolated, and poorly staffed. Its programming schedule included broadcasts in Esperanto and Yiddish, but not in Russian, which was introduced as late as October 3, 1960. Of its programming directed at Eastern Europe, only the Polish section retained a certain vigor, thanks to the exceptional funding provided by the Marshall Plan between 1949 and 1953.[18] For lack of means over that period, broadcasts in Romanian, Hungarian, Czech, Slovak, and Slovenian barely managed to survive.

Did France suffer such trauma under the Occupation and the Vichy government's collaboration that all of its energies had to be devoted to rebuilding its own identity, with scant concern for its image on the international scene? How surprising it was that after 1958 General de Gaulle, who himself had such extensive first-hand experience in the importance of foreign broadcasting, made no attempt to revive France's international broadcasting policy, even though it could have constituted an additional asset for French influence.

Foreign programming, then under the responsibility of a Foreign Relations Directorate created on February 24, 1963, still suffered from the same incoherence. In April 1963 a report by Eduard Balladur provided an in-depth analysis for the first time, making short- and long-term recommendations (maximizing the use of existing technical means, building new transmitters outside the mainland France, producing steady programming in French.)[19] One of the report's impacts was to prompt a study on the potential audience of the French foreign radio service (called *Rose des vents*, or "wind rose"). The study was very successful. Starting November 20, 1964, and over 11 days, the French radio station (whose transmitting power was boosted for the occasion) asked for listeners' reports from around the world: it received 45,147 answers and 69,611 listeners' reports from some 114 countries.[20] Interest around the world in France's international broadcasting was now a proven fact. This operation, whose publicity impact was felt by key political officials, convinced the government that it should launch a program to build more powerful transmitters as part of the Fifth Plan. The decision was announced at the National Assembly on October 14, 1965.[21] However, the Finance Minister then refused to allocate the 10 million francs required to relaunch the international broadcast programs. The Foreign Affairs Minister in charge of the directorate (which from 1968 was called the Foreign Affairs and Cooperation Directorate) fought the development of foreign broadcasting. Clearly, the French Ministry of Foriegn Affairs did not believe in short-wave radio.[22]

In 1970 the prospects of French international broadcasting looked particularly bleak: only 200 hours a week, versus 723 for the BBC. That same year, a position paper by France's National Union of Journalists drew attention to the sorry state of France's policy in this area. With regard to broadcasts aimed at communist countries, the paper denounced the fact that "we have persisted for years with broadcasts in French of a news bulletin in Eastern Europe, during working hours, when the total number of listeners who understand French is limited at best. Meanwhile, we broadcast almost no French lessons in the region."[23] Rather than review the programming, when Radio France Internationale (RFI) was created after the demise of the ORTF, the decision was made in 1974 to simply abandon all broadcasting toward the Eastern Bloc countries. France chose to focus all of its efforts on the South, mainly Africa. In those years, the volume of its foreign programming reached an all-time low (at 125 hours a week, in 1980).

Under the administration of François Mitterrand, RFI soared again. After General Jaruzelski's power grab in Poland, the Polish section was revived in December 1981, followed by other language sections: in Russian (September 1983), Romanian (January 1985) and Serbo-Croatian (January 1986),[24] but not in Czech, a failure deplored by many at the time. "Why are the Czechs, probably the population most attached to French in Central Europe (along with the Poles), not deemed worthy of a special service in their language?"[25] In 1988, RFI reached a total of 302 hours of weekly programming in 9 languages, which was still a far cry from the BBC and the Deutsche Welle.

Deutsche Welle and Deutschlandfunk

In 1929, Germany was one of the very first countries to set up an international radio broadcasting system. That system was to be silenced in 1945. In the immediate postwar period, West Germany's radio stations were brought under the control of the occupiers, before German personnel were gradually reintroduced at their helm.

Deutsche Welle (DW) was created in only 1953, as a member of the public broadcasting network. Starting May 3, 1953, programs were gradually introduced in German, English, Spanish, Portuguese, Arabic, Russian, Polish, Czech, Hungarian, and Serbo-Croatian.[26] Modeled after the BBC, DW sought to position itself as the international radio station of reference in the German language. It clearly saw itself competing with East Germany's Radio Berlin International, created in 1956. Like its rival, DW sought to conquer various audiences in developing countries. Competition between the two stations, both of which sought to speak in the name of Germany, was especially intense on the African continent during the decolonization struggles of the 1960s. West Germany's international broadcasting efforts underwent substantial growth over that period, jumping from 315 hours in 1963, to 779 hours in 1970.

Bonn's policy toward the German Democratic Republic (GDR, or East Germany) clearly contributed to modifying programming content. Over the period of the Hallstein doctrine (non-recognition of the GDR), the primary mission of DW was to dissuade any country from establishing relations with East Germany. When Willy Brandt's *Ostpolitik* was formulated in the early 1970s, the role of DW shifted from fighting the GDR to promoting West Germany's interests in the world, while still denigrating communist ideology.

The country's partition spurred a parallel effort to set up a radio station that would appeal to West Germans and East Germans alike, and to rebut the propaganda emanating from the communist station, Deutschlandsender, into which West Germans could tune. However, West Germany had no national radio system at the time, only regional stations within each land. The project of a federal radio broadcaster, supported by Conrad Adenauer, faced stiff opposition from social democrats who feared the government would use the project to gain control over regional media. After a string of conflicts during the 1950s over its financing, programming, and location, a federal law was passed on October 26, 1960, that founded the new radio station, called Deutschlandfunk.[27] The same law also gave Deutsche Welle a government agency status. Both were supervised by their own Board of Administrators, comprising representatives from the government, political parties, churches, business employers, and labor unions.

When it started broadcasting on January 1, 1962, Deutschlandfunk's main mission was to build a "radio bridge between East and West Germans,"[28] covering news and issues within both areas of partitioned Germany. To prevent East Germany from claiming the broadcaster was established to undermine it, Deutschlandfunk launched parallel programming aimed at other Central and Eastern European countries (in Polish, Romanian, Hungarian, Czech, Slovak, Serbo-Croatian), as well as at Western Europe and Scandinavia (in English, Danish, French, Italian, Dutch, Norwegian, and Swedish).

However, programming in these languages was already being provided by Deutsche Welle, and therefore often duplicated efforts. This obviously created rivalry between the two stations, while undermining their effectiveness. It furthermore became apparent that their respective personnel were not keen on cooperating, even though the two radio stations' large headquarters in Cologne were neighbors.

On April 23, 1975, an agreement was finally reached: Deutschlandfunk would continue its medium frequency broadcasts in Polish, Czech, Slovak, and Hungarian, while maintaining editorial control over its programming on short-wave in the same languages. Deutsche Welle would keep its broadcasts in Serbo-Croatian and Romanian, with editorial control in these languages on medium frequency.

Unlike other Western counterparts, West German broadcasters faced neither budgetary cutbacks nor stagnation during the 1970s, but rather steady growth (reaching 804 weekly hours in 1980). Their efforts through the 1980s even helped them unseat the BBC's top position (with 831 hours in 1988). However, a closer look at their programming towards Eastern Bloc countries reveals major differences: while the number of hours was nearly the same with regard to Eastern Europe (88 hours a week for the BBC, versus 86 for Deutsche Welle), the BBC devoted more resources to Russian programming (45 hours, versus 26). In only two decades (from 1950 to 1970), West Germany succeeded in becoming one of the world's top broadcasters, not only by developing "traditional" international radio broadcasting in 39 languages, but also by creating a "cross-Germany" radio station whose impact on the political and social life of East Germany was particularly strong.

2. Substitution radio stations: RIAS, RFE, RL, RFE/RL

As their name indicates, substitution radio stations seek to provide a substitute to official state-sanctioned media in the countries where they broadcast. Even as they broadcast in foreign lands, these stations claim to be "the voice of the people" and, as such, provide programming only in the native language of the target country. The communication rationale of substitution radio stations is based not on the source, as in our previous examples, but rather on the *target*, that is, on the perceived expectations of audiences. The legitimacy of programming is grounded in the need for *truth*: substitution radio stations say what the official media don't say or distort, whether that is about today's news or other historical and cultural events. They seek to provide alternative informational and editorial services while often "dressing up" their programs with music, weather forecasts, practical information, etc.

Professing to be "the voice of the people," substitution radio stations serve as a relay and amplifier for the voices of domestic opposition. Their mission is to support potential resistance movements that specifically lack the means to make themselves heard. In other words, substitution radio stations endeavor—from abroad—to exert indirect influence on domestic political life. Unlike representation radio stations, they seek not to woo a potential audience (which is taken for granted), but rather to *exert pressure* on the authorities of the target country.

Such radio stations therefore operate under a specific political project: to challenge the legitimacy of the regime in a target country. The regimes in question never fail to see the real danger and the destabilizing impact of these stations; they will thus act more aggressively against substitution radio stations than against representation radio stations. Understandably, they want to investigate the origins and objectives of such undertakings: Who funds them? Who runs them? For what purpose?

R.I.A.S. (Radio In American Sector)

On the initiative of the US military government based in Berlin, then under the helm of Gen. Lucius Clay, RIAS (Radio in American Sector) went on the air in February 1946. Its programming, transmitted through cable at the time, was aimed at the German population living in the US-controlled area. RIAS provided an information service on day-to-day affairs (which products were available in the supply centers, for instance), and scheduled political and cultural programs to "explain" to Germans the horrors of the Nazi regime. In 1948, as the Soviets proceeded with the Berlin blockade, RIAS served as the mouthpiece of the Allied resolve. With the onset of the Cold War, the tone of the radio station became increasingly belligerent toward the communist authorities in Moscow and East Berlin alike. When it started broadcasting in May 1949 (first on low, then medium frequency, then FM), the station could cover nearly all the Soviet-controlled areas of Germany.

Under the motto "The free voice of the free world," most RIAS programming was prepared by a West German team working under US supervision. The station's objective was to inform, entertain and educate the East German public by providing the radio station it would have wanted, had it had a choice in the matter. In the early 1950s, Radio in American Sector offered comprehensive programming, complete with news bulletins, commentaries, games and contests, music programs (jazz, especially), weather forecasts, and classroom broadcasts. By 1953 it was already broadcasting 24 hours a day and was therefore adjoined by RIAS 2, which broadcast 12 hours a day with programming aimed at more specific segments of the East German population: farmers, women, Communist Party cadres, and police officers.[29]

During the 1950s, RIAS' popularity grew steadily, particularly through satirical shows that tackled issues banned in the communist media. East Germans, who at the time could still travel to West Berlin, would send in postcards, phone in, or even take the risk of visiting the station's headquarters. Thanks to such input and constant monitoring of East German media, RIAS was fairly well-informed of all aspects of the daily, political and social life in East Germany. While broadcasting news from the West, the station focused its efforts on gathering information from the East, primarily East Germany, but later other Eastern bloc countries as well. When, for example, Hungarian youth secured certain rights, RIAS would immediately let the East German youth know about it, so that they too could start demanding the same rights. Thus was born the technique known as "cross reporting," obviously geared at promoting a certain social combativeness, and later to be adopted by the RFE/RL. The radio station did not encourage violence, but it did incite people to make demands. On June 16 and 17, 1953, as strikes and demonstrations rocked East Berlin, RIAS helped to amplify the protest movement by relaying the demands of workers, and publicized their actions throughout East Germany.[30]

The building of the Berlin Wall, in August 1961, severed the station's ties to many sources of information within East Germany. This sudden disruption, which lent renewed importance to its action, removed the finger the radio station had kept on the pulse of the East German public. In the early days of détente, US officials soon started questioning the strategic necessity of the station, while the staff still believed in its usefulness. By 1967, programs catering for specific segments of the population were abandoned in favor of more general programming. RIAS appeared to have become a West German station like any other, except for the fact that it carried more news about the communist world.

In 1972 the terms of the inter-German treaty allowed RIAS journalists to travel to East Germany, as long as they obtained the required authorization from state authorities. The quality of news immediately improved, even though journalists would sometimes self-censor to keep their credentials. The rising power of television through the 1970s and 80s contributed to the decline of the radio station. The East German public preferred to watch West German TV programs, a phenomenon so massive that the communist regime simply had to concede defeat.[31] RIAS played only a support role at that point, providing the daily schedule of West German television stations, as no specialized magazine or TV Guide was available in East Germany.[32] To slow down its decline, RIAS launched its own TV program in 1986, as well as a radio station aimed at a younger audience (with lots of music and short news bulletins).

Over these four decades, a number of conflicts emerged at the radio station, due to the fact of it serving two masters: the United States of America and West Germany. Although it was staffed mostly by Germans from day one, RIAS remained very much an American station. Funded by the United States Information Agency (USIA),[33] it remained an official instrument of US foreign policy, a tangible symbol of the United States' determination to remain in West Berlin. Meanwhile, certain observers interpreted declining levels of US support during the 1960s as a weakening of the US resolve to resist communist pressure on Berlin.[34]

At the same time, RIAS was becoming increasingly "Germanized," particularly after joining the West German ARD network. The US authorities gradually decreased financial support to the station, to the point that in the 1970s, 90% of the station's budget was provided by West Germany. The role of the United States remained mostly political: to ensure continued operation of RIAS in West Berlin. Conflicts inevitably arose, as US supervisors complained that the German team responsible for day-to-day programming failed to listen to them. The policy direction of RIAS—which spoke for two governments with complementary but different foreign policies—was incontrovertibly impacted, preventing in-depth coverage of sensitive issues (such as German reunification or nuclear missile deployment in West Germany). These pressures on the orientation of RIAS hurt the quality of programming, which in turn most likely contributed to lower ratings.

RFE (Radio Free Europe)

Near the end of the 1940s the RIAS model inspired another US station to start transmitting from Munich toward all of the "Sovietized" countries of Europe: Poland, Czechoslovakia, Hungary, Romania, and Bulgaria.[35] Staffed by exiles from each country, the station purported to be independent, while in fact it was funded by the CIA. From 1946-1947, former heads of counterintelligence (from the Office of Strategic Services, or OSS) and experts in psychological warfare started thinking about the best way to enlist Eastern Bloc exiles in the ideological fight that was beginning against the USSR. To this end, they sparked the creation of the National Committee for a Free Europe (NCFE) that would bring exiles under its wing as part of a broader anti-Communist program. Funded by the CIA from 1949 on, the committee's plan was to set up a radio station aimed at the populations of Eastern and Central Europe with a view to support and even foster resistance against Moscow. The CIA sought to help these people free themselves from the communist yoke. In this, the Agency knew it could count on the support of proponents of the *Rollback* policy aimed at pushing the Soviets out of Europe—a policy championed by James Burnham who deemed the *Containment* doctrine incapable of holding back Soviet pressure.[36] A classified report from the National Security Council (NSC-68) dated April 14, 1950, provided a comprehensive framework for just such a strategy, calling for a "nonmilitary counteroffensive against the USSR, including covert economic, political, and psychological warfare to stir up unrest and revolt in satellite countries."[37] Radio Free Europe was born into this thick Cold War atmosphere. A parallel can be drawn between the creation of RFE and the founding of the Congress for Cultural Freedom in Berlin, in 1950. Both initiatives were part of a common strategy of cultural resistance to communism in Europe. As such, they benefited from the support of the CIA and private foundations, "with this mix of philanthropy and intelligence work the mastery of which the United States seem to relish."[38] To avoid harming official relations with Moscow, the NCFE was introduced as the private initiative of respectable American citizens concerned about the struggle for truth, and against communism. The creation of the National Committee for a Free Europe was announced on June 1, 1949, at an official ceremony held at the Empire State building in New York. The following year, it launched a "Crusade for Freedom" throughout the United States, led by Gen. Lucius Clay, as part of Harry Truman's "Campaign of Truth." This US-style extravaganza, which took the Freedom Bell as its symbol, was aimed at mobilizing American public opinion and at raising financial support for the objectives of the Committee. Every year the NCFE would lead a fund-raising campaign for its projects. However, the amounts raised remained small in comparison to those funneled through the CIA: for the year 1951-1952, for example, private donations amounted to $600,000, while secret government allocations reached $28 million.

Radio Free Europe started beaming toward Central Europe on US Independence Day, July 4, 1950. The broadcast was rather modest: aimed at Czechoslovakia and Romania, it lasted all of 20 minutes. Within three years however, the station had grown rapidly, transmitting in Polish, Hungarian, Czech, Slovak, Romanian, Bulgarian, and even Albanian (from 1953 to 1956). At the time, each language section was introduced to its listeners not as "Radio Free Europe" but as "The Voice of Free Poland," or "Free Hungary," and so on, as if the radio station were the only alternative to communist media. Programming, based on the RIAS model, sought to be as comprehensive as possible, mixing information with commentary, programs for specific social segments, weather forecasts, and music programs (mainly jazz and rock).

At the time, the CIA was also conducting airdrops over Eastern Europe, using balloons filled with political leaflets and brochures calling local populations to protest and struggle, with slogans such as "Labor Unions to Workers," "More Money, Less Talk," "Food for People, Not the Soviets," etc. As part of Operation Prospero in July 1953, 12 million leaflets were dropped from 6,512 balloons sent over Prague, Pilsen, and Bratislava. The organizers of such operations were convinced "that they had pioneered a technique in political warfare in combining the qualities of radio and the printed word," as the two media "complemented and reinforced each other."[39] From 1951 to 1956, 300 million leaflets were showered on Czechoslovakia, Hungary and Poland.

In Poland, Radio Free Europe carried out its first "stunt" based on revelations from Colonel Jósef Światìo, a former member of the secret police. When he defected to the West in 1954, he was debriefed for months by CIA experts, who decided to broadcast his experience on the airwaves of RFE. Światìo knew of a number of scandals and corruption cases within the ranks of the secret police, as well as among communist leaders. RFE broadcast over a hundred interviews with him, while thousands of leaflets about his stories were balloon-dropped over Poland's main cities. According to Bronislaw Geremek, these were "authentic revelations that had a major impact on public opinion. For the first time, the secret lives of power-holders were exposed. This was a great moment in the history of RFE in Poland, earning it the public's trust."[40] The Polish government felt the need to take action. The former Department of Public Safety (created under Stalin) was disbanded, and a number of officials from the secret police were fired.

The "liberation" message that RFE directed at the peoples of Eastern Europe was quite ambiguous. What kind of liberation was being promoted? The 1956 Hungarian insurrection became an eye-opener in this regard. As François Fejtö has pointed out, the heads of RFE's Hungarian station were severely blamed for "criminal negligence"[41] for these "broadcasts widely followed in Hungary," and the way they besmirched Imre Nagy's policies and encouraged the Hungarians to revolt.[42] This was in stark contrast with the attitude of RFE's Polish section headed by Jan Nowark. A few weeks earlier, during "Polish October," the station had supported the compromise position represented by Gomulka, advising caution to the population.[43] By the end of 1956, Radio Free Europe was the subject of intense controversy in the Western press. Sanctions were taken against it, with commissions of inquiry launched by West Germany, the Council of Europe and the United Nations.

This challenge to RFE's actions forced the United States to clarify its radio broadcast policies toward the Eastern Bloc countries. The position advocated by Jan Nowak prevailed: the RFE should promote gradual change within communist regimes, not incite local populations to an open and violent uprising. The objective of liberation for people living in the Eastern Bloc was clearly abandoned for that of liberalization of the communist regimes. The goal for RFE was to promote the development of an independent public opinion capable of putting pressure on the ruling elite, to embark on economic or political reform. In short, RFE's mission was to contribute, from the outside, to the creation of a public space that could form the basis for domestic forms of counter-power.

Starting in 1957, a "professional code of conduct" was drawn up by station officials with a view to establishing "guidelines" for staff, and thus put an end to outside criticisms. The code specified, for instance, that "public actions of the USSR government and party officials must be discussed by the RFE/RL staff in a responsible and dignified manner" (Point 3), that "nothing must be broadcast which could legitimately be interpreted as an incentive to violence or as irredentist," that "RFE/RL neither supports nor encourages any separatist or secessionist movements nor raises any territorial questions" (Point 4), ... and that "any suggestion which could lead listeners to believe that the West might intervene militarily in any part of their territory in the event of civil strife or international crisis, is to be avoided" (Point 8). It ended by declaring that "RFE/RL professionals must represent a model of tolerance and respect of plurality, diversity and human rights for all" (Point 10).

Despite this policy, two programming approaches regularly came to heads within RFE. On the one hand, there were the "hard-sellers" who saw radio mainly as an instrument of political persuasion aimed at educating listeners indoctrinated through decades of disinformation. On the other, there were the "soft-sellers" who thought their primary mission was to inform, and that this information should be objective and professional, allowing the audience to make up their own mind: were they not in the best position to see what a failure the communist system was? A review of programming shows both approaches coexisting on the air at RFE until the 1980s, mirroring conflicts on these issues among US officials as well as among the Eastern European émigrés recruited by the station. Such tensions were also observed at the sister broadcaster, Radio Liberty.

Radio Liberty (RL)
On March 1, 1953, a few days before the death of Stalin, another US radio station started broadcasting from Munich, this time towards the Soviet Union: Radio Liberation (RL, later changed to Radio Liberty [see below]). The creation of this station was largely inspired by RFE, although each operation was launched by clearly distinct secret cells. On January 18, 1951 at the instigation of the CIA, a committee was also created for the

recruitment of expatriates from the Soviet Union: AMCOMLIB (American Commitee for Liberation of the People of the USSR), an equivalent of the NCFE.[44] The committee's objective was to call for the liberation of Russia from the Soviet regime, especially through the creation of a radio station that would broadcast in the USSR. The idea was also launched of creating a research institute on the country's evolution, which would work in tandem with the station and provide it with expertise.

However, US officials encountered considerable difficulties recruiting competent émigrés who also spoke English. Conflicts that soon arose between members of AMCOMLIB, of diverse nationalities and political persuasions, delayed the project's launch. American officials were also not nearly as clear about the objectives of their propaganda efforts aimed at the USSR, as they were about those aimed at Central and Eastern Europe. Five years after Yalta, it still seemed possible to loosen Central and Eastern Europe from the Soviet grip. But the same goal within the USSR, a country that had lived under communism for over thirty years at that point, seemed more remote. That is why the purpose of Radio Liberation seemed so poorly defined. There were some who thought that it could help build relations of trust and cooperation between the Soviet and American peoples by countering the "anti-imperialist" propaganda of communist media. And there were others who thought that the goal should instead be to weaken the USSR, to make it more amenable in its dealings with the United States.

One thing is sure: RL's first broadcasts had such a strident anti-communist and anti-Stalinist tone that Jon Lodeesen wondered who, within the Soviet Union, could really be receptive: "People who felt no particular animosity towards Stalin could not identify with these programs."[45] RL initially broadcast in Russian, Belorussian and Ukrainian, and expanded its programming over the years to other populations of the Soviet Union. It was in charge of broadcasts to the Baltic states (Lithuania, Estonia, Latvia).[46] In 1972, it broadcast in 17 languages, including three in the Caucasus (Armenian, Azeri, Georgian), and six in Central Asia (Kazakh, Kirghiz, Tajik, Tatar, Turkmen, and Uzbek).

Over its first decade of operation, however, RL was barely audible within the Soviet Union. It seemed as though the US government did not want to provide the radio station with the means of immediately reaching an audience. It started broadcasting with a 10 kW transmitter, increased to 100 kW in 1959, and to 250 kW in 1964. Only then did its signal finally become strong enough to be heard, but still with a high noise ratio. To overcome intense jamming, the station was outfitted with new transmitters that, by the end of the 1960s, reached a power of 1,300 kW.[47]

The debates stemming from RFE's role in the 1956 Hungarian insurrection also led to a mellowing of RL's initially aggressive stance. In 1959 this change led to the adoption of a new, more modest name whose symbolic resonance still remained strong: Radio Liberty. But had liberation from Soviet domination of populations that made up the USSR really been at issue? Radio Liberty's programming never did appear to have insurrectionary qualities. Throughout the 1950s and 60s, it broadcast mainly literary and artistic programs that, within each of the Soviet Union's republics, sustained national and religious sentiments. With the exception of a few major news pieces, such as the content of the Khrushchev report, rebellions in the work camps or certain food riots, RL was unable to provide reliable detailed information on the Soviet Union, since it lacked contacts inside the country. Exiled writers, philosophers and artists were the main producers of its content.

In the 1960s, officials in Washington started questioning the usefulness of maintaining the station. However, as the first few *samizdats*[48] reached the West, RL was reborn. At certain stations, staff members who had known only Stalinism could hardly believe that such clandestine self-publishing could be for real in the USSR. They tended to see the *samizdats* as KGB provocation, until incontrovertible evidence proved the contrary—especially after Andrei Sakharov's *Reflections on Progress, Peaceful Coexistence, and Intellectual Freedom* was published in the West in 1968.[49] The question for RL was how to analyze, process and publicize all the underground material now flowing from Russia and the various republics of the USSR. So it gathered a number of Western specialists on the USSR and organized a conference in London in 1971, to draw up guidelines on how to use *samizdats*.[50] In addition, RL (as well as RFE) undertook to archive all the *samizdats* they received, building one of the world's most unique collections of such documents over that period.

However, just as RL was finally finding its second wind, even its true raison d'être, it entered a zone of turbulence—much like RFE—, following revelations in the United States that both stations were supported by the CIA. The battle each station then had to wage for its survival brought them together to officially merge their activities.

RFE/RL

Over the 1960s, CIA support for the Munich stations became increasingly common knowledge in well-informed circles, including journalists and politicians. But it was California's counter-cultural *Ramparts Magazine* that in February 1967 revealed the financial ties between the CIA and various civil (student, labor, etc.) organizations. This information was then published by the *New York Times* and the *Washington Post*. RFE's name soon appeared alongside the list of organizations that benefited from the CIA's covert funding programs, channeled through "front" foundations.[51] In view of the press coverage, President Johnson requested that the CIA put an end to these practices. In 1968, for the first time in their history, RFE and RL faced budget cuts. But the revelations failed to generate a full-blown scandal in American public opinion, which actually had almost no idea of what the Munich-based radio stations were doing. Public attention quickly turned to other dramatic news, both on the domestic front (with the assassinations of Robert F. Kennedy and Martin Luther King, Jr.) and internationally (with the invasion of Czechoslovakia and the war in Vietnam).

In the early 1970s, as East-West relations eased into détente, the very existence of Radio Free Europe and Radio Liberty was severely threatened. Democratic Senator J.W. Fulbright took the lead of those claiming that the radio stations had become "outworn relics of the Cold War."[52] Over the next two years, intense controversies rocked the US Congress and the Senate on this issue. Some wanted the radio stations simply shut down, while others wanted transparency in their sources of funding. The heads of both stations undertook intense lobbying efforts to convince the nation's representatives to maintain their operations. They persuaded 50 members of Congress to vote in their favor—a position that finally prevailed on March 22, 1972. However, Congress' monitoring of the annual funding would be a way to control the stations' activities.

In May 1972, Richard Nixon set up a commission, chaired by Milton Eisenhower, to plan the long-term future of the radio stations. Nixon implemented the report's main recommendation: the creation of a *Board for International Broadcasting* (BIB), to act as a trustee in charge of overseeing the quality, efficiency and professional integrity of RFE/RL's operations, in keeping with "the broad foreign policy objectives of the United States." Under the authority of the BIB (founded October 19, 1973), the two Munich-based radio stations became official tools of US international communications policy, with a status different from VOA's.[53] The statutes of the BIB brought the two radio stations closer together institutionally, and in 1976 they were placed under single management. The separate RFE and RL entities were subsequently merged and called RFE/RL.

The managerial merger between the two Munich stations helped to improve the efficiency of their operations, but it also brought financial and administrative oversight that constrained their autonomy. Certain journalists started missing the "good old days" of the CIA when money was no concern and not as many justifications were required. In January 1981, James Critchlow, a member of the BIB, traveled incognito to Munich and wrote a scathing report on the poor quality of Russian programming, which he said was tainted by the expression of Russian "nationalistic and xenophobic views."[54] The report was leaked to the press, setting off a small scandal within the radio station. Control mechanisms were all the more deeply resented by journalists at both radio stations as they felt the US directors nominated to head the RFE/RL were generally incompetent, lacking in motivation, and brought too much of a managerial view to their job.

The fact that RFE and RL now fell under a single management changed little in the stations' operation. Each team of expatriates still lived in its own separate world. Over the years, two distinct microcosms had indeed developed, each with its own labor union, wage structure, jargon, etc. The "RFE world" had very little communication with the "RL world," even though staff members worked every day in the same building. The "RFE world" remained dominant. Its staff was seen as more professional than that of RL, and more of them spoke English. They had better relations with the US overseers than those of RL, who spoke mostly Russian. Each of these two "worlds" could then be further broken down into as many "sub-worlds" as there were language sections within each radio station. In addition, all of these sub-worlds (Polish, Hungarian, Romanian for RFE; Russian, Ukrainian and Georgian for RL) carried the weight of its own specific history—a history of course ridden with conflict. The successive generations of émigrés that had joined the stations since 1950 clashed often, as each brought in its own particular disappointments or expectations (see below).

In 1975, soon after the US government decided to openly support the Munich-based radio stations, the agreement on the Conference on Security and Cooperation in Europe (CSCE) brought international legitimacy to their efforts. The days when the CIA would use the radio stations to carry out covertly what could be called a strategy of "indirect destabilization" of the communist camp[55] already seemed far behind. Although the strategy was "pacified," somewhat in keeping with the new developments in international relations, its fundamental objective changed very little in substance. The goal of RFE/RL remained to support the efforts of a potential opposition within the Eastern bloc, of those called "dissidents" in the USSR, and "resistance" in Poland. Under the Carter administration the approach was maintained in the name of human rights. It continued under Ronald Reagan, only this time as part of the battle for "Truth." This is how support for the actions of RFE and RL remained consistent through various administrations.

Resources, however, remained modest. In the early 1980s, the annual budget of RFE/RL was about $200 million, or the cost of one B1 bomber. Some analysts deplored the disproportionate allocation of military versus ideological means. Frank Shakespeare, for instance, opined that most US politicians never truly believed in the strategic importance of these propaganda efforts aimed at the Eastern bloc.[56] The Soviets, however, took this threat very seriously, never ceasing to demand the closure of the Munich-based radio stations, calling them "nests of spies"—a charge that might not have been totally groundless. It would take Gorbachev's *Glasnost* policy before a change of attitude toward the radio stations could be seen in Moscow. Signal jamming was stopped, which forced the heads of RFE/RL to review their mission.[57]

3. The particular case of Vatican Radio

The religious purpose of Vatican Radio puts the station in a distinct category. Created with the assistance of Guglielmo Marconi, Vatican Radio was inaugurated by Pope Pius XI on February 12, 1931,[58] then put under the care of the Society of Jesus. Its basic mission was to promote Catholicism as the universal religion, and to allow representatives of the Church and of the Roman Catholic faith to stay in touch with Rome wherever they were in the world. Over the first few years of its existence, programs were most often limited to special broadcasts (messages from the Pope, eucharistic congresses, canonizations, etc.).

The political situation under fascist Italy was a source of major difficulties in the operation and development of Vatican Radio. Since it depended on the Italian administration for signal transmission, the station had to be quite circumspect, for its programs could be censored or banned. In 1939, Radio Vatican launched Polish and Hungarian programs. During the war it added programs in Lithuanian, Ukrainian, and Slovak. Radio Vatican launched a message service for prisoners and the deported, and sought dialogue among all belligerents. Nazi Germany still questioned the radio station's neutrality, reprimanding it for its broadcast of certain sermons critical of Hitler's regime. The station's broadcasts in French were terminated in May 1941, when Father Emmanuel Mistiaen used the airwaves to denounce the National Socialist ideology. They were resumed the following September, but then only in muted language, full of innuendoes.[59]

After the war the radio station grew rapidly, thanks to the support of several Catholic communities like that of the Netherlands, which gave it a 100kW transmitter in 1950. From 1947 to 1950, Radio Vatican launched new programs to reach the populations of the Soviet camp: in Romanian, Czech, Slovak, Letton, Russian, Armenian, Albanian, Bulgarian, Croatian and Belarus. In 1957, Pope Pius XII inaugurated the new Santa Maria di Galeria broadcasting center and, in the same year, a new program was set up to complement the station's essentially religious and musical broadcasts. After the election of Pope John-Paul II, who adopted the habit of reciting the rosary on the air, the station broadcast Sunday mass in Polish. By 1979 Radio Vatican was broadcasting in 33 languages.[60]

As both a denominational and a state radio station, Radio Vatican was caught up in contradictions that weighed heavily on the quality of its programs. They were condemned for being uninteresting, often insipid and inaccessible to a lay public. The absence of competent staff and critical evaluation of these programs partly explained this situation. The fact however remained that, for audiences in the Communist Bloc, the uniqueness of this station was the priority it gave to broadcasting the mass in the language of countries where religious practice was banned or under close surveillance.

Broadcasting to silent audiences

Western radio stations broadcasting to Eastern Bloc countries encountered the same difficulties. The worst was the silence forced on their listeners. Nothing is more frustrating for a journalist than to produce a program without any hope of feedback on the targeted audiences' reactions—apart from a few letters received weeks or months later, whose content is often vague enough to cross the barriers of censorship. That was the daily lot of those who worked at these radio stations. Any communication implies both emitting and receiving a message; in the present case, was the message actually received? This gnawing doubt on the reception of Western radio is at the heart of their history and doubts about their usefulness.

All those in the upper echelons of the administration or the political class who were hostile to radio broadcasts to the East used the supposedly small audiences as an argument to call for budget cuts and the elimination or complete overhaul of certain programs. These threats never failed to trigger debate on the priorities of radio action. In view of the envisaged or imposed restrictions, at which countries should programs be aimed? Should the effort be concentrated on the world service in English (for the BBC) or in French (for RFI)? Which language section should be prioritized? What type of program? And so on.

The resistance regularly expressed by certain senior officials at Foreign Affairs regarding these radio stations was nevertheless based on a far more deep-seated critique of the legitimacy of their actions. As a form of interference in the domestic affairs of a state, because they endeavored to establish direct communication with its population, these radio broadcasts appeared to some to be incompatible with the traditional concept of international relations based on dialogue and cooperation between states. This was for example the very reserved attitude in the 1960s of the French Foreign Affairs Minister, who preferred to send taped radio broadcasts to the French embassies (so that they could have them broadcast on local or national stations) rather than supporting the international service of the moribund ORTF. In the 1970s the United States also had to deal with the fact that the State Department's approach to the Soviet Union tended to be out of phase with that of VOA, not to mention Radio Liberty.

Politicians in the West generally had very little knowledge of overseas radio activity because if was of no interest to them. As they broadcast to foreign countries, Western radio stations by definition had no influence on public opinion within their own country—the only opinion that counted in electoral periods. In fact these publics were usually unaware of the existence of such radio stations, which meant that there was no reason for politicians to try to defend their cause. This also explains why the tutelary authorities could so easily cut their budgets without any fear of opposition from a public that had very little if any knowledge of their actions. The only possible pressure groups in Western countries were those formed by communities of immigrants from the East. Some of their representatives were on occasion able to persuade the authorities to maintain or develop a program in the language of their home country.[61]

Little wonder that the staff of these radio stations (managers and journalists) often felt an absence of recognition for their work, especially from listeners east of the Iron Curtain. But those audiences were loath to take the risk of expressing their interest, except in hushed tones in letters that were never sure to arrive. For a Western journalist, working at an international radio station in his or her country was a thankless task; it could even be seen as a form of exclusion. The employees of these stations were therefore constantly in quest of recognition. Additionally, the foreigners recruited to work in the language sections frequently experienced an identity crisis, split as they were between their host and home countries.

In the absence of reliable audience figures, those in charge of Western radio stations tended to justify their missions in ideological or political terms. They pleaded that the stations were the spearheads of the battle for democracy in the East: their programs reflected the fundamental values of democratic systems and thus contributed to teaching these values to listeners. Among the practitioners of international broadcasting there was still a prevailing ideology, even a "philosophy of the principle of truth," expressed in the titles of English-language books on the subject, e.g., the above-cited work by Gerard Mansell on the history of the BBC, *Let the Truth be Told*; and those of two American experts, Edward Barret, *Truth is our Weapon*[62] and Wilson Dizard, *The Strategy of Truth*.[63] It mattered little that the practice of propaganda sometimes led to a restrictive or manipulative conception of the truth. All these writings were intended to demonstrate a political and moral obligation: if totalitarianism was synonymous with propaganda, then democracy was synonymous with truth, and Western radio had to embody an image diametrically opposed to that of the adverse system. The truthfulness of information was moreover a professional requirement, the minimal condition for the credibility of their "messages" and for developing listener loyalty.

To promote their cause, the heads of these radio stations continued to use more pragmatic arguments as well: the necessity to retaliate ("We have to increase the strength of our signal to counter the Soviets"), to meet the challenge of competition ("We need an extra transmitter because the BBC has just decided to get one"), and to satisfy national prestige ("The voice of France must be heard once again"). The advocates of international radio broadcasting compared the military budgets of Western states, earmarked for the purpose of containing or undermining communism in the East, to the budgets of radio stations intended for the same purpose. They pointed out that the latter were ridiculously small compared to the former, whereas the battle on the ideological front was crucial against a totalitarian system. In October 1950, in the heart of the Cold War, Sir Robert Bruce Lockhart justified the action of the BBC's international service to the British government in the following terms: "The External Service costs no more than a small cruiser, and for that price […], you could have the services of what amounted to a battle fleet."[64] Twenty years later US diplomat Averell Harriman defended RFE/RL before the US Presidential Commission, confirming that these two stations contributed to the West's security. Yet, not withstanding the validity of these arguments, detractors had every opportunity to ask: can you tell us how many people listen to your programs and whether they enjoy them?

The lack of contact with listeners also impacted on the quality of these radio stations' programs. Immigrants from the East recruited by the stations had often left their countries years before. Although they were driven by the desire to serve their homeland, their political motivation did not necessarily make them good at their job. Moreover, their situation as exiles was a handicap in understanding the evolution of the audiences for whom they were catering. They could represent potential listeners' expectations only in terms of their own past lives in their home country, and of their ideological and cultural background. They were therefore likely to offer programs that were out of phase with the target audience's expectations, because their representations no longer matched those listeners' daily lives.

The sociological and political composition of the language sections of Western radio stations was therefore of crucial importance to the nature and quality of their programs. In the immediate post-WWII years, programs to the East were hosted above all by immigrants who had fought Nazism and had subsequently engaged in the struggle against communism. But they had little or no experience of life in such a system, as most of them had emigrated before the war. Until the early 1970s these "pre-communism" immigrants were in a majority at the radio stations. There was some change when repressive measures consequent to the successive crises in Soviet Europe (1956, 1968 and 1981) triggered new waves of immigration from which Western radio stations could draw new talent and thus renew their Hungarian, Czech, Slovak and Polish teams.

The daily life of certain sections was therefore characterized by the cohabitation of two or three generations of émigrés. This situation tended to generate tension between those who had always refused communism, those who had believed in it for a while, and those who had grown up under it. Each wave of immigrants arrived with their own representations of audiences' supposed expectations, and the more limited the contact with the target country, the more their convictions clashed. The internal histories of RFE and RL were marked by these conflicts between generations and, in the case of RL, between the various religious and national traditions of the Soviet republics represented in Munich. At times the American officials had to arbitrate, even though they had scant knowledge of the Eastern country to which the section was broadcasting.

The paradoxical consequence of this situation was that the more a country experienced successive waves of emigration, the better the quality of radio programs broadcast to it. It was the arrival of freshly landed immigrants, by definition more in phase with the realities of their home country, that enabled the stations to propose programs more likely to meet audiences' expectations. Their contribution was indispensable, if only to transmit changes in the vocabulary and idiomatic expressions of the national language. As Poland was the Soviet Bloc country that had undergone the most social and political crises triggering waves of emigration, it was the Polish sections of these radio stations that had the highest rate of renewal. This was particularly true of the BBC and RFI: in the mid-1980s, the majority of their staff had left Poland between 1970 and 1983. The quality of Polish programs was thus improved. Those who worked for these radio stations often had contact with people who had remained in their home country and were still trying to combat the regime there. Across borders, between East and West, a form of complicity was established between them: that of participating in the same struggle for freedom. The renewal of the other Eastern sections was by comparison far more limited (with the exception of the periods immediately after 1956 for Hungary and 1968 for Czechoslovakia). This could explain the lack of vitality of the Russian sections, at least until Soviet Jews were authorized to emigrate in the early 1970s.[65]

The fact remained that Western radio stations were often unable to recruit real journalists for their Eastern-European sections—simply because they could find none. Recruitment criteria were based above all on candidates' political convictions, their motivations for wanting to work at a foreign radio station, and their intellectual qualities. Yet, despite the multiple criticisms leveled at them, and the all too often mediocre quality of their programs—from the point of view of both their technical reception and their content—Western radio stations really did have an audience in communist countries. For listeners in the East, who persisted in tuning into them, they symbolized the voice of the West, the forbidden fruit: the voice of freedom.

Table: Number of hours per week of Western radio stations' broadcasts in 1984*

	RL/RFE	VOA	BBC	DW/DLF
Eastern Europe	558	103.3	87.5	85.8
U.S.S.R.	497	201.3	45	26.3

* *Source:* Short (ed.), *Western Broadcasting Over the Iron Curtain*, op. cit., p. 20.

Notes

1. The vital role that television played between the two parts of Germany will be the object of a specific analysis (see Part 3, Chapter 2).

2. Actually, international broadcasting started to develop in the early 1930s. For its general approach, the best reference on this is Donald R. Browne, *International Radio Broadcasting: The limits of the Limitless Medium*, New York, Praeger Publishers, 1982. In French, see also Fouad Benhalla, *La guerre radiophonique*, Collection de la RPP, Paris, 1983.

3. The concept originated in the United States; see David M. Abshire, *The Washington Papers, International Broadcasting: a New Dimension of Western Diplomacy*, Sage Publications, 1976.

4. For a historical overview of these language sections, see Appendices 6.1 and 6.2, p. 131-132 in Kenneth R.M. Short (ed.), *Western Broadcasting over the Iron Curtain*, New York, St Martin's Press, 1986.

5. See the article by Alan Heil and Barbara Schiele, "The Voice Past: VOA, the USSR and Communist Europe" in Kenneth R.M. Short, *Western Broadcasting over the Iron Curtain*, op. cit., p. 98-112.

6. French national radio hosted VOA broadcasts until 1953. Simon Coppens was the radio station's representative for Europe. He hosted three 30-minute shows aimed at disseminating the spirit of the free world through its most appealing aspects: "America and its Music," "Panorama of American Jazz" and "Negro Spirituals." See Jean-François Remontet and Simone Depoux, *Les Années radio (1949-1989)*, éditions de l'Arpenteur, 1989, p. 35-36.

7. The US continued broadcasting in these languages of the USSR through what became Radio Liberty (see the following section on substitution radio stations).

8. Jack Anderson, "Putting a muzzle on the Voice of America" in *The Washington Post*, February 17, 1979, p. 31.

9. Laurien Alexandre, *The Voice of America: From Détente to the Reagan doctrine*, Ablex Publishing Corporation, 1988, p. 27.

10. On the war years, see Asa Briggs, *The History of Broadcasting in United Kingdom* (Volume 3), London, Oxford University Press, 1979.

11. Report from the British Embassy in Moscow, dated March 29, 1946 (BBC archives).

12. Quoted by Donald R. Browne, *International Radio Broadcasting: The Limits of the Limitless Medium*, New York, Praeger Publishers, 1982, p. 168.

13. For a discussion of this debate, see Gerard Mansell, *Let the Truth be Told: 50 years of the BBC External Broadcasting*, London, Weidenfeld and Nicolson, 1982, p. 260-62.

14. Gerard Mansell, *op. cit.*, p. 256.

15. Julian Hale, *Radio Power: Propaganda and International Broadcasting*, Editions Elek, 1985, p. 49.

16. The "*Poste Colonial*" started broadcasting May 6, 1931, during the Colonial Exhibition on the outskirts of Paris, while the "Empire Service" started only on December 19, 1932. For a history of French international broadcasting, see relevant sections in Christian Brochant, *Histoire générale de la radio et de la télévision en France*, Vol. I (1921-1944) and Vol. II (1944-1974), Paris, Documentation Française, 1994. See also Frédéric Brunquell, *Fréquence Monde: Du Poste colonial à RFI*, Paris, Hachette, 1992 and Roger Nouma,

Radio France Internationale : Instrument de la présence française dans le monde, political science PhD thesis, University of Lille II, 1990.

17. Raymond Aron, "Le Père Ubu au travail" in *Paris-Presse*, April 4, 1947.

18. See André Moosmann, *Histoire des émissions internationales de la radiodiffusion française (1931-1975)*, 2 volumes, Centre de Documentation Radio France, 1981.

19. Roger Nouma, "Rapport Balladur : des propositions pour renforcer l'action radiophonique vers l'étranger" in *Cahiers d'histoire de la radiodiffusion*, N° 39, December 1973-February 1994, p. 68-71.

20. Jean Charon and Roger Nouma, "L'opération 'Rose des vents'" in *Cahiers de la radiodiffusion*, issue 43, December 1994-February 1995, p. 73-81.

21. The plan called for a set of 500-kW transmitters to replace the aging 100- to 250-kW Allouïs-Issoudun transmitters. These were to start operating in 1972 only.

22. Jean Charon, "Les ondes courtes. La voix de la France" in *De Gaulle et les médias* (symposium of the Charles de Gaulle Institute, November 19-21, 1992), Paris, Plon, 1994, p. 216.

23. "La voix de la France : constat d'une faillite," *Livre blanc du Syndicat national des Journalistes* (Document Radio France), Paris, 1970, p. 19.

24. See *RFI aux vents de l'Histoire (1931-1992). Généalogie et repères* (Document Radio France Internationale), April 1993.

25. Ludovir Sochor, "Radio France et les émissions vers l'étranger" in *L'Alternative*, n° 24, March-April 1984, p. 61.

26. Botho Kirsch, "Deutsche Welle's Russian service (1962-1985)" in K. R. M. Short (Ed), *Western Broadcasting over the Iron Curtain*, op. cit., p. 158-171.

27. On the creation of this radio station, see Rolf Steininger, *Deutschlandfunk: die Vorgeschichte einer Rundfunkanstalt (1949-1961)*.

28. Isabelle Bourgeois, *Radios et télévisions publiques en allemagne*, CIRAC, 1993, p. 62.

29. For example, the program "Five Minutes for Twenty Thousand" aimed at the 20,000 East German police officers and border guards, to counter propaganda directed at them.

See Donald Browne, "RIAS Berlin: a Case Study of a Cold War Broadcast Operation" in *Journal of Broadcasting*, Issue 10, Spring 1966, p. 127.

30. See Part 2, Chapter 1.

31. See Part 3, Chapter 2.

32. Douglass A. Boyd, "Broadcasting between the two Germanies" in *Journalism Quarterly*, vol. 60, issue 2, Summer 1983, p. 237.

33. About $2.6 million a year in the early 1960s.

34. This is how various West German newspapers interpreted the interruption of low-frequency RIAS broadcasts in February 1964.

35. Yugoslavia was not among the countries targeted, as the United States did not consider it part of the Soviet sphere after Tito broke ties with Stalin in 1949.

36. James Burnham, *Containment or Liberation?*, New York, John Day Company, 1952.

37. See Sig Mickelson, *America's Other Voices: Radio Free Europe and Radio Liberty*, New York, Praeger, 1983, p. 28. The main purpose of the National Security, created in 1947, the same year as the CIA, was to advise the President of the United States on security matters.

38. Pierre Grémion, *Intelligence de l'anticommunisme: Le Congrès pour la liberté de la culture (1950-1975)*, Paris, Fayard, 1995, p. 625.

39. Allan Michie, *Voice Through the Iron Curtain: the Radio Free Europe Story*, New York, Dodd, Meat and Company, 1963., p. 140-141.

40. Author's interview with Bronislaw Geremek, July 3, 1993.

41. François Fejtö, *1956 Budapest, l'insurrection*, Bruxelles, Ed. Complexe, 1981, p. 100-101.

42. See Part 2, Chapter 1.

43. Jan Nowak, *Polska Z Oddali, Wojna W Eterze-Wspomnienia* (Poland from the distance: War of the Airwaves), Londres, Ed. Nowa, 1988.

44. The committee would undergo various name changes, in particular "American Committee for Liberation from Bolchevism" in 1953.

45. Jon Lodeesen, "Radio Liberty Munich: Foundation for History" in *Historical Journal of Film, Radio and Television*, Vol. 6, n° 2, 1986, p. 197-209.

46. Each of these three language sections was transferred to RFE in 1984. This decision granted an old request from expatriates of these countries who had refused Soviet annexation in 1940 and had argued for their European cultural traditions to be integrated within RFE.

47. Joseph G. Whalen, *Radio Liberty: A study of its origins, programming and effectiveness*, Munich, unpublished report, p. 42.

48. The term was originally coined by Russian poet Nicolai Glazkov in the 1940s before it joined the vernacular of Soviet dissidents by the mid-1960s. *Samizdat* literally means "self-published." The principle of the *samizdat* is that readers become publishers, as they themselves reproduce many copies of the document they were given. The main instrument was the typewriter, since strictly regulated access to photocopiers made photocopying nearly impossible. The chain of complicity rendered the process uncontrollable by those who took part in it. One of the consequences was that *samizdat*-edited documents could "leave" for the West, where they could be published. This led to the lesser-known monicker of "tamizdat," which appeared in the USSR in the early 1970s, meaning "published abroad," i.e., in the Western World. One of the best studies on the Russian *samizdat* is still Michael Meerson-Aksenov and Boris Shragin (eds), *The Political, Social and Religious Thought of Russian "Samizdat": An Anthology*, Belmont, Mass, 1977. For Central Europe, see Gordon Skilling, *Samizdat and Independent Society in Central and Eastern Europe*, Macmillan, 1989.

49. Published in *The New York Times* on July 22, 1968.

50. That same year Radio Liberty published an anthology of collected writings: *Five years of Samizdas*, Munich, 1971. Two of the best works on *samizdats* are those of Michael Meerson-Aksenov and Boris Shragin (Ed), *The Political, Social and Religious Thought of Russian "Samizdat": an Anthology*, Belmont, Mass., 1977; and Gordon Skilling, *Samizdat and Independent Society in Central and Eastern Europe*, Macmillan, 1989.

51. During the media frenzy, the name of Radio Liberty never came up.

52. See the Fulbright Report to the Senate Committee, *Hearings before the Committee on Foreign Relations*, 1971, p. 111 *et seq.*

53. While VOA reported to USIA (see above), the BIB reported directly to the President of the United States through the National Security Council (NSC). Five of the seven members of the BIB were nominated directly by the President, after confirmation by the Senate.

54. Quoted by Sig Mickelson, *America's Other Voice: The Story of Radio Free Europe and Radio Liberty*, Op. Cit., p. 201.

55. Anne-Chantal Lepeuple, "Une approche américaine de la stratégie de l'information : Radio Free Europe/Radio Liberty" in Anne-Chantal Lepeuple and Jacques Semelin, *Les nouveau enjeux de la communication occidentale vers l'Est*, Paris, Fondation pour les études de défense nationale, 1989; and Anne-Chantal Lepeuple, "Radio Free Europe et Radio Liberty (1950-1994)" in *Vingtième Siècle*, October 1995, p. 31-45.

56. Frank Shakespeare, "International Broadcasting and US Realities" in Kenneth R.M. Short, *Western Broadcasting over the Iron Curtain*, op. cit., p. 57-68.

57. The archives of these two US stations are now at Stanford University's Hoover Institution, where they can be consulted.

58. *Observatore Romano*, February 14, 1931, and the *Tribuna*, February 16, 1931.

59. Renée Bedarida, "La voix du Vatican (1940-1942). Bataille des ondes et résistance spirituelle" in *Revue d'histoire de l'Eglise de France*, Vol. 64, N° 173, July-December 1978, p. 215-243.

60. For more information on this subject, the reader is referred to one of the rare synthesis documents on the history of the radio station, published at the time of its 50th anniversary: Fernando Bea & Mezzo Secolo, *Della radio del Papa, 1931-1981*, Editions du Vatican, 1981.

61. There seems to have been a correlation between the size of the immigrant community in a Western country and the size of the language section for that country at the radio station. In France, the Polish community (historically settled in the area of Lille) was the largest, and at the international radio station the Polish section had the largest staff. See Gabriel Garçon, *La radio française parle le polonaise. Histoire des emissions en langue polonaise de la radiodiffusion française (1932-1974)*, Lille, Publications du rayonnement culturel polonais, 1991.

62. Edward W. Barret, *Truth is our Weapon*, New York, Funk and Wagnalls, 1953.

63. Wilson P. Dizard, *The Strategy of Truth, the Story of the US Information Service*, Washington DC, Public Affairs Press, 1961.

64. See Mansell, *Let the truth be told, op. cit.*, p. 222.

65. The arrival of Soviet Jews generated intense conflict at the Russian section of RL in October 1976. They accused the Russian traditionalists, whose immigration dated to the end of WWII and who were in the majority at the section, of their attachment to the past, their nationalism, even their anti-Semitism. With the exception of a few minor changes, these traditionalists maintained their leadership of this section.

II

East-West reception: Between attraction and withdrawal

What do we actually know about the reception of Western radio in the Eastern Bloc from the beginning of the Cold War? It would be easy to work on the commonly held assumption that the communist states did everything in their power to prevent their people from listening to radio from the West, and that an overwhelming majority of citizens in the East wanted to hear "the voice of the free world." Easy but wrong, or at least simplistic. Of course the communist regimes did try to block Western broadcasts in various ways, mainly by jamming them. There is nothing surprising about that: such extreme protectionism, reprehensible from the point of view of the individual's right to information, corresponded to the logic of the communist project. Building a "New Man" meant preventing any Western "contamination," for the construction of socialism necessarily implied withdrawal, isolation from "decadent imperialism," to shape a new political and social identity. Soviet ideologist Andrei Jdanov was probably the one who, in 1947, at the time of the creation of the Kominform, most aptly expressed this necessity for a cultural and mental break with the West's "moral rot."[1]

From the mid-1950s, however, some communist states started to demonstrate more openness when they lifted the jamming of Western radio broadcasts, sometimes for fairly long periods. Does anyone remember that Poland was the pioneer in this respect, from 1956, and that the USSR followed suit in 1963 (except for Radio Liberty), until 1968? Such decisions were surprising: they seemed to contradict the very objectives of the communist regimes. Did they stem from a wish to normalize East-West relations, with some ulterior motive of deriving a benefit? Or were they bowing to pressure by the people, considering this as a minor concession since the reins of power were in any case firmly in their hands? Answering these questions requires a case-by-case analysis, in the context of the time.

It would also be wrong to believe that everyone living behind the Iron Curtain wanted to tune in to Western radio. Listening to stations broadcasting from the West was rarely a mass phenomenon, except in dramatic circumstances, for instance in Poland after General Jaruzelski's institution of martial law on December 13, 1981. Certain categories of the population had unquestionably made a habit of it, but these audiences fluctuated, depending on the country, the period and the social group. Moreover, those who listened to Western radio often had contradictory feelings about it, reflecting a more general ambivalence with regard to the West. Whereas many of listeners in the East felt that Western stations represented "the voices of freedom," they were also aware that they were propaganda tools in the hands of Western states.

Finally, even though ears were tuned in to the West, this did not mean that they were closed to the media of the East. Reception was a complex matter which sometimes combined attraction toward the outside with phases of keener interest in the country's domestic policy. In periods of political revival such as the Prague Spring in Czechoslovakia, audience figures for Western radio stations tended to drop. This was perfectly understandable, since at such times the national media seemed more interesting.[2] The history of reception of Western media in the East is therefore marked by movements of attraction and withdrawal, punctuated by states' policies and populations' expectations. This chapter examines some of the main features of that history.

Diplomacy and jamming

To block or neutralize the reception of Western media in their country, communist governments acted on two fronts: diplomatic, by bringing various forms of pressure to bear on the countries broadcasting, and technological, by jamming their radio broadcasts. On numerous occasions the USSR and its satellites, as members of international organizations, called for an end to Western broadcasts to the East. The justification was always the same: breach of state sovereignty and interference in domestic affairs. This position of the Eastern Bloc countries was inspired by their protectionist conception of the trading of information, which they perceived strictly within the bounds of interstate cooperation. Poland was responsible for formulating the communist world's complaints and grievances against foreign radio. Diplomatic pressure differed however in the case of representation radio stations and substitution radio stations. With regard to those like VOA and Deutsche Welle, the Soviets called for a less aggressive tone, more conducive to entente and cooperation. On the other hand, when it came to RFE and RL the demands were of a very different nature. Perceiving these stations to be "nests of anticommunist spies," the countries of the East wanted their closure. The USSR and the GDR furthermore acted jointly to obtain undertakings that programs broadcast from West Berlin would not be detrimental to the interests of socialist countries. Their argument was that the former capital of the Reich should be neutral as far as radio was concerned.[3] The Soviet attitude nevertheless lacked coherence, since in parallel the USSR developed its own international propaganda machine, which by the end of the sixties was competing with that of the United States. Radio Moscow, constantly expanding since 1945, broadcast in 80 languages in the early 1980s, with a specific focus on developing countries. As in the case of all the other international radio stations, there was no question of respecting states' sovereignty.[4]

In the name of the principle of the free flow of information, the Western countries, above all the United States, consistently refused to bow to the communist states' demands. Their credo was that freedom to communicate went hand in hand with democracy. That meant that anything to promote the free flow of information was beneficial to democracy. In this doctrine, communication across borders was an important factor of understanding between peoples, and therefore of peace. A similar view of international relations had already been outlined by former US President Wilson, in the aftermath of World War I. In the 1940s it was adopted again by certain officials at US press agencies, who saw the globalization of information as a powerful economic vehicle for furthering their goals, and a political means for countering states' monopoly on information.[5] Article 19 of the Universal Declaration of Human rights, which was adopted by the UN General Assembly on December 10, 1948, and promulgated the individual right to freedom of information and expression, constituted the international legal grounds on which Western governments challenged communist countries' protectionist practices. But this liberal conception of the West necessarily had limits. States had to reach some form of agreement, if only for the redistribution of frequencies within the European Broadcasting Union (EBU)—a crucial issue since the number of radio broadcasters had been climbing since 1945, leading to the saturation of short-waves. Moreover, irrespective of what they said officially, Western governments bore in mind the communists' critiques. Political and financial control over radio stations enabled them to have the right to a say in the content of programs, and thus to ensure that, in certain circumstances, the heads of communist states were not offended.

The preliminary negotiations at the Conference on Security and Cooperation in Europe (CSCE), the final act of which was signed in Helsinki on April 1, 1975, set the stage for new East-West conflict over these two conceptions of the flow of information. The "Third Basket" agreements were nevertheless favorable to the West, although these countries recognized the post-1945 borders of the Soviet Union. In spite of the fact that the Helsinki Convention lent new legitimacy to radiophonic action toward the East, the Soviets kept up their guard. During the same period they fought the West within another international organization, UNESCO, by supporting the demands of several developing countries clamoring for a "new world information and communication order" (NWICO). These countries challenged the Anglo-Saxon hegemony over international channels of communication and demanded more equitable rules between North and South.[6] The Eastern Bloc endorsed this revolt directed essentially at the United States and Western Europe, but such actions undertaken under the aegis of UNESCO bore little fruit in practice. The countries of the West refused to budge in what they saw as nothing more than an ideological battle.

In parallel with these diplomatic battles, the countries of the East were using jamming, the most effective way to block the reception of Western programs: first VOA, from April 1948, and then the BBC, a year later. From their inception, RFE's and RL's programs were also tampered with, by a jamming station set up in 1948 in Prague.

In the context of East-West relations, jamming was a fairly reliable indicator of the state of détente or tension between the Soviets and the West, especially the Americans. The USSR briefly lifted the jamming of VOA and the BBC in the spring of 1956 and the summer of 1959, during Khrushchev's visit to the United States. During the Camp David talks (September 26-27, 1959), the Soviet premier proposed a limitation to US broadcasts to the East, in exchange for a lifting of the jamming of VOA. President Eisenhower refused. Yet, from June 18, 1963, Moscow stopped jamming VOA and the BBC for a period of five years, following the signing of the US-Soviet nuclear test ban treaty. Maury Lisann explains that the Soviets believed the improvement of their information system and the development of television would turn the population away from foreign radio.[7] But the jamming of VOA and of the BBC was resumed with the Czechoslovakian crisis of 1968. It was again lifted on September 11, 1973, in the context of preparations for the Helsinki Conference, only to be restored after the 1980 Polish crisis. In the Soviet Union, a single station was jammed uninterruptedly for 35 years: RL, from its creation in 1953 until November 1988, when Gorbachev took the historical decision of lifting the taboo on this radio station, as part of his *Glasnost* policy.

Jamming was also a barometer of Central and Eastern European countries' wish for openness and, more generally, their aspirations for independence from Soviet domination. Poland was the first to stop jamming all Western radio stations' broadcasts, including RFE, in November 1956 when Gomulka came to power. This decision was preceded by a demonstration in the town Bydgoszcz, where the jamming station was burned down. Listeners, nevertheless, continued to complain about persistent, albeit weaker, jamming by the Soviet station in Prague. On July 28, 1963, Romania imitated Poland. Ceausescu's intention was to mark his wish for independence from the Soviet Union. A year later, on February 1, 1964, the Hungarian reform policy, under the impetus of Janos Kadar, led to the lifting of jamming of the BBC and VOA. Czechoslovakia followed suit two months later, on April 1. It was only 10 years later, in September 1974, that Bulgaria decided to do likewise, and then only for VOA. After the death of the Prague Spring in 1968, the jamming of Western stations was resumed in Czechoslovakia. Although Poland resorted to irregular jamming from March 17, 1971, subsequent to December 1970's unrest, neither Romania nor Hungary jammed foreign stations in any systematic way (with the exception, in Hungary, of the region bordering the USSR). In general, the jamming of Western radio was less intensive in Central and Eastern Europe, RFE naturally always being the hardest hit.

Although jamming—nicknamed "KGB jazz"—was relatively effective, its cost was high. In the early 1980s the number of jamming stations in the USSR and Central Europe was estimated at over 2,000. A study by the USIA in 1983 affirmed that the Soviets devoted between US$100m and US$130m to the practice annually.[8] Another study by the BBC estimated that they used more transmitters for jamming than did the BBC, VOA and RFE/RL together for broadcasting their programs.[9] The Soviet's jamming equipment in socialist countries also blocked Israeli, Albanian and Chinese broadcasts.[10]

Western radio stations were not powerless to counter these measures. They retaliated by transmitting their signal on several frequencies to increase their chances of being heard. As a result, jamming was by no means a flawless procedure. A motivated listener generally ended up "picking up the West," especially since the intensity of jamming decreased the further one was from a town or city. One simply had to go out into the country over weekends to tune in to banned broadcasts.

Attempted audience rating

For those who doubted that Western radio really did have audiences, the staff of these stations had some surprising anecdotes, like the amazing story of Richard Nixon (then President of the United States) when he arrived in Warsaw on May 2, 1959. On his way in from Moscow he expected to receive the same official welcome that the Soviets leaders had reserved for him: interaction at the highest level without any contact with the population. The Polish people had not been informed of his visit and the media had been instructed not to mention it. But RFE, in the know thanks to the President's entourage, broadcast news of the visit 24 hours prior to Nixon's arrival. Listeners were given his time of arrival and even details of his itinerary. The news spread within hours and the Warsawians were there to meet him. In his memoirs Nixon recounted: "As we turned into the highway, I noticed small clusters of people shouting at us from the side of the road. Then something hit me in the face. But it was not a rock: it was a bouquet of roses. [...] Two-hundred-and-fifty thousand people lined the streets of Warsaw, according to the official and unofficial estimates. It was unprecedented and unexpected."[11] Another testimony was by an Armenian visitor to Rome in 1971. He reported that every Sunday for the previous 40 years, the inhabitants of his country had gathered to listen to the mass broadcast by Radio Vatican in Armenian: "It's the only way that we have to follow a Catholic Armenian liturgy and the sermon of a Catholic priest."[12]

But these anecdotes provided no specific or even general information on the nature of Western radio's audiences. Who listened? How often? To what type of station? To what type of program? In which countries? Reports from the embassies and audibility tests carried out by telecommunications engineers traveling incognito in the receiving countries were insufficient to build a representative image of listeners. To assess the audiences of their station, officials had to have four types of indicator:

- the number of radio receivers;
- letters from listeners;
- attacks in the communist media;
- opinion polls.

The number of radio receivers
Until the end of the 1940s, the system prevailing in the Eastern Bloc countries was a sort of cabled radio broadcasting network linking buildings, businesses and towns. There was a single program, and users' only

option was to switch a loudspeaker on or off.[13] Then in the 1950s the number of individual wirelesses mushroomed, enabling people to listen to a variety of programs. The state controlled the acquisition of these receivers by making it mandatory to report their purchase, but the mere fact of their being on sale marked a significant political change. It meant that the authorities conceded individuals' freedom to choose their programs and to have an alternative to official programs. This change was particularly significant, as the Soviet Union had embarked on the production of its own short-wave radio receivers. The heads of the Kremlin could thus make themselves heard in the furthest corners of distant republics of the Union. The downside was that it facilitated individuals' access to foreign programs.

Western radio stations' audience ratings therefore implied that the number of short-wave receivers in countries of the East was known. This was impossible, as available statistics gave only the total number of receivers without differentiating their characteristics. Polish statistics, for example, showed 1.46 million radio receivers in 1950, 5.64 million in 1960, 5.65 million in 1970, and 8.66 million in 1980.[14] A BBC study on the entire Eastern Bloc estimated the number of receivers at 20.26 million in 1955, 59.7 in 1965, 73.5 in 1970, and 92.6 in 1975.[15]

Yet short-wave reception was not the only criterion for access to foreign radio. Several Western stations (especially the BBC, RFE and DF) also broadcast to Central and Eastern Europe on medium-wave, which extended the possibility of picking them up on an ordinary radio set. Sometimes they even broadcast on long-wave, as did VOA to counter its jamming on short-wave.[16] We can therefore safely say that Western programs had a potential audience of several million individuals from the mid-fifties, and of tens of millions from the early seventies. But, of course, the fact that they had the technical means to pick up radio broadcasts from the West did not necessarily mean that people actually listened to them.

Listeners' mail
All the experts who analyzed the letters sent to Western radio stations found that the volume of mail received from a communist country was directly correlated with the phases of openness or closure of that country. For instance, whereas the Czech service of DLF received 58,000 letters from Czechoslovakia in 1969 after the repression of the Prague Spring, this figure had plunged to 1,000 a year later. The same trend could be seen with letters from Poland before and after the institution of martial law on December 13, 1981: in 1980, the Polish service received

21,000 letters, in 1981, 31,000, and in 1982 no more than 18,000 (a figure that was still high, considering the situation within the country).[17] But did these variations in the volume of mail correspond to audience figures? Definitely not. All the studies undertaken on the mail received by Western radio stations show that these letters were not representative of the station's audience.[18] Decreasing numbers of letters did not mean that people weren't listening to radio programs from the West; it was just that far fewer listeners dared to write, or that their letters were intercepted by the police or border controls. For instance, a questionnaire survey was undertaken in 1978 in West Germany by Radio Canada International (RCI), on 540 of its listeners who had written to the station during the three months preceding the survey, and 236 listeners identified during another survey on 20,000 individuals representative of the West-German population. The results showed that data extrapolated from the listeners' mail was an indication neither of the audiences' demographic characteristics nor of their listening habits. A similar conclusion was drawn from a study undertaken in 1981 by the audience service of the BBC, in the Indian states of Utar-Pradesh and Rajasthan.

The radio stations sometimes organized games to elicit audience's opinions. It was an excellent idea for prompting silent listeners to react; most of the stations broadcasting to the East tried it, usually successfully. Yet, once again, those who contacted the station were not necessarily representative of its public. An expert from VOA, W. Antony Hackley, believed that whenever even modest rewards were at stake, it was highly likely that some of the participants, informed by word of mouth, would not be regular listeners of the radio station organizing the game.[19]

Audiences' reactions had to be taken with a great deal of circumspection, whether they were spontaneous or prompted. Their main utility was to stimulate journalists at the radio stations (letters were better than nothing at all), sometimes to give them new ideas, and to provide indications on the audibility of the station's signal in a specific geographical area.

Attacks by communist media
An indirect indicator of Western radio's audiences was the frequency of attacks on the stations in the communist media. The assumption was that the more people tuned in to Western broadcasts, the greater the communist authorities' need must be to convince their populations of the stations' misdeeds. One of the first studies to analyze the Soviets'

reactions to VOA broadcasts in Russian, undertaken in 1951 by Sovietologist Alex Inkeles, showed that Moscow presented the VOA as the "voice of the dollar," an instrument of US capitalism whose purpose was to support the imperialist and military machinations of the United States.[20] This was typical Cold War discourse. DW likewise received its stream of insults; it was presented as "the radio station of the friends of Goebbels and those nostalgic for the Third Reich," while the BBC was said to "pursue reactionary goals, as the lackey of imperialism, under cover of objectivity."[21] Even when jamming was lifted in the period from 1963 to 1968, this vitriol against Western radio barely ceased, as the authorities of communist countries still felt the need to turn their populations away from them: "The vast majority of Soviet listeners are absolutely not interested in this type of program ... which they immediately ignore. There is only an insignificant number of crazy philistines who seek sensations and cacophonic jazz."[22] The most virulent abuse was concentrated on RFE and RL, which were branded as "nests of spies" and "agents of fascism and imperialism hostile to the spirit of détente," among other things. In 1981 these diatribes turned into physical aggression when the headquarters of RFE/RI were attacked. The culprit was allegedly the terrorist Carlos in the pay of the KGB.[23]

But was there actually any evidence that the intensity of attacks against a particular radio station was proportional to its audience? No one can say. The systematic disparaging of Western radio was part of the unavoidable exercise in counter-propaganda initiated with the Cold War and sustained throughout the period of détente. The communist governments set up a unit to analyze the daily programs of the foreign stations: "A synthesis report on the previous day's programs (especially those of the BBC, VOA and RFE) was submitted daily to senior government officials, while another group formulated counterpropaganda' arguments to be used by communist journalists."[24]

Western radio could also serve as a foreign scapegoat to draw attention away from serious domestic problems. In fact this tactic was standard practice. "Foreign manipulation" was accused, for instance, of being the reason for internal opposition to the regime. The famous declaration on August 14, 1984, by Jerzy Urban, spokesperson for General Jaruzelski's government in Poland, typified this type of attitude: "If you would close your Radio Free Europe, the underground (Solidarity) would cease to exist."[25] But this says nothing about the audiences of these stations; it shows only what effects the authorities *assumed* them to have. In other words, analyzing communist leaders' reactions to Western radio stations was not an accurate way of measuring their influence on a society; it merely reflected the degree of the communist authorities' fear of the stations' impact.

Opinion polls

From the late 1950s, some officials at US radio stations thought that opinion polls on visitors from Eastern Bloc countries to the West could provide significant indications on their stations' audiences. The first polls were run by RFE/RL at the 1957 Brussels International Trade Fair, on 300 Soviet citizens. From then on, similar surveys were undertaken on Hungarian, Polish and Czech visitors and later, in the 1970s, on Romanians and Bulgarians as well. This technique was fiercely criticized for being unscientific. What methodological value could be attributed to answers sometimes obtained in inappropriate and semi-clandestine conditions, by interviewers who were rarely trained in polling techniques? How representative were respondents who, by definition, had been authorized to travel to the West and were therefore bound to be members of the communist state apparatus or close to it? It is also likely that the published figures were largely overestimated in order to "prove" the reality of RFERL audiences and thus to justify approval of their budgets by the relevant deciders. But the officials at RFE/RL denied such maneuvers. The new team which took over the audience research service in the early 1980s claimed that it had developed a perfectly reliable methodology, in collaboration with a team of MIT researchers under the supervision of Ithiel de Sola Pool.[26]

Whatever this method was worth, an American source confirmed that the data supplied by the EEAOR (East European Area Audience and Opinion Research) for five radio stations[27] had the merit of highlighting certain general tendencies in these stations' audiences. The ones with the largest audiences in the Eastern Bloc as a whole were RFE/RL, VOA and the BBC. They were listened to in the evenings mainly, when reception on short-wave was best. Their prime time was usually between 10 p.m. and 11 p.m., after the movie or serial on TV. The global audience of foreign radio tended to increase at times of international crisis and social or political tension in the receiving country. Reception rates were highest in Central Europe (Poland, Czechoslovakia and Hungary). Audiences in the USSR were smaller, except in Moscow and Leningrad, in the Baltic republics, Ukraine, Georgia and Armenia, that is, primarily the non-Russian republics of the Union.

For the year 1984, for example, a US research institute estimated the audiences of the leading Western radio stations in Eastern Europe and the Soviet Union as follows:

Table 1: Weekly audience ratings of the main Western radio broadcasters in 1984*

	RL/RFE	VOA	BBC	DW/DLF
Czechoslovakia	54	45	36	8
Hungary	52	23	15	7
Poland	66	48	33	9
Romania	61	23	18	10
Bulgaria	37	23	20	15
USSR	8-12	14-18	7-10	3-6

* Figures given in percentages.

To what extent were these percentages overestimated? I wanted to compare them with the results of confidential studies undertaken during the same period by government survey institutes in the communist countries. For Poland, I was able to obtain data from the OBOP (Osrodek Badania Opinii Publicznej), the national institute for public opinion and media studies. During the 1980s this institution was responsible for regular polling (twice a year, on average) on Polish audiences and the credibility of the audiovisual media. The survey (generally on samples with over 1,000 individuals) contained two questions specifically on the audiences and credibility of Western radio stations.

The validity of information collected in this way in communist countries is questionable. Did respondents feel free to answer questions frankly in an opinion poll on "sensitive" issues, considering the social climate of repression and suspicion? What were their answers worth when they were asked if they listened to the foreign radio broadcasts that the authorities tried to jam? These data are nevertheless of interest, as they can be cross-compared to some of the US surveys. The following two tables show the results of two polling institutes for the 1980s.

To these data was added a third type of survey, the first of its kind, carried out in February-March 1989 by the audience service of the BBC in Poland, in collaboration with the OBOP. For the first time, a Western radio station was authorized to undertake research in a communist country. The survey was on two samples of 1,000 individuals (one of them comprising people who had already been surveyed).

It would be risky to compare these figures obtained with very different survey and analysis methods. At least there was one constant: all three institutes recognized the supremacy of the same three Western radio stations: RFE, VOA and the BBC. But they credited them with very different

Table 2: Audiences of six Western radio stations between 1982 and 1989, according to RFE/RL*

	1982	1983	1984	1985	1986	1987	1988	1989
RFE	68	66	66	59	56	51	57	46
VOA	43	48	48	53	46	48	54	43
BBC	27	23	33	33	34	35	41	33
DLF	12	8	9	9	9	8	6	4
RFI	-	1	4	4	6	8	5	6
Radio Vatican	10	11	14	9	8	15	13	11

* The question was "In the last three months before leaving your country, which Western radio station(s) did you listen to?" Figures given in percentages, with 1% representing about 280,000 individuals.

Table 3: Audiences of Western radio stations between 1980 and 1989, according to the OBOP*

	Total	BBC	VOA	RFE	RFI	DLF
1980 Sept	27	12	11	15		
1983 March	29	7	14	15		
May	24	10	18	17		
1984 Sept	23	9	14	12		
Nov	30	15	22	18		
1985 June	34	14	24	20		
Sept	23	9	16	13		
1986 Jan	24	11	17	12		
May	20	11	15	10		
Oct	23	11	17	14		
1987 Jan	24	12	18	13		
June	21	9	16	12		
Dec	22	11	15	14		
1988 Feb	22	11	15	16		
May	31	14	22	24	3	4
Sept	31	14	22	24	3	6
Dec	25	12	17	18	3	4
1989 Feb	30	15	23	22	4	5
June	23	13	16	18	4	4
Sept	24	12	16	19	3	3

* The question asked was "Do you listen to Western radio stations? If so, which ones?" A list of radio stations followed, including Radio Moscow and Radio Tirana. Note that R.F.I. was called "Radio Paris." Figures given in percentages.

Table 4: Audiences of six Western radio stations in February-March 1989, according to the BBC and the OBOP*

	RFE	Radio Vatican	VOA	RFI	BBC	DLF
February-March 1989	34	13	26	5	23	3.3

* Figures given in percentages.

scores, since the OBOP situated the audiences of these stations between 10 and 20% of the total adult population, the BBC between 20 and 30%, and RFE/RL between 20 and 50%. These studies were comparable in their descriptions of audience profiles, which closely resembled those of all research on international radio stations[28]: audiences consisted mainly of listeners who had received a secondary or higher education, were men rather than women, and lived in towns or cities rather than in the country. It followed that these listeners were mainly in the middle- or senior management category, rather than laborers or farmers. Every radio station seemed to have a specific public. With its serious and rigorous image, the BBC tended to be the station of the intelligentsia, whereas RFE reached lower socioeconomic categories. Both the BBC and VOA seemed to be listened to mainly by people in managerial positions and the elderly. These "sociological profiles" were nevertheless flexible, and varied from country to country.

Membership of the Communist Party was not a decisive criterion in these audience profiles; people listened to Western radio whether they supported the communist regime or not. Above all, this type of practice revealed listeners' lack of confidence—expressed to a greater or lesser degree—in the national media of their country. In 1964, the *New York Times* correspondent in Warsaw commented wryly that in official conversations, the tone was one of anger when western radio stations were discussed. But many Party members confided that those who complained the most about these stations dashed to their radio sets when Khrushchev fell, to find out what had really happened.[29]

Numerous Communist Party central committee meetings were faithfully reported in RFE broadcasts! On occasion, one or more participants would even disclose the contents of the meeting to the Munich-based radio station. Why? To serve their own individual interests by passing information to the West that was an embarrassment to their political opponents. Listening to RFE was therefore also a way of tuning into what was going on in the political wings, and obtaining information that was theoretically more credible than that provided locally. There was nothing rare, for instance, about civil servants passing on the exact statistics of their ministries to Western radio stations, to counter the manipulation of official figures. In light of this, it was hardly surprising that these stations had large audiences.

Reception processes

When the BBC first introduced Russian programs, the *Daily Express* correspondent reported that in Moscow "listeners freely passed on to their neighbors what Radio London had said."[30] This situation was however short-lived, for the Soviet government's attitude hardened soon thereafter. People who listened to the BBC or VOA were sometimes reported to the authorities by neighbors, and sentenced to several years' imprisonment for "ideological crimes." The fact of spreading information heard on foreign radio was considered to be an offence in most countries in the Soviet Bloc. During the Cold War, listening to Western radio was virtually a secret activity, carried out in the evenings, usually at home behind closed doors and shutters. Families would gather around the wireless and strain to understand what the host was saying, over the jamming or noise.

These practices strongly resembled those that appeared in WWII, when people in Nazi-dominated Europe listened to the BBC. In this respect, the historical continuum between the behavior of people in countries occupied by Nazi Germany and those in the Soviet Union is striking. Such habits were nevertheless to die out as Eastern governments relaxed their pressure on individuals, partially lifting their jamming and thus allowing foreign broadcasts to reach their citizens. These changes were largely the outcome of social pressure: the people of the Eastern Bloc gradually reclaimed the right to a different type of information, despite all the state's attempts to control and intimidate them. From the 1970s, people in Poland and Hungary no longer hid to tune in to Western radio stations. Poetess and dissident Natalia Gorbanevskaia explained that this change was also evident in the Soviet Union: "People dare to do things that were completely unimaginable ten or fifteen years ago. For example, now [in 1978], everyone listens to foreign radio and talks about it freely."[31] In light of this, could these regimes still be qualified as "totalitarian," when they seemed to have relinquished their control over all sources of information available to individuals?

Managing to pick up a station with good reception was not always self-evident. Even if listeners knew the frequency of a particular radio program, they were never sure of being able to hear it clearly. Bad weather or interference could disturb reception. Some listeners would think that the interference was due to jamming, when it was simply the result of saturation of the short-waves. In the period 1963 to 1968, over a third of all Soviet listeners reportedly believed that VOA and the BBC were still being jammed, when in fact the practice had been discontinued.[32] They often kept turning the tuning button until they picked up a station that was vaguely audible. With practice, they learned to recognize the tone and vocabulary of particular radio stations, even if the host had not yet announced the station's name. They learned to recognize voices, some of which became familiar, and it was also through these voices that they identified the station. Several RFE and BBC journalists, back in their home country after 1989, testified to the same moving experience. They told about how, talking to a friend in a public place, they would see someone come up to them and appear to listen to their conversation. The presence of this stranger would soon become uncomfortable. Then suddenly the intruder would say to the journalist: "I think I recognize your voice; isn't it you who used to talk on RFE?" And when the journalist answered in the affirmative, the passer-by took the opportunity of saying just how much the journalist's program and voice had been important to him or her in difficult times, even if he or she had not always agreed with them.

The various surveys cited above show that listeners generally had a fairly precise idea of what they expected from each radio station. News from the BBC, unlike VOA, was not only listened to but considered to be credible. This trust in the British station stemmed partly from its reputation for reliability, gained during the Second World War. Its supposed objectivity may also have been the consequence of Britain's decline as a world power since 1945; listeners perceived the BBC as being in a better position to give a balanced view of international news. Attitudes differed substantially when it came to VOA. People listened to the station not only to be informed of global events but also to know what the US government's position was on a particular issue pertaining to East-West relations. On this point, VOA was obliged to broadcast a daily news bulletin starting with the following words: "This reflects the views of the US government"—a phrase that never failed to irritate more than one listener, as it seemed so futile; all the station's programs were manifestly steeped in the official views of the US government.

As for RFE/RL, listeners were fully aware that these stations broadcast the voice of anticommunist émigrés. That was precisely why they either chose or refused to listen to this type of radio station. They accepted it when it nurtured sentiments hostile towards the powers that be, and refused it when they wanted to stay out of politics. This was evident during the 1960s in Poland, for example, in the period known as the "small stabilization" when the population wished to be left in peace and to have better living conditions materially. Most people withdrew, focusing on their jobs and the private sphere. Adam Michnik tells us that people preferred not to listen to the voices of emigrants who spoke of democracy and freedom. Émigrés had little credibility, because they had chosen the easy life of the West, and many Poles were of the opinion that they "told lies about Poland on RFE broadcasts."[33] Twenty years later the situation was totally different: RFE had a huge audience in that country.

Just the vocabulary used on RFE and RL warrants a comparative analysis of the periods and of the language sections. Sometimes it was particularly harsh and tended to shock listeners, even those opposed to the regime. Czech journalist Jaroslav Jiru, for example, regretted that "the hosts of the Czech section did propaganda the other way round, especially by treating some political officials as 'government lackeys.'"[34] On the other hand, RFE idealized all potential opponents, immediately qualifying them as "freedom fighters," a term found in the discourse of some US politicians to refer to groups or movements opposed to Marxist regimes in both the Eastern Bloc and the South. This "RFE language" turned some of the listeners of these stations toward the BBC which had a more neutral and professional tone. But RFE maintained a significant advantage: as it had far more air time than its rivals, it was able to broadcast long extracts of the clandestine press in *samizdats*, which appeared at the end of the 1960s.[35] Polish journalist Stefan Bratkowsi claimed that this was the main interest of RFE: thanks to the station, an opposition bulletin or review, which might have had at the most a few hundred or thousand readers (concentrated mainly in a town and surrounding areas), could become known to millions of people.[36]

Once they had an idea of the advantages and limitations of the main radio stations broadcasting from the West, listeners compared them to select the best programs. A common practice consisted, for example, in checking on the BBC for information broadcast by RFE. After the institution of martial law in Poland on December 13, 1981, RFI's programs in Polish were particularly popular. The Polish section, hosted by Casimir Piekarec, adopted a lively and incisive tone. A few years later, famous Polish humorist Jacek Fedorowicz praised this return of France onto the airwaves: "RFI was the only radio station that, in the darkest days of the 'state of war', was able to talk to us with lightness and sometimes even to make jokes. Strangely, these jokes, which theoretically should have shocked us, brought us closer to RFI. It was really an interesting psychological phenomenon. While RFE announced an event in a sinister voice, with one of the most serious pieces of Beethoven in the background, RFI spoke to us about it in a normal tone."[37]

The audiences of Western radio stations often had contradictory expectations. They certainly did expect a lot, sometimes too much, and therefore expressed a wide variety of complaints about them. Many listeners seemed to be in a permanent state of ambivalence regarding these stations, which Solzhenitzyn clearly expressed. On the one hand, this author defended the stations when he spoke of their action as a "mighty non-military force which resides in the airwaves and whose kindling power in the midst of communist darkness cannot even be grasped by the Western imagination"[38]; on the other, in the name of the high conception that he had of their mission, he constantly levelled criticism against them. For instance, he regretted that the heads of VAO, "in their zeal to serve détente, ... remove everything from their programs which might irritate the communists in power,"[39] and deplored the fact that the BBC broadcast only in Russian and not in the other languages of the republics, and that its program on the Russian orthodox religion was far too short.[40]

Criticism also appeared in the writings of other dissidents or observers of the Eastern Bloc. They accused Western radio stations of broadcasting propaganda as well, of disregarding certain events, and of failing to take a clear stand on certain issues. In *Antipolitics*, Hungarian György Konrad expressed his skepticism regarding international radio stations in both East and West: "When the anti-politician listens to the programs of some of the radio stations on short-wave, he soon feels a growing propensity to switch off his wireless. It's so childish of the political elites to criticize one another and act innocent."[41] During the 1970s, Vladimir Bukovski also regretted that Western radio stations were too accommodating with the Soviet Union. He noted wryly that news was "given in homeopathic doses to the countries to the East of Europe, considered incapable of massively absorbing the West's thinking and cultural values."[42] In a report published in 1986, historian of dissidence in the USSR, Ludmilla Alexeieva, denounced the extreme Russian nationalism of RL's Russian broadcasts, especially in its historical and religious programs. She concluded, "In brief, the listener who took the trouble to stay up late at night and endure the agony of listening through jamming was rewarded with something very similar to Soviet propaganda, only with a different political direction."[43]

Foreign radio broadcasts tended to be seen as an additional rather than an exclusive source of information for listeners, who also used the local media. The press, radio and television all maintained their preeminence in countries East of the Iron Curtain. International listeners could of course sometimes decide to ignore what these media had to say, but generally they compared the news put out by the national media with that broadcast by foreign radio. One of the most common practices was to watch TV news in the evening and then later to tune in to Western radio stations to see what their version of the day's events was. The next day, they would check what the party press had to say—and in what terms—about the same events. This constant cross-comparison between the domestic and foreign media involved complicated processes of decoding information.

People had to decipher the communist media's stereotyped news; they had to learn to read between the lines, and generally started learning to do so as children, as part of their socialization. In his book *Jazyk a moc* (*Language and Power*), Petr Fidelius shares some of the recipes for this "linguistic cuisine" needed to interpret the totalitarian language in which, according to him, the keywords were "people," "democracy" and "socialism."[44]

How did someone striving to resist the influence of propaganda perceive and process information? One of the main principles for deciphering the communist media was to postulate that a piece of information denied by the party press had to be true. In the thickets of ideological jargon, the challenge was to find the information that may be true. Listening to one or more foreign radio stations helped to verify this deduction and to obtain more details on the subject. But audiences of international broadcasts knew that Western radio stations could also warp or exaggerate facts. They had to be cautious, and usually applied their deciphering to Western media as well, before putting together the version of a fact or event that could be considered plausible.

This process of construction of "the truth" of a piece of information was not only individual. Often it involved a network of people within the country or abroad, who passed around information and tried to compare and cross-check it, communicating by letter or telephone when necessary. In this sense, they co-constructed news that was "true." Donald Shanor's metaphor of the "underground telegraph" aptly illustrates this routine. In *Behind Enemy Lines*, he describes the effects of a piece of news broadcast by radio on short-wave: "Their information also immediately enters the underground telegraph system. Friends who have been listening call friends who were not. If the event is important enough, the news is supplemented by opinions gleaned from reading between the lines of the official version. Soon afterward, the letters begin to arrive from Brighton Beach or Los Angeles and the telephone rings with an international call with code words sprinkled among the conversations about aunts and babies."[45]

Conversations between family members or friends were essential for comparing what everyone believed to know about an event. It was a way of checking the veracity of news, of passing it on and discussing it. Seemingly trivial comments were crucial in a country where the media could never be considered reliable because they were known to be covered by the thick cloak of censorship. In this type of situation, word of mouth was of prime importance as a vehicle of information throughout the country. Hungarian writer Gyula Sipos observed with amusement in 1969 that, without listening to Western radio, he learned all the news by word of mouth, far faster than if he had waited for it to be published in the newspaper.[46] This was what his compatriot, sociologist Elémer Hankiss, called the "second system of communication in which authentic news circulated, rumours and gossip were traded, where tiny fragments of truth buried in manipulated information and hollow speeches were tracked down and deciphered, where party policies were constantly debated and analyzed, where a Hirschmanian 'horizontal voice' was raised against the official 'vertical voice.'"[47] This second system of communication was fed not only by news on Western radio but also by all sorts of rumours, information leaked by people working in government or the Party, letters or telephone calls from abroad, meetings with visitors or tourists, and so on. In Czechoslovakia, normalized in the early 1970s, Milan Simecka considered that from this "vast network of popular information, we can reconstruct an image of reality close to the truth, after a reasonable sorting. This network is able to find the most secret news: practical information on consumptions, preliminary signs of various government measures, gossip and undisclosed scandals."[48]

Thanks to the informal network of horizontal communication, news that was embarrassing for the authorities was often known to the population days before the official media reported it. Simecka explains that the "fun" was then to observe the state officials' contortions to find arguments that would enable them to present the news in a way that was most favorable to them. News obtained from Western radio was then reexamined by the informal communication networks. Via these channels, it reached further down into society and generated diffuse effects. In this sense, the influence of Western radio cannot be reduced to the assumed size of its audiences; society as a whole was permeated by the circulation of news in this way.

"Sound windows" and milestones

So why did the inhabitants of communist countries rely more or less regularly on Western radio? Probably because they thought that it broadcast news either censored by their government or likely to be released later in a watered-down version. In the period from 1945 to 1986 this idea was certainly well founded. For people living east of the Iron Curtain, Western radio was indeed the first source of news about the Berlin-East uprising in 1953, the Khrushchev Report in 1956, the invasion of Czechoslovakia in 1968, the earthquake in Romania in 1977, the Gdansk strikes in 1980, and the Chernobyl nuclear accident in 1986. It was from this perspective that Raymond Aron perceived these stations' relative importance in the context of the psychological war between East and West. On the respective impacts of practices of persuasion and subversion, he wrote in *Peace and War: a Theory of International Relations*: "information seeks to be a weapon as soon as it addresses the governed over the heads of the leaders and breaks the monopoly which the state claims to exercise. The minimum weapon aimed at by the psychological weapon in Cold War is to prevent the totalitarian regimes from being alone with their peoples: the *third man*—the stranger, the enemy, the foreigner, the democracies, world opinion—is always present. He does not suppress, but he limits the modern form of royal prerogative, the right of official lies, of excluding speech and interpretation from the outside."[49]

Research by several authors, especially Tristan Mattelart,[50] shows that audiences in the East tuned in to Western radio for other reasons as well, not only to be informed. From the end of the 1940s they saw these stations as a source of entertainment. There is ample evidence that many listeners were attracted by the introduction of jazz, banned in the East at the time. Young people would sometimes get together out in the country, where they could listen and dance to the sounds of Louis Armstrong or Sidney Bechet without the risk of being seen or heard. One of the most popular programs was "Music USA" hosted from 1955 by Willis Conover. An opinion poll in Poland in the late 1950s acclaimed him "the year's best American."[51] The same enthusiasm was witnessed in the sixties for rock and then pop. The English-language programs of RTL, broadcast from Luxembourg, and Radio Monte Carlo, which were fairly easy to pick up in Central and even Eastern Europe, contributed substantially to the diffusion of this popular music from the Anglophone world. RFE's research institute undertook a survey of the station's audiences in the 1970s, and in 1979 credited it, for example, with 15% in Czechoslovakia and Hungary, 21% in Poland, 16% in Romania, and 18%

in Bulgaria. The communist leaders were unable to curb this irresistible attraction for British and American music. At best, they could try to control its diffusion in their countries by introducing their own jazz and then rock stations, or by trying to nurture an "Eastern rock." Some British and American singers were even authorized to tour in the East, for example the Rolling Stones in 1967 in Poland and Elton John in 1979 in the USSR. Elton John was amazed to hear the public singing along with him at his concerts, in the country where none of his records were on sale. In fact, his fans had heard his songs on VOA and learnt them by heart. Even though the communist authorities tried to stifle or even to "harness" the youth's appetite for popular music from the West, they were powerless to control its deeper meaning. From the very beginnings of the broadcasting of jazz on VOA, Western music was synonymous in the East not only with pleasure but also with freedom. The Czech group John Lennon (named after a member of the Beatles) was probably the best symbol of this.[52]

Listening to Western radio was also a way for people in the East to educate themselves and especially to become familiar with or even to learn a foreign language. This was the case of those who followed the BBC's "English by radio" programs. Others tried to keep up their French and to improve it by picking up the weak signal of the French radio station. In this respect, books were an indispensable companion. As English, French and German were taught in schools, some students realized that this activity meant more than simply mastering a modern language; it was a window to an inaccessible outside world. In Romania, several French teachers (in the 40-50 year-old age group) told me how much their knowledge of French had been a way for them to preserve a sphere of autonomy under the dictatorship. Choosing to learn French and then to teach it had been more than an intellectual and professional investment; it was a personal choice that, in a crazy world, had given some meaning to their lives: that of freedom.

Western radio also afforded the possibility of monitoring cultural and scientific developments in Western countries, in art, literature and technical progress and its applications in daily life. It kept listeners up to date on the contents of Western publications of direct interest to them, like the British journal *Index of Censorship* or one of the magazines published by Polish immigrants in France, *Kultura*, banned behind the Iron Curtain. The broadcasting of certain articles from these publications came as a surprise to more than one Western expert on communist countries. Former managing editor of *Esprit*, Paul Thibaut, related how, on his arrival in Poland in 1984, a friend who went to meet him at the airport immediately congratulated him on his article published in the periodical a few days before his departure. He had just heard it read in Polish on RFI!

All these uses of Western radio by audiences in communist countries can be summed up as follows: through the access that it afforded to information, music, language and culture, it provided listeners with "sound windows" onto the West. Elémer Hankiss recounted how "at the worst moments of the Cold War, in the stifling environment of societies sealed off from the rest of the world by the communist regimes, listening to Western radio was equivalent to looking at pictures in the *National Geographic*: a window onto the world."[53] This possibility of imaginary escape from the totalitarian universe was expressed remarkably well by Russian poet Joseph Brodsky when he described the inside of his radio receiver as if it were a "window" enabling him to watch Europe: "Through six symmetrical holes in its back, in the subdued glow and flicker of the radio tubes, in the maze of contacts, resistors, and cathodes, as incomprehensible as the languages they were generating, I thought I saw Europe. Inside, it always looked like a city at night, with scattered neon lights. And when at the age of thirty-two I indeed landed in Vienna, I immediately felt that, to a certain extent, I knew the place."[54]

Western radio did not only enable listeners to escape to a world they wanted to experience. By looking through those windows, they also found landmarks to find their way in a shifting context, both at home and in international relations. Former RFI chairman Henri Tézenas du Montcel's lighthouse metaphor illustrates this aspect: "If some can't see the advantages of this type of radio station, why don't they say the same thing about lighthouses on the coast? Lighthouses do nothing but light up a void; yet they are vital for the circulation of ships. In storms they become totally indispensable."[55] During the different periods of crisis or social tension in the Eastern Bloc countries, the growth of Western radio stations' audiences was indeed a clear indicator of people's need to refer to foreign sources as a guideline when forming their own opinions.

When things were calm, Western radio was still a source of references for listeners, for it constantly provided them with a different view of the world to the one presented by the communist media. In this respect, the stations of the West were a "weapon" for everyone engaged in the battle to preserve the nation's memory. Leszek Kolakowski's analysis was that by manipulating all information, the totalitarian system destroyed the very principle of "truth": "A people whose memory—both individual and collective—is nationalized, turned into perfectly malleable, totally controllable state property, is entirely at the mercy of its rulers; it has thus been dispossessed of its identity."[56] All references were scrambled, noted Jacques Rupnik, starting with those of the nation's memory. Through this "scotomization" of the past—a theme dear to Milan Kundera and Vaclav Havel—people tended to lose their identity and their autonomy. It was a full-blown psychological war, in which listening to Western radio was a form of survival ... so as not "go crazy." The programs did also contain propaganda, but at least it had the advantage of always providing the listener with *an alternative* conception of reality and history. Radio stations in the West were thus a way of not sinking into the closed and schizophrenic world of totalitarianism. Could they become more than that, instruments of liberation at the service of a collective struggle, as some American experts wanted them to? It is impossible to answer this question without taking a closer look at the history of Eastern Europe itself, through the main crises that shook the Soviet Bloc from 1953.

Notes

1. Andrei Zhdanov, *On Literature, Music and Philosophy*, London, Lawrence & Wishart, 1950.

2. Based on a study by RFE, Paul Lendvai affirms that audiences in Czechoslovakia dropped from 60% to 37% during that period. See Paul Lendvai, *Les Fonctionnaires de la vérité. L'information dans les pays de l'Est*. Robert Laffont, Paris, 1980, p. 216.

3. Richard Wettig, *Broadcasting and Détente: Eastern policies and their Implications for East-West Relations*, C. Hurst, London, 1977.

4. Jacques Semelin, "V.O.A. contre Radio Moscou" in Michel Winock (ed.), *Le Temps de la guerre froide*, Paris, Seuil, 1994, p. 309-319.

5. See in particular the book by Kent Cooper, former Director of Associated Press: Kent Cooper, *Barriers Down. The Story of the News Agency Epoch*, New York, Rinehart, 1942.

6. See the MacBride Report: *Many Voices One World* (abridged version), Paris, Editions UNESCO, 1984.

7. Maury Lisann, *Broadcasting to the Soviet Union. International Politics and Radio*, New York, Praeger Publishers, Special Studies Program, 1975, p. 16-20. Some experts considered that the lifting of jamming was not total, as the Soviets reserved the right to selective jamming of VOA and the BBC, depending on the nature of the program and the main events of the day.

8. James P. MacGregor, "Jamming of Western radio broadcasts to the Soviet Union and Eastern Europe," in *Research Report R-4-83*, April 1983, USIA, Office of Research.

9. Richard Evans, "Jamming 'costs' Russians £500m" in *The Times*, 31 October 1985.

10. Stanley Leinwall, "Jamming past, present and future," in *World Radio TV Handbook*, 1980.

11. Richard Nixon, *Six crises*, New York, Doubleday and Co., 1962, p. 284-285.

12. Bea, *Mezzo Secolo, Della radio del Papa, 1931-1981, op. cit.*, p. 222.

13. This cabled network, still functioning in Russia in 1995, was subsequently to broadcast two or three radio programs.

14. *Annuaire de la radiotélévision polonaise*, Warsaw, 1994.

15. BBC data. See Rutger Lindhal, *Broadcasting Across Borders. A Study on the role of propaganda in external broadcasts*. CWK, Gleerup, Kungälw/Lund, 1978, p. 12.

16. This was, for example, the Americans' tactic: every time VOA was jammed on shortwave, the United States immediately transmitted its signal on long-wave. Maury Lisan reported that, when the Soviets lifted the jamming of VOA in 1963, the Americans immediately reduced their long-wave signal from 1,000 kW to 50 kW. See Lisann, *Broadcasting to the Soviet Union, op. cit.*, p. 15.

17. Jürgen Reiss, "Deutsch Landfunk: Broadcasting to East Germany and Eastern Europe," in R.M. Short (ed.), *Western Broadcast over the Iron Curtain, op. cit.* p. 183.

18. Guy Robert, "Un indicateur utile mais pervers, le courrier des auditeurs," in *Multiplex*, n° 32, October 1986, p. 54-58.

19. *Ibid*.

20. Alex Inkeles, "The Soviet Characterization of the Voice of America" in *Columbia Journal of International Affairs*, n°2, Vol. V, spring 1951, p. 44-55.

21. Vladimir Artemov & Vladimir Semyonov, *The BBC History. Apparatus, methods of radio propaganda*, Moscow, Iskusstvo, 1978.

22. Sergei Ivanovich Tsybov & Nicolai Fedorovich Christyakov, *Front Tainoi Voiny* (*The Secret War Front*), Moscow, 1965, p. 12-13.

23. On August 16, 1991, former KGB Major General Oleg Kalugin, on a visit to the RFE/RL headquarters in Munich, admitted that the KGB had organized that attack in which nobody had been injured, fortunately, although the damage to property was considerable.

24. Interview with Thomas Schreiber, March 12, 1991. To be able to carry out this analysis, the government necessarily had to leave one frequency unjammed. To ensure that it was not identified, it was usually changed every day. Of course, for listeners the game was to find that frequency.

25. Quoted by William A. Buel, "Radio Free Europe/Radio Liberty in the mid-1980s" in R.M. Short (ed.), *Western Broadcasting Toward the Iron Curtain, op. cit.*, p. 74.

26. See Eugène Parta, John C. Klensin and Ithiel de Sola Pool, "The shortwave audience in the USSR: Methods for improving the estimates," in *Communication Research*, n° 4, Vol. 9, October 1982, p. 581-606.

27. VOA, RFE/RL, BBC, DLF/DW, and RCI (Radio Canada International). Although these stations were rivals, their officials met regularly during the 1980s to inform one another on their respective practices (program content, audience assessments, developments in Eastern Bloc countries, etc.).

28. Donald R Browne, *International Radio Broadcasting. The Limits of the Limitless Medium*. op. cit. p. 331.

29. Article by Max Frankel in *The New York Times*, January 11, 1964.

30. See Mansell, *Let the Truth be Told, op. cit.*, p. 219.

31. Interview with Natalia Gorbanevskaia, in *Alternatives non-violentes*, n° 32, February 1979, p. 41.
32. Lisaan, *Broadcasting to the Soviet Union, op. cit.*
33. Adam Michnik, *Penser la Pologne. Morale et politique de la résistance*, Paris, Ed. La Découverte/Maspéro, 1983, p. 117.
34. Interview with Jaroslav Jiru, January 15, 1995.
35. See Part Three, Chapter 1.
36. Jan Marcin, "Zachodnie Rozglosnie Polskojezyczne," in *Kultura*, 1986, p. 90-97. Jan Marcin was the pseudonym used at the time by Stefan Bratkowski, then chairman of the clandestine association of Polish journalists.
37. Jacek Fedorowicz, *Recenzja dans Felietony i dialogi*, Paris, Ed. Kontakt, 1988, p. 106-107
38. Cited by Lurien Alexandre, *The Voice of America, From Détente to the Reagan Doctrine*, Norwood, New Jersey, Ablex Publishing Corporation, 1988, p. 24.
39. Aleksandr Soljenitsyn, "Misconceptions about Russia are a threat to America," in *Foreign Affairs*, Spring 1980, p. 823.
40. Aleksandr Soljenitsyn, "About the World of the Russian Section of the BBC" in *Kontinent*, n° 8, 1976 (this article was the outcome of Soljenitsyn's meeting with the British station's team in January 1976).
41. György Konrad, *Antipolitics*, San Diego: Harcourt Brace Jovanovich, 1984.
42. Vladimir Boukovsky, "Lettre ouverte à Francis Ronalds, directeur de *Radio Liberty*" in *Continent*, Paris, Gallimard, 1979, p. 185-186
43. Ludmilla Alexeieva, *US Broadcasting to the Soviet Union*, A Helsinki Watch Report, New York, September 1986, p. 25.
44. Petr Fidelius, *Jazyk a moc (Language and Power)*, Munich, Edition Arkyr, 1983, (Chapter II), p. 80 onward.
45. Donald Shanor, *Behind Enemy Lines, The Private War Against Soviet Censorship*, New York, Saint Martin's Press, 1985, p. 90.
46. *Elet és Irodalon*, Budapest, February 22, 1969.
47. Elémer Hankiss, *Hongrie. Diagnostiques. Essai en pathologie sociale*, Genève, Ed. George, 1990, p. 113.
48. Milan Simecka, *Le rétablissement de l'ordre*, Paris, Ed. Maspero, 1979, p. 147.
49. Raymond Aron, *Peace and War: a Theory of International Relations*, New Brunswick, New Jersey, Transaction Publishers, 2003, p. 165.
50. Tristan Mattelart, *Le cheval de Troie audiovisuel. Le rideau de fer à l'épreuve des radios et télévisions transfrontières*, Grenoble, Presses Universitaires de Grenoble, 1995.
51. Thomas C. Sorensen, *The World War, The Story of American Propaganda*, New York Harper and Row, 1968, p. 230.
52. On the significance of this penetration of Western pop music in the East, see the noteworthy research of Timothy W. Ryback, *Rock around the Bloc, a History of Rock Music in Eastern Europe and the Soviet Union*, New York, Oxford University Press, 1990.
53. Interview with Elémer Hankiss, December 5, 1991.
54. Joseph Brodsky, *On Grief and Reason*, London, Penguin Books, 1996, p. 7.

55. Interview with Henri Tézenas du Moncel (Chairman of RFI from 1986 to 1989), September 18, 1989.

56. See Jacques Rupnik, *L'autre Europe. Crise et fin du communisme*, Paris, Odile Jacob, 1990, p. 288.

PART TWO

Tragedies behind closed doors

Reclaiming the public sphere: The first attempts (1953-1968)

Exiting from a state of totalitarianism meant leaving an existence of general social schizophrenia. It was as if, in the prevailing climate of intense social pressure, people tended to have a split personality, caught between two contrasting demands: complying with the values of the system in public, and being more-or-less oneself in private. In Soviet Europe this disease of social compliancy took a while to settle in. Initially, in the early days of the Cold War, some people sincerely believed that the Communist project could improve their lives, and that it was probably better than capitalism. Accordingly, they resolutely supported the powers-that-be, that is, Moscow. But, gradually, or suddenly in some cases, the veil lifted and this initial collective adhesion became more and more artificial. From then on, the communist ideology consistently lost its legitimacy, as the number of supporters dwindled. In a recent book, François Furet describes the collapse of this perceived utopia in Central Europe during the mid-1950s.[1]

Yet the communist regimes managed to survive, partially due to the West's indifference, at the time, to the fate of people in the East. Another strong factor contributing to their longevity was the way in which these political systems spread their hold over individuals. Of course, the peoples of Central and Eastern Europe reacted differently to Soviet domination, depending on their own history, especially that of their national and religious traditions. Between unreserved adhesion to Moscow and open revolt, the range of reactions was wide. But whether people persisted in believing in the "bright future of socialism" or not, the system was designed to ensure that everyone cooperated with it. This intentional and obligatory collaboration of each and every citizen was vital, if only for people to maintain their jobs. Consequently, resistance from within the system was all but impossible, except for a few rare historical moments in a Manichean struggle that pitted occupants against occupiers.

If there was a struggle, it was wholly an internal battle against the invasiveness of totalitarianism. The logic of totalitarianism is to meddle in individuals' private lives, to the point of seeking to eliminate any distinction between the public and private spheres. As this pressure is exerted on everyone, through various systems of surveillance and betrayal, the only way an individual can defy the system is by maintaining an inner space of autonomy and freedom that escapes the authorities' control. People have to learn to "split" themselves between the conformism of apparent submission, outside, and the search for free thought, inside. What they do is not necessarily what they think; and what they think is not what they believe. It is important to be careful, under an appearance of docility.

How people in the East maintained this inner space differed, depending on their social or professional background. Czeslaw Milosz described, for example, the subtle ways in which certain intellectuals in Stalinist Poland *concealed* their thoughts and feelings, even though they otherwise adhered to some of the system's values. He saw certain similarities with the practice of *ketman* in the Middle-Eastern Islamic civilization. *Ketman* techniques, he explained, consisted in pretending to agree with one's opponent in order to put him off track and allay his suspicions.[2] To disguise one's thinking, one not only had to silence one's convictions but also to employ many strategies to trick one's opponent, including performing rites known to be futile.

However, these methods of concealment required a capacity for "intellectual acrobatics," which not everyone had. The most widespread attitude was simply *silence*: silence concerning one's deepest convictions, one's religious faith, and one's patriotic feelings. Fearing arrest and deportation, people preferred to say nothing, even if this meant sometimes dropping a sentence or two in a meeting they were forced to attend, to suggest their allegiance to the regime. That was the best way to make sure they were left alone. As Milosz pointed out, the best refuge was home, the "four walls of one's apartment." "My home is my castle." In this bastion, the rebel could drop the mask and try to be him- or herself.

This type of psychological and mental attitude was sometimes a matter of survival in a hostile political environment. It was a defense mechanism, an attempt to remain oneself. However, whereas individuals could thus find the resources to assert themselves—in secret— through silence or guile, it was obviously too dangerous for them to do likewise in public. Yet emancipation lay in taking that big step from private to public, in opening a breach in the wall separating the two spheres. Crossing the line of demarcation meant openly expressing one's real opinion, lifting the mask and thus being the same person in public as in private. There was nothing automatic about this; it was not only a question of removing the protective cloak of disguise. Switching thus from private to public implied deep personal change and restoring one's split identity. But if outside pressure remained too strong, this "unmasking" of oneself in public was almost inconceivable; it was far too hazardous. For an individual to dare to cross over, social coercion had to be relaxed. In the Soviet Bloc this happened from 1953 onwards, after the death of Stalin.

Being oneself in public, expressing one's real opinions, meant embarking on a process of reclaiming the public sphere. This individual and collective action took place in two ways.

The first was through discussion circles, places of interaction created on the initiative of intellectuals, writers or artists. Poland and Hungary in 1955-56, and then Czechoslovakia in 1967-68, witnessed the birth of places of public debate set up by reflection groups or journals. These critical forums for expression on public life corresponded to the concept of a public sphere as defined by Jürgen Habermas.[3] The second way was through spontaneous development of various forms of social or political protest. From 1953 to 1968, collective movements appeared, even mass resistance, driven by the wish to talk openly in the streets, in the media, in public generally. Public protest was the ideal way to reclaim the public sphere.

The history of opposition in Central Europe can thus be reinterpreted by approaching it from this angle. Many observers have for instance analyzed Poland's and Hungary's major crises, in 1956, and later that of Czechoslovakia, in 1968, as attempts to reclaim these countries' national identity.[4] These mass resistance movements were indeed the symbol of the Eastern Europeans' wish to regain control of their own destiny, by recovering their identity. But few authors emphasize the fact that they were also crises in the peoples' attempt to win back the public sphere by reviving critical public debate and/or action. In fact, the two dimensions were inextricably interlinked, for asserting an identity necessarily involved a new form of public expression: the renaissance of East-East communication liberated from Soviet control. Starting with the workers' uprisings in the GDR in 1953, I propose that we take a new look at these great historical moments in the revival of free speech in the East, which lasted no more than a few hours or a few months, before state repression stamped it out again. Their comparative study has enabled me to highlight the importance of the relation between communication and resistance, and to further our understanding of the role that these Western radio stations played—or not—in these crises.

The birth of public debate: the time of the "publicists"

The death of a tyrant always leaves a power vacuum. Both adulated and despised, yesterday's tyrant at least served as a reference for all. To be sure, he provoked hate: the people had to say they loved him when actually they loathed him, to applaud the orator when they would have liked to have spat in his face. But the tyrant also inspired veneration, and became the object of collective idolatry. Many, without any obligation to do so, decorated a wall of their dining room or bedroom with his picture.

The tyrant's omnipresence marks time and space. He determines history around his authority, gagging not only free speech but also the very meaning of words and actions. That is why a tyrant's death often arouses fear of the void. How can the world carry on without him determining its direction? Status or symbol, the tyrant is also a code, a landmark for everyone; he compels people to do this, to follow that, from cradle to grave. There is so little soul in him that the announcement of his death triggers a sort of psychological shock, reminding everyone who had almost forgotten that he was human after all.

Hence, Stalin's death on March 5, 1953, caused both relief and anxiety. The passing of the "Father of the People" was mourned not only in Moscow but also in Warsaw and Prague. Then, as the emotion started to die down, many slowly came out of their state of Stalinist catatonia. They learned to walk again and, even more so, to talk, to talk to one another. In Moscow, the power hub, some officials were aware of the need to loosen the totalitarian state's stranglehold. Measures of appeasement were taken in the weeks immediately following Stalin's death, notably an amnesty decree and an announcement of amendments to the penal code (March 27, 1953), as well as substantial price decreases (March 31, 1953). By then the press was already giving less and less space to Stalin. Despite their differences, the new leaders (Molotov, Malenkov, Khrushchev) pressurized the heads of the satellite countries to adopt a "new course": politically it meant more collegial leadership; economically it promised improved access to consumer goods for people in the East. Even though Stalinists still carried substantial weight in the empire, the USSR had embarked on the process of de-Stalinization.

This de-Stalinization policy, symbolized by Nikita Khrushchev, was a vast process of restructuring communication between the government and the people, in which the former endeavored to regain the trust of the latter. François Fejtö summed the situation up as follows: the Soviet leadership "realized that it had lost touch with its browbeaten, apathetic population, and that the powerful propaganda machine was working in a vacuum"[5] To restore this communication, and despite their differences, the masters of the Kremlin were to initiate a process of thawing. On July 10, 1953, their announcement of the execution of Lavrenti Beria, the man who personified Stalinist terror, was seen as a strong sign of détente.[5]

By relaxing the central system to some extent, de-Stalinization was also to contribute to the gradual re-emergence of public speech. The advocates of the new policy had however seemingly failed to assess its possible effects within a system that had just been subjected to many years of terror. It is difficult today to imagine the impact of the Khrushchev Report on Stalin's crimes. Presented behind closed doors to the delegates of the 20th congress of the Soviet Union Communist Party, on the night of February 24-25, 1956, the report was a major issue in the internecine battle led by Khrushchev and Mikoyan against Molotov and the conservatives. But the content of the document also largely transcended the framework of an internal political power struggle. As a real indictment of the "little father of the people," the report struck a hard blow at official ideology, undermining the collective representations that until then had prevailed in the communist world.[7] It literally traumatized those who had sincerely venerated Stalin and had accordingly followed the line of official propaganda. Leon Festinger explained that it generated profound "cognitive dissonance," which demanded the revision of the Party's collective representations. In this sense, the document was an indirect invitation to discussion and public debate, as the then AFP correspondent in Moscow pointed out: "The condemnation of some of Stalin's methods had the effect of giving the population of Moscow a taste for free discussion, even with Westerners, without fearing sensitive subjects."[8] The content of the "secret report" spread very fast in March and April, both within the Eastern Bloc and in the West. On March 16, 1956, the *New York Times* correspondent was able to publish a summary of the report, and on June 4 the US State Department released the full report. Within days, VOA and RFE broadcast it to Communist Bloc countries.

In Central Europe the information disclosed in the Khrushchev Report triggered the rise of internal protest. Countries such as Poland and Hungary, already experiencing social fermentation, witnessed the gradual formation of a public sphere in the Habermassian sense: a space for critical discussion and formulation of political action, separate from the state sphere. Intellectuals and artists in Budapest and Warsaw were at the forefront of this public debate: it was the age of the publicists. This term, almost forgotten in the West, but still alive and well in Central Europe, denotes those who initiate public debate.

The publicists are the ones who raise the most crucial questions, who present the people with problems of public relevance. Their function is something like that of editorialists in the Western press, although publicists are not necessarily journalists; they may be artists, writers, sociologists or poets and, additionally, publicists. In these societies, barely emerged from Stalinism, where censorship had been particularly severe, this tradition of the publicist experienced an extraordinary revival in 1955-56.

Many of these intellectuals and writers became the leaders of "revisionism," a movement difficult to define because its form differed so much from one country to the next. The revisionists disagreed on many fundamental points within the officially endorsed ideology. In particular, they were against the dictatorship of the proletariat and for workers' councils. They refused the dominant role of the Soviet Union, and rejected the principle of censorship.

Inevitably, the revisionists' positions were a source of intense controversy with the partisans of a conservative Stalinist-type approach. They set off a protest dynamic in Central Europe, unprecedented since the beginning of the Cold War.

Journals and discussion circles

These circles of protesters fed society in two ways: either through writings, literary works or articles in the press and in journals, or else through debates within reflection groups similar to those of 18th-century pre-revolutionary France. Hungary experienced an "intellectual revolt" from the autumn of 1955. On October 18, writers and artists published a memorandum protesting against the Party's interference in literary life.[9] The weekly literary *Gazette* soon became the banner of protest. Leading writers of the day expressed their ideas in its columns, and tens of thousands of readers impatiently awaited their articles. "We attacked the Rakosi regime and its record," said Gyorgy Paloczi-Horvath. "Our weekly was attacked all the time by the official party daily, was confiscated on occasions. But its popularity was such that Rakosi didn't dare to suppress it. People fought for it when it appeared on the streets."[10] In Poland, literary journals preached reform in the political context of de-Stalinization (marked by the release of 30,000 prisoners, including Gomulka, vice-president from 1945 to 1948). Owing to its outspokenness and reports on daily life, the weekly of the secular intelligentsia, *Po Prostu*, became the country's most popular journal. Philosopher Leszek Kolakowski was already one of the best publicists in Poland. "The role of *Po Prostu* was to talk openly about issues never discussed by official propaganda. The journal wanted to tell the truth about the living conditions of workers, the absence of democracy in the Party, the instability of economic policy, the ossification of Marxist doctrine, the existence of cliques and local mafias, etc."[11]

During this period discussion groups also made their appearance in these countries. In Hungary the first and most famous was the Petofi Circle, which exalted the 1848 revolution. Set up at the end of 1955 under the aegis of the Communist Youth League, it served as a meeting place for young intellectuals disillusioned by Stalinism. After the 20th congress of the Soviet Union Communist Party, the circle's meetings drew ever-wider audiences. On June 14, 1956, no fewer than 1,600 people attended a debate on philosophy, in which George Lukacs pleaded against dogmatism. On June 27 the circle drew the amazing figure of 6,000 people for another debate on press freedom! Poland's most popular discussion circle was Tordu (the name of the street where it held its meetings), with its numerous branches in the provinces. In April 1956, an inter-circle cooperative center was created, and thus was born a fully fledged social movement that went way beyond the mobilization of a few intellectual dissidents. Political and social debates also took place within the framework of official organizations, some of which openly called for real reform and took concrete decisions. For instance, on April 23, 1956, the writers' union expelled several conservative Stalinists from its leadership.

The same spirit of renewal was found a decade later in Czechoslovakia among the proponents of "socialism with a human face," under the leadership of Alexander Dubcek. It is noteworthy that the Prague Spring was launched from 1967 by the same category of individuals, that is, writers and journalists. Pavel Tigrid[12] pinpointed the inauguration of the revolt to the June 2, 1967, declaration by several members of the Writers Congress, which they had broken away from the party line. Hence, an opposition did exist, openly demanding an overhaul of state structures and active participation by intellectuals in political life. Journalists also played a key part in the development of discussion circles. From 1966-67, they organized debates in various circles, both in towns and in the countryside, and in schools, industrial plants, cultural centers, etc. Throughout these gatherings they openly expressed their difficulties with censorship and learned what the population's greatest concerns were. By early 1968, these meetings had become a social phenomenon, sometimes bringing together several thousand people.[13]

From Warsaw to Budapest and Prague, intellectuals successfully revived an increasingly broad public debate because the population was receptive to their engagements. It would definitely be wrong to believe that these intellectuals controlled public opinion by becoming its enlightened avant-garde; they shaped opinion as much as they were shaped by it. They owed their public success to their ability to choose the right moment to express the populations' expectations and demands, in a form that was more or less acceptable to the powers that be. In this sense, they intervened as *mediators*. This historical mission was all the more important since public opinion had no independent press at the time in which to voice its concerns. The creation and expansion of a public sphere could be carried further only if this mutual influence of brave intellectuals and their potential audiences reinforced each other dialectically. That was how the former gained influence over the latter, first in student circles and then, in 1956 in Poland and 1968 in Czechoslovakia, among the workers. Generally, the formation of a public sphere goes hand in hand with the gradual constitution of a civil society, through the creation or revival of associations that value their independence from the state authority. This phenomenon appeared in 1956 in Hungary (especially among students) and, as Karel Bartosek[14] emphasized, on a massive scale in 1968 in Czechoslovakia (among journalists, students, former political prisoners of the 1950s, etc.).

These changes transcended professional groups and social categories. In the periods of awakening of public speech, the whole atmosphere of a country changed. In Poland, in the summer of 1956, the people dared for the first time in years to express their real feelings and criticism. During the same period, the famous June 27 meeting of the Petofi Circle in Hungary had a liberating effect not only on the speakers but also on the audience: "Two hours after the meeting started the Vaci Utca was blocked with crowds of people, several thousand in the street. [...] The next day there was an atmosphere in Budapest that had not been felt there for a long time."[15] People were aware that something had happened and for the first time they said what they thought. In spring 1968 in Czechoslovakia, this newfound freedom of speech in daily life was equally impressive: "For weeks the streets were empty after the working day was over, everyone was at a meeting, especially party cells and committees. Then came the writers and scholars, economists and victims of the terror, ex-servicemen and Pioneers."[16]

The risks of destabilization

The formation of a public sphere in countries under particularly rigid political regimes had repercussions that could escape the control of these countries' leaders. The almost inevitable consequence was effectively to trigger a short period of crisis within the party-state political apparatus. How could lasting cohabitation be envisaged between, on the one hand a sphere of protest and, on the other, bureaucratic structures grounded in the principle of absolute state control? As criticism spread further and further through society, there was also the probability of it infecting the ruling elite. In 1956 in Poland and 1968 in Czechoslovakia this process of destabilization led to the instatement of "reformist" governments. In Hungary a similar attempt failed when the 1956 insurrection was crushed.[17]

In Poland, Gomulka became the symbol of the desire for change. During the summer and early autumn of 1956, the proponents of reform engaged in an intense struggle against the "Natolinians," the most conservative elements of the Polish regime. Strengthened by his popularity, Gomulka agreed to return to power provided that there was a renewal of the Communist Party politburo. The Stalinists, however, intended to oust him by remaining in the majority. The conflict was eventually settled at the central committee meeting of October 19 to 21, 1956, after a tug-of-war with Moscow that could have turned into a bloodbath.

However, fully aware of Gomulka's popular support, and bearing in mind his declaration of loyalty to them, the Soviets finally decided to support him. His main condition was met: all the "Natolinians" were expelled from the central committee and Gomulka was elected first secretary of the Party by acclamation. Throughout the country, enthusiasm was equal in measure to the tension and restlessness that had prevailed for several days. On October 23, some 200,000 people gathered on the square outside the Palace of Culture cheered the hero of the day: "the man who stood up to the Russians." The Polish regime subsequently underwent a real process of liberalization, symbolized by the weekly *Po Prostu*. It was however short-lived; closure of the weekly a year later marked the end of this period.

In Czechoslovakia the context of political reform was less harsh but equally uncertain. Faced with the writers' spirit of revolt, Novotny wanted to retaliate but met with growing opposition within the Party. From September 1967 to January 3, 1968, when Dubcek was appointed as first secretary, internecine strife divided the proponents and the adversaries of change. The population was excluded from the debate throughout the crisis. Initially their only source of information about the events was foreign radio (especially RFE), but the role of the national media soon predominated when the partisans of reform appealed to public opinion in an attempt to lift the confidentiality that was shrouding conflict within the Party. In their struggle against Novotny, who was by no means ready to lay down arms, they understood that it was in their interests to take the debate into the public sphere. This would enable them to rally to their cause not only the progressive intelligentsia, but also broader segments of the population. Accordingly, they mobilized the Czechoslovakian media, including many journalists sympathetic to their cause. The tactic proved successful and led to Novotny's fall in March 1968. Zdenek Mlynar stressed the importance of this mechanism, "capable of forcing change on the system. And it was not a party or state mechanism, consisting of a democratic process within the structures of power, but rather it was a kind if public lobby backed by a free press and the free expression of opinions outside the power structure."[18]

The dynamics of the Prague Spring were thus inextricably entangled with the liberalization of the media, marked *inter alia* by the reappearance of the weekly *Literarni Noviny* on March 1, 1968. Under its new title *Literarni Listy*, the periodical immediately became a platform for discussion on public issues. Numerous debates in the press and on radio and television attested to a real explosion of the expression of public opinion after years of being bullied, gagged and biased.[19] Czechoslovakia was the country in which the public sphere changed the most in those years, for censorship was (almost) done away with on June 26, 1968. However, whereas Dubcek's team had relied on the media to come to power, it started to criticize them for their lack of loyalty to the new government. Then, in July 1968, in the face of looming Soviet intervention and threats to the new freedoms secured in the Prague Spring, politicians and journalists were once again reconciled.[20]

The two processes leading to Gomulka's rise to power in Poland, and Dubcek's in Czechoslovakia, had one crucial point in common: in neither case did the battle between progressives and conservatives switch over to violent conflict triggered by public demonstrations or urban riots. To be sure, it came close to that in Poland, but the process was avoided *in extremis* thanks to Gomulka's skill and firmness. In Czechoslovakia the proponents of reform adroitly used the national media to prevail over the conservatives. This was something new in a communist country, where opponents' fate was usually banishment or death. It showed that the process of destabilization triggered by the revival of public debate could be contained; it had not "degenerated" into physical conflict. Was this one of the main keys to the compromise reached in these two cases? In hindsight, it even seems that the avoidance of any public conflict during the critical period of October 19 and 20 increased Gomulka's room to maneuver. By relaying the wish for reform expressed by the population, he was able to convince the Soviets that he was also the guarantor of public order. Could one say that the Prague Spring movement marked above all the primacy of speech over public protest—speech that was both a quest for a new political way and an outlet for a whole country's frustrations, suppressed for so many years under the yoke of dictatorship? Historically, it is probably to Dubcek's credit that he postponed stabilization in order to allow free rein to the free speech movements.[21]

But not all protest in the communist bloc was quelled by this type of symbolic expression of speech. In other circumstances, in several countries, accumulated frustrations generated various forms of social unrest after 1953. Braving the dangers of which they were fully aware, groups formed in the streets to demonstrate their hostility towards the government.

The revival of public action: from the streets to radio

De-Stalinization had the effect of reviving not only public speech but also public protest. As the scope of this book does not enable us to analyze all the demonstrations and riots of the post-Stalin period,[22] I will focus on the two most important ones: the East German uprising of June 16 and 17, 1953, and the Hungarian uprising of October 23 to November 4, 1956. These two crises differed in one important respect: only the latter was preceded by what I have called an awakening of public speech. Yet the two events had many similarities. A comparison of the evolution of these crises, from their very first hours, shows that on the whole they followed the same pattern: assertion of the group in the urban sphere, experience of non-communication with government representatives, wish to talk on radio and, finally, repression.

Spilling over into the streets:
East Berlin, 1953, and Budapest, 1956

In the early 1950s social frustration was intense in the German Democratic Republic, a country suffering from serious economic problems and characterized by food shortages and low wages. Peoples' exasperation was evidenced mainly in indirect forms of passive resistance such as apathy at work and absenteeism. To improve production and solve the economic crisis, Walter Ulbricht, a faithful Stalinist at the head of the East German Communist Party (SED), raised the quotas of industrial work by at least 10%. The decree promulgating this reform, published on May 28, 1953, sparked latent labor protests.

The first measures towards détente taken by Moscow after Stalin's death revealed certain contradictions within the SED. Suddenly, on June 11, without any explanation, the population was informed of a "new way" that announced a change of orientation in the GDR's Stalinist policies. In light of this, would the decree on new, higher industrial quotas be applied? Signs of social discontent had been multiplying for the previous two weeks. Work stoppages were appearing in several districts throughout the country, especially in construction firms, industrial plants and the mines. This was also the case in East Berlin, especially among workers assigned to building Stalin Avenue, a prestigious new road that the communist leaders had commissioned on the ruins of Frankfurter Avenue. On June 16, a news item published by the trade unions' mouthpiece, *Tribüne*, triggered a crisis: despite the "new way" policy, the council of ministers confirmed the decision to raise industrial quotas by 10%, with immediate effect.

Construction workers on "Section 40" of Stalin Avenue had already downed tools the previous afternoon. When they heard the news they decided to dig in their heels and maintain the strike. They put together a makeshift banner proclaiming: "We demand lower quotas," and went from one worksite to the next, inviting their colleagues to join them. The procession swelled as they went along: first 70, then 800, and soon 2,000. Without any police interference, the crowd headed for the trade union headquarters but the offices were closed. It then moved on to the government buildings. By mid-day the demonstrators had reached the district of the ministries, close to Leipzigstrasse; there were 10,000 of them. The authorities were taken aback by the movement that had grown hour by hour.

This was the first protest demonstration in the streets of East Berlin since 1943.[23] Workers had dared to go out into the streets, normally strictly reserved for public events (parades and official gatherings) organized by the party-state. Without authorization, they demonstrated their hostility to the government by literally occupying the public space. This was more than simply a physical occupation of the urban space, for the strikers' courage to demonstrate publicly stemmed from their desire to make themselves heard. As a group they wanted to express publicly, if only for passers-by, their criticism of the regime—a criticism that was, by definition, prohibited. Public roads and squares were the places in which they could do so.

The scene described by a witness of the East Berlin demonstrations on the afternoon of June 16, 1953, was remarkable: "From square to square, every 200 meters or so, workers who had left their worksites improvised open-air meetings. I counted eight in two kilometers, each with no more than about 100 individuals that an orator—evidently improvised—harangued without passion but with firm assurance."[24] This was a form of appropriation of the urban space by individuals or groups who were not in any way designated to express themselves there as such, that is, as social and political actors critical of the powers-that-be. The space of the streets became the field for collective protest action, whether in the form of peaceful gatherings or insurrection.

In East Germany the increase in industrial quotas sparked a crisis that had been brewing since the creation of the communist state due to deteriorating social, economic and political conditions. From the next day, June 17, the strikes spread to some of the country's main industrial centers: Bitterfeld, Hennigsdorf, Halle, Leipzig, Merseburg and Gorlitz. It was estimated that some 300,000 workers downed tools in 272 localities.[25] The scenario was more or less the same everywhere: workers went on strike and took to the streets where they marched or assembled. They often grouped together on public squares, the traditional loci of popular protest before the Nazis came to power. In some places the demonstrations turned to insurrection, for instance in Magdeburg, Brandenburg and Gera where jails were attacked.

Unlike Poland and Hungary in 1956, in the GDR this movement was not preceded by a revival of public speech. East German intellectuals, journalists and writers played no part in the awakening of the people's social conscience. Harsh living conditions and unpopular measures naturally fed private conversations among workers, both at home and at work.

Research has shown moreover that, in the first two weeks of June, conversations among workers often revolved around the timeliness of industrial action to protest against the new quotas. But there is no trace of the formation of a public sphere, through speech, might have prompted workers to set themselves objectives, to choose spokespersons, and to interact with other segments of the population. This absence of prior public debate (which would in any case have been inconceivable in the East German communist regime) explains why the movement remained confined to workers in the construction and other industries, the main targets of the new quotas.

It also explains why the crisis was so sudden, switching almost overnight from latent revolt to mass public protests. The dynamics of this uprising seem to have been more reactive than controlled. It could be qualified as a sort of social reactivity in which action was not driven with intent but resulted from the reaction of certain groups—

here, workers—to situations that they perceived as intolerable. In these circumstances it took very little—the decision to increase production quotas—to mobilize them instantly. The dynamics of such movements were based on a paradox: because they were improvised, there were no appointed spokespersons; the workers were "pushed" into the streets rather than marching with clearly-formulated demands. But as social actors switching over to public protest, they themselves became the spokespersons of a society that could no longer bear government pressure.

The slogans chanted during the June 16 and 17 demonstrations clearly illustrate this way of protesting on behalf of the group and of society as a whole: "Down with the quotas!" but also "Free elections!," "No more borders!"

Three years later, the Hungarian uprising of 1956 was another case of the switch to public protest action, although preceded this time by the formation of a small critical public sphere. It was a typical example of the process that developed from the creation of a space for debate to its expression in protest form in the streets. The October 23 demonstrations in Budapest marked the beginning of this tilting over into public protest.[26] In such cases one could imagine (even predict) that the prior birth of a space for debate would give the movement some degree of reflexive maturity. From the moment the movement went public, such maturity would result in more elaborate demands and objectives than in the case of social reactivity alone. In the Hungarian example, several platforms for expressing demands were set up in the days preceding the October 23 demonstrations: short texts, usually written by students, presenting 14, 16 or 18 demands. Formulated in a way that was careful not to contradict the principles of the socialist constitution, they ranged from "the creation of a new government" to the "withdrawal of all Soviet troops," through "the reorganization of the economy" and "total freedom of opinion and the press." These points, some of which seem nothing short of unrealistic, were written up hastily in a pre-revolutionary atmosphere, for instance those drafted during the October 22 meeting at the Polytechnic School. They nevertheless constituted the beginning of a political program that can be seen as the fruit of debates held in preceding months, especially within the Petofi Circle.

We must nevertheless be careful not to over-simplify this switch from public debate to public action. The Polish October case, which preceded the Hungarian uprising by a few days, looks somewhat different. Although there was also a move to open protest, the process was laborious—and for good reason! The challenge was by no means small: daring to demonstrate in the streets against the dictatorship. Collective public protest first took on devious forms that could be defined as something "in-between": no longer only a verbal expression of criticism, but not yet an open manifestation of opposition. In the case of Hungary, the official funeral of Laslo Rajk on October 6, 1956, seemed to serve this purpose. The context of this national day of mourning (also the commemoration of the execution in 1849 of 13 generals by the Austrian authorities) afforded the population the opportunity to commemorate the death of other heroes: those who, seven years earlier, had been the victims of Stalin's purges carried out by the Hungarian government itself. For the 150,000 people present, the October 6, 1956 "demonstration" was therefore a matter of re-appropriating a symbol of national identity in a way that immediately made it meaningful as criticism of the government. The significance of the event nevertheless remained highly ambiguous, for the ceremony took place in the presence of state dignitaries. The government, which had organized the official funeral, had no control over the significance that most of the participants attributed to it. The way was thus paved for more explicit forms of protest: the mass demonstration two weeks later, on October 23.

The prior formation of a critical public sphere also facilitated the expansion of the protest movement. As the development of public debate in the preceding months had gradually reached into different segments of society, representatives of these social groups swelled the ranks of the public protest movement. This was evidenced on October 23. The demonstration, initially decided in a spirit of solidarity with the "Polish October," and first banned then authorized even though it had already begun, brought together writers, students and intellectuals, before being joined by people from a wide spectrum of occupational backgrounds. At around 2 p.m. tens of thousands of students formed a huge procession that set off towards the two squares named after heroes of the 1848 revolution, Josef Bem at Buda and Sandor Petofi at Pest. They were soon joined by the writers who had gathered in Gorki Street, outside the Polish embassy. At Bem Square a writers' manifesto, moderate in tone, was read without arousing the masses' enthusiasm. "We're not in 1848," commented Miklos Molnar. "The *Arise Magyars* of 1956 hasn't been written. The writers' movement has had its day; it's served its purpose. Now, its losing its way in the revolution that's feeding itself."[27]

But the crowd kept growing. It had reached two to three thousand people when, at 4:30 p.m., near the Marguerite Bridge, the strikers from the large industrial districts joined it. Other occupations were represented too: salesmen, waiters, store-keepers, tram drivers, cobblers, among many others. Half of the inhabitants of Budapest aged 20-40 took to the streets to demand change.

Asserting an identity in public

Irrespective of its origins, any street demonstration is linked to a process of assertion by the group protesting. Appearing together in public is necessarily defining oneself in public, and symbols, slogans and chanting are all attributes of this collective presentation of the self. The demonstrators may proceed in ways already used by the powers that be (official parades, for example), but will then re-appropriate them, giving them new meaning. On June 16 and 17, 1953, marching protesters in the GDR sang popular working-class songs and slogans that distorted those of the Party. Together they chanted: "Against the regime: unity of the working classes."[28] In Budapest the demonstrators strongly expressed the national and political nature of their action, re-appropriating their national history through multiple references to the 1848 revolution, including those mentioned above. Many students wore a red, white and green cockade in their lapel. The crowd sang the national anthem to the glory of Kossuth, along with the Marseillaise, and sometimes the Internationale. It chanted: "Nagy to power, Rakosi in the Danube," "Now or never," "We want a Hungarian government" and, for the Russians: "Go home!" or "The Russians in Russia."

The constitution of a group identity in the urban sphere also involved a new labeling. The protesters wanted to "de-semiotize" and "re-semiotize" places (public buildings and roads) so that they would correspond to the meaning that they attributed to them. One of the first actions of the East Berlin workers in June 1953 was to remove the red flag at Brandenburg Gate. In Budapest the demonstrators bore the national Hungarian flag—from which they had cut out the Soviet coat of arms—, snuffed out the red star above parliament, and toppled the giant bronze statue of Stalin towering above the municipal park. This act might actually warrant analysis by an anthropologist and a psychoanalyst, for the scene brings to mind a collective murder of the father. Pulling down the statue of the dictator proved difficult, but "finally, they managed to melt Stalin's knees with a blow torch. Only the two huge boots remained on the base, while Stalin's body was cut into pieces and the enormous head dragged by a roads department truck into the town center. It remained there outside the national theatre for a few hours, with a signpost ripped up at the corner of a road: 'Dead end.'"[29] That day, the Hungarians indulged in the destruction of the most glaring symbol of their oppression, reducing to a thousand pieces this historical figure of their enemy who had imposed on them the reign of terror—a regime that they definitively wanted to rid themselves of.

As soon as it had started to make its mark on the urban space, its identity constituted, the group sought partners for dialogue. In 1953 as in 1956, it spontaneously headed for the seats of political power: the district of the ministries in East Berlin, Parliament Square in Budapest. This was an extraordinary event in a communist country; a radical departure from standard practice that consisted in managing conflict strictly within the Party. The demonstrators thus revived the traditional protest march in which the downtrodden gathered together in a procession to state their claims and grievances. In both East Berlin and Budapest their encounter with the authorities turned sour. Dialogue was impossible and communication rapidly became conflictual, for the crowd was impatient to make itself heard. How could communication possibly be established during these initial public confrontations? In the drama that had started to play out in public, was this not simply Act One, in which the actors proved to themselves that the main theme of the story was indeed mutual misunderstanding between the government and society?

When the workers arrived at the seat of government on June 16, at around 1 p.m., they demanded to see Walter Ulbricht and Otto Grotewohl, to no avail. Instead, first the secretary of state, Walter, then the cabinet minister Fritz Selbmann, followed by the political secretary of the district of Berlin, Heinz Brandt, and finally Professor Robert Havemann, came out to talk to them. All were shouted down. Fritz Selbmann undertook to ensure that the government's decision to increase industrial quotas was withdrawn, but the crowd was still not satisfied:

"Colleagues!" he said to the workers, who retorted:
"We're not your colleagues!"
"I'm a worker like you"
"But you've forgotten it. You've betrayed the workers."[30]

A few hours later the government announced that it was to back down on the issue of industrial quotas. But it was too late; this retreat simply emboldened the strikers, who wanted much more, including concessions of a different kind. They demanded the government's resignation and free elections. Finally, they called for a general strike and a gathering the next morning on Strausberg Square (near Stalin Avenue). In a van equipped with a loudspeaker they covered the city, rallying others to join them.

In Budapest the crowd made no attempt to obtain anything whatsoever from the Stalinist leaders whom they abhorred. They gathered on

Kossuth Square at 5 p.m. to hear the man in whom they put all their hopes, Imre Nagy. In 1953, Nagy had been prime minister before being expelled from the Party, but had recently been reinstated as a party member. Nagy reluctantly appeared before the crowd shortly before 8 p.m. Starting his speech with the ritual "Comrades," he was immediately booed by the same people who had waited for him for hours. His speech was disappointing; it failed to meet the people's expectations and offered nothing concrete. "When Nagy urged them to calmly go home the disappointment peaked. The entire square muttered angrily and no one applauded his peroration. Ill at ease for a moment, Nagy suggested they sing the national anthem."[31] This initiative enabled the Hungarian leader to communicate *in extremis* with the people gathered before him. But it certainly did not satisfy the crowd's frustration, which stemmed from the profound gap between the people and the man who was supposed to be closest to their expectations. It was as if the communication code that formerly, through communist ideology, had maintained a sort of fictive unity between them and their leaders, had broken down. A new one had to be found, one that was older, more profoundly rooted in the people's memory. In this instance, only the Hungarian national anthem enabled Nagy to save his poor public performance. He found himself projected to the center of a political situation, the full implications of which he failed to grasp.

This absence of dialogue was an incentive for the demonstrators to increase their presence in the public sphere and to voice their collective protest even more vociferously. The dynamic of the demonstration boosted them to reclaim a greater space of expression. Demonstrating means joining forces to make oneself heard. Shouting or chanting a slogan together is like using a collective megaphone; it unites the voices of those who are never heard, withdrawn as they are into themselves in the multitude of schizophrenic shells of the totalitarian world. This inebriation from being together, in the open, gives the group an impression of strength. In these circumstances, what could be more understandable than the wish to gain control of a far more powerful megaphone: the media, starting with radio?

In the 1950s, radio was the mass medium par excellence. Under the Party's absolute control, it spewed out a constant, monotonous flow of lies that bore no relation to daily life. Stalinist propaganda seldom used the impassioned tone that had so often characterized the Nazi hysteria; it was boring, soporific, made—it seemed—to push people into resignation. But this time the demonstrators wanted to put an end to the lies. Spurred by their newfound audacity, by the delirium that came from feeling their collective strength, they wanted to set off to conquer radio, or at least to express themselves on it so that they could tell the truth: their truth.

As they set out to reclaim this right to speech in the media,[32] the demonstrators sought to expand their audience. Their aim was still to express themselves in public, but with a far broader reach than simply the spectators of street demonstrations: they wanted to talk to the entire nation. As a mass medium, radio attracted the mass of protesters, who saw it as a way of obtaining the recognition of their struggle. Given the change of scale of the audience, no one doubted that this new switch from one public space to another would inevitably be conflictual. This was truly a matter of power, strikingly and tragically illustrated by the first crises in Central Europe.

From the first day of their action, demonstrators in both East Berlin and Budapest approached a radio station to make their movement known. In 1953, the workers of East Berlin wanted to talk on RIAS, a popular US radio station in East Germany. The station was accustomed to receiving complaints from people about their living conditions, or poems, for instance. In the context of particularly harsh media censorship in East Germany, it was a sort of *ersatz* for some. But for an East German to physically go to the radio station's headquarters in West Berlin was extremely risky. Sentences of up to five years in a camp had been meted out to individuals who had dared to do so. On June 16, the workers nevertheless braved the danger. They knew that RIAS was the only radio station picked up in the GDR that could talk about their action. Over the past two weeks it had reported on the growing strikes in some of the country's industrial centers, and its 7:30 p.m. news bulletin on June 15 reported the beginning of the Bloc 40 strike at the Stalin Avenue construction works. Two groups of strikers spontaneously went to the US radio station the next day to talk about the movement that was spreading in East Berlin. Although they were uncoordinated (the first arrived at noon and the second at about 3 p.m.), they both had the same request: to express themselves over the air so that they could make their demands known and call for a general strike. Some of them even thought they could make RIAS the information and coordination center of their struggle.[33]

But the strikers were met by the journalists' and station supervisors' refusal. RIAS was happy to talk about the workers' movement, but not to hand the microphone over to them. Apart from this position of principle, the officials at the US radio station were unsure as to the best line to adopt to cover the event. This was the first time since the station's inception in 1947 that this type of situation had occurred. Should they relay the call for a strike? If so, how? The RIAS officials had to improvise, which was probably why the radio's line reflected some hesitations, picked up in the analysis of its programs during the crisis.

In Budapest, demonstrators arrived at the national radio station from 6 p.m. on October 23. They wanted their demands read over the air, but the swelling crowd was barred access to the building. Eventually a delegation was allowed in and negotiations dragged on. Nothing had been concluded when suddenly, at 8 p.m., the station broadcast a speech by the first secretary of the Communist Party, Erno Gero, in which he abrasively described the day's events as "nationalist provocation." The demonstrators were able to hear his speech via receivers placed at the windows of the building.[34] They were furious, and shocked, especially since their own text had still not been read. The crowd started to grumble and the most determined groups tried to force their way into the building by climbing through windows and crashing a car into the front door. At the same time the AVH[35] tried to clear an area around the building. At around 9 p.m. the first shots were fired. Members of the urban police and the army who sympathized with the demonstrators had given them weapons. Tens of people were killed or wounded in this first battle for the radio station, but victory escaped the invaders. As they seized the building, journalists loyal to the government fled with their equipment and took refuge in the buildings of parliament from which they carried on broadcasting ... under the protection of Soviet tanks.

From 4 a.m. the tanks had rolled into Budapest. Their arrival was immediately seen as provocation. Perhaps the conflict could have remained a riot, but with the Red Army's intervention it turned into insurrection. From that point on armed groups were formed at the entry to bridges and certain avenues of the capital, to block the Soviets. Their "assistance" had been secretly demanded by Erno Gero and Andreas Hegedus, without the knowledge of the central committee. The committee, at an emergency meeting convened on the night of October 23 to 24, had appointed as the new prime minister the man whom the crowds had demanded in the streets of Budapest, Imre Nagy. But the next morning, between 8.15 a.m. and 9 a.m., when the radio announced both Nagy's appointment and the Soviet intervention, confusion between the two arose easily. Listeners could readily believe that it was Nagy himself, barely instated, who had appealed to the Red Army, when actually he had nothing to do with the decision. Nagy's political legitimacy was thus tainted. This turned out to be a serious handicap for him in his efforts to solve the crisis, for he constantly had to defend himself of this accusation both at home and internationally—an accusation that the Hungarian section of RFE endorsed and propagated.

The "support" of Western radio stations

National radio refused to relay the voice of the opposition; but what about Western radio stations? Did they help the protest movements to reclaim the public sphere? We have seen how Western radio stations contributed to the development of public debate, for instance in 1956 when they widely broadcast the content of the Khrushchev Report, and in 1967 when they made known the internal conflict between conservatives and reformers in the Czechoslovakian Communist Party. But what was their line when it came to open crisis? Did they help to publicize the public protest?

Western radio maintained its function as a reference[36] throughout the upheaval of events large and small punctuating the destabilization of the Eastern Bloc. During the turmoil, the BBC remained the reference for information on what the world's leading powers were saying and doing, on how international opinion was reacting, and so on. Of course this preference for the BBC did not mean that the other stations had no listeners. People in the eye of the storm in Budapest or Prague tuned into whatever they could: VOA, RFE or Radio Vienna. The substitution radio stations, however, went further than simply supplying news; their political goal was, from outside, to encourage nascent forms of opposition within the communist countries, whether judiciously or not.

The effects of mass means of communication being difficult to define, assessing these stations' support for opponents is particularly complex. At the very least, the intentions behind their messages have to be clearly distinguished from the processes in which they were received. Many studies have shown that the meaning of the message transmitted is rarely the same as that of the message received. Multiple factors influence the modalities of reception and their possible effects, including the receiving person's psychological or sociological characteristics, or variables pertaining to the context of reception, for example. As a result, the receiver "co-constructs" the sense of the message addressed to him or her.[37] From this point of view it is interesting to examine the respective roles of RIAS in the East Berlin uprising of 1953, and that of RFE in the Hungarian insurrection of 1956. A study of this nature highlights both the opportunities and the limitations of these foreign radio stations' intervention in the course of the early crises in Central Europe.

RIAS during the East German uprising of 1953

Situated in the US section of West Berlin, RIAS had a finger on the pulse of the East German capital. It was even able to receive news from throughout the GDR fairly quickly. This proximity with the communist world, at the very frontier between East and West, gave it a particular political responsibility in the Cold War context. What to say or not to say on the air was a matter of debate almost daily among the station's journalists and frequently among its supervisors. Yet, on June 16, 1953, when the workers' demonstration broke out in the streets of East Berlin, RIAS director Gordon Erwing said he found himself left to his own devices, unable to obtain any clear instruction from US officials.[38] After consulting the journalists and some friends, he defined the official RIAS line in the crisis: report the facts without broadcasting the call for a general strike and without allowing the workers to go on the air. By thus setting the limits of RIAS's action, the aim was clearly to restrict the American station's involvement in the conflict. In this way he hoped to avoid provoking a reaction by the Soviets, which could in turn lead to action by the United States. Who knew, an irresponsible communication policy by RIAS could inadvertently spark off a third world war! In this Cold War context, when Stalin's death seemed to have ushered in a more uncertain phase in international relations, fear of that eventuality was very real in both Washington and Bonn. Talking on RIAS at 10.50 p.m. on June 16, the West German minister for inter-German relations, Jakob Kaiser, appealed to the workers to act wisely and not to fall into the trap of provocation. His attitude was inspired by the Westerners' fear of seeing the affair degenerate into international conflict: "I say to every citizen of East Berlin: don't get carried away by rash actions; no one must put themselves or those around them in danger. Real change to your lives can be achieved only by restoring German unity and freedom."[39]

But an analysis of program content from June 16 to 18 shows certain discrepancies with the station's official policy line; some programs were actually an incentive to take action. The fact that the workers were calling for a general strike was mentioned from the first major report on the June 16 demonstration broadcast that same day at 4:30 p.m.,[40] and repeated in a night program on June 17 at 1.26 a.m.[41] RIAS also relayed the rallying cry to congregate the next day, June 17, on Strausbergplatz. Although the journalists themselves did not call for the gathering, they explicitly reported the call, along with the workers' demands: not only the refusal of higher industrial quotas but also the demand for free elections. In its evening programs on June 16, RIAS made no more mention of the call for a general strike, but some commentators and guests of the station spoke in terms that could be interpreted as precise instructions to the East German workers.

The most explicit message was that of Ernst Scharnowski, leader of the DGB (Deutscher Gewerkschaftsbund), the confederation of West-

German industrial trade unions, which was planning a demonstration on June 17 in solidarity with East German workers. Authorized that day to speak on RIAS in its popular early morning program "Working day in the zone,"[42] he explicitly called for public gatherings: "Join the East Berlin construction workers' movement, [...] and meetings everywhere on your Strausberg squares; everywhere, the more you are, the more powerful and disciplined the movement, the more successful it will be."[43] Scharnowski thus circumvented the prohibition on mentioning the call for a general strike, and repeated the previous day's rallying cry by the East Berlin workers: meet on Strausbergplatz. Note that he said "meetings everywhere on your Strausbergplatz" (when in fact this square was in Berlin). In this way he was intentionally addressing the entire population of the GDR. For RIAS listeners not living in or near the capital, this meant: "Meet on the main public square of your towns." As this meeting was scheduled for the morning, during working hours, the call amounted to an incentive to strike immediately. This declaration, repeated three times between 5:36 a.m. and 7:30 a.m., was heard throughout the GDR. To what extent did it effectively spur the workers to strike? Were they not already determined enough?

For weeks, unrest had been simmering in the country's main industrial cities. RIAS reported any information it could get hold of on the situation. But this type of news also circulated via social communication channels within East Germany. As historian Manfred Hagen pointed out, workers spread the word throughout the country as they were often assigned to jobs far from their place of residence and therefore traveled extensively. This was particularly true of the construction workers on Stalin Avenue, who slept in barracks close to the site during the week. When they "went home, the workers spread a feeling of discontent in their town and perhaps even spoke of the strike."[44] In this type of social climate, we can see why the sensational news of a strike in the streets of East Berlin had such a mobilizing effect on people who were already worked up. Simply the decision to "drop" this news over the air on RIAS, when the Western press agencies saw it as Soviet provocation, had the effect of awakening or boosting the fighting spirit of workers throughout the country. In other words, the *context of reception* of these programs meant that they were interpreted as an incentive to action by the East German workers concerned by quota increases. In this respect, the news of the East Berlin demonstration was seen as an example to follow: "If *they* are doing it, why not us?" It is moreover highly likely that certain details of reports on this action had an incentive effect, without that being the intention of the journalists reporting them. For instance, the surprising news that the police had not intervened to stop the demonstrators' march on the ministries might have been perceived as a weakness in the government, and therefore interpreted as an opportunity to take advantage of the situation to openly defy it. Various witness accounts show however that the link between reception of the news of the East Berlin demonstration and the beginning of the strike in other towns or regions was all but automatic. Complicated processes were at play, especially through *conversations* and *debates* between workers: "Were those who launched the action not agitators?," "Should we also strike and if so, on what conditions?" After hearing the June 17 morning news on RIAS, many workers discussed these questions openly as soon as they arrived at work. These near-simultaneous conversations in dozens of firms throughout the GDR caused the strike to spread suddenly during the morning. Thus, the extraordinary mass movement of June 17 stemmed from the combination of at least three factors: first, the June 16 demonstration as such, which was both the culmination of the latent protest and a factor triggering the future mass movement; second, the rapid dissemination of the news by RIAS throughout the GDR; and third, the receptiveness of workers' bastions in other districts, ready to embark on industrial action.

In this context, RIAS was nothing more than an amplifier of the mass movement. It did not "command" it, but contributed to spreading it by acting as a technical support and a political relay. As a technical support for the transmission of information, it was the main means of spreading news about the East Berlin demonstration, although not the only one. Here again, as in the period preceding the crisis, news was also spread via communication channels within the country. Theodor Ebert explained how railway workers and employees of the ministry of commerce used the telephone and telex to spread news from the capital.[45] RIAS's role was also political, if only because its officials "dropped" the news shortly after the beginning of the movement—an attitude that could be interpreted as an intention to spur it on (they could have decided instead to withhold the news). RIAS played an even more active political role when, on the morning of June 17, through Scharnowski's voice, it called on all citizens of the GDR to meet on public squares. But even though this call was effectively broadcast far and wide, there is no proof that it decisively shaped that day's events. Depending on its own history and sociological composition, every town or region experienced a particular mobilization process, both in the streets and in the workplace. The June 17 uprising was thus the result of a sort of co-construction between the radio station and the social movement itself. Its immediate outcome was the exceptional formation of a new public sphere in the GDR, for the first time in a communist country. On that morning, street demonstrations, speeches in industrial pants, the fact that workers sometimes tuned into RIAS on the company radio, and perhaps above all the joy on their faces, were all evidence that the East Germans were busy reinventing the internal conditions of their own communication.

But the promulgation of martial law by the Soviets at 1 p.m. on June 17 soon put paid to this new social dynamic. In the provinces the strikes were only starting: in Leipzig, Merseburg, Rosslau, Bitterfeld, Halle, Wittenberg, Jena, etc. These June 17 strikers were expecting RIAS to talk about them as well in its evening programs, as it had done the previous day for the Berlin East workers. But, apart from a brief mention of the strikes on the morning of the 18th, the American station said nothing. All its reports and commentaries were worded as if everything was over, noted Rainer Hildebrandt.[46] The strikers, who had hoped that RIAS would support their struggle and relay the call for a general strike, were bitterly disappointed. "For me, June 17 was a wonderful experience [...] but it was also the most bitter disappointment of my life" said one of the strike leaders. "My disappointment didn't concern the Soviet authorities whom I already knew from prison. It was the attitude of the West that was disappointing. Of course we weren't expecting armed support, and the West could have said that; at least it could have said that. It wouldn't have damaged our strike; on the contrary, it would have clarified the situation. The strike would not have been able to develop uncontrollably, we would have been strengthened in our attitude of disciplined refusal of violence (*bestärkt im Durchhalten disziplinierter Nichtegewalt*), even if it was only for a warning strike."[47]

Yet, if the movement ran out of steam, it was not only through a lack of support from the West, if only via radio. It was of course also because of Soviet repression,[48] compounded by the lack of the movement's perspectives, as Arnulf Baring explains.[49] The strikers were not properly organized and remained relatively isolated. Although they wanted to talk on behalf of the entire population, they were unable to persuade other social classes to join their struggle. Their movement had no detailed and coherent program that could lead to a change of government. Moreover, the GDR had few people capable of taking over the reins of power, like Gomulka in Poland or Dubcek in Czechoslovakia. It follows that the decline of the movement resulted not only from the line followed by RIAS but certainly even more so from the limits of this first mass revolt in communist Europe.

RFE during the Hungarian insurrection of 1956

RFE programs during the 1956 Budapest uprising generated intense controversy in both East and West. The Hungarian section of RFE was accused of inciting the population to take up arms against the Soviets, with the intention of overthrowing the communist government. That was the official version of Janos Kadar's government, set out in its white paper published after the events.[50] It was also that of many articles published in the Western press in the three months following the crisis, especially in West Germany where the headquarters of RFE were located (Munich). The UNO report on the events also implicated RFE albeit with circumspection: "It would appear that certain broadcasts by Radio Free Europe 43 helped to create an impression that support [from the West] might be forthcoming for the Hungarians. The Committee feels that in such circumstances the greatest restraint and circumspection are called for in international broadcasting."[51] Yet, at a press conference on January 25, 1957, Chancellor Konrad Adenauer affirmed that "this investigation has shown that the assertions which appeared in the press, that Radio Free Europe promised the Hungarians assistance by the West—armed assistance by the West—are not consistent with the facts. [...] But a discussion, an exchange of views, took place which also resulted in personnel changes and I believe that the matter can be considered settled for the time being."[52] So what actually happened?

The episode of RFE's role in the Hungarian uprising is taboo in the American station's history. Many officials contended that RFE programs did not add fuel to the flames, although certain programs might have been "blunders." This was the point of view argued by Robert Holt in a book written in 1958, probably published under the control of the CIA, on which the station depended directly at the time.[53] At the end of 1956, under pressure from the international press and the West-German government, RFE undertook an analysis of its own programs in Hungarian, broadcast during the uprising. The report concluded that of the 308 different items, 16 could be considered as suspect even though there was no glaring difference with the station's policy. Four other items were found to have given military advice to the Hungarian freedom fighters. Of those four items, only one was considered to be an outright violation: a review of an article in *The Observer* presented in the Western press review on November 4, 1956. RFE asserted as factual the assumption made by the correspondent of this newspaper (in the same day's issue), that "if the Soviet troops really attack Hungary [...] and the Hungarians will hold out for three or four days, then the pressure upon the government of the United States to send military help to the freedom fighters will become irresistible."⁵⁴ No RFE program called for armed struggle, affirmed Holt, adding, "however, there were some broadcasts from the West that could have been confused with RFE, and these freely indicated that Western help was in the offing. A small transmitter located just outside Frankfurt, used by the NTS (a Russian émigré organization known as the 'Solidartsis') was turned over to a Hungarian veterans' group in Germany. Some of the broadcasts from this station were irresponsible—indicating that the West was coming to the help of the Hungarians.

Apparently, some of these broadcasts were confused with RFE's."⁵⁵ In short, the radio station had little to blame itself for, except a slight "excess of exuberance," as Sig Mickelson put it a quarter century later.⁵⁶ Hence, the Hungarians allegedly heard only ... what they wanted to hear.

Yet these "conclusions" could not be certified by experts outside the station. Commissions from the UN, the Council of Europe and the West German parliament were unable to carry out independent inquiries into the CIA's control. All the audio and written archives of these programs were destroyed by RFE officials, except for a few scripts to which I was allowed access in the early 1990s, after much insistence. These documents are representative of RFE programs as recorded by West Germany in 1956, which were stored in the Hungarian national radio's archives in 1995.⁵⁷

Two tendencies can be identified in these programs broadcast between October 23 and November 5. The first, that could be qualified as maximalist, consisted in systematically denigrating Imre Nagy's government by accusing it of taking only "half-measures" (October 24) and above all of having called on Soviet troops to suppress the uprising. Imre Nagy's new government, claimed the US radio station, was a Soviet stooge that had nothing to do with the Hungarian people (October 27). This position was in itself a way of prompting the Hungarians to act with intransigence and therefore to demand more from Nagy, whereas Moscow allowed him very little leeway. Second, RFE constantly praised the Hungarian people's extreme fighting spirit. This was another way of spurring them on, by flattering their pride and making heroes out of the insurgents in advance: "Who is busy fighting against the barricades? The communists say 'the dregs of society'. We say: the entire nation with a sense of heroism and sacrifice that serves as an example to all nations" (October 25).⁵⁸ In other excerpts, RFE suggested that a military victory of the "freedom fighters" was possible: "The army attacking Hungary is not invincible. [...] The Hungarian army is strong. Reasonably, after cold calculation, the possibility exists of confronting the Soviet troops and prevailing. The ceasefire promised by the Budapest government with blood on its hands was nothing more than a shameful betrayal" (October 31). From November 2 the program content became less vehement. Some self-criticism by the station could even be perceived, with regard to its accusation that Nagy had called in the Soviet troops. "We were here, hundreds of miles away and, in view of the tragic circumstances today, we are not in a position to settle this issue. The sentence in this trial will be pronounced in more peaceful conditions, by the nation, perhaps only by history. [...] There has never been a greater need for national unity, which is precisely what the prime minister is calling for today" (November 2).

This change of tone, also pointed out by Robert Holt, was probably due to direct intervention by the US officials in New York in charge of RFE, alerted as to the highly questionable content of the Hungarian section's programs. But it was already too late. How can one not agree with Micklos Molnar's severe judgment, or that of François Fejtö cited above, both of whom described RFE's policy at the time as "irresponsible?"[59] Did this "hard-liner" approach of the Hungarian section stem from the fact that its director, Andor Gellert, fell ill at the beginning of the uprising, thus leaving the team to its own devices? Some people thought so, but this explanation is insufficient. The team's "excesses" stemmed far more from the circumstances of the time and its members' political leanings. It is difficult today to imagine the extraordinary emotion that the Hungarian uprising, followed by Soviet intervention, provoked throughout the world. In the West, the incredible epic of this little forgotten country that defied the Red Army was followed from day to day. In Munich, the members of the Hungarian section of RFE were themselves overcome by their emotions and, even more so, because they were exiles of the country, by their passions. They were aware of being at the centre of world news and wanted to contribute to a conclusion that—from their point of view—was favorable to Hungary. It was in this sense that they sought to take part in the conflict, not simply as chroniclers of the crisis, but as actors who fully supported the insurgents.

These RFE employees' political convictions consequently led them to make serious errors of judgment, reflected in the program content. Most of the staff at the Hungarian section were right-wing émigrés who failed to perceive the positive role that Imre Nagy could play as new president of the Council. For example, the military chronicles were by Julian Borsanyi, formerly an officer on Admiral Miklos Horty's staff. "Their anticommunism did not enable them to understand Nagy's policy during the crisis," commented a Hungarian journalist formerly with RFE. "They couldn't grasp that this revolution was actually a tremendous attempt to reform communism. They were men of the past who thought that Hungary's prewar regime could be reinstated."[60] That was why their political engagement led them to commit serious professional misconduct, especially not adopting the neutral tone that would have been RFE's best bet."[61]

Yet we cannot conclude that RFE was responsible for the Hungarian tragedy, and even less so that it caused the revolution. Its fanatical programs certainly did not have the direct effect of triggering Budapest's street battles. Like RIAS in West Germany, RFE's role in Hungary can be understood only in the context of reception of its programs locally. According to observers and journalists present in the country at the time, many Hungarians were counting on moral and material support from the West. In previous years the West's repeated declarations against the Soviet Union's control over Central Europe had naturally fed their hopes. Now that the hour of truth had dawned, it was logical for the Hungarian insurgents to call on the West for help. It was therefore in this climate of intense expectation that RFE propaganda had the effect not of moderating people's hopes but rather of fuelling them by making people believe in a forthcoming Western intervention. "In the psychological climate of what must be called war-time conditions everything the free world said in its broadcasts was liable to incite or, at least, raise false hopes on a very large scale."[62] An opinion poll on Hungarian refugees in 1957 revealed that the vast majority of those who engaged in armed struggle believed they would receive help from the West. "One third of the refugees volunteered the view that Western broadcasts and propaganda in general had led the Hungarians to believe that aid would be forthcoming. More significantly, when asked directly whether American broadcasts had given the impression that the United States was willing to fight to save Hungary, fully half of the respondents gave affirmative answers and only a little more than one third of them denied it."[63] Interviews showed that hope in the West stemmed from much more than the content of RFE programs during the crisis. It resulted primarily from RFE and VOA programs in preceding years and, more generally, from what the Hungarians had understood of the major Western powers' declarations from the beginning of the Cold War.

The end of the crisis was proof that the Western countries had no intention of coming to the Hungarian insurgents' aid. The October 28 debate at the UN led to no concrete measure.

Worse still, the Franco-British intervention of October 29 against Nasser's control of the Suez Canal turned the world's eyes away from Eastern Europe, towards the Middle East, and left the field open to the

Soviets in Hungary. Why deny them the right to intervene in that country when France and Britain were doing the same thing in Egypt?

Hence, while RFE was justifiably the focus of criticism, it was actually little more than a magnifier of Western, especially American, contradictions. It was in the United Sates, in the early days of the Cold War, that various experts had formulated the objective of "freeing the prisoners of communism." With the CIA's support, RFE was to be one of the instruments of that policy.

But by putting the United States' back to the wall, the Hungarian crisis revealed that this strategy had no substance. RFE consequently found itself in an awkward position regarding the concrete implementation of US diplomacy in the crisis.

After 1956, RFE had to clarify its missions by adopting a more moderate policy of "liberalization," as it was known. During the Prague Spring it was therefore out of the question to discredit the Dubcek government by reproaching it for not following a radical line. It was likewise excluded to praise the courage of the population for its attempted resistance to the Warsaw Pact invasion. RFE remained withdrawn with regard to the events, whereas the Czechoslovakian media were in the front line.

From the point of view of the West's communication policy towards the East, two important lessons can be learned from the respective roles of RIAS in East Berlin in 1953 and RFE in Budapest in 1956. The former crisis has shown that this type of radio station can effectively contribute to the development of public protest action, when at least two conditions are met: the opponents have to be *expecting* something from the station, whether to hear news or to express themselves on the radio, or at least to feed it information likely to serve their action; and the radio station must be sufficiently *in phase* with the social movement of the country towards which it broadcasts its programs.

These were the conditions for interaction between the broadcasters (in the West) and the audiences (in the East). This was how the East German uprising, the first mass revolt in Soviet Europe, revealed the amplifying character of the interventionist model of a substitution radio station to support protest movements in the East.

But the experience of 1956 shows that this support must exclude any incentive to armed struggle. Making heroes out of violent insurgents, as the Hungarian section of RFE did in 1956, is excluded. It was on the basis of this prohibition of violence that the following years were to witness a gradual convergence between the development of various forms of civil resistance in the East (as non-provocative forms of conflict) and the simultaneous formation of public spheres, with the support of Western radio stations.

Notes

1. François Furet, *Le passé d'une illusion. Essai sur l'idée communiste au XXème siècle*, Paris, Ed. Robert Laffont/Calmann-Lévy, 1995.
2. Czeslaw Milosz, *La pensée captive. Essai sur les logocraties populaires*, Paris, Gallimard, 1953, p. 119. Milosz based his reasoning on the book by Comte Arthur de Gobineau, *Les religions et les philosophies de l'Asie centrale*, Paris, Gallimard, 1933.
3. Jürgen Habermas, *The Structural Transformation of the Public Sphere: An Inquiry into a Category of Bourgeois Society*, trans. Thomas Burger, Cambridge, Massachusetts Institute of Technology, 1989.
4. François Fejtö, *A History of the People's Democracies*, Vol. II, London, Pall Mall Press Limited, 1971, p. 58.
5. Feito, Historic des democraties populaires, tome 2, op. cit. p. 89.
6. For an historical overview of this period, see the above-cited book by François Fejtö and that of André Fontaine, *Histoire de la guerre froide (1950-1965), Vol. II, Paris, Points Seuil, 1981*.
7. Leon Festinger, *A Theory of Cognitive Dissonance*, Harper Peterson and co., 1957.
8. *Le Monde*, March 21, 1956.
9. On the history of literary life in Stalinist Hungary and the emancipation of certain journalists and writers, see the book by Tamàs Aczel and Tibor Méray, *The Revolt of the Mind: A Case History of Intellectual Resistance Behind the Iron Curtain*, New York, Frederick A. Praeger, 1959.
10. Cited by Melvin J. Larsky and François Bondy, *The Hungarian Revolution*, London, Martin Secker and Warburg Ltd., 1957, p. 28.
11. Interview with Krzysztof Pomian, December 10, 1995. On his role during this period and, more generally, on the events of 1956 in Poland, see Christian Duplan and Vincent Giret, *La Vie en Rouge. Les Pionniers* (Vol. I), Paris, Le Seuil, 1994, p. 243-245.
12. Pavel Tigrid, *Le Printemps de Prague*, Paris, Ed. du Seuil, 1968, p. 151.
13. Karel Jezdinsky, "Mass media and their impact on Czekoslovak politics in 1968" in *The Czekoslovak Reform Movement 1968*, Vladimir V. Kusin (ed.), International Research Document, London, 1973, p. 269.
14. Karel Bartosek, "La société civile en Tchécoslovaquie et la révolte de 1968" in *La Nouvelle alternative*, n. 27, September 1992, p. 55-59. This article was a subject of debate in the government commission of inquiry into the events from 1967 to 1970 (created after the fall of the communist regime), the results of which were presented at the international conference of Libnice (December 2-6, 1991).
15. Letter by Simon Bourgin, cited by Melvin J. Larsky and François Bondy, *The Hungarian Revolution*, op. cit., p. 32.
16. François Fejtö, *A History of the People's Democracies*, Vol. II, op. cit. p. 151.
17. See below.

18. Zdenek Mlynar, *Nightfrost in Prague*, New York, Karz Publishers, 1980, p. 102.
19. Pavel Tigrid, *Le Printemps de Prague*, op. cit., p. 226.
20. See Part 2, Chapter 2.
21. François Fejtö, *A History of the People's Democracies*, Vol. II, op. cit, p. 151.
22. In particular, the unrest that broke out end-May 1953 in Czechoslovakia in Plzen, Brno, Prague, Ostrava and, three years later, in Poland in Poznan where a workers' revolt was severely suppressed (tens of deaths).
23. Many authors have written that this demonstration of 1953 was the first in the streets of East Berlin since 1933, that is, since Hitler's rise to power. But they are forgetting the spontaneous demonstration of dozens of German women married to Jews, in the period from February 27 to March 6, 1943. Protesting against their husbands' arrest, these women gathered in Rosenstrasse, opposite the detention centre from which the men were sent to the death camps. Cf. Jacques Semelin, *Sans armes face à Hitler. La résistance civile en Europe (1939-1943)*, op. cit, p. 198-200.
24. *Le Monde*, June 24, 1953.
25. Jean-Philippe Matthieu and Jean Mortier, *RDA Quelle Allemagne?* (in collaboration with Gilbert Badia), Paris, Ed. Messidor/ed. Sociales, 1990, p. 76.
26. On this subject see Pierre Kende, "Hongrie 30ème anniversaire : les causes d'un soulèvement," in *Revue Est- Ouest*, October 1986, n° 35, page 1 onwards.
27. Miklos Molnar, *Victoire d'une défaite. Budapest 1956*, Paris, Fayard, 1968, p. 126.
28. See Manfred Hagen, *DDR - Juni '53, Die erste Volkserhebung im Stalinismus*, Stuttgart, Franz Steiner Verlag, 1992, p. 60.
29. Cited by Miklos Molnar, *Victoire d'une défaite*, op. cit., p. 128.
30. See Rainer Hildebrandt, *Was lehrte der 17. Juni? Eine Denkschrift*, published by the auteur, 1954, p. 55.
31. Tibor Méray "Imre Nagy. L'homme trahi," *Les Temps Modernes*, Paris, Ed. Julliard, 1960, p. 113.
32. Anything concerning radio also applied to the press. However, radio's public staging of the process described here was more intense, probably because it allowed for a more immediate, broader collective communion to arise than did the press.
33. Rainer Hildebrandt, Was lehrte der 17. Juni? Eine Denkschrift, op. cit., p. 97.
34. In 1956, radio programs were still heard via a wired radio system (see Part 1, Chapter 2). Therefore, the crowd could hear Gero's speech only by means of wired receivers installed at the windows of the station's premises, facing the street.
35. Allam Vedelmi Hivatal: the political police despised by the population.
36. See Part 1, Chapter 2.
37. We are talking here of "co-construction" of the meaning of the message, resulting from interaction between transmitters and receivers. On this subject see the journal *Hermès* (C.N.R.S.), in particular "A la recherche du public," n° 11-12, 1993.

38. "Der 17. Juni und der RIAS," in *17. Juni 1953, Arbeiteraufstand in der DDR*, edited by Ilse Spittmann and Karl Wilhelm Fricke, Köln, Edition Deutschland Archiv, 1982, p. 213.

39. Der Aufstand "der Arbeiterschaft im Ostsektor von Berlin und in der sowjetischen Besatzungszone Deutschlands." Tätigkeitsbericht der Hauptabteilung Politik des Rundfunks im Amerikanischen Sektor in der Zeit vom 16. Juni bis zum 23. June 1953.

40. The instruction not to mention the call for a general strike was given after this program. This is the excerpt concerned: "At around 3 p.m. most strikers left the square situated in front of the government buildings and went towards Leipzigerstrasse, in the direction of Alexanderplatz. They kept chanting: 'Free elections!' while some called for a general strike. The VOPO (police) did not intervene."

41. In this night program, witnesses of the previous day's demonstration on Alexanderplatz and in Friedrichstrasse were heard. They said that a shop window had been smashed and that the police had then arrived. The word "strike" was pronounced in a journalist's question: "Do you have the feeling that all this is going to end in a strike?" It cropped up again in the words of a witness who, after a lengthy description of the workers' strike, concluded: "So, they immediately proclaimed a general strike."

42. The word "zone" denoted East Germany. The West Germans referred to "the zone" because they did not yet recognize the German Democratic Republic; they saw it only as the eastern part of Germany placed under Soviet control and commonly known as the "Soviet zone."

43. Der Aufstand "der Arbeiterschaft im Ostsektor von Berlin und in der sowjetischen Besatzungszone Deutschlands." The East Berlin workers' Uprising in Soviet occupied Germany. Annual Report of the Broadcasting Policy Department in the American Sector from 16 June to 23 June 1953.

44. Manfred Hagen, *DDR - Juni '53, Die erste Volkserhebung im Stalinismus*, op. cit. p. 35.

45. Theodor Ebert "Non violent resistance against communist regimes?" in Adam Roberts (Ed.), *The Strategy of Civilian Defence*, London, Faber and Faber, 1967, p. 180.

46. Rainer Hildebrandt, *Der 17. Juni*, Verlag Haus am Checkpoint Charlie, Berlin 1983, p. 152.

47. *Ibid*, p. 154.

48. The repression reportedly resulted in a total of between 200 and 400 victims. At least 21 East German citizens were shot, as well as 25 Soviet soldiers for refusal to obey orders.

49. Arnulf Baring, *Uprising in East Germany: June 17, 1953*, Cornell University Press, 1973.

50. *The Counter-Revolutionary Forces in the October Events in Hungary* (4 volumes), 1956 and 1957; and *The Counter-Revolutionary Conspiracy of Imre Nagy and His Accomplices*, 1958. Published by the Information Bureau of the Council of Ministers of the Hungarian People's Republic.

51. Report of the Special Committee on the Problem of Hungary, New York, 1957, p. 43 (ref : A 3592 ONU).

52. *Ibid*. p. 47.

53. Robert Holt, *Radio Free Europe*, Minneapolis, University of Minnesota Press, 1958. In view of the close ties between the CIA and RFE, it seems highly unlikely that the author would have had access to the sources cited in his book without the assistance or supervision of members of the CIA. The agency would thus have been able to influence the orientations and analyses of his work.

54. Robert Holt, *Radio Free Europe*, op. cit., p. 197.

55. *Ibid.*, p. 198.

56. Sig Mickelson, *The Story of Radio Free Europe and Radio Liberty*, New York, Praeger Publishers, 1983.

57. An analysis of these programs was also undertaken by Gyula Borbandi, former director of the Hungarian section of RFE, who drew on his personal documents. His article appeared in Volume IV, 1995, of the *Institut 1956* of Budapest, of which Pierre Kende was president. His analysis is much the same as the one developed here.

58. These words were pronounced by Imre Mikes, nicknamed "Gallicus," a highly talented propagandist whom many Hungarians loved to hear, whether they agreed with him or not. For a long time Imre Mikes edited the journal *Myugati Hirnok*, published in the 1950s in France and very well informed on Hungary's domestic situation.

59. Miklos Molnar, *Victoire d'une défaite*, op. cit., p. 189.

60. Interview with Julia Lang, former journalist with the Hungarian section of RFE from 1984 to 1993 (29 August 1993).

61. Sig Mickelson, *The Story of Radio Free Europe and Radio Liberty*, op. cit, p. 97.

62. George Urban, *The Nineteen days*, London, Ed. Heinemann, 1957, p. 269.

63. "Hungary and the 1956 uprising," opinion poll run by The International Research Associates INC., New York 1957 p. 3-4, cited by George Urban, *The Nineteen days*, op. cit., p. 269.

The public sphere as a battlefield: Budapest, 1956 and Prague, 1968

In the first attempts at emancipating the people of communist Europe, the potential influence of Western radio was less of an issue than the restructuring of these countries' own local media, that is, East-East communication. The development of communication with a strong national identity expressed, above all, the Central European peoples' wish to assert their autonomy from Soviet control. But it was precisely this process of emancipation of speech and public action that Moscow found intolerable and that consequently served to justify its use of armed force. In both instances, the aim of Soviet and Warsaw Pact intervention, respectively in October 1956 in Hungary and August 1968 in Czechoslovakia, was to crush the movement arduously striving to reclaim the public sphere. The Hungarians and Czechoslovaks strongly resisted this violent repression, mainly by endeavoring to maintain or even to expand an autonomous sphere of communication, out of the Red Army's control. The first two mass resistance movements in communist Europe thus turned the public sphere—both the streets and the media—into a battleground.

The face of this battleground differed, depending on the specific history of these countries' cultures and the types of action peculiar to each insurrection. In 1956, the insurgents wanted to control both the streets and the media, and consequently engaged in violent physical conflict with the Soviet troops. In 1968, the Czechoslovak resistance left the streets to the Red Army but attempted to maintain control over the media for as long as possible. The aim was to avoid physical confrontation, and to engage instead in a symbolic struggle over which the enemy had less control. The movement thus drew its strength from a *delocalization of confrontation*.

The importance of the media also differed in these two mass resistance movements separated by a twelve-year interval. In 1956 the media (posters, press and radio) were simply one aspect of the struggle, in parallel with urban guerrilla fighting and the general strike. In 1968 the media (posters, press, radio and television) were at the heart of a vast movement passively resisting the occupier. As radio allowed for mass participation, it was the resistance movement's preferred means of communication in both cases. Its flexibility and scope made it the best medium for ideological expression and technical coordination of the opposition.

Moreover, radio's near instantaneous capacity for reaction to events meant that the opposition was able to maintain intense interaction with the society in resistance.

The tragic outcomes of the Hungarian uprising and the Prague Spring show the limits of these resistance movements. Both Hungarians and Czechoslovaks made a stern effort to reclaim the public sphere and did partially succeed. And their efforts did effectively redraw the boundary between the public and private spheres. The process of freeing speech had an intoxicating effect on individuals, enabling them to partially abandon their former mechanisms of protection against totalitarian coercion.[1] But how could these attempts remove the other barrier, separating Eastern Europe from the West? It was precisely this strategic partitioning of the continent that enabled the Soviets to intervene and so to avoid a shift in the international balance of power.

In other words, it was as if the changes in the modes of communication within these countries took place in a fishbowl. This was indeed a laborious process of reclaiming the public sphere, but one that remained closed off to the world because it was trapped in a strategic context that contributed to its isolation.

Budapest, 1956: the media as participants in and products of insurrection

On the morning of October 24, Radio Kossuth, the Hungarian national station under control of the conservatives, inflamed supporters of the insurgents by referring to them as "fascist and reactionary elements" and "gangs of counter-revolutionary looters."[2] Once martial law had been proclaimed at 8:15 a.m. (Nagy's first decision as president of the Council), it threatened those who refused to lay down arms with the death sentence. These invectives and threats, often pronounced in an unctuous voice, were interspersed with musical interludes that were completely surrealistic, given the gravity of the situation: pieces of operetta, French cancan or languid tunes. Meanwhile, battles had been raging in various districts of Budapest occupied by Soviet tanks since 4 a.m. This profound dissonance between the dramatic reality of the facts and the absence of their representation on Radio Kossuth rapidly transformed the public sphere into a battleground. In spite of their failure to talk on national radio, the insurgents were to attempt to express themselves in the official media (press and radio).

The fact that Imre Nagy was slow to assess the situation added fuel to the fire. The population was eagerly awaiting his first declaration to the country, broadcast by radio at noon on October 24. What was this man, whom the people believed was really on their side, going to say? A few thousand had heard his talk on Kossuth Square the day before. Now the whole country was waiting with baited breath ... and Nagy's speech was a flop. He failed to say the right things, those that most of the people wanted to hear, that corresponded to what they felt and thought. He made no mention of the fact that he had not been the one to call in the Soviet troops, although many Hungarians could, at a push, understand this omission. More serious was his plea for a compromise with the Party "hardliners." There was no way the people could accept such an attitude of appeasement, after so many years of accumulated hatred. They wanted to hear him condemning the "Gero clique," not asking the insurgents to lay down arms!

A rumor immediately started going round Budapest, that Nagy had made his speech in the presence of two Soviet counter-espionage agents standing behind him with revolvers in their pockets. The anecdote, although unfounded, summed up the balance of power in a formidable nutshell. It suggested, first, just how important Nagy's public communication was at that precise point in time, but also that he was unable to say what he really wanted to as he had spoken under constraint. He was consequently not really responsible for the people's disappointment. This rumor, fairly typical of the way in which Hungarian public opinion perceived relations at the summit of communist power (plots, bribery, violence, etc.), had the effect of keeping Nagy on the people's side.

However, the kindly representation of a muzzled and victimized leader concealed another side to this character. Nagy had not yet grasped the depth of the popular movement. He seemed unaware of the fact that the people fighting in the streets were not "the rabble" but his own supporters, his former students, his friends. It took a few days before he gradually woke up to this and rallied to their cause. Moreover, underestimating the importance of radio in those early hours of crisis, he "made the mistake of abandoning this weapon to his worst enemies. He failed to take the time to listen to radio programs and no one told him to what extent they exasperated the masses."[3]

Pressure from the rebel radio stations

It was in this context of deadlock and misunderstanding that the insurrection produced its own speech and expressed itself through various media. Initially the insurgents used the simplest of means to publicize their demands: posters, which proliferated on the walls of Budapest in the days running up to October 23. Mostly they were leaflets pasted on the city's walls.

Shortly afterwards the rebels could be heard on certain radio stations and wrote in various newspapers, though in the provinces, not immediately in Budapest. From October 24 the uprising spread steadily to several of the country's cities and industrial centers, spurred on first by the "shock" caused by the national radio programs, and then by a process of inter-individual communication. For those living outside the capital, national radio was the first sign that something serious was happening. The weaker intensity of its signal, the unusual interruption of its programs, and its constant attacks on the supposed "fascist gangs" automatically alerted listeners avid for news. The news itself was circulated by word of mouth, by telephone, travelers, postmen, drivers, etc. News of Soviet tanks rolling into Budapest, confirmed by foreign radio, had the effect of rapidly mobilizing the people between October 24 and 26. Press organs and regional radio stations came under the control of "workers' councils" or "revolutionary committees," which constituted a sort of "second power" inspired by the Yugoslavian model, in opposition to the government that was accused of having called in the Soviet troops.[4]

The emergence of these rebel radio stations was a tangible sign that the popular revolt was spreading throughout the country. On the third day of the uprising, when communication with Hungary had become almost impossible, many observers were surprised to pick up calls for resistance on the local radio station in the vicinity of Miskolc (a large industrial center in North-Eastern Hungary): " 'Don't believe the lies', said a determined young voice. 'Soviet troops must leave Hungary. Go on strike! […] We also want socialism, but one that corresponds to our specifically Hungarian conditions.'"[5] In the following days new voices were heard, from Pecs (coal and uranium mines), Gyor in the eastern part of the country (which called itself "Free Radio Petofi"), and then Szolnok, Debrecen, Nyiregyhaza, etc. The content of their messages was twofold: vehement criticism of Nagy's October 24 speech, and a call for the population's immediate mobilization, primarily by means of a strike and in some cases armed struggle. All of rebel Hungary formed an opposition force and expressed itself. These multiple voices gradually drowned out that of Radio Budapest, which lost its tone of self-assurance.

Between the national radio station and these regional stations, a form of public confrontation developed over the air, the expression of a full-blown political battle between the actors in the crisis. This battle was first and foremost a war over the legitimacy of talking in public, to the public, the Hungarian nation. All the rebel radio stations presented themselves as "free" and claimed to talk in the name of the "workers," while Radio Budapest claimed to talk on behalf of the government. Some leaders of the workers' councils were aware of the importance of this weapon. Gyorgy Szabo from the Gyor area, for instance, said he was expecting the West to give them not military aid but a 10 kW transmitter to "send messages to the Hungarian people."[6] The rebel stations consistently broadcast petitions, demands and other memoranda drawn up by the workers' councils. They maintained steady pressure on the Nagy government, forcing it to adopt a more audacious political line and thus to break away from the Party hardliners. Radio was a means to directly address the chairman of the Council and to issue summonses and ultimatums at will: "In the name of the Dunantul," said Radio Petofi, "the Gyor National Council calls on Premier Imre Nagy to take further steps [...], [especially] to request the commander-in-chief of the Soviet troops to cease fire. We transmit these demands by radio [12:15] and we expect Imre Nagy's personal answer by 20:00 at the latest."[7]

Sometimes these stations' confrontation with national radio looked more like professional competition, as the following surprising excerpt from "Free Radio Miscolc" on October 31 shows: "When we announced Marshal Zhukov's order, Free Radio Kossuth resented it half an hour later. It resented the fact that we had beaten them to it. Dear Kossuth Radio, if you don't mind, this was not the first announcement with which we came out first. And if you are not up to the mark, we shall try to beat you to it in the future."[8]

Hastily sent to Budapest on October 25, the Soviets Anastas Mikoyan and Mikhail Souslov forced Erno Gero to resign as First Secretary of the Party, and replaced him with Janos Kadar. They hoped that the Kadar-Nagy twosome would effectively restore order. The political current supporting Nagy was consequently able to progress more easily. Two days later the prime minister formed a new government that tried to both reassure the Soviets and placate the rebels. Some members of the new government were not communists: Zoltan Tildy (one of the founders in 1930 of the small independent landowners' party), Bela Kovacs (former secretary general of the same party) and Ferenc Erdei (one of the founders of the national farmers' party). But the presence of these lesser-known personalities failed to counterbalance a majority of particularly unpopular communist ministers. The government disappointed the rebels. Numerous delegations from the workers' councils went to Budapest to urge Nagy to make it more representative. The rebel radio stations maintained their pressure on him: they refused to recognize the government and demanded radical decisions, starting with the withdrawal of Soviet troops.

The next day, October 28, in a new radio broadcast at 6 p.m., Nagy decreed the ceasefire, announced the signing of an agreement with Moscow for the withdrawal of Soviet troops, the dissolution of the AVH, and even the recognition of the "new democratic bodies created on the people's initiative." This new speech pleased the people far more than the one four days earlier. In contradiction with his earlier address, Nagy claimed to refuse the idea that the formidable popular movement was a counter-revolution. Actually, he said, it "embraces and unifies the whole nation," and "its aim is to ensure our national independence and sovereignty ... It is the grave crimes of the preceding era which have triggered that great movement."[9] As André Fontaine pointed out, it would have been wise to stop there,[10] but the rebel radio stations urged Nagy to go even further. That same day, October 28, Radio Gyor demanded free elections and the dissolution of the Warsaw Pact. The pressure was coming from the streets. On October 30, insurgents in Budapest stormed the premises of the communist federation of Greater Budapest and murdered its occupants.

Restructuring of the public sphere
This dramatic episode convinced Nagy that more radical measures would be needed to assuage the people's fury, and he resigned himself to announcing crucial decisions. He abolished the principle of a single party to enable the country to revert to the political system of 1945 (at the time of the pluralist coalition of parties). He also expressed the government's wish to denounce the Warsaw Pact and, for this purpose, wanted to engage in negotiations with Moscow, in view of total withdrawal of Soviet troops from the entire Hungarian territory. From that moment and up to November 3, included, Hungary was to experience an incredible period of freedom regained. The Hungarian people seemed to have won the revolutions: public pressure, expressed in the streets through strikes or in the media, had led the central government to announce unprecedented decisions in a communist country.

These changes at the highest level of the party-state accelerated the ongoing restructuring of civil society and of the public sphere. Former social and political actors re-emerged: among others, the Catholics (Cardinal Mindszenty, sentenced to life in prison in 1949, was released, along with many political prisoners), the social democrats who recreated their party, and the small landowners who did likewise. As the Communist Party was in decay, its leaders needed to change their identity and to reorganize. Janos Kadar formed a new communist party, called the "Hungarian workers socialist party."

Free speech was revived everywhere and the country's history resurfaced after ten years of forced silence. People all over were talking: in the revolutionary committees of the towns and villages, in the ministerial committees, in the improvised offices of the parties and associations. Workers' councils were convened day and night. Everyone formulated their own demands in the name of the Hungarian people and the "revolution."

The rapid evolution of press and radio reflected this accelerated transformation of the public sphere. The situation of the press was confused. Some titles disappeared, while others were given new life and yet others underwent substantial change, starting with the communist party organ *Szabad Nep*. When it reappeared, after being suspended on October 24 and 25, the tone was one of reconciliation with the rebels. The editorial on October 27 described the events as a "national democratic movement."[11] On October 28 it was even more explicit: "We don't agree with those who dismiss the past days' events as an attempted fascist and counter-revolutionary coup d'état. We have to admit that a mass democratic movement has developed in our country."[12] Under Kadar's impetus, it changed its name on October 31 to *Nepszabadsag (People's Freedom)*. The next day several publications reappeared: *Nepszava*, the social-democrat party organ, *Kis ujsag*, the journal of the agrarian party, known as the "small landowners," and *Szabad Szo*, that of the farmers' national party. *Igazsag (The Truth)*, the organ of the "Hungarian revolutionary youth," had the widest readership among the insurgents. From the outset they saw it as their mouthpiece because it had struggled for the abolition of Stalinism in Hungary. Some publications had only one page, for example *Nepszava* (a trade-unions newsletter) and *Magyar Nemzet* (the students' newsletter), and were often distributed free-of-charge to boost the morale of the protesters manning the barricades. Young people went to the offices of these publications to give them poems, pieces of news, or accounts of "the revolution." This was an extraordinary period of blossoming of the press. Within a few days "no fewer than twenty-five daily papers [appeared] in place of the five sad, dreary, stereotyped sheets of recent years."[13]

To increase their impact, the rebel radio stations started to coordinate their broadcasts. On October 30, Free Radio Gyor and Radio Petofi merged their programs. They were soon joined by the Balatonszabadi station, which until then had been responsible for broadcasting communist propaganda to the West. On November 2, Radio Debrecen, Radio Dunapentele, Radio Gyor, Radio Kaposvar, Radio Miskolc, Radio Nyiregyhaza, and Radio Pecs all broadcast the same program.[14] This cooperation between rebel radio stations reflected more than simply a desire for technical coordination; it was also the tangible sign of a general restructuring of the country's public sphere, in line with the political changes under way. Hence, the history of the Hungarian uprising seems to be linked to the formation of local and regional critical public spheres that clustered together as the political situation became increasingly radical, thus constituting a new national public sphere.

There was no way that Radio Budapest could remain excluded from these events. An analysis of its programs between October 24 and 28 shows a gradual transformation of the content. At the beginning of the uprising, semantic camouflage was used extensively to mask the nature of the fighting ("counter-revolutionary bandits," "fascist looters," etc.). But the national radio station subsequently started to recognize the real identity of some of them: those who were on the barricades were "workers from the 'Red Star' tractor factory or students from the Polytechnical School." Soon afterwards some reports described the reality of the street battles ("fighting is taking place outside the party offices in the 13th district and outside the Karoly Robert barracks"). It was as if the last remaining ideological veil was gradually being torn down, so that the factual agenda slowly started to coincide with that of the national radio station.

A decisive step was taken on October 30: journalists of the national radio station criticized themselves and announced a radical change: " 'Dear listeners', they declared solemnly on the air at 3.05 p.m., 'we are opening a new chapter in the history of Hungarian radio. For years, the station has been an instrument of lies and only a means for transmitting instructions. It lied night and day. It lied on all the airwaves. Even in this hour of our renaissance, it has continued its campaign of lies. But the struggle that has brought us national liberation has also freed our radio station. Those who have told us so many lies no longer belong to our Hungarian radio station [...]. We, who are now at the microphone, are new people. We'll tell the truth, nothing but the truth."[15] To mark this desire to break away from the past, the station changed its name to

"Free Radio Kossuth," adding the adjective used since the beginning of the revolution by the regional rebel stations. October 30 thus marked the climax of the conquest of the public sphere by the insurgent movement, which ended up piercing the very heart of the official communication center: national radio. To what extent was this change of identity of the state radio station authentic and profound? At the very least, it attests to the desire to turn the page, confirmed moreover by the merger between Free Radio Kossuth and Free Radio Petofi on November 3: "This is the first time since the outbreak of the victorious revolution that the great Budapest transmitter and all the provincial transmitters are broadcasting the same program," said the announcer on Free Radio Kossuth. "Today we have taken a long step forward to national unity. The fact that the two radio stations, which were developed in opposite direction for some time, are now united, have found each other as an expression of this unity."[16]

Since the Soviet tanks seemed to have left Budapest, Hungary was able to make a fresh start. On November 3, Nagy announced the formation of a coalition government similar to the immediate post-war one, with no more than four communists. Shops started to reopen and public transport to function again. Radio and several newspapers called for a return to work. Hungary seemed to be calming down and everything led people to believe that on November 5 things would be back to normal. That was what they wanted. Why, they wondered, was the Hungary-Sweden football match scheduled for Sunday the 4th cancelled? The Hungarians were still totally unaware of the tragedy about to happen: the dawn attack by Soviet tanks.

Death of the Nagy government, live

An analysis of the programs of national radio and provincial radio enables us to follow "live" the Nagy government's tragic end. At 3:15 p.m. on November 4, in a trembling voice, the president of the Council announced to the Hungarian people that hundreds of Soviet tanks had entered the country. His very brief message gave no hint of capitulation: "Our troops are fighting," he declared. "The government is at work. I am informing the Hungarian people and international public opinion." The national anthem concluded his speech, solemnly signifying the stakes: the country's independence. Nagy took the whole world as his witness, not only through the last sentence of his message but also because it was immediately broadcast in English, French, German and Russian. Did this mean he was hoping for help from the West? At 7:56 a.m. a call for help was broadcast by writers and intellectuals, ending with a pathetic "Help!

Help!" Their message was repeated in German and Russian. The artisans of the rebirth of public speech were thus the last to express themselves freely on the national radio station. After that the station broadcast music until it was interrupted at 8:10 a.m., although it was still possible to pick up the silent airwaves until 9:44 a.m. The station resumed its broadcasts at about 9 p.m., to announce the constitution of a new "revolutionary, workers and peasants' government" presided by Janos Kadar, who had asked for the Soviet troops' assistance to stamp out the "counter-revolution." Radio Budapest was again under Moscow's control and reverted to its former name, "Radio Kossuth."

In the provinces, the workers' council radio stations were silenced one by one. Before closing down they too appealed to the West for help. Some called on the UN, others asked straight out for military help, most took Radio Free Europe as their main ally. Radio Free Dunapentele, for example, launched the following appeal to RFE: "Attention Radio Free Europe, attention! Keep on broadcasting our news ... we give only important news." Then: "Attention free Europe, we're asking for immediate help, armed assistance. We will try to speak again. We have to interrupt our broadcasts [sic]."[17] Weak voices from clandestine radio stations could still be picked up here and there, revealing the existence of pockets of resistance. Then, silence. As these radio stations were gagged, the BBC and RFE became the population's only source of different news on the events. Even while telephone communication with foreign countries was cut off, the Hungarians were still able to pick up Western radio stations. RFE supplied them with surprisingly accurate news on the fighting, both in Budapest and in the provinces.[18]

But the Hungarian resistance was not entirely suppressed; it returned on the walls of the city. The Budapest insurgents were militarily vanquished on the fifth day of a fierce battle in which the scales were tipped. This armed struggle was followed by a war of words and slogans. The posters of the Kadar government, demanding a return to work, were covered with smaller ones calling for a continuation of the strike. Others made a mockery of Soviet propaganda: "Ten million counter-revolutionaries are at large in the country!," "Lost—the confidence of the people. Honest finder is asked to return it to Janos Kadar, Premier of Hungary at 10,000 Soviet Tanks Street."[19] At the same time, leaflets circulated in factories, calling for resistance, for the return of the Nagy government, considered as the only legitimate one, etc. From the first days of the insurrection these modes of communication bore witness to the country's political regression. Everything gained in the public sphere seemed to have been destroyed by the Soviet intervention.

But was that really so? Listening carefully to the new programs of Radio Budapest, some experts perceived a significant difference compared to those prior to the uprising: "the official propaganda had lost its arrogance. It was presented in muted tones. It was as though the announcer was looking away while speaking. They were ashamed."[20] And with reason: the few days of freedom were paid for very dearly with thousands of deaths during the Soviet repression.

Prague, 1968: resistance through the media

The Hungarian case stands in sharp contrast with the Czechoslovakian population's resistance in 1968 against the Warsaw Pact invasion. Not only did Prague not experience violent revolt, the bases of communication processes during the crisis were also very different. In 1956 the media had been one of the components of the resistance (in parallel with the guerilla and the strike); in 1968 they were its backbone, although not its main vehicle. They were, so to speak, the "brain" behind the resistance.

When the Soviet troops invaded Czechoslovakia on the night of August 20, 1968, their goal was to put an end to the "counter-revolution" of the Prague Spring. The plan was first to justify their intervention, by claiming that the Czechoslovaks had appealed to its socialist brother states to save everything gained in the communist revolution, and then to force the country to accept a "revolutionary, worker and peasant" government, a form of collaboration à la Kadar, destined to serve its own interests. For that purpose, Moscow intended to rely on men like Alois Indra and Drahomir Kolder, at the head of the Communist Party and hostile to the line followed by Dubcek. But the scenario turned out differently from that of Hungary 12 years earlier.

To implement its plan, Moscow had to block the functioning of the country's political power without delay. But when the first troops approached the capital, the Party presidium was in session. As soon as he was informed, Alexander Dubcek proposed a declaration to the nation, condemning the power grab. The proposal was approved by the presidium shortly after 1 a.m., despite some members' opposition.[21] By confirming the legal and constitutional nature of the incumbent government, the declaration made the military invasion appear illegitimate. It affirmed that the attack was "contrary to the fundamental principles of relations between socialist states and a denial of the basic norms of international law. All leading officials of the Party [...] remain at their posts, to which they were elected as representatives of the people and members of their organizations according to the laws and regulations of the Czechoslovak Socialist Republic." Moreover, the text contained a recommendation for the population: "The presidium calls upon all citizens of the Republic to keep the peace and not resist the advancing armies, because the defense of our state borders is now impossible. For this reason, our army, the Security Forces, and the People's Militia were not given the order to defend the country."[22] This appeal, which urgently convened the national assembly and the government, defined the political framework from which the resistance movement was to develop.

Affirming national cohesion against collaborationism
The leaders' declaration was immediately sent to the national radio station, with the sound of Soviet airplanes coming in to land at Ruzyne airport already audible in the Prague sky. The station's programs would normally have ended at 1 a.m., but the journalists wanted to broadcast the presidium's declaration as quickly as possible. In the meantime, they broadcast serious music by Smetana and the announcer asked listeners to stay tuned in. "The people who heard this music woke their neighbors. Many remembered the night of 1938, after the Diktat of Munich."[23] And suddenly, at 1:30, the presidium's first words echoed on the waves ... but were immediately cut off. Not even the first sentence was broadcast in full. The transmitters were disconnected by Karel Hofman, head of the telecommunications central administration, in the Soviets' pay. Only those listeners with a wired radio receiver (the system used formerly in Eastern Bloc countries[24]) were able to hear the official text. But the technicians urgently sought an alternative ... and found one, so that the entire country could hear the presidium's communiqué at 1:55 a.m. The night team wanted to carry on broadcasting, but this was impossible. Then at 4:30 a.m. on August 21, when the radio station resumed its usual programs, the appeal was broadcast at regular intervals. The journalists announced their determination to remain at the service of the legal government, until such time as they were physically prevented from doing so. They reminded listeners that they were speaking over "the legal Radio Prague," to emphasize that they were clearly under the authority of the constitutional government. They were also careful not to give their names over the air, but the listeners knew their voices.

The radio journalists then had the feeling of having achieved their "first victory," as two of them, Jiri Dienstbier and Karel Lansky, emphasized.[25] The fact that the text was broadcast almost immediately was of considerable importance for the subsequent course of events. The radio station immediately maximized its political impact by making it known to a very broad public. From this point of view, the complementarity between the respective roles of the government and the media was remarkable. When the political authorities immediately took a stand they defined a *collective direction* for the country and proposed a guideline for this crisis situation. The media then made this interpretation by the constitutional authorities public, and thus helped to ensure that it was immediately transformed into a *public fact* that the invader would necessarily have to take into account. From the night of the invasion, the ground was laid for the sudden upsurge of a totally unexpected, vast civil resistance movement, one that affirmed and defended national cohesion against any collaborationist government.

It was consequently impossible for the USSR's argument of a so-called "invitation" to be plausible, since the legitimate leaders of the country had just informed the nation and the whole world that they had put out no "appeal for fraternal aid." It was furthermore of little consequence that a station with the patriotic name of Radio Vltava[26] started to broadcast from East Germany that morning of August 21, announcing that, according to Tass, "leaders of the Party and the government have asked the Soviet Union and other member states of the Warsaw Pact to grant immediate aid to their Czechoslovakian brothers, including military aid."[27] The announcers' foreign accents were unmistakable and, for the oldest listeners, brought back bad memories of the arrival of Hitler's army in 1939. Even though leaflets with the same message were dropped over Prague by helicopter, Radio Moscow programs in Czech and Slovak swamped the country's airwaves, and a television transmitter was installed in the yard of the Soviet embassy, Moscow's propaganda services were powerless to "convince" the population of the validity of the invasion.

Unable to convince, the USSR was there to constrain, and thus to rally the support of all those who—out of realism—were prepared to collaborate with it. The immediate expression of national unity, whether "at the top" or "at the bottom" of society, would nevertheless prevent a collaborationist movement from forming and growing. The arrest of Dubcek and several other political leaders who had not tried to flee,[28] barely a few hours after the Soviet tanks' arrival, had struck a hard blow at the partisans of the Prague Spring. But throughout the country, their refusal to endorse the military intervention—now public knowledge—boosted a collective will not to collaborate. Among the Party leaders an institutional and legal resistance developed instantly. On the morning of August 21, President Svoboda refused to obey Soviet orders to form a new government with Indra and Kolder; he knew that it would be unacceptable to the country. From the afternoon of August 21, the national assembly, convened for an extraordinary session, managed to remain in session. Many motions and declarations by official authorities simultaneously affirmed their loyalty to Dubcek and their rejection of the occupation. The 24th Party congress, initially scheduled for September 9 and convened for an extraordinary session on August 22, was moreover an organizational masterpiece. The members, meeting clandestinely at the CKD plant in Prague, in the working-class district of Vysocany, renewed the Party leadership and strengthened the fighting spirit against the occupier. The effect produced by the Warsaw Pact's military intervention was thus the exact opposite of its goal. Instead of seeing the "good communists" queuing up to take over from a tottering team, Moscow caused almost the entire Party to go underground. "The invasion was a military success but a political fiasco."[29]

This institutional resistance was echoed by an almost unanimous popular resistance uniting Czechs and Slovaks. Once the shock of the invasion had passed, the population became aware of its own strength. People sensed that the eight months of the Prague Spring had been a period of collective rebirth. Even though they realized that this adventure was probably over, they wanted to "do something." Was this simply a gallant last stand? Not only. For several months the people had retrieved their pride, their identity and their dignity. They were no longer afraid of confronting the occupier. Czechs and Slovaks had felt they could relate to their new leaders' desire to build a "socialism with a human face"; they felt legitimate and failed to understand why Moscow wanted to prevent them from going their own way, especially since they harbored no anti-Russian sentiments. Two slogans soon appeared on the walls of their cities, typical of this spirit: "Lenin, wake up, Brezhnev's gone crazy!" and "Ivan, go home: Natacha's waiting for you." Through a multitude of everyday actions, a nation was shown a rare example of collective unity, demonstrating its attachment to the gains of the Prague Spring. Perhaps there was a minority that was prepared to serve the invader, but the movement against it was so strong that anyone with collaborationist leanings was dissuaded from expressing themselves openly. Civil society, which had become increasingly assertive over the preceding months, said "No" to the occupier. It said so in a thousand different ways, openly or indirectly, with humor or sadness, sometimes with the seemingly idiotic malice of the Good Soldier Schweik, a comical character invented by Jaroslav Hasek who incarnated the Czech spirit of resistance to Austrian domination ... by an excess of zeal. As a result, instead of being a tragedy, these first hours, these first days of the invasion, were a great time in history.[30]

Maintaining the voice of free Czechoslovakia

A powerful movement of passive resistance was thus born the very day of the invasion, but it needed to be fleshed out, in spite of the inevitable chaos caused by the attack. That was the role of the media, which were to be the amplifiers of this social and national cohesion in the midst of crisis. Their intervention was particularly important in so far as the population was cooperating with them. It spontaneously put itself at the service of journalists, keeping them up-to-date on the development of the situation with a variety of news.

Journalists consequently found themselves in a strategic position, as the spokespersons of the resistance that was developing throughout the country. Their role was fundamental in maintaining this collective cohesion at all times. In turn, the tempo constantly set by the media reinforced each individual's protest. Continuous interaction was thus established between the media and the population during the crisis. The media also contributed to encouraging and reassuring individuals in their resistance. In this way they helped to minimize the feeling of isolation and anxiety that an occupier has to be able to play on to ensure a maximum of collaboration. Political leaders as well as the population, continually informed of their own actions by the media, had a feeling of solidarity and of forming the same community of struggle at this historic time.

Unlike the Hungarian insurrection in 1956, in the Czechoslovakian resistance of 1968, very few new media appeared. The main changes occurred *beforehand*, during the Prague Spring.[31] At the time of the invasion there was nevertheless a sudden change in the functioning of these means of communication. This development was totally improvised, as the authorities had provided for no measures in case of attack. To cope with this exceptional situation, journalists invented equally exceptional ad hoc modes of working. They were as unprepared for this tragedy of occupation as everyone else, yet for several months they had been the main artisans of the rebirth of civil society, the core of the Prague Spring. This political experience had provided them with essential guidelines for functioning in a crisis. As one of them, Jaroslav Jiru, said: "We weren't technically prepared to react to the occupation forces, but we knew how to behave politically. We knew what we had to do: maintain the voice of free Czechoslovakia and keep the media out of the hands of the occupying forces for as long as possible."[32]

This was the main spirit of the Czechoslovakian resistance from August 21 to 27, 1968. As long as independent speech could be heard, there was concrete evidence that the voice of a legal and legitimate Czechoslovakia had not been gagged by military force. Even though this "political line" was not decreed by anyone, it was adopted by all, journalists as well as most of the Party and union leaders who were still free, and of course the vast majority of the population, who trusted both. As the Party presidium had resolutely advised against violence, within hours the entire population engaged unexpectedly in civil resistance through speech and thus via the media. From this point of view, radio, television—a new arrival in the resistance's arsenal—and the press played complementary parts in the country's battle against the invader.

Radio, television and press: complementary roles
On the morning of August 21, many people wanted to defend "their radio station" bare-handed. Hundreds had already congregated outside the national head office in Vinohradska Street. Not that there was anything surprising about that: "in the Czechoslovakian conscience radio was linked to the most serious moments in the history of the Republic, the events of Munich, the Nazi occupation or the 1945 uprising in which the fiercest battles had been fought for radio."[33] For the Czechoslovakians, radio was thus far more than a means of communication, it was a symbol of national resistance. Relaying the presidium's declaration, the journalists regularly launched calls for calm and asked the crowd gathered outside the building to disperse. Yet, when a column of tanks arrived in the district at around 7.30 a.m., the crowd was still there, unpredictable. The tension mounted and shouts were heard. Soldiers fired into the air while some youths managed to burn two tanks by setting fire to their gas tanks. Shots were fired at the building. A journalist on a typewriter at the window recorded what he saw, and his text was immediately broadcast. When the soldiers entered the building the national anthem was immediately put on the air. People thought that it was all over and sadness was visible on their faces. "But a minute later a voice well-known on radio announced that they were still in the studio and that they would broadcast for as long as they could. If you hear other voices on the radio, different to the ones that have broadcast until now, don't believe them."[34] The soldiers had cut only the internal telephone line. Thinking that they had interrupted the programs, they occupied the ground floor and first two floors. In the meantime, journalists higher up in the building started to broadcast again. But the studio was soon discovered again and this time the program was definitively interrupted. It was 9 a.m. A team of technicians had prepared another studio in the same building but decided not to use it, for fear of being identified. This interruption of the programs intensified the population's irritation and anxiety. Journalists then became aware that it was necessary

to maintain a continuous news program at all costs, as a constant and reassuring presence for the public. At 11 a.m. the journalists who had occupied a studio near the national radio head offices resumed the station's programs. A fairly similar scenario was found at Pilsen in the West of the country, where radio programs were interrupted before being resumed shortly afterwards, alternately from Ceske-Budejovice in Southern Bohemia and from Banska-Bystrica in Central Slovakia.

These first two hours of the functioning of radio in Soviet-occupied Czechoslovakia reveal the high level of coordination swiftly established between journalists and technicians. With the active support of their director, Zdenek Hejzlar, they rivaled one another in seeking ingenious ways to carry on practicing their profession without betraying the spirit of the Prague Spring. Their work was totally improvised and carried out in constant fear of being discovered. The fact that the station's 16 studios were scattered across Prague and its suburbs facilitated their task considerably. Before 1968 the employees had complained about this situation, wanting the studios to be grouped together to improve their working conditions, but "with the Soviet intervention it proved to be a huge advantage."[35] Journalists and technicians also managed to set up an original system of liaison and broadcasting between the studios of the capital and those of the various regional stations. The principle of this networked system was to broadcast non-stop through a series of transmitters that relayed one another at regular intervals.

Established from August 21, this organization was perfected in the following days: "Twelve regional stations broadcast in turn for a duration of ten minutes in a two-hour cycle."[36] The brevity of each station's broadcasting time made it difficult for the Soviet agents to detect them.

To this ingenious broadcasting system were added totally new conditions of program reception, compared to 1956. Observers were amazed to find that in 1968 everyone was listening to radio with a transistor, either held against the ear or, if it was bigger, carried under the arm. This technological innovation that gave listeners total mobility, proved to be a formidable instrument of resistance: the population could finally remain in constant contact with journalists working underground, both at home and outside. The journalists, in turn, were often in contact with certain political officials (especially members of parliament), either by phone or via messengers who managed to get through roadblocks by hiding in ambulances, for example. This original system of broadcasting and reception was what made the Czechoslovakian resistance so strong and enabled it to react to the crisis with strength and flexibility.[37]

TV journalists, like their director Jiri Pelikan,[38] proved to have the same spirit of improvisation as their radio colleagues. They went on the air at 6:40 a.m. to broadcast a special program, also starting with the presidium's declaration, calls for calm, and messages of support from various institutions in the country. The very first images of occupied Prague were shown: "dense groups of young people waving flags right up to the wheels of the tanks whose turrets were pointing at the crowd."[39] These images were simultaneously transmitted to the West via the Intervision network. Czechoslovakian television technicians had the presence of mind to immediately make contact with their counterparts at Eurovision in Geneva. The West thus received live images of the Soviet tanks' entry into Prague—a first in the history of the Eastern Bloc—and broadcast them on TV news that same day.[40] But the tanks were already approaching the head office of the national TV channel in Jungmannova Street. There was no crowd waiting outside as in the case of radio. Soldiers occupied the building at 8.30 a.m., by which time a team of journalists and technicians had already left for a studio situated a few streets away. It was 8:50 a.m. "For a moment we heard their voices, then the image disappeared. A few minutes later the sound was back. The announcers urged people to support the constitutional organs."[41] Thus, when the national radio station stopped broadcasting (between 9 and 11 a.m.), television took over. At the end of the morning, images came from Cukrak Hill situated 25 km from Prague, where the main TV transmitter was located. There the journalists managed to broadcast live the Soviet soldiers' seizure of the transmitter: incredible images of a television channel that filmed its own end. "Russians jumped from the vehicles (the program continued), crawled to the gate and, machine gun in hand, slipped through the woods towards the transmitter. [...] The members of the television personnel had the time [...] to leave the building [...] and return to Prague incognito."[42]

Apart from these exploits on the first day of the occupation, television was not as flexible as radio. In those days, TV broadcasting equipment was still cumbersome and the transmitters (in Prague, Bratislava and Ostrava), of which there were far fewer than for radio, soon came under Soviet military control. The journalists nevertheless persevered. From the afternoon of August 21, they broadcast "TV without images," that is, radio, as Miroslav Sigl explained.

With his team he took refuge in the Tesla factory (that manufactured transmitters!), and from there he broadcast a radio program on the same frequency as the one used by Czechoslovakian radio on May 5, 1945, when it called on the people of Prague to rise up against the Nazi occupier.[43]

Television was also handicapped by the modalities of reception. At the time, TV sets were particularly heavy, difficult to move, and equipped with roof antennae that were generally unreliable and difficult to adjust.

The functioning of the press and printers was likewise disrupted by the invasion. On the morning of August 21, the dailies were published normally and contained the presidium's declaration. But during the morning the head offices of the main press organs were occupied and their employees expelled. On their own initiative, the journalists sought alternative premises and new means of distribution. With the aid of large numbers of volunteers, the newspapers continued to be published, although irregularly, and their news was at times fanciful. New titles appeared, like the weekly *Politika*, scheduled to be launched later. Several newspapers, published at first in the form of brochures or leaflets, soon adopted a more regular format. Their distribution was somewhat erratic though, and depended on the complicity of railway employees, bus drivers, workers, policemen or simply motorists.[44] People waited for them impatiently: "Cars passed without stopping. Their passengers dropped bundles of newspapers. The people pounced on these bundles like grasshoppers."[45]

The Soviets had certainly not expected this type of resistance through the media, but they did have the means to deal with it. On August 21 and 22 they took control of most of the television sites, the main newspapers and the government press agency CTK. Radio was more problematic, but they soon scored points on that front when a large transmitter was discovered on August 24 in Ostrava. To facilitate the detection of "pirate" programs, galvanometric equipment was brought into the country. The occupiers had quickly become aware of the importance of radio and immediately started to confiscate transistors—to which groups of young people mockingly responded by holding building bricks to their ears.

Could the early success of the resistance have continued? It is difficult to say, as the signing of the Moscow agreements a few days later impacted heavily on the resistance dynamic.[46] Yet never before had military invaders been confronted with this surprising form of civil resistance through the media. Vaclav Havel commented that "that week showed how helpless military power is when confronted by an opponent unlike any that power has be trained to confront; it showed how hard it is to govern a country in which, though it may not defend itself militarily, all the civil structures simply turn their backs on the aggressors."[47]

Delocalization of the conflict

The unusual modes of "confrontation" between occupiers and occupied in the Czechoslovakian case warrant closer inspection. It was, for example, impossible for the occupying forces to destroy any specific place in which a crowd of protesters might be concentrated, for the nature of the conflict was diffuse and all-encompassing. The strange battle between the military forces and civilian resistance was thus expressed in an asymmetrical balance of power between tanks and the media.

From the first hours of the invasion this dynamic was marked by politicians and journalists' constant appeals to the population to remain calm and to disregard "provocation." One of their recommendations—among dozens of others—heard on national radio from the morning of August 21, was "With you, we want to remain calm [...]. We are sure that you are also going to remain calm and that, rather than demonstrating, you will go to work in a few hours time. There you will make an effort to do what you have to. For the moment there is no other solution."[48] The logical consequence of this type of recommendation was that public demonstrations were avoided. Yet many young people had a powerful urge to protest in the streets. They were dissuaded from doing so, over and again, without always understanding why. Any street protests were designed to be quick and non-provocative, like the noon "flash strikes" lasting two minutes on August 21 and of one hour on August 23. In this respect, one could say that the 1968 resistance movement disinvested the public sphere of the streets as a potential place for the expression of mass protest.

Did this mean that the Czechoslovakian resistance gave up the idea of any form of collective expression of its refusal of Soviet occupation? Certainly not. That was the purpose of mass communication that, as we have seen, was the main agent of social cohesion against the invader. The media were the means through which society could express its rejection of the foreign occupier, without the support of mass demonstrations in the streets. In this respect, journalists and the population had an almost "fusional" relationship, equal in intensity to the traumatism of the foreign aggression. It is certainly rare in the history of a country for society and the media to merge in this way. A slogan frequently broadcast was "We're with you, be with us."[49] The Czechoslovakian resistance thus shifted its occupation of the streets to that of the media, creating a balance of power that was less and less physical and increasingly symbolic. This general tendency to delocalize the conflict was also, in a sense, a *delocalization* of the public space in which the battle was taking place. In this context, civil resistance was particularly difficult to control militarily.

Yet the collective protest movement never totally abandoned the urban space. Some intermediate phenomena combined action in the streets with that of the media. Posters, for example, were a subtle way of occupying the urban space through a very simple medium, and the Czechoslovaks used it extensively: "cobblestones, streets, walls, shop windows, telephone booths, everything was covered with thousands and thousands of drawings, caricatures, posters. The naïve drawings of children were found next to the best artistic productions."[50]

This use of posters nevertheless also showed up the lopsided conflict between occupiers and occupied, between the power of arms and that of words.

Other processes contributed to reinforcing the delocalization of the struggle, for example the "demarcation" of the urban space and even simply ignoring the occupier's physical presence. One of the great novelties of this resistance was that it invented a *"desemiotization"* of the urban space. In other words, to make it more difficult for the occupier to move about in the country, it became increasingly common for road signs, street names and numbers, and the signs identifying institutions to be removed.[51] Instead, there were suddenly dozens of Dubcek Squares or Svoboda Avenues. The aim was to create a sort of social underground in which the occupied society would remain unattainable by the occupation forces.

During the first two days, many Czechoslovaks tried to convince the Soviet soldiers that they had no reason to be in their country. The irony was that, by making Russian compulsory in schools, the Soviets had made it easier for the Czechoslovaks to explain to their invaders that their leaders had fooled them and that they would do better going home! As these tactics of demoralization had only a limited, albeit very real effect,[52] they were dropped in favor of another one: ignoring the occupation forces, talking to them as little as possible, and giving them neither food nor assistance; in short, living as if nothing had happened, as if the country was not occupied.[53]

From this perspective, street demonstrations were futile. Demonstrating would be protesting, whereas the idea was less to protest against the invaders (which would amount to recognizing their presence) than to participate in a national effort to ensure that society kept functioning outside the occupier's control.

Journalists: substitutes or relays for political power?
The instrumental role that journalists played in the Czechoslovakian resistance created the impression that they were the ones directing it; indeed, "radio and television had become the country's government in the full sense of the term."[54] This assessment, put forward by Pavel Tigrid and shared by Vaclav Havel,[55] certainly does seem to be grounded in so far as

journalists substituted themselves partially, in the emergency, for the main leaders of the Prague Spring who had been arrested by the Soviets. The journalists played this part in two ways: through some of their public speeches, and in the way they worked. Many of their declarations reflected the ambiguity of this dual "positioning," since in the crisis they wore two caps: that of information professionals and that of politicians.

For instance, when Jiri Dienstbier summed up the day's events on the evening of August 21, he expressed himself first as a journalist (which he was) who was trying to stand up to the occupier: "Dear friends, right now I think that we can say one positive thing with absolute certainty: the occupiers' argument has fallen flat because they were unable to destroy the radio broadcasts in time and have therefore been unable to gain credence for the idea that they were 'invited' into our country." But as he concluded, he slipped out of the journalist's position and started talking almost like a cabinet minister addressing the national community: "Our strength is in keeping calm, in pure legality, in everyone's awareness, both at home and abroad, of our legitimacy."[56]

Radio journalists assumed a political function of prime importance through the choice of information that they decided to broadcast or not. The country's invasion led to all sorts of rumors (notably Debcek's death[57]) and disinformation. In this hotchpotch of news and pseudo-news, the journalists were in the best position to sort out what seemed to be objective and of interest to the public. They thus contributed meaningfully to maintaining the country's unity and limiting the chaos generated by the invasion. In that type of situation where "information was more strategically important than ever, indeed the only way of governing and of managing power, the journalists were the only social group with the possibility of governing effectively."[58]

Can such missions actually be qualified as a *management* of the resistance? Even though the journalists coordinated and amplified the passive resistance, they did not politically define it. It was the Party presidium that took that responsibility, just before it was neutralized on the night of the invasion. To justify their action, the journalists repeatedly affirmed their loyalty to the legal government. In this sense they were *relays* rather than substitutes for the political authorities. Their legitimacy to resist as journalists stemmed from the legitimacy of the legal authorities to remain in office, notwithstanding the *fait accompli* of the occupation.

Had these constitutional authorities changed their policy, the journalists would no longer have had the same legitimacy to resist. That was moreover exactly what happened with the signing of the Moscow Agreement. The entire population put its trust in Dubcek and Svoboda.

When it learned that Dubcek had been forcefully taken to Moscow with several other leaders of the Prague Spring, and that Svoboda had agreed to join them, it was filled with both hope and anxiety. From then on, the resistance dynamic was in a sense hanging in the air, pending a political solution to the crisis. On August 27, when the country learned that the delegation was back in Prague, these uncertainties evaporated. At 2:40 p.m. a communiqué read on radio and television tried to present in an acceptable light the "Moscow Agreements," the text of which was never made public. At 3:10 p.m., Svoboda addressed the nation, affirming that it was his duty to do everything to avoid bloodshed in Czechoslovakia. "As a soldier," he declared, "I know the hecatomb that fighting between the population and an army with the most modern arms can lead to. That is precisely why I considered it my duty, as President, to do everything in my power to avoid that happening."[59] After this speech, anger mounted in Prague: "From that moment, a gesture, a word, a stone could have set off the revolution. The people who had managed to get through to Wenceslas Square were no longer content to stand in front of the tanks to prevent them from moving forwards. They wanted to attack them, march against them, chase them from Wenceslas Square, from Prague, from the country."[60] Multiple protests throughout the country were immediately reported on radio.

But Dubcek's speech was announced. He was the uncontested symbol of the Prague Spring; the people trusted him totally. When he started his 27-minute address at 5:40, it was clear that he was physically and psychologically exhausted. Punctuated with sobs and silences, his speech was tragic: the man seemed broken, whereas the country he was talking to was not. His words confirmed those of Svoboda: they recommended a "normalization" marking the end of the Prague Spring. The people felt cheated; many were extremely bitter.

Had they resisted for nothing for six days? Had their leaders, taken off to Moscow, known nothing of their exploits? Had they doubted the strength of their resistance to the point of seeing it as nothing but a negligible factor in negotiations with the Russians? The crowd was probably less convinced by Dubcek's words than by his unspeakable emotion. It knew that everything was over. On Wenceslas Square "the people started to move. But they were no longer demonstrators driven by the same desire. They were simply pedestrians."[61]

In his speech Dubcek attacked the radio stations, showing that he knew—without having being present—that they had been at the heart of the people's resistance: "Certain broadcasters [...] are spreading mistrust and doubts on the results of the Moscow negotiations," he said.

"We are warning you seriously against such acts. [...] It is easy to put out inflamed words on the air, but one has to be aware of one's responsibilities concerning new victims and new damages, which are already serious enough"[62]—an ultimate homage addressed unwittingly by Dubcek to the journalists who had led the week-long struggle on his behalf. But for them too it was the beginning of the end. The media would no longer have the legitimacy needed to carry on fighting the occupier, since the political authorities had decided to submit to its will.

The journalists did nevertheless attempt to keep up the struggle. For a few more months the press managed to remain surprisingly free, reflecting a civil society that had given up the most open forms of resistance but carried on expressing its refusal of the occupation. The funeral of Jan Palach, the philosophy student who burned himself to death on Wenceslas Square on January 16, 1969, in protest against the Soviet invasion, was an impressive manifestation of national unity, although entirely unofficial. When, on the night of March 28, 1969, a large crowd in Prague and others around the country celebrated its hockey team's victory over the USSR, Moscow was to use their "anti-socialist excesses" as a pretext to force the country to toe the line more quickly. On April 1, an extremely severe censorship law was enacted and on April 17, Dubcek was forced to resign. This was the final death of the Prague Spring: it began with the end of censorship; it ended with its restoration. In the following months the journalists' profession was thoroughly purged: of the 4,000 journalists registered with the professional union, 2,600 were scrapped from the roll or dismissed. All the editors-in-chief of the press, radio and television were forced to resign. At the same time, civil society was literally suffocated: 70 social organizations or associations created in 1968 were banned or eliminated.[63]

Hence, the end of the Czechoslovakian crisis was not a bloodbath as Hungary had been in 1956, but the invasion did leave nearly a hundred dead and several hundred injured. From a human point of view, the leaders had partially met their objective. But from a political point of view, the outcome of the crisis was far worse than that of Hungary. By agreeing to sign and to implement the Moscow Agreement, the Czechoslovakian leaders tied their own hands.

They willingly engaged in "a policy of collaboration synonymous with capitulation," as Michel Tatu so aptly put it.[64] Hungary, which had resisted in 1956, had experienced nothing similar: it had put up a fight, it had lost, but it had not signed anything. That was why the respective effects of these two attitudes were different in the long term. In post-1968 Czechoslovakia, the leaders' capitulation blocked the country's political future; from then on, time seemed to have stopped. In post-1956 Hungary, the traumatism of a nation that was militarily vanquished but had not surrendered politically was inevitably to lead to an opening of the communist authorities towards society. This happened in the 1960s with Kadar's famous policy: "Whoever is not against us is with us."

The primacy of radio

Despite their differences, there were similarities in the part played by the media in the Hungarian resistance of 1956 and that of Czechoslovakia in 1968. The role of posters and the press in both cases of mass resistance was a continuity of their role in the large revolutionary social movements since the 18th century: they were protesters' favorite means of expression, the modes of communication through which they occupied the public sphere by asserting their social identity and creativity.

Radio, on the other hand, assumed a new function in 1956 and 1968. We know how this instrument had been used as a propaganda tool on the masses in the 1930s in the Soviet Union and Nazi Germany. During WWII, radio had also asserted itself as an international means of communication that served the goals of counter-propaganda and acted from outside in concert with resistance movements inside a country. It was, however, not until 1956, during the Hungarian insurrection, that a country's radio served as the main medium for communication in the struggle against a foreign opponent, outside of a war context. In 1968 Czechoslovakia, it had the same role but with far more flexibility, thanks to the invention of the transistor set.

In these crises, radio fulfilled three functions: it was a tribune, a prescriber, and a messenger. Its first function was to be an immediate locus of expression through speech. Its wide broadcasting range enabled it to reach a large audience and to appeal to social and political actors across the spectrum, all hoping to influence the course of events in their favor, through radio. In this sense, radio served as a tribune for protest groups. It was the mouthpiece for their opinions and, more generally, public opinion. Radio was the place where people went when they wanted to present themselves to the public as a political, social or cultural actor of the resistance. A case in point was the Baninka miners who sent a delegation to Radio Free Gyor on October 25 to make it known that they were going on strike and that "they have also formed their own Workers' Council [and that they] are keeping order and discipline. However, they are watching events in Budapest with concern and that is why they asked that their demands be transmitted through Radio Free Gyor to the

Hungarian government and Imre Nagy. Their first demand is that Imre Nagy call on the Russian troops in Hungary to begin their withdrawal carrying white flags."[65] During the days of the uprising, rebel radio stations passed on hundreds of motions and resolutions intended to put pressure on the Nagy government. In Czechoslovakia, from the first day of the invasion, legal radio stations likewise broadcast an avalanche of motions to support the Dubcek team, from a wide range of institutions and organizations.

Second, radio served as an impetus for public protest action. When social or institutional resistance crystallizes, radio can be an ideal instrument in its development. By relaying the voices of the actors in the resistance, and by broadcasting their instructions, it acts as a prescriber to the public, telling it what to do and what not to do. Provincial radio stations in Hungary that fell under the insurgents' control launched multiple appeals to strike and, more generally, to join the resistance movement. Likewise, in Czechoslovakia countless instructions were given to the population by radio. They were sometimes of an imperative nature, especially to dissuade the population from any public demonstration, as on August 23 in Prague. On that day the rumor circulated that there was to be a demonstration on Wenceslas Square. "The news spread like wild fire" and everyone went in that direction. "That was when radio warned that the occupation troops were looking for a pretext to enable them to take firmer measures and to decree martial law. [...] The people who went to Wenceslas Square (mostly young people) were all carrying their wirelesses. When they heard the warning on the radio they immediately responded, showing a degree of discipline that amazes me. The crowd stopped in the small streets leading on to the square and dispersed."[66] The content of the instructions was sometimes more an incentive than an instruction, as on August 23, when radio stations suggested that people remove road signs and name plates. Actually, it was simply relaying an initiative born within the population; some groups had spontaneously started this action the previous day.[67] Yet radio had more than a role of transmission. By relaying such initiatives, it amplified them. Radio and the resistance thus participated in the same social movement, interacting closely.

Finally, radio served as a messenger. The situation spawned by an insurrection or invasion generally upsets the ordinary conditions of communication within a region or country. Mail, telegraphs, telephone and public transport are disrupted or even interrupted. Capable of rapidly broadcasting information on a large scale, radio can partially serve as a substitute for these faulty means of communication, and this role as a messenger is vital to help a resistance movement grow. On the second day of the Hungarian uprising, observers were amazed to pick up the following message on Radio Free Baranya (Pecs): "The resistance groups of Kinizsy and Zriny have to report and maintain contact. Until new measures have been taken, the orders to attack remain the same."[68] In the very first hours of the occupation in Czechoslovakia, radio messages were broadcast, urgently calling on members of parliament to go to the National Assembly, and on the delegates of the 14th congress to meet the next day.

Normally, these messages would have been passed on by telephone. Considering the difficulties in getting there (means of transport disrupted), the secret meeting of this congress, organized in record time (24 hours after the invasion), with a considerable number of delegates (1,192 out of 1,543), would simply not have been able to take place without this "radio notification" throughout the country.

In these emergency situations, radio's function as a messenger went further than summoning people to meetings. It was also able to offset certain dysfunctions caused by the crisis, and even to provide a few public services. For example, the rebel station Radio Free Mizkolc launched a call on the air, on October 29, for an iron lung for the Debrecen hospital,[69] and stations in Prague put out frequent calls for blood donors. Radio furthermore served as a substitute for mail and telephone, by offering a mailbox service for private individuals. That was the case in Prague where, from August 22, radio broadcast personal messages on the air (for example a father wanting news of his son).

The result of these multiple functions of radio was that the content of programs was heterogeneous, combining *inter alia* news and commentaries, coded messages and personal announcements, music and official declarations. This variety reflected the diversity of the missions fulfilled by the medium. In a sense, radio concentrated all the tensions and all the energies of a country in the process of resisting. In this respect, it was indeed at the centre of the crisis, at the interface between the fighting forces of society and the country's institutions. But for how long?

Intoxication and closed doors

Apart from the original role played by the media in the Hungarian and Czechoslovakian resistance, exceptional modes of communication were also observed between individuals. Resistance to Moscow generated the most accomplished form of East-East communication: "accomplished" because during the crisis it reached a climax, but also because Soviet repression put a stop to it. Perhaps it was because individuals knew that repression was imminent, even before it occurred, that interaction between them became so intense.

In both the Hungarian insurrection and the Czechoslovak resistance, people seemed to be in a state of euphoria. What could be more collectively exhilarating than talking freely and treating the foreign occupier with contempt! Writer Gyorgy Konrad's description of the atmosphere in the streets of Budapest at the beginning of the uprising gives a glimpse of this intoxication: "Total strangers, intoxicated by their own curiosity and expansiveness, strike up a conversation at every turn. We are two million village dwellers in the big city; everyone is an acquaintance. Each passer-by is an eye witness and a live newspaper, a rescue part and a punitive expedition, a guerrilla band and a political party."[70] Everyone demanded something in the name of the revolution and on the people's behalf. Gone were the barriers raised by individuals to protect themselves from totalitarian invasiveness. The fact that strangers readily discussed public matters proved that former boundaries between the public and private spheres had come tumbling down.

This free expression of inter-individual communication was the strongest and most moving sign that the people had reclaimed the public sphere. The flow of information changed radically, transcending the traditional role attributed to the media. As everyone communicated with everyone else, news was circulated by every individual. Multiple communication channels within the population served to convey news from place to place, with the inevitable risk of circulating the most fanciful rumors. The journalist's function as such disappeared, as everyone became both receiver and provider of news on public affairs. One of the most characteristic phenomena in this respect was the role of radio hams. In the first days of the uprising, a Hungarian student built a transmitter "to tell the world the truth." He explained this initiative as follows: "I broadcast all morning the general opinion of the people, in contrast to what the Governmental 'Kossuth' radio was saying. [...] When I was not broadcasting, I walked unarmed around the streets of Budapest to see what was happening. I talked to people; I watched the fighting; I saw young girls throw 'Molotov cocktails' at Russian tanks. Then, I broadcast to the world the truth, that we were not the counter-revolutionaries the Government said, but rather the whole Hungarian people fighting for our freedom."[71]

In those moments everyone was supposed to know, hear, learn and participate in the historical event; the people were experiencing a collective communion. A public audience for resistance media emerged from 1953. For instance, on the morning of June 17, strikers tuned into

RIAS on the company radio in their plant. In Czechoslovakia, the municipal radio station broadcast "Legal Radio Prague" on loudspeakers in the streets of various towns and villages. The use of bells and sirens signified an even stronger "sound occupation" of the public sphere. This process was used in East German towns in 1953, in Hungary in 1956 (notably in Gyor) and in Czechoslovakia in 1968 during the flash strikes of August 21 and 23. "It was impressive, at twelve mid-day, to hear the sirens screaming and the bells tolling. It had been so long since people had heard bells ringing at mid-day in Prague! [...] I saw many people, especially elderly citizens, with tears in their eyes."[72]

But Soviet intervention put an abrupt end to this renaissance of communication. The interaction was so intense that people had almost forgotten the reality of Europe's geopolitical division: Hungarians and Czechoslovaks were still cut off from the outside world. The repression—brutal in Budapest, more underhand in Prague—forced them "back into their shell."

In 1956, the Hungarians had banked on help from the West—something the West had not even considered. The yawning divide between their idealized representations of the West and the Western countries' attitude towards them created a fundamental communication gap between the two. Foreign journalists present in Budapest witnessed this, and were made to feel guilty about it. Initially the Hungarian population spontaneously welcomed them with open arms, asking them not only to witness the events but also to be the insurgents' messengers, almost their spokespersons. The Hungarians assumed that Western journalists were necessarily sympathetic to their cause, as the West, they believed, was on their side. The first break with the West occurred on October 29 when the population learned that the UN Security Council had adjourned without passing a resolution on Hungary. When the second Soviet intervention started on November 4, those Hungarian radio stations that could still broadcast freely multiplied their calls for help. This showed how strong their expectations were. But as this help was not forthcoming, all the frustrations and anger of a people that felt abandoned were taken out on Western journalists in the country. Acclaimed at the beginning of the uprising, they were booed by the crowds, as Thomas Schreiber reported in his articles for *Le Monde* and *L'Express*: "At the beginning of my stay, crowds everywhere applauded and even kissed the French flag on our car. But when we left, with exit permits issued by the Soviet authorities, we were insulted."[73] In several reports by foreign correspondents they spoke of their feelings of shame and guilt for the West's passivity. F. Colin wrote in *La Croix*: "Everyone stopped to say the same thing to me: 'Please go back quickly and tell the whole world what you've seen; we beg of you'. And I'd turn away, so as not to see those poor faces devastated by distress."[74]

In 1968, the Czechs expected nothing from the West. Was this because of 1956? Instead, they put all their hopes in the resoluteness of the leaders of the Prague Spring. Learning that their political leaders had been taken to Russia, the people looked towards Moscow rather than Washington. They expected nothing special from the Western journalists in the country, apart from informing Western public opinion. When the signing of the Moscow Agreement dashed their hopes of holding on to the freedoms of the Prague Spring, did they resent their leaders who had agreed to destroy the dream of a "socialism with a human face"? That does not seem to have been the case, at least not at the time. An opinion poll in September 1968 showed that 99% of the people still trusted Dubcek and 93% denied that there was a "danger of a counter-revolution."

Finally, both crises led to a dead end, a story unfolding behind closed doors, the tragic expression of communication that was impossible, from the point of view of both identity and openness onto the world. Yet these tragedies concealed a new dynamic. When the major crises of Soviet Europe are considered in their historical continuity, change is perceptible in the relationship between communication and resistance. In 1953, East German workers did not even attempt to express themselves in the media of the GDR; they went to West Berlin to talk on RIAS but were turned down. In 1956, the insurgents tried to voice their case on national radio, failed, and then secured the right to talk on regional radio stations. In the end, Radio Kossuth rallied to their cause. In 1968, the Czechoslovakian media opened up not in a moment of crisis, as in Hungary, but prior to the Soviet intervention, during the Prague Spring. In this respect, developments in Czechoslovakia in 1968 were a major step forward, compared to Hungary in 1956. But the constitution of this public sphere came up against the same brick wall: repression. And once again, the tanks prevailed over the media. Once again, access to the official communication sphere led to a dead end. In this respect, 1968 marked the end of an era. After that, other ways of reclaiming the public sphere were to emerge. In central Europe, Poland was the main crucible of this evolution, culminating in the Gdansk strikes of 1980.

Notes

1. *La révolte de la Hongrie d'après les émissions des radios hongroises (octobre-novembre 1956)*, Paris, Ed. Pierre Horay, 1957, p. 19.

2. Tibor Méray, *Imre Nagy. L'homme trahi*, op. cit., p. 140.

3. Méray, "Imre Nagy. L'homme trahi," in *Les Temps modernes*, op. cit., p. 140.

4. These workers' councils and revolutionary committees were formed at all levels: from the province to the municipality, from the large industrial plant to the modest kolkhoze. Their aim was to take over all functions of the administration and the party organs. They also sent the Nagy government numerous motions and memorandums to rally him to the rebel movement.

5. *La révolte de la Hongrie d'après les émissions des radios hongroises (octobre-novembre 1956)*, op. cit., p. 36.

6. *Daily Mail* of 29 October.

7. Cited in Melvin J. Larsky and François Bondy, *The Hungarian Revolution*, London, Martin Secker and Warburg Ltd., 1957, p. 114.

8. *Ibid.*, p. 166.

9. Cited by André Fontaine, *History of the Cold War*, Vol. II, "From the Korean War to the Present," New York, Vintage Books Edition, 1970, p. 219.

10. *Ibid*, p. 242.

11. *1956: Varsovie Budapest. La deuxième révolution d'octobre*, texts collected by Pierre Kende and Krzysztof Pomian, Paris, Ed. du Seuil, 1978, p. 247.

12. *La révolte de la Hongrie d'après les émissions des radios hongroises (octobre-novembre 1956)*, op. cit., p. 66.

13. Peter Freier, cited by Melvin J. Larsky and François Bondy, *The Hungarian Revolution*, op. cit., p. 168.

14. George Urban, *The Nineteen Days*, op. cit., p. 167.

15. *La révolte de la Hongrie d'après les émissions des radios hongroises (octobre-novembre 1956)*, op. cit., p. 100.

16. BBC summary, cited by Melvin J. Larsky and François Bondy, *La révolution hongroise*, op. cit., p. 188.

17. *La révolte de la Hongrie d'après les émissions des radios hongroises (octobre-novembre 1956)*, op. cit., p. 193.

18. That was how RFE was able to cover the advance of the Soviet army in Budapest almost by the hour: the seizure of East Station, of the Duna Hotel and then of Buda hill overlooking the city. As telephone communication with the West was impossible, RFE was probably informed via other channels, probably radio contact, either from the US embassy or by CIA agents.

19. *The Manchester Guardian*, 15 November 1956, p. 1.

20. François Fejtö, préface de *La révolte de la Hongrie d'après les émissions des radios hongroises (octobre-novembre 1956)*, op. cit., p. 10.

21. Seven votes for and four against. The opponents were Svestka, Bilak, Rigo and Kolder. Indra, as secretary of the Presidium, was not authorized to vote.

22. Robert Littell, *The Czech Black Book*, New York, 1968, p. 10-11. This set of documents was compiled by two renowned Czechoslovakian historians, V. Precan and M. Otaha.

23. Jiri Pelikan, *S'ils me tuent*, Paris, Ed. Grasset, p. 221.

24. See Part 1, Chapter 2.

25. Jiri Dienstbier and Karel Lansky, Rozhlas proti tankum. Kolaz *udalosti, vzpominck a zaznamu a vysilani Ceskoslovenskeho rozhlasu v srpnu 1968*, (The Radio against the Tanks), Prague, Ed. Edice Literatury Faktu, 1990, p. 20.

26. Name of the river running through Prague.

27. *Les 7 jours de Prague (21-27 août 1968)*, op. cit., p. 21.

28. Oldrich Cernik (Prime Minister), Josef Smrkovsky (President of the National Assembly) and Frantisek Kriegel (President of the Czech National Council).

29. Jacques Rupnik, *L'autre Europe*, op. cit. p. 318.

30. Karel Bartosek, "La société civile en Tchécoslovaquie et la révolte de 1968" in *La Nouvelle alternative*, op. cit., p. 58.

31. See Part 2, Chapter 1.

32. Interview with Jaroslav Jiru, January 15, 1995.

33. Dusan Havlicek, "La communication de masse en Tchécoslovaquie en 1956 et 1968. Contribution à l'analyse des processus d'information et des mass-médias dans le système politique du socialisme réel," in *Les expériences du Printemps de Prague 1968*, p. 237. Study n° 16 carried out in the framework of the research project "Les crises des systèmes de type soviétique," edited by Zdenek Mlynar. This unpublished document was kindly lent by the author.

34. *Les 7 jours de Prague (21-27 août 1968)*, op. cit., p. 39.

35. Dusan Havlicek, "La communication de masse en Tchécoslovaquie en 1956 et 1968," op. cit., p. 239.

36. Jiri Dienstbier and Karel Lansky, *Rozhlas proti tankum*, op. cit., p. 49.

37. Several authors have written that the Czechoslovakian army made some of its equipment available to the journalists. Zdenek Hejzlar, then director of the radio station, pointed out that even though this possibility was considered, it was not implemented: *La radio tchécoslovaque*, 1968, Stockholm (manuscript), cited by Dusan Havlicek, "La communication de masse en Tchécoslovaquie en 1956 et 1968," op. cit., p. 248.

38. See his memoires in his above-cited book: Jiri Pelikan, *S'ils me tuent*, op. cit.

39. Michel Tatu, *L'hérésie impossible*, op. cit., p. 174.

40. This was possible only because technical cooperation had been set up over the previous three years between television channels in the East and the West. The first images had been exchanged between *Intervision* (for the East) and *Eurovision* (for the West) on September 2, 1965. From then on, channels in the East supplied images to the newly created EVN (Eurovision News Exchange) on a daily basis. The fact that the head office of *Intervision* was in Prague facilitated the instantaneous transmission of images to the West.

41. *Les 7 jours de Prague (21-27 août 1968)*, op. cit., p. 35.

42. Erich Bertleff, *A mains nues*, Paris, Ed. Stock, 1969, p. 84.

43. Hence, the title of his memoirs: Miroslav Sigl, *Na viné 490 metro*, Prague, Nasé vojsko, 1990.

44. Gordon Skilling gives the list of the main newspapers published in the week of resistance: Gordon Skilling,

Czechoslovakia's Interrupted Revolution, Princeton University Press, 1976, p. 779.

45. Vaclav Byk, "Le premier mort," in *Prague : l'été des tanks*, Paris, Ed. Tchou, 1969, p. 17.

46. See below.

47. Vaclav Havel, *Disturbing the Peace: a Conversation with Karel Hvizdala*, London, Ed. Faber and Faber, 1990, p. 109.

48. Dienstbier, Lansky, *Rohlas proti tankum,* op. cit., p. 33.
49. Miroslav Sigl, *Na viné 490 metro,* op. cit., p. 43.
50. Erich Bertleff, *A mains nues,* op. cit., p. 172.
51. Gordon Skilling, *Czechoslovakia's interrupted revolution,* op. cit., p.776.
52. Some troops even had to be withdrawn from this "front" that was so unfamiliar to soldiers trained in warfare. Cases of suicide were also reported in the occupation forces.
53. Some Czechs however regretted this development, believing that the refusal of all contact with the soldiers was one of the causes of the resistance's failure. See Tomin, "J'ai dialogué avec les soldats russes" in Julius *Alternatives Non-violentes,* n° 46, December 1982, p. 51-60.
54. Pavel Tigrid, *La chute irrésistible d'Alexandre Dubcek,* Paris, Ed. Calmann-Levy, 1969, p. 142.
55. Vaclav Havel, *Disturbing the Peace,* op. cit., p. 109.
56. Jiri Dienstbier and Karel Lansky, *Rohlas proti tankum,* op. cit., p. 46.
57. This rumor developed on August 23 and was repeated in an Associated Press news bulletin on the same day at 1:36 a.m. and an A.F.P. bulletin at 3:47 a.m. Voir *Edition spéciale, Pourquoi Prague?,* Paris, Tallandier/Edition Première, 1968, p. 536.
58. Dusan Havlicek, "La communication de masse en Tchécoslovaquie en 1956 et 1968," op. cit., p. 264.
59. Cited in *Edition spéciale, Pourquoi Prague?,* op. cit., p. 594.
60. Erich Bertleff, *A mains nues,* op. cit., p. 190.
61. *Ibid.,* p. 195.
62. See *Edition spéciale, Pourquoi Prague?,* op. cit., p. 597.
63. Karel Kaplan, "Persécution politique en Tchécoslovaquie entre 1948 et 1972," Köln, Index, 1983, p. 43. Study n. 3 undertaken under the research project "Les crises des systèmes de type soviétique," edited by Zdenek Mlynar.
64. Michel Tatu, *Le Monde,* 21 August 1973. See also all his chronicles and reports on the Czechoslovak crisis published in the same newspaper, while he was its permanent correspondent in Vienna: *L'hérésie impossible,* Paris, Ed. Grasset, 1967-68. His writings remain an excellent document on that period.
65. Melvin J. Larsky and François Bondy, *La révolution hongroise,* op. cit., p. 120.
66. Erich Bertleff, *A mains nues,* op. cit., p. 163.
67. Mandrou (ed.), *Les Sept Jours de Prague (21-27 August 1968),* op. cit., p. 191.
68. *La révolte de la Hongrie d'après les émissions des radios hongroises (octobre-novembre 1956),* op. cit., p. 41.
69. *Ibid.,* p. 84.
70. Gyorgy Konrad, *The Loser,* Harmondsworth, Penguin Books, 1983, p. 215.
71. George Sherman in *The Observer* November 11, 1956, p. 7.
72. Erich Bertleff, *A mains nues,* op. cit. p. 163.
73. *L'Express,* November 15, 1956.
74. F. Collin in *La Croix,* November 24, 1956.

PART THREE

Resisting via the West

I

The immobile battle: Gdansk, 1980

When the workers of the Gdansk shipyards went on strike, twelve years after the suppression of the Prague Spring, people wondered whether Central Europe was about to experience a new tragedy. The event took on extraordinary proportions in terms of size, duration and, of course, its implications. It constituted a formidable challenge for a communist regime that purported to represent the workers' interests.

Whereas the protests themselves had been a minority phenomenon in Hungary and Czechoslovakia, the mass movement that unfurled from August 14, 1980 in the Gdansk area, as well as in hundreds of other industrial centers of Poland, was a watershed in the manner of resisting in the East. The Gdansk strikes were nevertheless part of the continuity of the major opposition movements of Soviet Europe, in so far as the social crisis that they triggered stemmed not only from workers' demands but also from the revival of the Polish national identity. The Gdansk Agreements that put an end to the conflict were moreover presented by both parties as a "national entente."

At the same time, these strikes also departed from the main modes of opposition that had appeared since 1956. The change was most striking in the occupation of the public sphere. In 1956, Hungarian insurgents had taken to the streets to demonstrate and then to fight. In 1968 the Czechoslovakian population had also occupied the streets to show their hostility to the Soviet occupier, although without clustering together in crowds of protesters. In 1980, the Gdansk strikers refused to protest in the streets, perceived as particularly dangerous. They preferred to entrench themselves in the shipyards to keep control of their struggle and avoid any provocation by the authorities. Poland's labor history of the previous 25 years explains this choice: the strikers wanted at all costs to avoid a repetition of the 1970 tragedy when dozens of workers had been shot by the Polish army.

Despite this withdrawal from the streets, they were not operating behind closed doors, on the contrary. From the outset, in addition to their main demand (the creation of an independent union), the Gdansk strikes were clearly a vast movement that set out to reclaim public speech, both within and outside the shipyards. In no time workers in the shipyards took over the company radio that was to serve as the main communication tool from then on. Outside, the workers had no intention of attempting to physically occupy the radio and television buildings. They spontaneously relied on those who came to see them—first the Polish journalists who wanted to and could, but above all Western journalists—to talk on their behalf. This was not a predetermined strategy but an ad hoc tactic adopted from the beginning of their action, which grew day by day.

Soon the strike was headline news throughout the world. Suspense built up around the eventuality of Soviet intervention, as the Polish authorities seemed unable to put an end to the situation. By obtaining international media coverage, the strikers had truly managed to break through the wall between East and West. Everywhere in the West, people who had never taken much interest in "the East" were suddenly fascinated in the outcome of the conflict.

They remained glued to events in Gdansk. French author Marguerite Duras' diary is an eloquent testimony. Like many Western Europeans, Duras saw Poland at the time as a country situated "elsewhere." She wrote in the columns of *Libération*: "Gradually a new event is emerging [...], it's taking place far from us, very far, in Poland." But this "very far" was soon to become part of her personal experience. The author, tuned into events in Gdansk, was stirred by the news from Poland: "I'm anxious because of Gdansk [...]. I can't say that I'm indifferent to the success or failure of the Gdansk strikes. I say that I'm happy that it's happened."[1] This was a sign that the Polish workers were making news; they were busy writing a history that fascinated the world.

In 20 years the media world had changed profoundly. Means of communication and especially television had developed rapidly. The West had heard only the stifled voices of the insurgents of the Hungarian uprising in 1956, through the large radio receiver that sat imposingly in every dining room. From Czechoslovakia in 1968 they had received no more than fleeting images after the events. By contrast, in

1980 they were able to follow the strikes behind the Iron Curtain every evening on television.² In the first three days images were rare; then they arrived almost daily and everything changed. The East, which had seemed so far away, was right there, almost next door. Television gave the impression of proximity: clearly an illusion but one that had the powerful effect of making people forget the Wall. The world lived in step with socialist Poland on the edge of the precipice. Even though they had confined themselves to their shipyards, the Polish strikers had thus managed to breach "the wall" and to make the whole world talk about them. In this sense their action was based on a paradox: it was an *immobile battle*.

How had things reached that point? It might seem that the historian has an easy job tracing the story back to its beginnings, since he or she knows the ending. Yet this type of task is always difficult, and even more so in the Polish case where several conflicting histories exist: that of the workers' memory, that of the intellectuals' combat, and that of the Catholic Church. Examining all these dimensions within the scope of this book is impossible and in a sense futile as this has already been done.³ Instead, based on these studies, I show the importance of another history within these histories: that of the role of communication in the construction of processes of resistance, before and during the 1980 strikes.

During the pivotal period stretching from the creation of the KOR (Social Self-Defense Committee) in 1976 to the birth of Solidarity in 1980, through Pope John-Paul II's first visit in 1979, three flows of communication had developed:

- *the assertion of an East-East communication identity* that marked the rebirth of public speech in Poland and partially altered the content of the official media;
- *the use of the East-West-East communication loop* that, via Western press correspondents, made it possible to get around Polish media censorship;
- *the opening of a West-East-West world communication* that, from Western journalists episodically or permanently present in the East, informed Western audiences so that they could witness live the exceptional events in the Soviet Bloc: the Pope's visit and the August 1980 strikes.

The aim here is to write not a separate history of these three flows of communication, but a single history of their interaction during the crisis. My argument is that it was their unexpected conjunction that made the 1980 events so unusual. The way in which the Polish strikers, without any predetermined strategy, used these forms of communication to organize, to publicly stage their action, and to open up to the world, made their resistance difficult to suppress.

It would nevertheless be wrong to affirm that the media prevailed over the tanks. The memory of the 1970 tragedy weighed heavily on the communist leaders' behavior as well. In particular, the head of the Party in the Gdansk area, Tadeusz Fiszbach, wanted to avoid a repetition of this type of disaster. Their restraint indirectly favored the development of the movement and its international amplification in the media. As it spread in the West, it became a factor of mounting external pressure on a government that lacked self-assurance. In this sense the Western media supported the social movement triggered by the strikers, and so contributed to dissuading the Polish authorities from using armed force.

Collective dissemination of information as a resistance strategy

Some texts are historical landmarks. Polish philosopher Leszek Kolakowski's "Theses on hope and despair," published in 1975, was one of them. Kolakowski argued that the communist system tended to disintegrate from the end of Stalinism, and that this opened up new spaces for resistance against it. In other words, the system's contradictions created the conditions for opposition to it. In a period in which the communist regime was seen as unshakable, this was a new idea. One of the author's main theses was that the slow disintegration of communism facilitated the development of free information: it was possible to overcome censorship by multiplying acts of defiance, within everyone's reach. The notion of civil resistance was thus at the heart of his reflection. Kolakowski recommended the collective dissemination of information as a strategy of resistance by civil society. And "the best means to prevent legal action against this type of [free information] 'offence', was to commit a very large number of them."[4] Hence, his wish to see individuals defend their freedom, and his appeal for the multiplication of insurgent groups, forms of self-organization of civil society. These were themes that were developed marvelously well by Adam Michnik in Poland, Vaclav Havel in Czechoslovakia, and Gyorgy Konrad in Hungary.

This text theorizes a trend born in Poland in the early 1970s. Rather than wait for "free information" from the outside, the idea was for people to produce it themselves *within* the country. We know how important the input of this outside communication was from the beginning of the Cold War, not only via the programs of Western radio but also through the invaluable intellectual input of the journal *Kultura*, created in 1947 and established in France, at Maisons-Laffitte, in 1948. In the spirit of its founder, Jerzy Giedroyc, it published quality books and a periodical nurturing a critical view of communist Poland, for the Polish intelligentsia in exile as well as those who had remained on the banks of the Vistula.[5] The *Kultura* project was thus to maintain contact with the country at all costs, in various ways.

From 1952, several articles from its monthly issues (and sometimes a whole issue) were printed on India paper so that they could be smuggled more easily into Poland. Books with camouflaged covers were taken in by sympathizers traveling to or from the West: diplomats, sportspersons, tourists, etc. This was how the work of Czeslaw Milosz, George Orwell and Witold Gombrowicz entered Poland and circulated underground. In the period of openness following Gomulka's take-over in 1956, more open contact was established with the country and certain articles in *Kultura* were even discussed in the official press. But in 1957 the government clamped down again and the journal was no longer tolerated. Those who sneaked it into the country or circulated it in Poland took serious risks. At the end of the 1960s the state prosecuted a group that had tried to introduce copies of *Kultura* through the Tatras mountain range in the Carpathians, on the Czechoslovakian border. The February 1970 trial of the youths involved, all members of a mountain club, was the subject of excessive media hype. Accused of having "attempted to organize a network of intelligence and ideological diversion," they were sentenced to jail terms ranging from three to four years. But the trial also had the effect of creating extensive publicity for the journal, until then hardly known by the general public in Poland. Its prestige was consequently enhanced, including in other Eastern European countries.

After Gomulka's fall and his replacement by Edward Gierek in 1970, the country was gradually to open up to the West, especially through close relations with France. Memories of the war and Stalinism faded. A new generation wanted to break away from the old patterns inherited from the recent past. During the 1970s, "fear, as a social phenomenon, gradually disappeared."[6] The most determined individuals and groups were to be the artisans of the collective dissemination of "free information" recommended by Kolakowski. Anti-government intellectuals no longer sought, as they had in the 1960s, to use petitions to protest against the government. At the time, petitions had been a form of public pressure, especially when the West was informed of them. A case in point was the appeal by 34 intellectuals, writers and artists who, on the initiative of Antoni Slonimski, protested publicly on March 17, 1964, against the restrictions imposed on the functioning of the press. But after the death of the Prague Spring in 1968, the communist government was really no longer perceived as being fit to be reformed. The time had come for society to organize and inform itself.

It was in this new context that the KOR or Social Self-Defense Committee (*Komitet Obrony Robotnikow*) was set up on September 24, 1976, shortly after the Ursus and Radom strikes (against price hikes) in June that year. This marked an important step in the development of Polish opposition, four years before the Gdansk strikes. The KOR consisted of a group of dissident intellectuals who had united to provide persecuted workers and their families with moral, legal and financial aid. The Committee's first task was to bring to the public's attention the repression to which the workers were subjected, and thus to garner support for them.

Under the impetus of a leading member, Jacek Kuron, the KOR (changed on October 31, 1997, to the KSS-KOR[7]) was to spawn a dissident community throughout Poland that was both the product and the vehicle of this diffusion of information.[8]

Within the country, the KOR adopted the *samizdat* technique for the duplication of its documents and communiqués. Based on Article 52 of the constitution on human rights, it launched unofficial publications in 1977: mainly its newsletter and more specialized documents such as *Robotnik* ("The Worker") and *Glos* ("The Voice"). A publishing house, Nowa, was established in the same year. The question of using roneo or typewriter copying arose. This simple technical choice actually had major political implications. Although the typewriter made it possible to constitute a network of complicity, as readers became copiers, this technique more or less excluded the working-class world where few typewriters existed. Polish dissidents therefore preferred to roneo newsletters, even if the networks of complicity between readers and publishers were then weaker. The KOR sought to publish high-quality documents with a fairly large circulation, as the number of readers was constantly rising. It sometimes used professional printers, although such contracts were risky. To elude the police, these publications were printed in secret.

Internationally, the KOR relied mainly on Western press correspondents in Warsaw. In the past, Western journalists had made contact with independent personalities to find out their views on developments in the country, and local intellectuals and journalists critical of the regime had sought to pass information on to Westerners, to defy censorship. But these were individual contacts that were always risky and sometimes punished. The KOR, on the other hand, used such relations with journalists as a working method, a resistance strategy, a means to transmit secret information to the West in the hope that it would return to the East via Western radio stations. An *East-West-East* communication loop was thus formed.

The KOR simultaneously relied on the Polish sections of these stations, especially the BBC and RFE—sometimes called "Warsaw 4."[9] In the 1960s, the opposition had also benefited indirectly from Western radio stations for its petition campaigns. Jan Nowak, head of the Polish section of RFE, explained how, in 1964, the "letter of the 34" had arrived in Munich via an individual living in London, and had then been sent to Poland.[10] At the time, Western radio was not yet systematically used by press correspondents. The KOR activists took that step. Their aim was to form a parallel communication network based openly on Western radio, and thus, from the outside, to create an embryo of public opinion within the country.

In this respect the memoirs of Jacek Kuron are illuminating. As Polish law did not formally ban the dissemination of local news abroad, Kuron wanted to exploit this legal loophole. His apartment became a newsroom for Western journalists, and the news used in their dispatches was broadcast a few hours later by the BBC and RFE. Jacek Kuron also had the audacity to phone France and the UK, where he knew that the two Smolar brothers (Aleksander in Paris and Eugenius in London) would relay his news to radio stations broadcasting to the East.[11] He reminisces about that period with humor: "I developed a highly effective information technique. In the middle of the night, I would pitilessly wake Aleksander, because I knew that the sooner the news was sent, the more effective our action would be. Later, I was told that his little boy Piotr, who'd been given a toy telephone, would pick up the receiver and say: 'Hello Jacek, yes, I'm here, I'm recording, I'm noting, you can send it through.'"[12] Rapid dissemination of news was particularly important, as the repression against KOR members, trade union leaders and human rights activists was intense. The most effective way of counteracting it was immediately to transmit information to the West, especially to RFE, on the individuals who had been arrested, those who were likely to be detained, and so on. "We agreed on the following principle," explained Kuron, "when an arrest took place in the street, the victim had to shout out his or her name and telephone number as loudly as possible. Soon, the 39-39-64 symbolized every instance where the authorities broke the law. When the police arrested someone anywhere, I was almost always informed very quickly. Once they were released, the person had to inform me straight away. They had to call neither family nor friends, but to let me know at Mickiewicz Street. With this method, I knew where every member of the KOR was, and what they were doing. Free Europe broadcast the communiqués on arrests and releases on an hourly basis [...], as the most effective way of combating arrests was precisely to inform Free Europe. After the news was announced, a person could almost always expect to be released."[13] Kuron himself experienced the system first-hand. One day when he was arrested, the police officer guarding him tried to comfort him, saying: "Don't worry Mister Kuron, your wife has already sent the news to Radio Free Europe and you'll probably be out very soon."[14]

Within four years the KOR (then KSS-KOR) developed a network of informers and activists in all of Poland's cities and industrial areas. It also dispensed training through a "flying university," with "teachers" who traveled throughout the country giving talks on the history of Poland, the Church's role and similar topics. Some 10,000 copies of the Charter of Workers' Rights, published by the KOR in September 1979, were circulated. The journal *Robotnik* attained a circulation of over 20,000 in 1980 and served as an example for the version launched by militants in Gdansk: *Robotnik Wybrzeza* ("Worker of the littoral"). Bogdan Borusewic, Andrzej Gwiazda, Anna Walentynowicz and Lech Walesa, who initiated one of the first founding committees for free trade unions, in April 1978, were subsequently to play a leading role in the August 1980 strikes at the Lenin shipyards.

The development of what was then called "democratic opposition" was possible only because government repression had slackened. KOR militants were still persecuted and sometimes even terrorized by the police, but they were not eliminated. Once again, this was a fundamental difference with the Stalinist period. Another reason why the network thrived was the complicity from which it benefited in Polish society. The KOR was the spearhead of growing social opposition across a wide social spectrum. The church, in particular, often served as a meeting point and center of coordination for independent initiatives, especially after the first pilgrimage of Pope John-Paul II, Karol Wojtyla, former archbishop of Cracow.

The advent of John-Paul II and the boosting of the Poles' morale

The election of John-Paul II, the first non-Italian pope in 450 years, was a source of national pride for an overwhelming majority of the Polish population. His first visit to Poland, from June 2 to 10, 1979, was truly an experience in "communication and communion" that had a powerful, liberating effect on people's minds. Daniel Dayan described this trip as an example of a "way of acting through rituals," understood as an effective form of symbolic action. It was a "transformatory event" that "put history onto new rails by suggesting a new vocabulary for action."[15] "The Pope's speech made post-war Poland look like a minor setback, a parenthesis." To open the near future, he called on the distant past and evoked the figure of Saint Stanislas, bishop of Cracow in the 11th century, decapitated and thrown into a lake in 1079 for defying the temporal power of King Boleslas II. This use of a symbol enabled the Pope to suggest an amazing synchronization of time between the Middle Ages and the present, making his visit a formidable challenge to the Polish government.[16]

The communist authorities had done everything in their power to limit the impact of the Pope's visit, by presenting it as a strictly religious event. They expected to obtain the population's gratitude for authorizing the Pope to visit his homeland. Both parties pretended not to see what the other side was playing at.

The government acted as though the Pope's visit to a communist country was not an issue, and John-Paul II pretended that he would have no difficulty talking to his followers. Actually, the Polish authorities were on the defensive. Like other leaders in the Soviet Bloc, they were worried.[17] Polish television could not ignore the event on which it broadcast three reports live.[18] Today we know that precise instructions were given to the Polish media in advance to bias their coverage and reports on the Pope's visit.[19] Two objectives stand out. The first was the wish to determine in advance what should be said on the pilgrimage, as if the government were afraid of the event. For example, on June 4 all the morning newspapers published the same headlines and the same lead article on the Pope's arrival, with the same photo of the pontiff being welcomed by Edward Gierek, first secretary of the Party.[20] The second objective was to conceal any signs attesting to popular mobilization during the pontiff's visit. The communist government refused to see the Pope manage what it was incapable of achieving, that is, gathering immense crowds without any constraint. This instruction to journalists made a laughing stock of Polish television: "cameramen invariably managed to show John-Paul II surrounded only by trees, clouds, nuns, choirs, members of the clergy and sometimes a few elderly people."[21] But this framing of the Pope—literally and figuratively—fell apart. The impact of his visit to Poland was so strong and generated so much enthusiasm that the censorship seemed ridiculous. Actually, through this first visit, John-Paul II boosted Poland's morale in three ways: by fortifying the Poles' identity; by solemnly announcing their return to Europe, over and above the East-West divide; and through international TV coverage that gave his visit a global dimension.

Firstly, fortifying the Poles' identity. By emphasizing the history of the common origins of the faith and the nation, the Pope showed how much communism had failed in its project to sever the link between Poland's national and religious consciousness. As Patrick Michel explained, "by making God the only category that it refused to integrate ideologically, the communist government set the Pope up as an ideal vehicle for challenging its own legitimacy."[22] After the release of Cardinal Stefan Wyszynski in 1956, the Polish Catholic Church had been tolerated by the regime, which granted it some freedom of publication. The Pope's visit was therefore unexpected recognition for the Church. It urged its members to celebrate the event by acclaiming this Pope who had been one of its own and who had proved to have a formidable talent for communication. Yet the first moments of his encounter with the population were not particularly intense. On the road from the airport to Victory Square in Warsaw, where he was to celebrate his first mass, the crowd's welcome was luke-warm. Later, however, during this mass that brought together 300,000 people, when the Pope exclaimed: "No one can exclude Christ from the history of mankind in any part of the world! Excluding Christ from the history of humanity is a crime against humanity!," he triggered his "first wave of applause; immense, prolonged, like a liberating cry, a signal that everything had become possible."[23] After that, the people's jubilation never waned throughout the pontiff's historical trip.[24] People went out into the streets as they had never dared to do before. They were no longer afraid. They spoke to one another and telephoned one another to discuss the event. As Bernard Lecomte noted, "for a week, from mass to mass, a nation has been shaking itself off and proudly lifting up its head. Millions of people, accustomed for the past three decades to talking honestly only with their families, in small groups, and to keeping quiet in public, have become aware of their numbers, their existence, their strength."[25] Through the Pope a new way of being in public was born. People sang and prayed together in the streets, their eyes sparkling. These warm crowds, which seemed to surprise even themselves, formed a huge community.

The election and visit of John-Paul II also contributed to opening Poland up to the West, notwithstanding the strategic partitioning of the continent. Poles had the impression of being recognized and protected a little more, knowing that they had an echo chamber in Rome since the Pope was one of them. And the Pope had just announced a new vision of

Europe: a Catholic Europe, of course, but one that disregarded borders and divisions into blocs. For John-Paul II, Poland was both the model and the centre, as he solemnly proclaimed in his sermon at Gniezno. This bond between Poland and Europe was again emphasized during his farewell ceremony at Jasna Gora, which drew the largest crowd in that first visit (close to a million people): "Our Lady of the Mountain," he declared, "I consecrate to you Europe and all the continents, I consecrate to you Rome and Poland united in the person of your servant."

Thus, well before Gorbachev, John-Paul II proposed a vision of Europe that, rooted in the continent's religious past, led to an opening up of Poland, enabling it to break free of the Soviet yoke. But he was aiming further than his home country, thinking of all Christians in the communist bloc. To add force to his message, he traveled with a squad of catholic prelates from other Soviet Bloc countries.

The power of words was enhanced by that of images. Through media coverage of the visit, the utopia started to come true. A real opening up of Poland's media was witnessed. This first visit of a Pope to a communist country drew the attention of media throughout the world, far more than had his preceding visit to Mexico. Some 1,200 journalists were there, from tens of countries. It was as though, through them, Poland had crossed the wall for a few days, as though the huge crowds that had come to hail "their" Pope, announced that communism was well and truly dead in their country, and that it had been unable to destroy the people's deepest beliefs. Hence, the Pope triggered the events that corresponded to his announcements.

These demonstrations were all the more spectacular since television was present on the scene this time. Western TV crews were able to film unfettered in a communist country, and to relay images of an event that was neither sport nor art. Radio was of course also present, and more so than ever. The BBC and VOA were granted authorization to send a special correspondent to Poland, although RFE was refused that permission. It consequently went to considerable lengths to cover the event in various ways. The radio station took the "white line" of Radio Vatican, which enabled it to broadcast all the Pope's speeches live, in Polish.[26] Naturally, RFE and RL broadcast special programs to the other communist bloc countries as well.[27] This use of cross-reporting, so dear to RFE, was essential for informing populations whose media barely covered the Pope's visit at all. RFE was highly skilled in this technique; it analyzed and passed on news as it came in from the Western agencies. It also innovated by drawing on an additional source of information: the images broadcast by West German and Austrian TV channels. By watching them, the RFE journalist could describe scenes that were censored in Poland.

This projection on TV screens around the world was something very new for a communist bloc country. Thanks to Mondovision, up to one billion people watched the Pope's visit to Poland. Daniel Dayan and Eliu Katz described this as an example of "ceremonial television," in which certain channels in predominantly catholic countries offered special programs that totally disrupted the normal program schedule.[28]

But the curtain ended up dropping again. The Pope returned to Rome, the eyes of the West turned away, and the crowds dispersed. Was everything over? No. Millions of photos remained, along with tapes on which the Pope's speeches had been recorded. Texts and important declarations on individual freedom, human rights, the refusal of materialism, and European Catholicism, among others, were all subjects of meditation and discussion for many months, in small groups throughout Poland. Although physically absent, the Pope's presence could still be felt; he had given the Poles hope, whether they were believers or not. More than ever before the church had the function of a refuge, not so that the Poles could withdraw from the world, but to enable them to discuss world affairs. Via its non-profit organizations, the Polish church fostered public debate, even critical public action—a fairly widespread function of religious organizations in "regimes with limited pluralism."[29] The profound impact that the Pope's visit had had on people's minds could not possibly fail to have an equivalent effect on public opinion. When? How? No one knew. For months the Poles spoke and spoke again about the boosting of their morale that many of them had experienced during the pontiff's 10-day visit. This was when another history started to play out: not only that of the intellectuals, nor that of the Church, but that of the working classes, precisely (was this pure coincidence?) in one of the areas that Jean-Paul II had not been authorized to visit: the Baltic coast.

Gdansk, 1980: from reclaiming speech to seeking national entente

Extensive research has been devoted to the working class history of this region, deeply rooted in the post-WWII history of Poland's peasantry. Many workers employed at the Baltic shipyards were of peasant origin (the best example being Lech Walesa himself), and these common origins largely explain the rural areas' support for the strikes. Several studies highlight the importance of the working classes' memory, without which the dynamics of the social movement in 1980 cannot be understood.[30] For 10 years this region had been marked by the memory of the Polish army's violent repression of the workers' uprising on December 16 and 17, 1970, especially in Gdansk, where there were nine deaths.[31] During the 1970s this tragedy was a veritable state taboo that the official media persistently blacked out. But throughout the Baltic region the memory of the tragedy remained alive, especially since the Polish media had failed to cover it. That was why the demand for a monument to the victims of 1970 soon emerged in the working classes. It was to be one of the first demands of the strikers in 1980.[32]

The workers' memory was still alive through the forms of action and organization chosen by the strikers. In December 1970, they had quit work to set fire to the Party premises, and had been violently repressed. Subsequent to that they had withdrawn to their places of employment, where they rediscovered strike action on the job. This experience led them to remain at the shipyards in 1980 and to be extremely careful not to provoke state repression. Their desire to limit themselves to a nonviolent struggle was more than a moral issue, but not simply a matter of tactical pragmatism either; they had learned from past failures, starting with the repression of the Hungarian uprising in 1956. The choice of civil resistance was a watershed in a country where violence seemed to have attended every major historical event until then. It was evidence that, in certain circumstances, a people can depart from its own tradition and prove to be surprisingly innovative.[33]

The strikes of the summer of 1980 can be interpreted in two contrasting ways. The first, defended by such sociologists and historians of social movements as Roman Laba and Laurence Goodwyn, celebrate the workers' experience. They claim that it was instrumental in the Gdansk strikers' choice of a strategy in 1980.[34] The second interpretation, developed by the actors themselves or engaged observers like Adam Michnik and Timothy Garton Ash, emphasizes the decisive function of intellectuals in the way the movement was conducted.[35] The experience built up by the KSS-KOR, which appealed to workers to avoid violence and to set up strike committees within the shipyards, was one of the most important factors.

It is difficult to settle for one of these two interpretations as they clearly appear to be complementary. When the government made the decision on July 1, 1980, to increase food prices for the third time in 10 years, it created a situation that was to facilitate the encounter and interaction of these two histories, these two memories. The series of strikes that broke out across the country in July 1980 afforded the opportunity for the most determined workers and the most active KSS-KOR militants to meet. The latter fulfilled a communication function between groups of strikers and kept the Western media up-to-date on the situation.

Irrespective of the importance granted to any specific type of actor in the crisis, another interpretation is possible, one that focuses on the importance of communication processes in the birth and evolution of the Lenin shipyard strike, a crucial spot in the confrontation and negotiation with the government. By identifying the key points in their development we reveal a history with three main protagonists: the strikers and their supporters; the representatives of the government; and journalists.

The strike as a speech movement
The strike, prepared by the small committee of free trade unions, started on August 14 at 6 a.m. Bogdan Borusewicz had been responsible for producing 12,000 leaflets distributed in the trains that started running from 4 a.m, taking the workers to the shipyards. The slogan hit home because it emphasized two demands to which the workers were particularly sensitive: the reinstatement of Anna Walentynowicz, a highly popular colleague who had been fired the previous week, and a pay rise of 2,000 zlotys to offset price increases.

As soon as the strike was launched, the modes of communication and organization opted for played a decisive part in structuring it. Lech Walesa was immediately recognized as the natural leader of the movement in the first direct confrontation with management, when he added two further demands: his own reinstatement, and the erection of a monument to the victims of December 1970. One of the strikers' first actions was to take over the radios in the shipyards. These consisted of a sound system normally used by management to broadcast messages and instructions to the 16,000 workers on site. The strikers immediately appealed to their colleagues, over the loudspeakers, to go to their workshops (of which there were over a hundred) and to elect one or two delegates mandated to defend specific demands. The elected delegates (about a hundred) then appointed a 20-member strike committee, of which Walesa was the spokesperson. A team of stewards was also formed to strictly control access to the shipyards, while a technical team was responsible for installing a large radio antenna for receiving RFE programs in the best possible conditions. The strikers knew that the Munich station would be talking about them within hours.

Taking control of the shipyards' sound system was highly symbolic. The installation, dating back to Stalin's days, was an effective tool for management to control the workers—and here those same workers were appropriating the system for their struggle against management! At the height of the Berlin East uprising on June 17, 1953, certain workers had used their company radio to tune in to RIAS. For them it was a way of identifying with the American station, but their listening was passive. In 1980, the Gdansk workers seized the company radio above all for the purpose of talking on it themselves. In this sense, the strike started as a "movement of speech": theoretically, everyone could have access to the microphone, express their frustrations and voice their opinion. The strike spawned a new public speech and consequently a new public debate that swiftly spread from the heart of the shipyards to their geographical limits, the main entrance. There, discussion groups were formed on either side of the fence, between the strikers and those who were prohibited from entering: their families, other inhabitants of Gdansk, and visitors from other areas in Poland or elsewhere.

Loudspeakers were soon installed facing the streets, so that the people who had congregated near the fence could follow the debates taking place in the shipyards. It was as if the workers' talk had set out to conquer the city and even the whole of Poland. As the strike spread, so did conversations about it, in the towns and cities of the Baltic coast and then throughout the entire country.

The fact of controlling radio in the shipyards gave the group the feeling of experiencing the same collective adventure. The living conditions resulting from the strike with occupation (living together, eating and sleeping together) had already brought the strikers closer together and helped to unite the group.[36] Walesa's charisma facilitated this collective cohesion: his gift for expressing things, his way of handling crowds, and his choice of a middle way that obtained consensus. "When I find myself in the middle of a crowd," he wrote in his memoirs, "I always know what the people want. I can just sense it, instinctively."[37] The shipyard sound system under the strikers' control created a common space for the group, enabling individuals to express themselves, creating an atmosphere with popular music, and broadcasting negotiations with management live. It was a way of not hiding anything from anyone, so that everyone could feel they were both witness and participant. The communists acted in secret; they, by contrast, wanted transparency. Walesa explained: "We knew that keeping everyone informed of the negotiations could be our strength. In this way, everyone could feel they were participating."[38] Negotiations with management started on the night of August 14. The director, Gniech, soon agreed to the reinstatement of Anna Walentynowicz and Lech Walesa, and the erection of a monument to the victims of 1970, but not to the 2,000 zlotys. The next morning, workers at the Commune de Paris shipyards in Gdynia near Gdansk, and at other firms in the area linked to shipbuilding, joined the strike. The public transport workers in the Gdansk district stopped work as well. At mid-day the local authorities, concerned about the strike spreading, cut off telephone links with the rest of the country. As in 1970, Gdansk and the surrounding areas were suddenly isolated. The situation became even tenser when the police besieged the shipyards to control access.

Negotiations were resumed at around 5 p.m. but floundered on the question of wages. On August 16, the third day of their struggle, the strikers were exhausted and management stepped up the pressure. The minutes of the negotiations show how it manipulated the foremen to marginalize Walesa and force the strikers to back down. In the early afternoon the company proposed a 1,500 zlotys increase and a cost-of-living bonus, provided that the strike was immediately called off. Walesa could see no alternative; on behalf of everyone he accepted the offer and decreed an end to the conflict. He had however failed to see that this compromise satisfied the workers of the Lenin shipyards but not their colleagues who were striking elsewhere, in solidarity with them, and had obtained nothing. As he left the negotiating room Walesa was attacked. "We've won!" he affirmed. "Like hell!" retorted a worker. "Look at what's happening in the shipyards [...]. People are calling you a 'traitor', a 'sellout', they despise you."[39]

At this point the strike was winding down but was started again on a new basis and with new actors. Lech Walesa immediately grasped the situation and revived the movement. He suggested that those who wanted to stop the strike went home, and those who wanted to continue it elected new delegates. The conflict entered into its second phase. In the late afternoon of Saturday, August 16, delegates representing 21 companies within a 62-mile radius arrived in Gdansk. On the night of August 16, they decided to form an inter-company committee (the MKS) and to draw up a new 21-point list of demands.[40] On the Sunday morning, a mass was celebrated in the shipyards and near the fences. The crowd was there but many workers had joined their families. Was the movement trying to find its feet? The answer was forthcoming the next morning when the Lenin shipyard workers returned en masse to carry on the struggle, while new delegates arrived from other companies on the coast. The Gdansk strikers had the support not only of their families but also of farmers in the area, who sent them food. From then on their industrial action was no longer for themselves but for others, with others, on behalf of society as a whole. Swept along by the momentum of their action, they were to become the spokespersons of an entire society that was tired of submitting to the communist yoke. Until then the official media had spoken little about the events, except in enigmatic terms. In contrast, from the evening of the 14th, RFE had announced the beginning of the Gdansk strike,[41] and the whole of Poland knew about it. The next day at 8 p.m., television broadcast a speech by Prime Minister Babiuch. In particularly harsh terms, he demanded an end to the strike, referring to the "allies' concerns" and to "hostile forces that are trying to exploit the situation."[42] On the Sunday evening, August 17, the first secretary of the Party in the city of Gdansk, Tadeusz Fiszbach, made a more moderate speech on regional radio and television. His declaration showed that the shadow of the 1970 tragedy was still present in the local authorities' minds. "As we remember these events," he said, "we have to show calm and level-headedness with regard to any decision to be taken. Our patriotic duty is to do everything in our power to prevent the industrial action from spreading further."[43] But this level-headed tone was belied on the Monday morning by the virulent message on pamphlets distributed in the city and dropped by airplane over the shipyards, inveighing against those who wanted to continue the strike. The authorities tried to influence the workers and attacked those whom it considered to be responsible for the action, that is, the KSS-KOR militants, whom they accused of having revived the strike. Rumor had it that those who wanted to go back to work would be beaten up by the strikers—an allegation that was soon denied over the shipyard radio.

In spite of its propaganda and maneuvering, the government was unable to contain the wave of strikes that broke out on Monday, August 18, throughout the coastal region and then the interior as well. From the point of view of communication, the importance of structuring the movement shifted from the inside *towards the outside* of the shipyards. The creation of the MKS made it possible to bring together representatives from all the striking companies at the Lenin shipyards. But the delegates wanted to keep contact with their colleagues who had remained on site, and the strikers hoped to rally workers from other firms, who had not yet embarked on industrial action. This meant that they needed to create a communication network of their own, through which they could coordinate and consolidate the movement and thus exert maximal pressure on the government. As telephone lines with Gdansk were still down, they set up a system of messengers to carry news and instructions to workers at all firms on the coast and further afield, whether they were already on strike or wanting to join.

In this endeavor the delegates made extensive use of tape recorders to record MKS debates and negotiations with management. That had not been the case in Prague in 1968: the Czech resistance had not been accustomed to using recordings, and individuals had no tape recorders to carry around. In 1980 the Gdansk strikers used this tool in two ways: first, to record negotiations with company management in full, so that everyone could have access to what was said; and second, to send the content of these debates or negotiations to other parts of the country, to encourage strikes there as well. In this respect, the Gdansk strike was a movement "of speech": speech was conveyed from place to place so that everyone could be made aware of what was playing out in Gdansk. Most uninitiated listeners found these recordings stupefying. Jean-Yves Potel wrote: "After my first return from Gdansk, on August 26, I had to take out my tapes, people had to listen to them, to read my pamphlets, before they believed me. Everything seemed so incredible!"[44]

The workers' delegates served as messengers, but when some were arrested the members of the local Gdansk groups volunteered for this action. Not being workers themselves, they were more likely to get through police roadblocks by inventing various pretexts. They traveled to Szczecin, Wroclaw, Elblag and dozens of other places in the country. Some succeeded, taking with them tape recordings, pamphlets and instructions from the MKS. Others were arrested by the militia driving around Gdansk and its outskirts in unmarked cars. These vehicles were however spotted by passers-by, who passed their registration numbers on to the MKS. The committee then broadcast the numbers by loudspeaker to warn everyone. The Gdansk workers thus used the same technique as the Czechs had done in 1968, to identify and single out unmarked police cars.

Laurence Goodwyne sees this "war of mail" as the most decisive factor in the development of the strikes. The letters and parcels contained in-depth knowledge of the movement, what she calls "hard-movement knowledge," that is, details of the strikes, instructions on how to join the MKS, and so on. In this way, a horizontal communication network was built from Gdansk, "beyond the ken of remote sympathisers in far-off places, whether they were KOR, Radio Free Europe, or the Polish Pope."[45] Bonds of solidarity were gradually formed between the strikers at various companies and in this way the movement necessarily became more cohesive. As workers at more and more companies downed tools, the specter of a general strike seemed increasingly real for the government.

The immobile battle 157

Agreeing and making oneself heard
While the movement was built up through speech, this speech also had to be directed towards the government, to put pressure on it. These two inextricably linked dynamics can be summed up in two verbs: agreeing, and being heard (and understood)*.

For the workers it was important always to agree, literally. Throughout the strikes the sound system constituted the common space for speech, through which the conflict was to develop and to be resolved. As new strikers' delegates from other companies arrived in Gdansk, they took turns to talk on the radio, introduce themselves, state their claims, etc. The public applauded them every time. As in 1956 in Hungary, radio enabled them to present themselves, but this workers' speech was less constrained by communist ideology. In the permanent forum that the Lenin shipyard was becoming, the workers talked about themselves, told their personal stories, expressed their resentment, described the difficulties of everyday life, and so on. Of course, the workers also had to agree on the basics, that is, on common demands, and consensus was obtained on the platform of 21 demands drawn up on the night of August 16 by the MKS. It defined one of their main demands as the creation of a "free trade union, independent of the Party and employers"—an idea formulated during the events of 1970.

Several other demands pertained to information and communication, especially the one that came third on the list: "respect freedom of expression, printing and publication," which implied putting a stop to repression against independent publications, and "opening the mass media to representatives of all faiths."[46] The strikers did not however demand the abolition of censorship. On this point and others, Bogdan Borusewicz acted as a moderator: "It was the abolition of censorship that led to the [Red Army's] intervention in Prague in 1968," he explained. "You've got to leave them a way out."[47] Finally, the strikers also needed to agree in a third way: they wanted to be able to enter rapidly into contact with one another, throughout the network of companies that were striking. While the mail system was one solution, it naturally could never be a substitute for the telephone. That was why the MKS laid down as a condition for any negotiation, the restoration of telephone lines between Gdansk and the rest of the country.

---

*Translator's note: in French the author plays on the verbs *"s'entendre"* (to agree, to get along, to understand one another) and *"se faire entendre"* (to make oneself heard and/or understood). The infinitive *"entendre"* means to hear, to listen to, to understand, to intend or mean.

But as the movement grew it also had to be heard by the government. For that purpose, the workers' protest was based on two dynamics: social pressure generated by the extension of the strikes, and pressure from the international media. Both of these intensified steadily throughout the conflict. In the week of August 18 to 23, the movement grew more powerful, as the number of companies that joined the strike escalated from 156 on the 18th, to 253 on the 20th, and 388 on the 23rd. Membership of MKS increased accordingly, to 1,000. On August 18, workers at the Warski shipyard in Szczecin downed tools as well—a tremendous encouragement for the Lenin shipyard strikers. From then on Gdansk tried in every way possible to make contact with Szczecin: either through messengers or by demanding the restoration of telephone lines.

International media pressure was in itself a major asset for the MKS. Perhaps not all the workers were aware of this, but those who had been trained by the KSS-KOR surely were. The minutes of the negotiations on the second day of the strike reveal that Lech Walesa used the fact that the strike was already news in the United States to put pressure on management.[48] Was it still the 1970 precedent that was weighing on the future of the conflict? Whether that was the case or not, barely 72 hours after the beginning of the strike, several representatives of the Western media were already there, and not the least known: in particular, Marian Kafarski for AFP, Christopher Bobinski for the *Financial Times*, Bernard Guetta for *Le Monde*, and Peter Gatter for ARD (West Germany's number one TV channel).

Unlike their colleagues at Szczecin, who wanted no contact with Western journalists,[49] the Gdansk strikers welcomed them with open arms. "We were received like messengers of freedom," recalled Bernard Guetta.[50] For two weeks these journalists were to live in phase with the strikes, discreetly at first, then more and more openly. Their role was all the more important as the telephone blockade prevented RFE from making direct contact with Gdansk. Moreover, the August 20 arrest of several members of the KSS-KOR in Warsaw (including Jacek Kuron and Adam Michnik) seriously undermined the communications network towards the West, established four years earlier. This weakness in the dissidence was compensated for by the Western journalists present in Gdansk. More than simply witnesses of the conflict, they became the strikers' allies. International media coverage of the strike, via the West, was one of the main factors of its impact.[51]

This dual pressure (internal and external) was to weigh more and more heavily on the main actors of Polish public life from the perspective of negotiations with the strikers. Such negotiation seemed absurd in a communist state where, by definition, the Party represented the interests of the working classes! But the dramatic events of December 1970 haunted the minds of strikers and authorities alike. The former affirmed that "everything is negotiable," while the latter seemed unresolved to use force. When Edward Gierek had been appointed first secretary of the Party after that tragedy, he had promised that as long as he was in office, workers would not be shot at. Theoretically, this refusal to resort to arms was therefore an incentive to seek a compromise. The Polish economy's vital need for funds from the West also pleaded in favor of a nonviolent solution. Yet the speech that Gierek made on television on his precipitated return from vacation on August 18 could hardly be seen as an opening. While he agreed to examine some of the strikers' material demands, he refused to consider those that he deemed to be political, claiming that they were put forward "by irresponsible, anarchist and antisocialist elements." That same evening, the 7:30 TV news emphasized the "huge wastage that certain work stoppages have occasioned." The next day Gierek affirmed that 34 boats were waiting in Gdansk harbor, adding that "60,000 lemons are rotting in one of the holds of one of them"—a detail that had the entire Poland laughing.

But this propaganda was not to last. The strike movement was too strong and its consequences could be serious.

New players came onto the scene, starting with the church, which traditionally acted as moderator in this type of situation. That was exactly the position that Cardinal Wyszynski adopted in his August 19 and 26 sermons. Exceptionally, these were broadcast by television, the first one partially and the second one in full. The government thought it could derive some benefit from this standpoint, but the strikers disagreed with the cardinal and thought that he had been censored. The episcopacy's silence on the matter left room for that possibility, allowing the workers to believe that he had indeed been censored. On August 22, 64 moderate intellectuals addressed an open letter (immediately broadcast by the Western radio stations) to the Polish Communist Party and the MKS, calling on both parties to initiate dialogue and negotiations. Two of the signatories, Tadeusz Mazowiecki and Bronislaw Geremek, immediately went to Gdansk to propose their services. There they created an expert committee to assist the MKS in negotiations. Their arrival was timely, as the reformist current within the Party was pushing more and more for negotiations with the strikers. On August 15, the politburo appointed a commission headed by Tadeusz Pyka, but he flatly refused to recognize the MKS as a legitimate partner. He was however replaced on August 21 by the deputy Prime Minister, Miechislas Jagielski, a man known for his openness. Jagielski agreed to negotiate with the MKS and even to visit the Lenin shipyards to start the first negotiations publicly.

Jagielski's arrival at 8 p.m. on Saturday, August 23, initiated the third phase of the strike. This first public dialogue, staged by the MKS, concentrated all the drama of the conflict. From the point of view of communication, there were the two axes described above: agreeing, and being heard and understood. This community of struggle, a micro-society of rebels, growing day by day, that had transformed the city of Gdansk into an open space where people spoke to one another differently, smiled as they hadn't smiled before and seemed to be rejoicing, had to hear what was going to be said. Once again, the sound system in the shipyards served as a physical link between individuals. People felt they had to be there to hear and see everything. Everyone could be a witness of what was about to be played out, not only the hundreds of MKS delegates gathered together in the works' council hall, but also the thousands of people congregated in the shipyards and outside, near the fences.

This public had no intention of remaining passive in the tug-of-war that was about to take place with the government. From witness it could become participant. The technical set-up had moreover taken that into account: the sound system had been installed not only in the negotiators-public direction but also the other way round. The public was therefore able to hear both parties and to voice its approval or discontent. Hence, at any point the members of each delegation could hear the reactions that their statements triggered in the audience outside. This participation of the public as a third party was strongly symbolic. It reflected the movement's firm desire for democracy, since the public that could make itself heard physically, representing—albeit on a small scale—the voice of an entire nation, was seeking political recognition. The government delegation clearly saw the immediate advantage that it could derive from this set-up. As Jagielski himself said repeatedly: "You hear me? Can you hear me?" to obtain the workers' assent—an easy way to win applause.[52] Bronislaw Geremek saw this participation by the public as a key factor in the negotiation dynamics. It "prevented a sort of consensus from settling in between the negotiators, to make sure that things didn't go too far in the name of the reason of state and the fear of the Soviet Union. In other words, both parties had a kind of obligation to produce results, relative to the demands of the public, that is, the workers."[53]

As they came together around the negotiating table for the first time, each of the two parties introduced themselves to the public, somewhat like two boxers before a match. The interactions between Walesa for the MKS and Jagielski for the government were less the beginning of a dialogue than the continuation of two monologues. The tone was affable but the discord obvious, and the question of communication kept arising. The strikers reiterated their demand for the telephone lines to be restored and repeatedly denounced the Polish media's malevolence towards them. They accused the Party press of misrepresenting their struggle. In that day's issue of *Trybuna Luda*, for instance, they accused the state of limiting the Catholic press' freedom. The MKS vehemently demanded the right to express itself on radio and television, to which Jagielski simply retorted that censorship was one of the underpinnings of the socialist state. Just before the session was adjourned, Walesa obtained agreement that each party could broadcast a communiqué on the regional radio. Although this concession basically solved nothing, it was significant: the strikers secured the right for the first time to express themselves via an official media organ.

When, around midnight, the government delegation left the shipyards, the crowd was in a state of collective inebriation. "The workers shouted at Walesa: 'A hundred years, let him live a hundred years!' Western photographers ran backwards to take the historical photo, jostling and shoving one another under the disgusted eye of Jagieslki. And as the bus drove off into the night the workers, cap or beret in hand, sang the national anthem."[54] The scene might bring to mind the Cannes film festival if the business at hand was not quite so serious. The strikers knew that they had won a major victory that night, for the government had come to them and the excited cohort of Western photographers was proof that the whole world had their eyes on them. But another—decisive—round was starting, for which the workers had very little experience: the negotiations.

Towards a national entente?

To win these negotiations the strikers had to maintain their cohesion at a peak. A very important event in this respect happened on the same day as the government delegation's arrival: the birth of a strike daily newsletter, carrying the name of the movement that was to develop in the following months from Gdansk: Solidarity (Solidarnosc). This publication clearly crystallized the expression of the group's identity in the crisis, and the workers immediately saw it as their own: "With each edition there were long queues in the stairway of the building where the MKS had its headquarters."[55] Modestly presented on an A4 sheet folded in half, with a tiny font size, the newsletter reviewed the events and published the MKS' communiqués, but also included poems and personal opinions. The 12th and

13th issues comprised a precise chronology of the conflict. Two printing presses produced the bulletin, with the assistance of workers and people from outside the shipyards.[56] As the government delegation was present, the verb *entendre* ("to agree" and "to be heard/understood") took on a different meaning: the goal was to reach agreement with the government and thus to lay the foundations for a national agreement, a *national entente*. Was this actually realistic?

Irrespective, it was the aim of the third phase. Implicit since the beginning of the conflict, national entente emerged clearly when the government emissaries showed their resolve to negotiate. They had arrived not only in Gdansk but also in Szczecin, where another deputy prime minister, Kazimierz Barcikowski, had started negotiations on August 21 with the shipyard strike committee. But all eyes were turned to Gdansk, both in Poland and in the Western media. The government emissaries' visit made the city more accessible to visitors, as police vigilance was relaxed around the Lenin shipyards. In the last week of August, eminent representatives of artistic and cultural circles arrived in Gdansk, notably the film director Andrzej Wajda, already well-known for *Man of Marble*. On August 25 a film crew also arrived at the Lenin shipyards. After an arduous battle within the state documentary cinema agency, it had managed to secure authorization and the means to go to the shipyards to make a movie on the strike. Headed by Andrzej Kolodynski and Bohdan Kosinski, the team obtained exclusive permission to film in the conference room where negotiations were held. The footage, immediately stored in a safe place, was later turned into the movie *Robotnicy 1980*, an invaluable document on the history of the conflict. In the same week, a new wave of Western journalists also appeared in Gdansk. About 30 European, United States and Asian TV crews operated within the shipyards. This international media amplification contributed to mobilizing some Western trade unions in support of the strikers, in the United Kingdom, France and even New Zealand.

The possibility of reaching a compromise increased with the changes agreed upon on August 24 at the plenary session of the Party politburo. Aware that he was challenged, Gierek staked his all. He broke away from the most conservative third of the politburo members, including the head of propaganda, Jerzy Lukaszewicz, and supported Jagielski in his role as negotiator. That evening the first secretary made a particularly important offer in a new televised speech: he promised "immediate trade union elections wherever the workers wanted them, by secret ballot, with multiple candidates, but within the framework of the current one-party state."[57]

For the first time the government had made a truly significant proposal. But the Gdansk workers rejected it. They were fighting for an independent union, not reforms to the existing one. As soon as the speech on TV ended they stood up together and sang the Polish national anthem, their voices drowning out the *Internationale*.

Rather than appeasing the workers, as Gierek intended, this new speech spurred them to push further and to remain steadfast on their main demands. Some Party leaders were already mobilizing to break away from Gierek and to propose the appointment of a new head to resolve the crisis.

These political developments triggered an opening in the official media, evident in both their tone and their content. The change was already perceptible on the Baltic coast where Tadeusz Fiszbach was still endeavoring to act as moderator. Regional radio and television reported the reality of the conflict more and more accurately, with precise details on the situation regarding transport, problems of bringing supplies into the city, etc. Trust in these local media was consequently revived and their credibility restored. On the lawns of the Lenin shipyards and in the city of Gdansk people listened to the radio "full-blast": either to Polish stations or, of course, RFE and the BBC. The national media also showed signs of détente. From August 20, the word "strike" was used and MKS's role was publicly recognized. After the appointment of a new director of television, some Party leaders, like Ryszard Wojna and Miechyslav Rakowski, were invited to read their articles the day before they were published. It was as if the authorities wanted to revive interest in their own press and to say to the population: "look at how we're busy changing." On August 27, the Communist Youth newspaper *Sztandar Mlodych* published the MKS's complete 21-point list for the first time, with a photo of the Lenin shipyards. This was unquestionably an "historical exploit."[58] But even though the media were experiencing real détente, censorship was by no means abolished. Nothing had been said yet, for example, of the 64 intellectuals' call put out on August 22, nor the arrests carried out on August 20 in the KSS-KOR. To protest against such omissions, Polish journalists spoke out in turn. About 30 of them, present in Gdansk and mostly correspondents for the Party press (notably *Trybuna Ludi* and the *Politika*), launched a public appeal on August 25: "We, Polish journalists, present in Gdansk during the strike, declare that much of the information published until now, and especially the way in which it has been commented on, does not correspond to what is really happening here. This is leading to disinformation."[59] Under pressure of the events, the first cracks were starting to show in the government's power sphere. The Hungarian insurrection of 1956 had produced the same phenomenon, but far more suddenly and dramatically.

These signs, encouraging for the strikers, had not yet resulted in any real progress in the Gdansk negotiations. From the first meeting on August 23, each new round would stumble against new difficulties. By August 25, the telephone lines had still not been reconnected and the government commission seemed to be backtracking on the principle of MKS's access to radio. Suddenly, on the night of August 25, things started to move again when local officials of the town of Gdansk announced that automatic phone lines with Warsaw had been restored. The two parties also came to an agreement on the principle of broadcasting the first 20 minutes of the negotiations on regional radio.

When negotiations were resumed at 10 a.m. on the 26th, Lech Walesa made an important preliminary speech. He declared that the strikers considered themselves the spokespersons of society, without for all that challenging the principle of "socialist property." "It's not against Poland's social system that we're striking," he pointed out. "It's to be able to create an independent trade union, which is our right."[60] That was the beginning of a tough six-day round of negotiations, in which the experts of both parties played a fundamental role. There were 13 members in all: three representatives of MKS, four of the government, and three experts for each party. The fact that the experts on both sides often frequented the same intellectual circles in Warsaw meant that they were talking the same language, acceptable to the authorities and therefore, indirectly, to Moscow. But these meetings, in which Poland's future was being played out, went against the principle of public negotiations. The grassroots workers had the feeling of being excluded, and when the talks were resumed in public, the sound system—by chance?—sometimes broke down, inevitably provoking the crowd's anger. It seemed that things were nevertheless moving towards an agreement on the point that was dearest to the strikers: the creation of an independent trade union. The Polish government could agree to this as it had signed the ILO (International Labor Organization) Convention 87 on the right to organize.

If the government seemed to want to reach an agreement quickly in Gdansk, it was perhaps to avoid paralysis throughout the country. The fear seemed justified, as Poland seemed to be heading straight for a general strike. Other cities and industrial centers were joining in the movement, especially Wroclaw, Rzeszow, Lodz, Warsaw and Nowa Huta. The industrial bastion of Silesia was threatening to follow suit. Rumors of Soviet intervention were growing and for several days many Poles had been stockpiling as if they were expecting a catastrophe.

On August 27, Moscow commented on the Polish crisis for the first time, in a Tass communiqué attacking the "subversive elements striving to join forces in Poland, to drive the country away from the socialist system."[61] The next day the tone of the Polish media was suddenly harsher.

The only newspaper to have published the 21 demands immediately denounced the idea of a free trade union, claiming that it was harmful to the Party, the state and the socialist system. It described the demands as excessive and attacked the Western media, accusing them of citing only anti-socialist discourse. Radio and television returned to the theme of the heavy economic losses incurred by the strikes, and presented optimistic reports on those firms that had gone back to work. On August 29, the newspaper *Zycie Warszawy* published a virulent attack on dissident circles and the journal *Kultura*. The army daily, *Zolnierz Wolnosci*, denounced elements of anarchy threatening the country's most basic interests, while *Trybuna Ludu* launched a pro-Soviet campaign in a long, unsigned front-page article, the title of which was in itself a whole program: "Poland's loyalty to its alliance with the Soviet Union is reaffirmed as the cornerstone of the reason of state."[62] Was this the harbinger of a return to a hard political line? Was the country heading for a use of force by the Soviets themselves or the Polish army? Rumors were rife, fed by a mysterious radio ham who announced the beginning of Soviet intervention. The religious authorities smelled the danger and, on August 27, urged Lech Walesa to launch an appeal for calm. Walesa did speak in these terms in an interview for Polish television, but it was not broadcast in Poland.[63]

On Friday, August 29, a feeling of stalemate prevailed at the Lenin shipyards. No one knew when the talks would be resumed or what they might yield. Many strikers expressed their frustration about not being kept informed of the negotiations, as they knew that they were drawing to an end. Western journalists complained of the same thing: "Why are more and more discussions being held in groups and sub-committees?" they asked. Was there a wish to betray the MKS? Gwiazda explained to them that "when there is no microphone, negotiations can proceed without fearing that every word on Poland's internal affairs might be broadcast throughout the world."[64] Several members of the editorial team of the *Solidarity* newsletter shared the workers' frustration. They accused the experts, and above all Mazowiecki, of practicing politics in the wings and behind closed doors. Admittedly, Mazociecki had attacked them as well, reproaching them for publishing irresponsible statements in the newsletter, perceived as the MKS organ. On August 30 an atmosphere of suspicion was still reigning among the grassroots strikers when Jagielski returned to Gdansk to finalize the agreements. In the morning the two parties eventually agreed on the right to create a "new, independent and self-managed" trade union. But when Jagielski left for Warsaw to obtain the Communist Party central committee's endorsement, the text was vehemently criticized by the delegates and grassroots strikers. Their aggressiveness was focused not only on the experts but also on Walesa, accused of manipulation, dissimulation and even betrayal. After 18 days of strikes, the longest in the history of Soviet Europe, it was not easy to settle for a compromise. Moreover, the strikers were weary, and afraid: afraid of losing, or perhaps even of winning. A close battle ensued between the MKS presidium and the experts, on the one hand, and the more radical, bitter strikers, on the other. Those who criticized the agreement touched on sensitive spots: recognition of the role of the Party leader, absence of guarantees on the release of political prisoners (especially those of the KOR), and geographic limitation of the new trade union to the Baltic coast. Andrzej Gwiazda was instrumental in ensuring that this community of struggle, built up over the preceding days and nights, remained reasonable. On the evening of the 30th, the draft agreement was reviewed, article by article. The text was made even more audacious, asking for the abolition of censorship. The MKS moreover issued an ultimatum to the government, demanding the immediate release of political prisoners. This was contrary to the advice of the experts, who were alarmed by the sudden radicalization that could compromise everything at the last minute. On the night of the 30th the wildest rumors circulated in the shipyards, on the imminence of Soviet intervention. Yet, just a few hours earlier the agreement on the creation of an independent union had been signed at Szczecin.

That same evening, special news flashes on Western TV bore witness to the importance of this historical event.

It seemed that the Lenin shipyards had experienced a collective psychodrama in the final hour, condensing all the fears and struggles that Central Europe had known since 1956. The next morning, August 31, the MKS lifted the previous day's ultimatum, accepted Jagielski's promise of the immediate release of prisoners, and softened its position on censorship, demanding that it be severely controlled. That afternoon the agreement was signed before television cameras from Poland and the whole world. The media were there to crown the event. For the occasion, Walesa wore a rosary, as if it were a religious ceremony. "Where's the text?" It was not there yet but that seemed to matter little. The two men symbolizing the incredible history of this conflict moved towards the microphones, half smiling. Then, suddenly, their words broke loose: simple, strong, historical. They congratulated each other for reaching a compromise and, without any prior consultation, their speeches coincided to emphasize the fact that a national entente was possible. "We have shown that, when they want to, the Poles can understand one another," declared Walesa. "Dear friends, throughout the strike we bore in mind the interests of the homeland." Jagielski went on in the same tone: "Dear all... there are neither winners nor losers. The main thing is that we have reached this agreement. Now we have to get down to hard work and that will be the best proof of our patriotism."[65] Walesa signed the agreement with a huge pen in the Polish national colors. Close to him the marble statue of Lenin stood imposingly; it had remained unscathed throughout the conflict.

This detail struck many observers. It contrasted sharply with the fate of Stalin's statue, pulled down and cut up by the Budapest insurgents in 1956, and revealed a phenomenon that may seem surprising for a social movement of such a large scale: it had produced no negative representation of its opponents, neither of the Polish communists nor of the Soviets. The movement's symbols were sacrifice (the monument to those killed in December 1970), religion (portraits of John-Paul II and the Black Virgin of Czestochowa), and the nation (the white eagle, and the national colors: red and white)—not vengeance. By decorating the fences around the shipyards with these symbols, from the very beginning of their action, the strikers put out a strong message to the public: the refusal of vengeance. From the outset, the movement thus produced symbols that did not invite opposition to—and that could even facilitate—the search for a national compromise. That day, August 31, the Poles were stunned; they were experiencing what could be called collective communion. National radio interrupted its usual program to broadcast the signing ceremony live. That evening on TV news all of Poland rediscovered Lech Walesa's face. People said of him: "He talks like a Pole." It was as if, through him, another type of public speech was being born: one which a large majority of the population wanted to hear and support.

International mediatization of the conflict and the upsurge of television

On the weekend of August 30 and 31, Poland was headline news the world over. An anecdote eloquently reflects the situation: on the Saturday evening at 10:15, TF1 (a French TV channel) interrupted the American series *Starsky and Hutch* with a special newsflash to announce the signing of the Gdansk agreements (with images of Walesa triumphantly carried by the workers). Evidently, the story of the Gdansk strikes fascinated public opinion, and huge audiences had been closely following Polish news. For once, events from the East were a success story!

Close to 150 journalists were present in Gdansk for the signing of the agreements with the government. Most of them were special correspondents who arrived after August 23, when Jagielski went to the shipyards to negotiate. In that week the Polish government had granted the visas that the journalists had been impatiently waiting for, sometimes for more than a week. A minority of foreign journalists had however already been there for some time: those from the news agencies (AFP, Reuters, Ansa, AP), from the French daily *Le Monde*, and from the leading West German TV channel (ARD). They were the ones who had helped to make the strike world headlines. Their early presence in Gdansk was no coincidence, for the news agencies were the oldest and most permanent source of Western news in the East; the source that endeavored to carry on functioning when the correspondents or special envoys from other media could not or did not want to go there. They had all sent a journalist from their Warsaw offices to Gdansk at the outbreak of the conflict. The presence of Bernard Guetta for *Le Monde* followed that of Thomas Schreiber in the 1956 Hungarian uprising and that of Michel Tatu in the Prague Spring of 1968. It was with Michel Tatu that, in 1966, *Le Monde* created a position for a permanent correspondent in Vienna, for the entire region of Eastern Europe.

The Austrian capital was a good post from which to observe the life of the peoples' democracies.[66] The journalist from West German TV, Peter Gatter, arrived at the Lenin shipyards as official correspondent for Poland. The two West German channels ARD and ZDF had opened an office in Warsaw in 1972, well before the French TF1 (1980) and the BBC (1981), in the dynamic of Willy Brandt's *Ostpolitik*.

On the whole, Western journalists were not harassed by the Polish authorities. Their working conditions were of course complicated by the telephone blockade imposed on Gdansk, which forced them to go to Warsaw almost every day if they wanted to phone, but their reports were not censored in any way. Only the Western TV crews encountered real obstacles, for they were compelled to obtain the technical cooperation of their Polish counterparts to develop, edit and broadcast their images on the Eurovision network.[67] At each of these three stages the heads of Polish television were able to invent a thousand technical or administrative reasons to slow down the production, thus precluding presentation of the footage on that evening's TV news in Western countries. To solve these "problems," the technicians of Polish TV served as accomplices. Without their help, Western TV channels would never have produced images of the shipyards almost daily. This help could moreover be provided only because their supervisors gave them instructions that were relatively unrestrictive, as they themselves received orders lacking clarity, from a party racked by internal conflict. The communist leaders were in a predicament: on the one hand they wanted to isolate Gdansk to smother the crisis; on the other, they wanted to know what was happening there. Peter Gatter later learned that the members of the central committee would meet to view the footage that his team had shot in the Lenin shipyards and that Polish TV was prohibited from broadcasting.[68] They allegedly did likewise with reports from the BBC and the British agency Vice News.

For several days, reports filmed in the Lenin shipyards by Bernard Guetta were the liveliest and most precise chronicle of the Gdansk strikes in the French press. His articles had a considerable impact in both the East and the West. In the West this was explained by *Le Monde*'s prestige. In the East, it was because France under President Giscard d'Estaing maintained excellent relations with the Polish government and First Secretary Edward Gierek.

Although radio proved to be the fastest medium in this crisis, television was fast catching up. Western viewers could watch the evolution of the strike daily, thanks to TV crews on site. Notwithstanding the problems mentioned above, footage shot in Gdansk in the morning could be broadcast the same evening on TV news. From August 18, French audiences could see photos and then live scenes filmed in the shipyards. On August 19, TF1 broadcast an interview with Jacek Kuron (shown again on the 21st, after his arrest), and on August 27 a first interview with Walesa. The second French TV channel, Antenne 2, did not send a correspondent to Gdansk but hooked onto Polish TV to broadcast excerpts from its news bulletin and especially the speeches of leading personalities (that of Gierek on the 19th, and of the Cardinal on the 26th). Owing to the collaboration of Jean Offredo, a journalist of Polish origin, the channel was able to nurture strong emotions among many TV viewers, who had the impression of experiencing the conflict live. Offredo's role was twofold: translating from Polish to French, and explaining Polish political culture to the French public. During the last two weeks of August, at the end of the summer holidays, Poland occupied television screens two or three times a day.

This unprecedented mediatization nevertheless had the effect of warping representations of the respective roles of the actors in the crisis.

For instance, the journalistic practice in illustrating the conflict through a personality symbolizing it, distorted people's vision of the movement.

From August 30, the Western media crowned Lech Walesa as "the King of Poland," as Bernard Guetta commented ironically. The West saw Walesa as the victor in the power struggle; he consequently deserved all the honors, which also meant all the attention. The phenomenon was inevitable, for the man did indeed have charisma, and any resistance spawns its own myths, starting with the idealization of its heroes. This excessive personalization of the resistance leader overshadowed the weight of other personalities who had also played a crucial role (especially Anna Walentynowicz and Andrzej Gwiazda), and masked the strength and diversity of the social movement.

Many French commentators likewise put too much emphasis on the church's role in the conflict. "Even today," noted Jean-Yves Potel, "people still remember Gdansk as a strike led by priests."[69] Scenes on television, showing strikers taking communion in the grounds of the Lenin shipyards, probably strengthened this type of representation. But the image, without being false, was in this case misleading; it suggested a questionable interpretation of reality. The fact that the advent of a Polish Pope was instrumental in the genesis of this crisis, to allay fears and spur people into action, is beyond doubt. But the new actors who emerged during the crisis, attesting to the renaissance of civil society, sought to unfetter themselves from ties with the church. Analysis of the conflict shows, moreover, that the strikers did not appreciate intervention by the Catholic hierarchy.

These warped perceptions of the Polish strikes were inevitable. More importantly, and in spite of them, the strikers induced currents of sympathy in many countries throughout the world.

They turned their struggle into a message: that of freedom. From Paris to New York, Tokyo to Oakland, individuals and movements recognized one another in their struggle. This international movement of sympathy expressed itself forcefully when it was put to the test by martial law, promulgated in December 1981.

Impossible dialogue?
December 13, 1981, and consequent events

The common search for a compromise underlying the ultimate phase of the Gdansk negotiations largely defined the main political question: what would future relations between the government and society be? On what conditions and in which areas could the communist authorities agree to no

The immobile battle 171

longer be the "social everything," thus acknowledging that society had a space for initiative and autonomy? In this respect, the fundamental reform introduced by the Gdansk agreements was truly revolutionary, for it totally changed the rigid institutional framework of the party-state that had prevailed in Poland for the past three decades. The right to create an independent trade union and therefore to strike (Points 1 and 2 of the agreement), paved the way for open expression in society, outside of Party rules. The following months saw the emergence of new actors who, with the creation of branches of the Solidarity union, attested to the existence of a real civil society. Throughout Poland we witnessed public speaking and responsibility at the grassroots level, which Karol Modzelewski described as historical. "Solidarity was a unique mass movement in the history of modern Europe," he wrote. "A large majority of Poles experienced personal freedom for the first time in their lives. [...] At the grassroots level people created the structures of a new trade union movement, with the feeling of building a new Poland on ground wrenched from the ubiquitous control of the Party and Moscow. In all the factories, hospitals, schools and offices, tens, perhaps even hundreds of thousands of natural leaders appeared spontaneously. They led their colleagues and accomplished unprecedented social self-organization."[70]

This formidable social momentum—concretized within a year by over 10 million new members of Solidarity—nevertheless encountered powerful political and institutional obstacles. Gierek's dismissal by Kania on September 5, 1980 (just as Gomulka had been replaced by Gierek after the 1970 crisis) raised hopes of a new political orientation inspired by the Gdansk agreements. But Solidarity had hardly been created when it came up against procedural maneuvers that hindered its registration with the administration. It furthermore soon proved impossible for its leaders to express themselves in the national media, as the Gdansk agreements had made no significant progress in this respect.[71] Without their own daily newspaper, they had to rely on Western radio stations when they wanted to address the Polish nation as a whole. From the point of view of the opposition's access to the media, the situation thus remained much the same as prior to 1980. The communist leaders were clearly determined to refuse Solidarity leaders access to television. The union threatened several times to use its only weapon—a general strike—to obtain the right to make itself heard. At its first congress, September 5, 1981, dialogue seemed almost impossible and confrontation inevitable. The refusal of Polish television to broadcast the debates was a subject of acute conflict.[72] Behind the scenes, General Jaruzelski's power grab had already been in preparation secretly for several months.

When martial law was declared on December 13, 1981, the whole of Poland was in a state of shock. The collective trauma was so intense that the people spontaneously spoke of a "state of war," as if the situation were comparable to the Nazi occupation of 1940.[73] The repression, which many observers had been expecting from the end of August 1980, was finally there.

Compared to former crises in Central Europe, this delay was paradoxically a victory, in a sense. The Hungarian uprising had lasted only 10 days in 1956, and the Prague Spring nine months in 1968. In Poland, Solidarity "made it" for 18 months. The fact that Moscow was not directly involved in the operation—even though General Jaruzelski would have liked it to be[74]—can be considered the result of a sort of "civil dissuasion" exercised by the Polish people on Moscow. In this respect, the evolution of Soviet military interventionism in Central Europe was significant: the USSR had acted on its own in 1956 in Hungary; in 1968 it no longer operated alone in Czechoslovakia, where it involved the other countries of the Warsaw Pact; and in 1981, it left it to the local leaders to do the job. This process of "self-normalization" in Poland was physically less brutal than the major events mentioned above: there was neither terror, nor mass deportation (as in post-1956 Hungary), nor large scale-purges (as in post-1968 Czechoslovakia).

This did not, however, mean that General Jaruzelski's operation was ineffective. The fact that the army was the main instigator was formidable for the founders of Solidarity, for its prestige among the population was high, and it was precisely the army that had the job of bringing the union into line. Technically, the operation was a success: thousands of arrests made in one night decapitated the union—all of its leaders were arrested except one[75]—and lastingly weakened its regional and local structures. It was probably from a psychological point of view that martial law most effectively attained its goal of numbing the population's spirit of resistance. On this front the media were the main instrument. During the 1980 crisis the communication battle had turned to the strikers' advantage; this time the Polish authorities were determined to ensure that they were the only ones to benefit. Like any well-planned state of emergency, the operation was based on the interruption of all communication with abroad and the intensification of censorship. The jamming of Western radio was resumed, as in the days of the Cold War. At home, the manipulation of the domestic media had two objectives: making people afraid, and shattering any hopes of change. Symbolic of this propaganda was the appearance, on the evening of December 13, of journalists in military uniform on television. The message seemed to be:

"No more games to see who's the strongest; we're in control and everyone must get back to work."[76] In the following weeks, hundreds of journalists lost their jobs.

Another key element in the media apparatus was the press conference given by government spokesman Jerzy Urban. Only journalists from the Western press were invited, and they were allowed to ask the most disturbing questions. That evening, excerpts were presented on Polish television. The program was interesting, sometimes amusing and almost always tragic because Urban, who had "deliberately chosen to be Jaruzelski's decoy,"[77] was thoroughly cynical. Very soon the slogan "Urban is lying" became popular, but this bothered him little; his program had been a success. For several years it remained the most formidable feat of collective demoralization that the country had known.

Urban's aim had been to put across the message: "Look, you can say anything you want to in Poland, but it's pointless." In parallel, Polish television increased the number of movies and series from the West in its program schedule, obviously to keep the minds of the masses off the hardships of daily life.[78] The same tendency was also evident in the programming of several other TV channels in the East during that period.[79]

But although General Jaruzelski was able to break the Solidarity union, he was less successful in his attempt to rally society to his enterprise of national recovery. His team lacked legitimacy, both at home and abroad. On the international front, martial law triggered multiple protests, even though the Western states, as usual in this type of situation, showed far more reserve than did their public opinion. New in the West was however the revival, on December 17, 1981, of Polish programs on RFI (Radio France Internationale), which had been interrupted in 1974. The RFI program was clearly appreciated by a population that was sensitive to anything that broke its isolation in this difficult period.[80] Additionally, an international network to support Solidarity was set up in the West, mainly from Belgium. It specialized in smuggling into Poland anything that could contribute to the expression of free speech (journals, magazines, books, paper, photocopiers, walky-talkies, etc.). At the same time an underground Polish journalists' society was formed, chaired by Stefan Bratkowski. As for the man who symbolized the Solidarity ideal, Lech Walesa, he never sided with the powers that be. Released in November 1982 under pressure from the Church, he immediately declared: "I didn't sign anything." A Dubcek-like scenario never happened in Poland. The ideal of solidarity remained intact, but as a myth, in the absence of the social forces needed to put it back into action. An underground resistance network was nevertheless formed, under the impetus of Zbigniew Bujak. Many clandestine newsletters appeared, constituting the largest and most diverse parallel, private press and publishing market in the entire communist bloc. Timothy Garton Ash commented that "the contemporary Polish version of Descartes is 'I print, therefore, I am.'"[81] A new communication tool also appeared: the video-cassette recorder. People would meet secretly at friends' homes or in church buildings to watch banned videos such as *Robotnicy*. Hence, despite the party-state monopoly on the media, the Poles maintained access to different sources of information.[82]

On the political front the divorce between the government and society was obvious. It showed above all in the striking gap between the content of the official media and the social aspirations of the public—a recurrent focus of interest among Polish sociologists of communication.[83] In the second half of the 1980s, the question of compromise as a solution to the crisis resurfaced. It was to be a way of reverting to what had started to appear just after the Gdansk agreements, and of admitting that several years had been wasted. One man was instrumental in facilitating this internal evolution from the outside: Mikhail Gorbachev.

Notes

1. Marguerite Duras, *L'été 80*, Paris, Ed. de Minuit, 1980, p. 53 and 61.

2. From 1968 to 1980, the number of TV sets increased considerably. EBU statistics show that the number of TV sets in Western Europe and Scandinavia increased from 62 million in 1968 to 166 million in 1980. *Revue de l'U.E.R. (Union Européenne de Radiotélévision)*, n° 114 (March 1969) and Vol. XXXII, n° 2 (March 1981), Vol. XLI, n° 2.

3. Especially in French: Krzysztof Pomian, *Solidarité, défi à l'impossible*, Paris, ed. Ouvrières, 1982 and Georges Mink, *La force ou la raison. Histoire sociale et politique de la Pologne (1980-1989)*, Paris, La Découverte, 1989. One of the most interesting books in Polish is that of Andrzej Friszke, *Opozycja polityczna w Polsce*, Varsovie, ZNAK, 1994.

4. Leszek Kolakowski, "Thèses sur l'espoir et le désespoir" in *Pologne : une société en dissidence*, edited by Z.Erard and G.M. Zygier, preface by Alexander Smolar, op. cit. p. 92.

5. On the history of this journal, see the excellent article by Constantin Jelenski "Kultura : la Pologne en exil. Lieux et milieux" in *Le Débat*, February 1981, n. 9, p. 59-71.

6. Alexander Smolar, "L'ancien régime et la révolution en Pologne" in *Esprit*, June 1981, p. 113.

7. The objectives of the KSS-KOR were broader, including the struggle against any form of political or racial repression and the defense of all human rights organizations.

8. A history of the KOR was written by one of its founding members: Jan Jozef Lipski, *KOR, A History of the Worker's Defense Committee in Poland, 1976-1981*, Berkeley, University of California Press, 1985.

9. This was a way of "nationalizing" RFE, presented thus as the fourth national program of Polish radio, in addition to the three official ones.

10. To protect the signatories of the petition, who did not send their letter to Western correspondents in Warsaw, Jan Nowak sent the text of the letter to the correspondents. They then wrote a dispatch accrediting the information, which enabled RFE to report the news by citing the agencies' dispatches. In this way, the Polish authorities could not accuse the signatories of having made contact with RFE. Cf. Jan Nowak, *Polska Z Oddali, Wojna W Eterze-Wspomnienia*, Vol. II, op. cit. p. 119.

11. At the time, it was impossible to call West Germany directly. Kuron was therefore unable to call the RFE headquarters in Munich—which in any case would have been very risky. Instead, he had to contact friends or journalists living in countries accessible via an automatic phone call, mainly France and the United Kingdom. Once news reached these countries it could easily be sent to Munich, either directly or via the Polish section of RFE in Paris.

12. Jacek Kuron, *Maintenant ou jamais*, Paris, Fayard, 1993, p. 32. The Smolar brothers, Alexander and Eugenius, founded another important Polish emigration journal *Aneks*, in 1973. It was to make the KOR's theses known in intellectual circles specialized in Eastern Bloc countries.

13. Jacek Kuron, *Maintenant ou jamais*, op. cit. p. 33-34.

14. *Ibid.* p. 34.

15. Daniel Dayan, "Le pape en voyageur. Télévision, expériences rituelles et dramaturgie politique" in *Terrains*, n° 15, October 1990, p. 13-28.

16. Jean-Noël Jeanneney, *Concordances des temps*, Paris, Ed. du Seuil, coll. Points, 1991, p. 35.

17. On this subject see the highly detailed research carried out by Bernard Lecomte, *La vérité l'emportera toujours sur le mensonge*, Paris, Ed. JC Lattès, 1991.

18. The following three events were on the national network: the Pope's arrival with the reception at the Belvedere Palace given by the Party leadership and the state, followed by a mass and the laying of a wreath on the unknown soldier's tomb in Warsaw; a visit to Auschwitz; and, finally, the departure ceremony at Cracow airport. All the other events were broadcast only on local or at best regional TV channels, at varying times. Polish TV devoted an average of 15 minutes per day to the Pope's visit. Radio stations followed the same restrictions.

19. Published in an abridged form by *The Times* on July 2, 1979. Full text in *RFE Background Report*, July 15, 1979.

20. The only noteworthy exception to this discipline observed by the Polish press was the Cracow Catholic weekly, *Tygodnik Powszechny* that, despite censorship, managed to produce a report that accurately reflected the Pope's visit.

21. Paul Lendvaï, *Les fonctionnaires de la vérité. L'information dans les pays de l'Est*, Paris, Ed. Robert Laffont, 1980, p. 130.

22. Patrick Michel, *La société retrouvée. Politique et religion dans l'Europe soviétisée*, Paris, Fayard, 1988.

23. Bernard Lecomte, *La vérité l'emportera toujours sur le mensonge*, op. cit., p. 135-136.

24. During his 10 days in Poland, John-Paul II pronounced 30 homilies and sermons, addressing a total of some six million Poles who went to listen to him.

25. Bernard Lecomte, *La vérité l'emportera toujours sur le mensonge*, op. cit., p. 137.

26. Interview with Andrzej Arzeczunowicz, former member of the Polish section (March 18, 1992). The "white line" was the original sound emitted by Radio Vatican without any commentary. RFE thus acquired the right to broadcast the "Pope's sound" throughout his entire visit. In 10 days, the Polish section broadcast close to 90 hours of programs.

27. In parallel, the Hungarian and Czech services broadcast a total of 12 to 13 hours of special programs, and the Romanian, Bulgarian, Lithuanian and Russian services, two to three hours.

28. Daniel Dayan and Eliu Katz, *La télévision cérémonielle*, Paris, PUF, 1996.

29. Guy Hermet, "Les fonctions politiques des organisations religieuses dans les régimes à pluralisme limité" dans *Revue Française de Science Politique*, Vol. XXIII, n° 3, June 1973.

30. Jean-Yves Potel, *Gdansk, la mémoire ouvrière*, Paris, Ed. François Maspero, 1982.

31. Popular hearsay increased the total number of deaths to 400 or even 500. But this figure has never been confirmed. The number of deaths established by the state prosecutor of Voivodie in February 1971 remains the lowest: 16 killed and 177 injured at Szczecin, 18 killed at Gdynia, 9 at Gdansk and one at Elblag. See the discussion on these figures in Jean-Yves Potel, *Gdansk, la mémoire ouvrière*, op. cit., p. 31-35.

32. In Gdansk an unofficial public commemoration was also held on the site of the tragedy (Gate 2 of the shipyards). Every year attendance reflected the growing mobilization in the region. The crowd swelled from 800 in 1977 to 3,000 in 1979—a considerable figure considering the measures of intimidation and preventive arrests.

33. On this issue, see the articles by Krzysztof Pomian, Leszek Kolakowski and Sewerin Blumsztajn in the special issue of the journal *Alternatives Non-violentes*, "Pologne : La résistance civile," n° 53-54, winter 1984.

34. Roman Laba, *The Roots of Solidarity. A Political Sociology of Poland's Working-class Democratization*, Princeton University Press, 1991 and Laurence Goodwyn, *Breaking the barrier, The rise of Solidarity in Poland*, Oxford University Press, 1991.

35. Adam Michnik, *Penser la Pologne. Morale et politique de la résistance*, Paris, Ed. La Découverte/Maspéro, 1983, and Timothy Garton Ash, *The Polish Revolution: Solidarity*, New York, Charles Scribner's Sons, 1984.

36. On this subject see "Religious celebrations" in Victor and Edith Turner, *Celebrations*, Washington DC, Smithsonian Institute Press, 1982, p. 205.

37. Lech Walesa, *Un chemin d'espoir*, Paris, Fayard, 1987, p. 208.

38. *Ibid*. p. 190.

39. *Ibid*. p. 207.

40. See below.

41. The Munich-based station had been alerted by several informers during the day, including Jacek Kuron himself, who had received a description of the beginning of the strike by telephone.

42. *The strikes in Poland*, Radio Free Europe Research, Munich, West Germany, edited by William F. Robinson, 1980, p. 141. For my study of the media I have used this excellent work of RFE. For the original French version of this book I however cited a source more accessible to French-speaking readers, that is, articles from the daily *Le Monde*, translated in this English edition.

43. *Le matin*, August 19, 1980.

44. Jean-Yves Potel, *Scènes de grèves en Pologne*, Paris, Ed. Stock II, 1981, p. 132.

45. Laurence Goodwyn, *Breaking the barrier*, op. cit., p. 366.

46. Pologne. Le dossier de Solidarité, *L'Alternative*, p. 44.

47. *Le Monde*, August 19, 1980.

48. "As everyone knows, people are coming here from everywhere, even from the United States. Over there they already know about us, don't they? So, there's so much publicity" (implying: so you'd better give in to our arguments), in Lech Walesa, *Un chemin d'espoir*, op. cit., p. 204.

49. See Olivier Mac Donald, "Poland Solidarnosc in action" in *Labour Focus on Eastern Europe*, Spring 1981.

50. Interview with Bernard Guetta, October 10, 1995.

51. See below.

52. On this point see the roneoed minutes of the August 26 session published in the journal *Autogestions*.

53. Interview with Geremek, July 3, 1993.

54. *Le Monde*, August 26, 1980.

55. Jean-Yves Potel, *Scènes de grève en Pologne*, op. cit., p. 102-103.

56. The first, which had a circulation of some 40,000 copies, was installed at the Lenin shipyards by the publishing house Nowa (sympathetic to the KSS-KOR). The second was that of the Commune de Paris shipyards at Gdynia. With more modern equipment, it produced between 60,000 and 80,000 copies, and over 100,000 in the last days of the strike.

57. *Le Monde*, August 26, 1980.

58. *The strikes in Poland*, op. cit, p. 163.

59. Bulletin n° 7 (August 27) in "Pologne. Le dossier de Solidarité," *L'Alternative*, January 1982, p. 28.

60. *Le Monde*, August 28, 1980.

61. *Le Monde*, August 29, 1980.

62. Cited in *Medias RFE*, p. 194.

63. An excerpt was broadcast on French TV the same day. See below.

64. Reported by Tadeusz Kowalik, one of the MKS experts: Tadeusz Kowalik, "Les minutes d'un compromis" in *Les Temps Modernes*, September 1983, p. 311-330.

65. *Le Monde*, December 2, 1980.

66. Bernard Guetta, who occupied this post in 1979, covered the Gdansk strikes for *Le Monde*. The French daily *Le Figaro* did likewise. It also had a permanent correspondent in Warsaw, Bernard Marguerite, who covered the events in 1980.

67. At the time, TV journalists were still working with 16-mm film.

68. Interview with Peter Gatter, November 25, 1995.

69. Interview with Jean-Yves Potel, October 6, 1995. See also *Quand le soleil se lève à l'Est*.

70. Karol Modzelewski, *Quelle voie après le communisme ?*, Paris, Ed. de L'Aube, 1995, p. 37-38. See the sociological study undertaken at the time by Alain Touraine, François Dubet, Michel Wieviorka, Jan Strzelecki, *Solidarité, Analyse d'un mouvement social (Pologne 1980-1981)*, Paris, Fayard, 1982.

71. Their only concrete result was the broadcasting of Sunday mass on radio and the drafting of a new bill on censorship that would make it mandatory to indicate when something had been censored.

72. In view of this refusal, Solidarity banned Polish TV from attending the congress. When the latter asked the TF1 (French TV) correspondent François Gault for his images, Gault—supported by his superiors—refused. The members of the congress applauded this decision. On January 15, 1981, François Gault (with Jean-Marie Cavada) organized for TF1 the first live interview with Lech Walesa for a Western TV channel. The story of this program is recounted in his book *Walesa*, Paris, Centurion, 1981.

73. For a description of this "state of war," see the survey undertaken by Gabriel Mérétik, *La nuit du général*, Paris, Ed. Pierre Belfond, 1989.

74. That is the version found in documents provided by Russian president Boris Yeltsin to Polish president Lech Walesa in September 1993. Cf. *Le Monde*, 29-30 September 1993.

75. All of them were in Gdansk. The only one who managed to flee was Zbigniew Bujak.

76. See Véronique Soulé's description of these TV journalists in uniform, in *Libération*, January 4, 1982.

77. Interview with Jerzy Urban, October 10, 1989.

78. Karol Jakubowicz, "Polish Broadcasting Studies in search of a 'Raison d'Etre'" in *European Journal of Communication*, Vol. 4, n° 3, September 1989, p. 276.

79. See, for example, the evolution of Eastern German television in Chapter 6.

80. See Part 1, Chapter 1.

81. Timothy Garton Ash, *The Uses of Adversity*, op. cit., p. 247.

82. In this respect Georges Mond spoke of "de facto pluralism" in the absence of a de jure pluralisme of the media. See, for example, Georges Mond, "Radio et télévision en Pologne" in *Annuaire européen d'Administration Publique*, 1984, p. 261-284.

83. Karol Jakubowicz and Stanislaw Jedrzejewski, "Polish Broadcasting: the Choices Ahead" in *European Journal of Communication*, March 1988, p. 91-111.

Escape: From television to the border, Berlin, 1989

In 1980 the Polish workers had managed to create the first real opening in the communist bloc. In 1989 the East Germans managed their escape. Thousands left for what they believed was the Western Eldorado. Those who got away chose the right moment, the opportunity afforded to the prisoner when the door is slightly ajar and the guard is dozing. That was the situation after May 2, 1989, when Hungary decided to abolish the Iron Curtain separating it from Austria. At last, a border that could be crossed. For years, people had watched West German TV programs and dreamed of going there and traveling. Now they were no longer content to escape via the small screen: they wanted to leave, "for real." It was out of the question to be striking for better wages or rights provided for in the constitution. That would imply that they still wanted to live in East Germany, when actually they wanted to leave. Their departure expressed more than a refusal of the regime oppressing them; it marked the final rejection of a system imprisoning them.

However, those who did still believe in the country and wanted to strive for change saw this as an irresponsible choice. Long before 1989, some members of East German society had mobilized public opinion against leaving. Churches, writers, artists and small independent groups, together or separately, planted the seeds of the unprecedented collective mobilization of autumn 1989. Tens, even hundreds of thousands of people filled the streets of East Berlin, Leipzig and Dresden, shouting: "We're staying here," "We are the people," "Free Elections," "No violence." These mass demonstrations were doubly surprising. First, they changed the face of East Germany overnight, bearing witness to the awakening of a society that had seemed completely undermined since the 1953 uprising. In the history of Soviet Europe, they also signified opponents' return en masse to the streets, whereas in Gdansk everything had played out elsewhere. This collective re-appropriation of the urban space, of the right to demonstrate in public, took a great deal of courage and audacity as the state had had the monopoly for the past 50 years, with its official parades. People had to overcome their fear and be prepared to face the repression that could strike at any moment, as it did on the night of October 4 in Dresden and three nights later in East Berlin. But factors outside the country also favored the emergence of this re-appropriation.

Compared to the early 1980s, the international context was transformed when Mikhail Gorbachev came to power in Moscow.[1] Gorbachev's project entailed significant changes in relations between the USSR and the Central and Eastern European countries. The leaders of these states soon understood that there was no longer any question of Moscow guaranteeing military intervention in the event of domestic unrest. It was the age of reform, not repression. From Warsaw to Budapest, the message was picked up immediately, and round tables marked the renaissance of institutional dialogue between the government and society. However, in East Berlin and Prague the leaders remained firmly attached to conservatism—even though the GDR had amended its constitution in 1974 with a clause permanently and irrevocably binding the East German state to the Soviet Union.

This paradoxical situation was a powerful factor of destabilization of the East German system, caught as it was between pressure at home from mass emigration and demonstrations, on the one hand, and external pressure from Moscow, demanding change, on the other. Erich Honecker, head of the country for 18 years, had no choice but to resign, but this hardly pacified anyone. His successor, Egon Krenz, personified continuity while claiming to want a change of direction (*Wende*). The only immediate effect of his arrival in power was the awakening of the East German media that finally started to open up, but even that was not enough. Emigration to the West was turning into a mass exodus and demonstrations kept swelling. Was the government, out of desperation, going to resort to the same type of repression as China had experienced, notwithstanding Gorbachev's refusal of that solution? Was the country going to explode in civil war? No, the system imploded. From the "holes" that mass emigration had already dug in society, another "hole" was going to emerge: in the Berlin Wall itself. On the night of November 9, 1989, the course of history changed.

Moscow had not wanted this, or at least not so soon, no more than had Bonn, Washington or Paris. The world was caught off balance by the opening of the Berlin Wall, precipitated by popular pressure. After so many years of withdrawal into itself, how could the East German system find its feet again? Who was going to be able to master the situation? Those who had always believed in an East German identity based on the values of Protestantism and a renewed socialism were unable to formulate a sufficiently coherent political project to reassure the population. Submerged by popular pressure, they had not wanted the opening of the Wall either, at least not in these conditions. West Germany was the only stable framework of reference that could possibly reassure the masses and open up new prospects. Chancellor Helmut Kohl immediately grasped this and staked his political future on a project of rapid reunification of the country, made public on November 28, barely a few days after other demonstrators had taken to the streets of Leipzig shouting "We are one nation." Another history was thus set in motion: that of the German nation. It was a history that had actually never ended, as attested by the "TV bridge" established between the two populations, kindling the flame of national unity and people's awareness of it.

The uncontested symbol of all these events was the fall of the Berlin Wall itself. This mark of Europe's division was not destroyed by a war, as certain experts had predicted; it disappeared in an explosion of festivity. Far from crumbling in fire and blood, it collapsed before the TV cameras. What explains this incredible event? That is a difficult question to answer, for many archives are still unavailable. It will probably remain a subject of multiple interpretations for a long time, like the storming of the Bastille and the French revolution. I am taking the risk here of suggesting one possible explanation, consistent with the theme of this book, and that emphasizes the importance of public pressure as a decisive factor in the destabilization of the regime. That pressure was the product of interactions between the growing mobilization of the population and its amplification in the media, starting with television.

Nocturnal emigration via television

The reception of West German television in East Germany is the most well-known "TV bridge" between states of the West and the East. Neither of these countries had ever been "sovereign" when it came to communication, as their respective broadcasts covered a large proportion of the other's territory, with the exception of the Dresden valley in the GDR which was hemmed in by steep hills. Nowhere else in Europe did this phenomenon exist: the same nation in a politically divided country could receive the other side's audiovisual media, in the same language.[2]

But only the West German media captured the majority of audiences on either side of the Iron Curtain. The East German press, starting with the Party daily, *Neues Deutschland*, was necessarily read because it contained the country's political, social and cultural news, and because—like everywhere else in the communist bloc—people knew how to sift real news from propaganda. There was however such a striking gap between East Germans' daily lives and what the official news organs said about them, that these media could hardly pass for credible. Unsurprisingly, most people turned to West German radio and television. Although the "radio bridge" had existed for a long time,[3] the "TV bridge" was relatively new. Every evening the East German population emigrated, so to speak, through television, especially after the construction of the Berlin Wall in 1961. Unable to leave the country physically, East Germany escaped through the small screen.

In the Cold War climate of the 1960s the TV channels of these two states waged a propaganda war, mainly through programs designed to influence audiences in the other camp. Their respective newspapers then retaliated to the other side's arguments. From March 21, 1960, the program *Schwarzer Kanal* (*Black Channel*: black like imperialism) hosted by Karl von Schnitzler, responded to *Die Rote Perspective* (*The Red Perspective*) launched in 1958 by Thilo Koch on ARD. Von Schnitzler's 20-minute program, broadcast every Monday evening at 9:30, counter-attacked "imperialist propaganda" by commenting on programs on West German channels. This talented ideologist of the East German regime went down in history for saying: "Whoever believes that it is not dangerous to listen to antidemocratic radio and TV programs or to read Western newspapers is opening his ears to the enemy. The danger is death."[4] The fact that the *Schwarzer Kanal* had a three percent audience rating at best did not prevent it from remaining on the air for 29 years, until its closure was demanded during the 1989 street demonstrations in Leipzig.[5] From August 1, 1969, Richard Loewenthal's *ZDF Magazin* had responded to this program in a deliberately anticommunist and controversial tone.

In the early 1970s the *Ostpolitik* launched by Willy Brandt introduced a process of détente that was to have massive implications for the field of communication and the media.[6] A program was launched to develop telephone links between East and West Berlin, interrupted since the 1953 uprising. From 1972, East Germany also authorized West German media correspondents to have permanent positions in the country. Although the security police (the Stasi) had them under close surveillance and expelled some of them, these correspondents were able to cover political and social life in East Germany more closely. Cooperation was also initiated between the two countries' TV channels. One of the most characteristic programs of this new period was the magazine *Kennzeichen D* (*Registration number D*, for *Deutschland*), launched by ZDF in 1971 with the aim of reflecting East German reality more accurately. The founder, journalist Hans Werner Schwarze, commented: "it's only by learning to know one another better that one prevents stereotypes from setting in," and this "acquaintance with the others inhibits the use of arms."[7] The originality of *Kennzeichen D* was the fact that it sought a common critical language by questioning the nature of democracy in the West without affirming that the East had the worst system. Joachim Jauer explained: "that is why the program was criticized by West German conservatives who wanted it scrapped or brought under stricter political control."[8] As the letter "D" for *Deutschland* appeared on the car registration plates of both states, it was a way of signifying German unity, which corresponded clearly to the general ZDF mandate. The channel's statutes stipulated that it had to "provide an objective view of international events for all of Germany and, in particular, a global image of the German reality. Above all, [they] have to serve the cause of German reunification in a spirit of peace and freedom."[9] *Kennzeichen D* was so successful in the East that the GDR decided to put DDR on the registration plates of cars, rather than just a D, to mark the difference with West Germany!

The communist leaders were never able to stifle this appeal of the Western media. In the climate of suspicion of the 1960s, the East German communist youth had been mobilized in the "antennae hunt," following the declaration by the first secretary of the Party, Walter Ulbricht, that "the class enemy ... is on the roof."[10] Operation "Ox Head" (*Ochsenkopf*), as it was called, consisted in locating TV antennae turned westwards, and either turning them back eastwards or removing them. But the campaign was a failure; it was impossible to put a spy in every family. During the period of relative cultural liberalization following his takeover in 1971, Erich Honecker declared on May 28, 1973, that in East Germany "everyone can switch their set on or off, at will."[11] It was a way of saying that all citizens of the GDR were free to listen to and watch what they wanted to. Endorsing a *fait accompli*, this declaration was a turning point, a victory of society over the government's propaganda and intimidation. The freedom thus secured in the private sphere corresponded to the way in which society had simultaneously built "niches," as Günter Gaus put it.[12] These were the various forms of community-based mutual help through which individuals helped one another to overcome the difficulties of daily life.

East Germans were thus authorized to tune in to Western media. What were the audience ratings like? Western radio stations were listened to mainly in the mornings, when they had ratings of 60-80%, while for TV evening news, ARD's *Tagesschau* and ZDF's *Heute* fluctuated between 50 and 80%. These figures were provided by confidential surveys undertaken at the time by the communist authorities.[13] In contrast, the East German TV news, *Aktuelle Kamera*, had an audience rating of no more than 3%.[14] Western media had considerable credibility, evidenced in the following anecdote told by the renowned journalist Fritz Pleitgen.[15] One day in 1978, *Tagesschau* announced that purchases from *Intershop* stores (that distributed products of a better quality) might be subjected to more severe control. The next morning, tens of thousands of people queued up outside these shops to take advantage of the former system![16] Was this the consequence of Western media's appeal? East Germany was the communist bloc country with the highest number of TV sets per inhabitant: by the end of the 1970s, 95% of all households had one.

To win back the public, the East German government tried to rival Western channels by supplying entertainment. In line with a Party directive in 1971, the communist leaders thought they could take advantage of television's function as recreational, both to compete with Western channels and to stabilize their own regime. They consequently increased the proportion of entertainment programs shown, especially Western movies and series (e.g. *Dallas, Kojak*). Diversion was becoming a necessity as Marxist-Leninist ideology seemed to fade into the background. By giving in to the public's tastes in this way, the communist government capitulated once again, this time with regard to its own value system. Preventing people from watching Western television was one thing; introducing the cultural products of "imperialism" itself was quite another. Basically, it amounted to admitting that its ideology was less and less legitimate. Thus, by broadcasting Western cultural products, the communist regime contributed to undermining itself.[17]

The communist leaders probably imagined that the consumption of American movies and series, and more generally TV programs from West Germany, could constitute an *ersatz* for the public. Certain facts seemed to prove them right. A significantly large proportion of those who wanted to leave East Germany came from the Dresden valley where West German programs could not be picked up. The area was consequently called "the valley of the ignorant," although this was an exaggeration as its inhabitants could listen to Western radio stations. They were nevertheless qualified as such because they seemed to be deprived of something essential: Western TV. To remedy this situation and keep its inhabitants, the city authorities cabled Dresden in 1984!

The communist leaders were nevertheless mistaken about the role of a "safety valve" that West German television could play. While the fact of watching it could serve as a distraction in the short term, no stabilizing effect was guaranteed in the long run. One of the rare studies on the reception of East and West German television, undertaken in the mid-1980s by Kurt Hesse, showed that, on the contrary, watching West German TV tended to strengthen many East Germans' conviction that the Western system was superior to the communist system.[18] Hesse pointed out that the advertisements, movies and political programs fed a constant comparison between the two systems, in which the West almost invariably came out best.

Hence, watching Western television did not keep people from emigrating; on the contrary, it supplied reasons to justify the future emigrant's project even more, even though TV news spoke abundantly about unemployment and crime. Those who wanted to leave disregarded such negative aspects of the West; instinctively they downplayed them, if only because communist propaganda systematically exploited them. The candidate for emigration nurtured an idealized and simplistic representation of the West. Television, its showcase, revealing both good and bad, simply reinforced the desire to escape.

Closure of the system and emergence of critical opinion

The wish to escape was obviously the reflection of a rigid East German society, set in its ideology and structures, where the impossibility of talking openly produced this outward projection of people's minds. In fact, the entire history of the GDR led to that: the country's strategic position at the heart of a divided Europe, on which the stability of the East-West balance depended; the repression of the 1953 uprising which proved that the West was not prepared to intervene in such circumstances; the Stasi's system of keeping individuals under surveillance; and, above all, the prohibition on the dissemination of "information that betrays the fatherland," with severe repression provided for in the penal code.[19] By expressing him- or herself in the Western media, a person was branded a "capitalist agent" and consequently liable to immediate banishment to the West. All these strategic, political and penal constraints caused the system to close up on itself and people became passive. The Berlin Wall was actually the physical translation of an extraordinary attempt to psychologically wall in an entire population. How could a critical public opinion possibly develop in such circumstances? Even though public debate was possible, it could be launched only by actors who had themselves internalized the norms of the system but wanted to work on changing it from within. They had to carry out a feat of strength that departed from post-1968 modes of construction of public opinion in the Soviet bloc, by fostering real critical debate in the GDR without resorting to the Western media as external relays: in short, the opposite of Poland, where Solidarity had learned to use the Western media to feed internal debate. In East Germany the process had to be initiated in isolation. Was that possible? Some believed that it was, and fought to prove it.

A critical discourse, locked within the confines of the system, was gradually to emerge during the 1970s and then even more so during the 1980s, especially within churches and among artists and writers. The Czechoslovakian invasion, with the participation of the East German army, probably traumatized many in the country for a long time, for it revealed the difficulties of living under communism. The evangelical churches[20] were to be the receptacle of these doubts, questions and even suffering. After experiencing strained relations with the government in the 1950s, they had secured a privileged place within the system, as the only organization independent of the Party, with their own premises and publishing facilities, even if they were limited and censored.[21] This autonomy was obtained at the price of their recognition of the communist government, and their definition of themselves in 1969 as "churches within socialism." Some members of their hierarchy, we now know, collaborated with the authorities, including the Stasi. On March 6, 1978, the historical agreement reached at the summit between Erich Honecker and Archbishop Albrecht Schönherr (then president of the Kurchenbund), opened a new era in church-state relations. Hoping to reap the benefits of a new legitimacy achieved through this official recognition by the religious authorities, the government agreed, to some extent, to the principle of dialogue with the church hierarchy. This was a decisive development since "this hierarchy-to-hierarchy procedure paved the way for the role of mediator that the Church would one day have to play, often against its will, but with ever more vigor."[22]

The churches' spiritual and material autonomy meant that they were ideal places for whoever wanted to express themselves outside of the Party structures. As they increasingly served as an asylum for speech, "people came to them, believers or not, to be listened to without being judged."[23] By receiving people in this way and helping to channel their resentment and frustrations, the churches contributed in a sense to the system's stability. These individual approaches led to the creation of discussion circles, where some particularly sensitive issues were raised and considered in relation to the Bible, such as the existence of the Berlin Wall and the freedom to travel. The "church days" (*Kirchentage*) started to attract more people again. In the late 1970s, questions pertaining to peace and disarmament were discussed, in a context of growing militarization of East German society and the plan to install US Pershing missiles in West Germany. From these debates held "under the church's roof," "prayer evenings for peace," usually led by youth groups, were born in the early 1980s. One of the first took place on September 12, 1983, at Saint Nicolas church in Leipzig. The Western media were not welcome at these evening prayers, nor at other activities. The religious leaders feared their voyeurism, their lack of familiarity with East Germany and their quest for sensational news. They were concerned that journalists might "give a meeting political significance when it was above all a religious event."[24] They also criticized the irresponsible attitudes of certain journalists who were prepared to film young people participating in a compromising meeting, without concealing their identity, and thus exposing them to reprisals. In short, the religious leaders were against cooperation with the Western media and, even more so, street demonstrations.

As in other countries of the East, certain artists and writers simultaneously contributed to the emergence of a critical awareness within East German society, especially through theatre, cabaret and, above all, literature. In this book-oriented society, "a specific public and type of reading developed, in which the relationship with books was characterized by a serious attitude, by rejection (necessity being made a virtue) of the effects of fashion and the market, and by a conscious and astute way of reading, [where the reader was] constantly prepared to receive signals and information in the lines and between them."[25] With Honecker's authorization in 1972 ("There are no more taboos in art and literature"—as long as one remained socialist), East Germany underwent a relative cultural liberalization. Writers could talk about their personal experience of living in a communist country and describe violence or their interest in rock music, even if the circulation of their books was very limited. But the banishment of the highly popular cabaret singer Wolf Biermann, on November 16, 1976 (while he was in the West), was an indication that the authorities were putting an end to a movement that they feared would end up destabilizing the regime. This measure (Biermann was stripped of his East German nationality and banned from the country) triggered protest by 12 renowned writers and artists who refused to retract, despite pressure from the government. The authorities nevertheless endeavored to eliminate all rebellious minds from the artistic and cultural world, either by expelling them or by granting them extended authorization to travel abroad. Leave or be silent: that seemed to be the only choice left to creative minds.

Yet the Biermann affair never entirely smothered a deep-seated longing for change, reflected primarily in the emancipation of fiction, with such prestigious authors as Stephan Heym, Christa Wolf and Christophe Hein in the forefront. From different generations and with differing styles, they seemed to have little in common. Yet hundreds of thousands of readers in East Germany could identify with their work, which they saw as the mouthpiece of their own aspirations. These famous authors continued to believe in socialism; their writings were imbibed with the history of communism and antifascism, on which the East German state had based its identity and legitimacy. But they argued for an authentic, democratic and fair socialism. The characters in their books distanced themselves from the Party. They saw themselves as responsible citizens, avid for truth, who called for certain taboos to be destroyed and took a critical stance on the history of the Eastern bloc, starting with the 1953 uprising. This was of course still literature and rarely contained political writings, but it was these authors' own way of freeing people's minds in a country that had known only Nazism and communism since 1933. In those years people throughout the Eastern bloc were sensitive to such writings. These authors' international recognition forced the government to make some concessions in the early 1980s, for instance by allowing them to travel abroad to give public talks and lectures on their books, in the German tradition. People from West Berlin to New York, Thessalonika to Paris, invited them and helped to make them known.[26] During their rare visits to the West, often preceded by long waits for a visa, these writers were extremely cautious with what they said and whom they met. It was out of the question to have contact with East German intellectuals and artists who had gone over to the West, of their own choice or not, or to give interviews to Western journalists.[27] Their obligation to be reserved in the West was the condition of their semi-freedom of speech in the East. They were attached to East Germany and wanted to stay there to help the country to change from within.

This mindset was shared by small groups that emerged from 1982-83 within the churches of several East German cities: East Berlin, Jena, Halle, Leipzig, Magdeburg, Erfurt, Dresden, etc. In a spirit of solidarity with the mass demonstrations in West Germany against the installation of Pershing missiles, they demanded measures for East-West disarmament and demilitarization of East German society. These small groups, often spawned by the "prayers for peace" dynamic, took as their symbol a statue that the USSR had given as a gift to the United States in 1959 (placed outside the United Nations headquarters), illustrating a verse from the prophet Micah: "they shall beat their swords into plowshares." During the same period, October 1982, a movement called "Women for Peace" was created by Ulrike Poppe and artist Bärbel Behley. After the failure of negotiations on disarmament and the installation of Pershing missiles, themes other than peace appeared within these circles, such as civil rights (launching of the "Peace and Human Rights Initiatives" collective in 1985, by Gerd Poppe and Wolfgang Templin) and ecology (creation of the environment library in the Zion Church of East Berlin in 1986). All these groups, fairly close to the West German "alternative" cultural movement, were above all places of interaction and communication.

They formed a convivial microcosm that sociologist and theologian Erhart Neubert, and clergyman Heio Falcke saw as having a function of socialization for their members. They also constituted the foundation of independent civil rights action; the emergence of an "anti-political" culture influenced by the experience of Solidarnosc and the writings of Vaclav Havel (disseminated in *samizdats*). Together with the church leaders they shared the desire for a nonviolent struggle and sought to act from the grassroots of society, as close as possible to the citizens, and with transparency. The Stasi kept a very close eye on these groups' activities and, when necessary, infiltrated them.[28] Its detailed reports provide us today with a written memory of this nascent opposition.

These grassroots groups had little contact with one another, apart from very occasional regional or national meetings.[29] The dissident movement as a whole covered a wide range of themes and was geographically dispersed. "It's a sort of multi-shaped expression of dissidence, in little islands, everyone in their own town,"[30] explained a former activist. Apart from "word of mouth," their main communication channel was newsletters published by religious organizations. But these bulletins, under the churches' control, censored certain information that their leaders thought might be seen as "provocation." It was also out of the question for the members of these groups to use the Western media, as they could be accused of being "agents of imperialist propaganda" and risk banishment. The groups were well aware of the need to develop relations between one another, but first had to set up their own liaison organs. Some publications appeared with the stamp "Exclusively for use by the Church," which was a way of protecting them, even though they were not necessarily intended for religious circles. But others were born without this protection, for instance *Grenzfall* (*Border(line) cases*), created in June 25, 1986, by the "Human Rights and Peace Initiatives" collective. In its first issue the team presented itself as "wanting to expand an information network to facilitate the development in East Germany of various working groups on peace, ecology, human rights and the Third World, which are unable to inform one another via the state media."[31] This new, semi-clandestine publication was the harbinger of a significant change in these groups: their breaking free of the churches, along with a more resolute anti-government stance.

Unavoidable opening

The system was however not closed; it could not possibly be so. The regime was trapped in an untenable position between openness and closure. In the 1960s, it had wanted to barricade itself because, too open to the winds of change from the West, it strove to preserve a fragile identity behind the Wall. But this closure eventually became too burdensome for the population and the people were seeking an outlet. It was in this sense that closure compelled opening: a necessary opening up that the regime had to concede. The right to watch Western television was the first safety valve; the right to retire in West Germany was another, as were the "visiting rights" that families and friends had been granted since the 1970s, by virtue of agreements between the two states.[32] The churches were unquestionably the oldest of these cultural and human bridges.[33] In spite of the construction of the Wall and their forced separation, "close correspondence, at once federal and local, material and spiritual, subsisted between the two churches."[34] They thus served as a link between the two sides of the Wall, enabling a minimum of contact and exchange of news.

These cultural and human links between the two Germanys contributed to feeding a near permanent public debate, via the West German media, on life in East Germany, on the nature of inter-German relations, and on the evolution of East-West relations in general. In this respect, the participation of East German writers clearly shows the ambiguities of this system that was both closed and open. Even though they wanted to be published in the East first, they also sought publication in the West, since their books were increasingly popular there, especially in West Germany. Their publishers in the GDR immediately saw the advantages of negotiating the publication of their books with their counterparts on the other side of the Wall ... to obtain foreign currency. Thus, it became customary to publish in West Germany first, and then in East Germany or, at best, in both countries simultaneously. The possibility of publishing only in the West when authorization was not obtained in the East was refused by most writers, with very few exceptions.[35] The publication of a book by Christa Wolf or Christophe Hein was always a literary event highlighted by the West German media. It triggered reactions and comments, especially among artists and writers who had crossed over to the West and were asked for their opinion on the work of a colleague who had remained in the East. Hence, despite refusals, the West German media did offer a common sphere of debate on either side of the Iron Curtain, from which the peoples of the two states necessarily benefited.

The penetration of the Western media into East Germany was also facilitated by grassroots groups. Although these groups chose not to approach the Western media, or were prevented from doing so, the media went to them because they were a new phenomenon in the GDR. Journalists from the West were largely unfamiliar with the life and activities of these small groups, which they tended to consider as very marginal. For years East Berlin had used a method that had proved to be highly effective against potential opponents: as soon as a protester was deemed to be disturbing the public order too much, he or she was banished to the West. Consequently, the formation of real political opposition seemed impossible in the GDR—a country that could even boast having no political prisoners! West German radio and television spoke about these small groups from time to time, helping to make them known on either side of the Wall. There was no doubt that in 1982-83, for example, the Western media were instrumental in spreading the emblem of the sword transformed into a plowshare, spontaneously adopted by the East German grassroots groups. These media moreover compensated for the groups' lack of internal communication, by reporting their actions.

Certain journalists, informed after the events, would report what they knew on radio and television, and this news—even partial or stale—would serve as milestones for the East German groups, enabling them to know what others were doing. The West German media thus participated in the emergence of an opposition collective conscience in East Germany in the mid-1980s. In this respect, the role of the Western news agencies and official West German correspondents was essential. Depending on the circumstances and notwithstanding controls, they both served as information relays, primarily via the city of Berlin that had telephone links with both sides of the city. The role of the US radio station RIAS was no different here from that of RFE in Central Europe; both had the same aim: to amplify any nonviolent protest in the East, from the outside.[36]

Two international events spurred on this internal protest during the period 1987-89. The first was Mikhail Gorbachev's coming to power in Moscow. With his *Glasnost* policy raising real hopes of reform in the Soviet bloc, those in the GDR who were already pleading for change became a little more daring. Based on the encouraging declarations of Gorbachev's team, the evangelical churches called for the opening of a public debate, and discussion circles started to formulate precise proposals for reform. The most active was that of Wittenberg, from 1986, led by the Reverend Friedrich Schorlemmer.[37] The second important event was the world ecumenical meetings "Peace, justice and safeguarding the creation" in 1988, in which the East German protestant churches had been closely associated since their institution in 1983. The interest of the three ecumenical meetings held in this framework, within a period of a few months at Dresden (February 12-15, 1988), Magdeburg (October 8-11, 1988) and again Dresden (April 26-30, 1989), lay in the inclusion, in this process of reflection, of the grassroots members of the churches and other groups. Their common aim was to show the need for in-depth reform if the demands of these global challenges were to be met. Starting with a call for testimonies (over 10,000 letters received) and experience gained from several years of reflection, 12 texts were finally adopted and publicized in May 1989. The one that drew the most attention was the third, "More justice in the GDR: our task, our expectation," because it presented a complete political program for the country's democratization.[38] Several issues of the weekly *Die Kirche* that reported these resolutions were partially censored, but the editors also sent the texts to the West German media. In light of the slogan *Glasnost*, the East German regime's rigidity seemed ridiculous. Such measures of censorship, like the ban on the Soviet journal *Spoutnik*, highlighted its incapacity to control "the communication front" and to adjust to the new way chosen by Moscow.

At the same time, some writers' work became more politically committed. In the period preceding the fall of the Wall, the most noteworthy was Christoph Hein's play *The Knights of the Round Table*,[39] written in 1988 and staged in Dresden in 1989. "This parody of the King Arthur legend anticipated the final fall of the GDR."[40] The independent groups likewise became more outspoken, especially during the official commemoration event for Rosa Luxembourg and Karl Liebknecht, when they carried a large banner calling for freedom of expression. The authorities were reluctant to repress such audacity. They arrested many demonstrators but released them immediately, at the churches' request[41] and under pressure from grassroots protest groups that organized "prayer evenings" throughout the country, in solidarity with the detained. The one in East Berlin, attended by 2,000 people, received extensive media coverage in the West. Thus, the East German regime had simply succeeded in mobilizing people a little more against it. This open public hostility was nevertheless still a minority phenomenon compared to the population's general passivity. A year later, with the churches' support, these groups formed a larger network of surveillance committees around the May 7, 1989,[42] municipal elections, which brought to light the manipulation of the results by the SED. Whereas it would otherwise have provoked few reactions, the evidence of this fraud set off strong protest and led directly to the birth of the first independent political organizations, late in the summer.

During these pivotal years, 1987-1989, the relationship between communication and opposition in the GDR changed substantially. A telling sign of this evolution was the birth of indirect use of the Western media by East German oppositionists. In this respect a former member of the Iena group, Roland Jahn, banished in 1983,[43] carried out pioneering work from West Berlin. His experience as a militant had convinced him that spreading news in the West was crucial in the struggle against the state that, he noted, "tends to free jailed activists as soon as the Western media talk about them."[44] Based in the West, he was to be at the heart of two initiatives designed to facilitate the communication and mediatization of grassroots groups' action. The first was the creation of Radio Glasnost in August 1987. Broadcasting from West Berlin, it was intended to be a forum of expression for all East German groups who had little knowledge of one another and were often in conflict, especially in East Berlin. By making their texts and activities known, Radio Glasnost also wanted to compensate for the weakness of a semi-clandestine press that was too slow and limited. At the same time, Roland Jahn suggested that the magazines *Kontrast* on ARD and *Kennzeichen D* on ZDF broadcast footage that had been filmed in secret in East Germany by anonymous individuals. In this way it was possible to address more sensitive topics than those generally treated by accredited correspondents, who usually censored themselves. Camcorders were introduced into the country from 1987 for this purpose. This type of action was extremely risky, but now the youth were prepared to take that risk, fully aware that they were committing a serious act of disobedience and were thus liable to several years of imprisonment.

Initially the recordings were made in such a way that people's faces were not shown. The early reports concerned the real state of the country and issues such as environmental pollution (incineration of household refuse) and political realities (presence of neo-Nazi groups). The question of neo-Nazis triggered official protest by the East German government, which had always claimed to have an anti-fascist country. Then, with the May 1989 municipal elections, militants agreed for the first time to speak openly in front of the cameras, to appeal to people to use the polling booths and to join the surveillance committees. Eventually, from August 1989, even people with no militant activity were prepared to be filmed openly in protest against the state of dilapidation of the old city of Leipzig.

These videos were of poor quality. West German TV channels warned viewers that they were amateur recordings, and everyone understood the implications. The tapes were smuggled out of the country in various ways, including via the French cultural center of East Berlin. Such operations were also perilous for the people who were filmed. The churches were opposed to this clandestine activity but some of the most committed clergymen cooperated, including by agreeing to be interviewed. An example was the Reverend Schorlemmer, on August 20, 1989, in Wittenberg, with Luther's house in the background. After the interview was broadcast by *Kennzeichen D* on August 30, he became the victim of a defamation campaign and of telephone threats.[45] This was highly symbolic for a man who drew on Luther for the basis of his nonviolent engagement, especially his "Letter to the Princes of Saxony on the spirit of revolt."

Berlin, 1989: between East and West, the battles of television and the German people

The events leading to the fall of the Berlin Wall on November 9, 1989, are the history of a dialectic between a crumbling power and the steadily mounting pressure of a population, relayed by the media. Given the geo-strategic position of East Germany at the heart of a divided Europe, one has to take into account the international actors, above all the USSR and West Germany, without forgetting the peripheral but important role of Hungary and Poland. This history is particularly complex, especially since knowledge of the GDR was limited before 1989 due to the difficulty of accessing sources and carrying out surveys.[46] My aim here is not to emphasize once again the importance of the policy of *Perestroika* adopted by Moscow or of the changing relations between the USSR and the GDR in connection with these events,[47] and even less so to write a history of the breakdown of the East German state and the SED.[48] It is rather to further understanding of this process of public pressure, which most observers and analysts see as having "pushed" events further than the states concerned wanted them to go.

I am deliberately referring to public pressure and not popular pressure, a concept that is too limited. The particularity of the 1989 events lies in this interactive association, whether intentional or not, between various forms of mobilization of the East German population and its amplification by the media, above all television. From this angle, the overlapping of facts makes it impossible to separate the respective roles of the people from that of the media. It was their permanent interactions, in a situation where the government was disoriented, that accelerated events in this history and made their outcome unpredictable.

Deciphering these facts therefore implies the need to combine two analyses. First, an analysis of the communication processes as such. In this respect it is easy to identify the flows already observed in previous crises in Central Europe, especially East-West-East and East-East. From this point of view, the GDR's crisis in 1989 was situated in the continuity of that of Poland in 1980. The second analysis is of the two very different forms of mobilization of East German society in the summer and autumn of 1989: escape to West Germany, and demonstrations within the GDR. Both were peculiar to East Germany in the 1980s (and, more generally, since its creation in 1949).

A combination of these two types of analysis produces an original interpretation, not only of the events that led to the fall of the Wall, but also of this historical event itself.[49]

Fleeing the East under the cameras of the West

A mass movement is often triggered by something specific. In this case, the small something that sparked it off was a symbolic act of tremendous impact in the history of Soviet Europe: scissors cutting the barbed-wire fence on the Austro-Hungarian border. On May 2, 1989, the Budapest government, having embarked on a process of courageous reform with Moscow's blessing so to speak, decided to dismantle the Iron Curtain separating it from Austria.

Surprisingly, the sequence lasted no more than a few seconds on West German TV news, and gave rise to few comments in the West in general. On the other hand, although it was deliberately overlooked in East Germany, its impact was considerable in that country. Since 1984, the number of legal applications for emigration to the West had been climbing steadily. Suddenly, the Hungarian government's decision afforded a new opportunity to emigrate, which no longer depended on the GDR authorities' good will. From Hungary, where East Germans were allowed to go on holiday, it was possible to cross over to the West. During the summer, hundreds of East German citizens illegally crossed the Austro-Hungarian border into West Germany. Others preferred to submit an official application for emigration, with the result that the West German embassies were swamped with hundreds of East German "tourists" wanting to settle in the West. There had been precedents in the early 1980s, but only a few individuals had then been tempted to try their luck. This time the phenomenon took on what the GDR government saw as alarming proportions, especially since it could assume that the West German media indirectly encouraged people to attempt the journey.

The media did indeed focus intensely on the exodus. "Western television, showing just how easy it was to cross the Austro-Hungarian border, informed [their audiences] of itineraries for leaving the territory and interviewed refugees before, during and after their escape."[50] A study by Dietrich Leder, on the TV news of the four West German channels, confirmed this.[51] As an example, he presented his analysis of the TV news on August 8. ARD broadcast a report on the arrival of refugees at the Giessen refugee center in West Germany. The majority were young people in the 20-25 age-group. Some did not wish to be filmed and turned away when the camera focused on them. Yet the cameraman clearly ignored their reluctance, as their faces could still easily be recognized. Some agreed to an interview, in which they said how easy it had been to cross the border and how happy they were to be in the West. The report showed their enthusiasm and concluded with an excerpt from the welcoming speech by the Hesse secretary for the interior: "I greet you as free Germans in a free country."[52] On ZDF a young emigrant was interviewed live in the TV studio. The journalist asked him to describe his escape. It was not clear whether the young man was afraid or intimidated, but he seemed uncomfortable. He said that he was not drawn by "material things" and that he had left because he wanted to travel in the West, to Spain for example. His talk was not particularly political, apart from his final metaphor: "When you put a bird in a cage it doesn't feel good. It wants to live." The presence of witnesses became the rule on TV news. In the following weeks there was not a single broadcast without someone who had seen or experienced the event. On the 10:30 evening news program *Tagesthemen*, the famous newscaster Hans Joachim Friedrich seemed to be aware that his words could have the effect of encouraging people to leave. He stressed that "escaping via Hungary is currently the surest way," but added, as if he did not want to be accused of inciting people to leave: "We cannot recommend it. It's still dangerous and, as we've just heard, filled with hardships."[53] Yet the West German media expressed definite sympathy for those who left the GDR—a lack of restraint criticized by the media and the East German evangelical churches. Some saw it as televised support for the exodus.[54]

Whereas throughout the summer, West German radio and television repeatedly reverted to the problem of East German refugees in the Hungarian, Polish and Czechoslovakian embassies, the East German media totally overlooked the subject. On August 14, Honecker declared that "life has so many inadequacies that it's not necessary to spread them in the press as well."[55]

Yet even within the SED itself this wish to hush up a phenomenon that everyone was talking about seemed less and less comprehensible. The Party leaders were already shaken by the crisis. From late August, explained the editor-in-chief of East German radio news, "we received no more precise orders from our political superiors. This lack of precise instructions, to which all of us had been accustomed from the beginning of our careers, had the effect of paralyzing us in the face of the events."[56]

In September, the East German media finally reacted to the worsening crisis. On September 10, Budapest decided to allow refugees to leave without visas, in violation of an agreement in 1969 with the GDR, that had prohibited East German citizens from leaving for a third country with a visa valid only for Hungary. Upon the announcement of this decision, the East German media, furious, accused Hungary of flouting the GDR's sovereignty, and the Federal Republic of Germany (FRG) of framing the whole thing. Admittedly, throughout August such conservative West German newspapers as *Bildzeitung* had repeatedly announced that this type of measure was imminent. Chancellor Kohl probably thought that he could derive some sort of electoral benefits from the situation, at a time when his policies were being challenged at home. His foreign affairs minister, Hans-Dietrich Genscher, a man "from the East" (he came from Halle), who had always wanted to strive for German reunification, played a crucial part. We know today that West Germany had secretly negotiated with Hungary to obtain the departure of East Germans for West Germany, in exchange for DM500,000. For several years this "purchase" of candidates for emigration from the GDR was standard practice between the two states. But the problem of refugees in Poland and Czechoslovakia, where thousands of people were waiting for a decision similar to that of Budapest, was still not solved. The media focused on the West German embassy, where close to 3,500 people, including small children, were crammed up in the last week of September. This practically unmanageable situation was finally resolved by Genscher at the United Nations, where he managed to secure Prague and Warsaw's agreement to authorize the refugees' departure for West Germany. Faced with the *fait accompli*, East Berlin allowed the "freedom trains" to pass through its territory. The East German media nevertheless still attacked the refugees, calling them "fugitives" and "traitors to the fatherland." "The chorus was always the same," noted Irina de Chifoff, "the refugees don't know what they're losing by leaving for the West and they don't know what's waiting for them."[57]

But Genscher's solution was not enough. As soon as the 6,000 East Germans in Prague and Warsaw had left, 2,000 more arrived in Prague and 150 more in Warsaw! Thus, the pressure on the GDR government kept mounting. This situation was of particular concern to the communist leaders only a few days before a key event: the ceremonies of the 40th anniversary of the creation of the GDR, in which Mikhail Gorbachev was to participate.

Formation of a political opposition and its amplification by the West (September 11 to October 8)

The public pressure generated by the emigration movement was compounded by simultaneous pressure from the development of opposition within the country since the May 1989 elections. In fact the two phenomena were related. The exodus towards West Germany, which was shaking East German society to its roots, fuelled intense debate between those for or against emigration. The people who left were generally not from the fringes of society. Many worked in the service industry and were highly skilled (which made them confident of finding jobs in West Germany), for example, technicians, engineers or doctors, and some even had a Trabant, a small car that was a sign of wealth in the GDR. Their departure contributed to the disorganization of the country. Those who wanted to stay tended to see them as irresponsible, even cowardly, considering the problems that the country had to solve, although they were aware that such accusations were short-sighted. The documents drawn up from 1988 in the framework of the ecumenical year were a clear indication that, to put an end to the desire to leave that had constantly eaten at East German society, it was necessary to address the causes of exile, that is, to force the government to undertake in-depth reform. It was in this respect that the apparently uncontrollable tide of departures for the West precipitated the formation of opposition within the country—an opposition that was to be characterized by the emancipation of grassroots groups from the churches' supervision.

Contact during the summer between various personalities and opposition groups led to the birth of several political organizations in September. "In appearance, few things distinguished these different movements at their beginnings. Similar in their methods, their means, their vocabulary and their style, they seemed to devote most of their energy to creating a space for communication. The struggle was twofold: for public debate (*Offentlichkeit*) and for sincerity (*Offenheit*), the one being contingent on the other."[58] The largest organization, with the meaningful name of *Neues Forum* ("New Forum"), was created on September 11, on the initiative of artist and painter Bärbel Bohley, lawyer Ralph Heindrich, and biologist Jens Reich. Wanting to be recognized as a legally registered non-profit organization, *Neues Forum* adopted a moderate line and its call remained relatively vague: "It is important now for more people to participate in processes to reform society and for individual and collective actions to be brought together in a common action. That is why we have created a political forum for the entire GDR."[59] Echoing this initiative, the Writers' Union published a protest letter written on the initiative of Christa Wolf, harshly criticizing the government and calling for debate.[60] The launching of *Neues Forum* responded to an obvious need, overlooked for far too long: to shift public debate from its position almost exclusively under the churches' roofs, towards society as a whole, within a political framework. Within days, over 1,500 people, including many Party members, signed its constituent appeal.

Other organizations emerged as well during the same period. *Demokratischer Aufbruch* ("Democratic Renewal"), created on September 15, was also oriented towards reform. This group was led by Reverend Reiner Eppelmann and other church leaders, along with former Party members who agreed to join provided that "we don't reject everything positive in socialism and that we maintain it."[61] On October 2, *Domokratie Jetzt* ("Democracy Now")—which had already made itself known in an appeal on September 12—was formed, headed by peace and human rights activists like Ulrike Poppe. It was the only one of the three organizations to call for free elections and the opening of the Wall (its symbol was a butterfly). On October 7, the Social Democratic Party (SDP then SPD) was born, under the leadership of Ibrahim Böhme.[62]

The new organizations had very little means to make themselves known. Without logistics nor resources they could barely publish some leaflets with the help of certain parishes. This was why the direct or indirect complicity of the Western media was indispensable if their names and their appeals were to be known throughout East Germany. The announcement of the creation of New Forum received extensive media coverage in the West, while the media in the East completely ignored it. On September 11 and 12, Jens Reich and Bärbel Bohley gave telephone interviews to Western radio and television. For these opposition leaders, it was an important step to agree to express themselves in the "capitalist" media—something of which the Stasi agents took note.[63] As Reverend Herald Wagner pointed out, this facility of access to the Western media was envied by certain militant groups in the provincial cities.[64] Western journalists rarely went to places like Dresden, Halle and Magdeburg, where telephone links with the West were more complicated than from the capital.

Leipzig nevertheless had a different status because it hosted an international fair twice a year, in March and September. On that occasion Western journalists visited the city, thus affording the opportunity for people to make contact with them. It was precisely in Leipzig, in the late summer climate of effervescence, that the mobilization was to take on unprecedented proportions. Many of those hoping to emigrate wanted to be seen and heard by the journalists present in the city, to get themselves exiled. On September 3 they took advantage of a West German TV crew outside Saint Nicolas church to demonstrate. "As soon as the cameraman lifted his camera they shouted 'We want to leave!'"[65] The members of the grassroots groups who had been participating for six years in the "prayer evenings" at Saint Nicolas were indignant about these people seeking all the attention. They wanted it to be known that they, on the contrary, wished to remain in East Germany and to fight for reform. The idea was thus born to organize a counter-demonstration after Monday prayers at Saint Nicolas, even though the clergymen were against it. The first attempts ended in arrests, but the groups were not put off. Their project seemed all the more timely as attendance at Monday prayers escalated.

People of different generations came from several East German towns. The audience swelled, especially parents worried about seeing their children leaving for the West. On September 25 there were between 5,000 and 8,000 people on Karl Marx Square. By October 2, they had attained a record figure for the GDR: between 15,000 and 20,000. The country had not seen demonstrations of this size since 1953. The participants sang the *Internationale* and *We Shall Overcome*. They called for the legalization of the New Forum ... and the resignation of Karl von Schnitzler, host of *Schwarzer Kanal*. Western TV was absent during these early demonstrations, but photos were taken and sent to the West, and witnesses reported on the demonstrations over the telephone.

Initially the government seemed to take no account of the development of an opposition. From September 20, it refused to recognize the New Forum, considering the organization "an enemy of the state." But this policy of burying its head in the sand was futile, and in the meantime over 20,000 people had already left for West Germany. In Dresden, on the night of October 4, serious incidents were caused by the departure of trains to the West, transporting the people who had taken refuge in the FRG embassy in Prague. As the Czechoslovakian border was closed, young people swarmed towards overcrowded trains but were violently chased off and beaten by the police.[66] The government was clearly in a very uncomfortable position, just a few days from the October 7 anniversary celebrations. The way the ceremonies took place was moreover to illustrate the difficulties in which it was entangling itself.

On the one hand, the communist leaders wanted this commemoration to contribute to East Germany's international outreach. Heads of state, journalists and personalities from across the globe were invited to East Berlin. On the other hand, fearing provocation, they closed all border posts with West Berlin and the police and army were placed on alert. But instead of enhancing the regime's standing in the eyes of the world, the event had the opposite effect. Gorbachev grasped the opportunity to distance himself from Honecker and to publicly warn him with the now-famous sentence: "When one is late, one is punished for life."[67] At home, youth demonstrations in support of Gorbachev and calling for reform broke out in several East German cities, notably East Berlin, Potsdam, Dresden, Leipzig, Plauen and Jena. In East Berlin, 2,000 to 3,000 young people who had managed to gather outside the Republic Palace where Gorbachev was received by Honecker chanted: "Gorby! Gorby! Democracy!" and "Stasi get out!" After dark many of them were arrested and beaten up by the police, who also turned on the Western journalists present, especially a team from the leading West German TV channel. Other demonstrations took place on October 8 in East Berlin, Karl-Marx-Stadt (Chemnitz) and Magdeburg.

The repression on October 7 and 8 was severe: hundreds of people were injured and over a thousand arrests were made. The East German press denounced the collusion between the demonstrators and the Western media. On the evening of October 8, the TV news program *Aktuelle Kamera* broadcast an interview with the Chinese delegation which affirmed its support for the GDR's policies: a way of saying to opponents that East Berlin could well implement a solution similar to that of Peking against the Chinese students of Tiananmen, on June 4 that year.

Almost simultaneously, TV news on ARD and ZDF reverted to the previous night's repression. Images showing police brutality were broadcast and analyzed. They had been taken not by West German journalists, too well-known by the Stasi (and who had been harassed), but by British and US journalists accredited for the October 7 commemoration and under less intense police surveillance. All of East Germany could see what had happened in East Berlin.[68] Was the country headed for confrontation between a government that was showing its teeth and an opposition that was really starting to exist? In Leipzig, where grassroots groups had maintained their call to demonstrate the next day, on October 9, the climate was increasingly tense.

Nonviolent conflict and victory over fear (October 9-18)
How could the East German government put an end to this "anarchy" that was slowly overtaking the country through demonstrations and exodus? The most radical solution, which always seems inevitable in such circumstances, was repression: massive, brutal repression to stop the public unrest. The idea would be to strike hard, to instill fear, to isolate, to arrest. This was what was being prepared on Monday, October 9 in Leipzig where over 8,000 men from the police, the Stasi and popular militia were on stand-by. Western journalists were banned in the city. Everyone had the violence in Dresden in mind and feared the worst. It was however in Leipzig that, on the evening of October 8, the first official encounter between the population in the streets and the state took place. Owing to the mediation of Reverend Christoph Zimmer, the representatives of the demonstrators, who wanted information on the people arrested, were received by the mayor.

In Leipzig certain officials were also aware of the gravity of the situation. On October 6, the local newspaper *Leipziger Volkzeitung* had warned that "if necessary, we will use arms to respond to counter-revolutionary actions hostile to the state." On the morning of the 9th, orchestra director Kurt Masur interrupted the preparation of a concert, refusing to continue with rehearsals "while people could be murdered in the streets." He decided to initiate a meeting with the theologian Peter Zimmermann, the cabaret singer Bernd-Lutz Lange, and three Party secretaries, including the city mayor, Kurt Meyer. Together they drafted a concise appeal that summed up the situation in a nutshell: there was an imperative need for dialogue to avoid violence. "We all need a free tribune where we can exchange our ideas on the future of socialism in our country [...]. We urge you to act responsibly to ensure that peaceful dialogue can be established."[69]

In the meantime fear had gripped the city, where the rumor was going around that the order had been given to fire. The hospitals prepared beds and blood. At 2 p.m. the police took up their positions near Saint Nicolas church. Stasi agents entered the church and occupied the front pews. When prayers began, just after 5 p.m., the fear peaked: everyone was dreading an incident that might spark off the violence. Some 9,000 people were gathered in the church and on the square outside, including 1,000 police officers and members of the Stasi. During the prayers, appeals for dialogue and a refusal of violence were repeatedly voiced: "the appeal of the six," first, then that of the catholic bishop of the city, a support letter from Dresden, etc.

Candles were distributed among those present, as a religious symbol that had also become symbolic of the movement's nonviolence. "When one takes a candle," said Reverend Christian Führer, one has to be careful of the flame; one can't take a stone, so it's already an opening towards nonviolence."[70] "When we left the prayer meeting," recalled Susanne Rummel, "an extraordinary phenomenon occurred: our fear vanished. A huge crowd was there; it was as if the whole city had arranged to meet. We felt very strong, united."[71]

Was it the mass of people gathered together? Was it the "appeal of the six" that was bearing fruit? At 5:45 p.m., shortly before the end of the prayers, the police had withdrawn at the mayor's demand. Moreover, the municipal radio station (*Stadtfunk*) broadcast the "appeal of the six" through loudspeakers installed in the streets. Many believed that all this was a trap—once they were on the "Ring" (the ring road around the city), the demonstrators would be an easy target for the police, who could trap them in a pincer movement. Nothing of the sort happened. The members of the Stasi present in the crowd seemed to demonstrate with it, and the most overpowering slogans were: "We are the people" and "No violence." The crowd called for the release of the individuals arrested in the preceding days. When the demonstrators returned to the city centre at around 9 p.m., some police detachments were content to direct the traffic. According to the Stasi report, the repression orders were not executed, and there were many cases of insubordination.[72]

That day, October 9, the opposition had taken a major step, not only because there were some 70,000 demonstrators, a new historical record, but above all because they had overcome their fear. By participating in the demonstration, they knew that they were defying the Stasi, those who had managed to break all spirit of revolt in them for years, if not for their entire lives. But on that day they no longer cared. The exceptional situation called for exceptional behavior. Who would have thought that the inhabitants of this dilapidated, polluted, forlorn city would one day show such courage? People had expected the test of strength to play out in the capital. As a result, the Leipzig demonstrators seemed like the collective heroes of a successful non-violent battle. That was why October 9 subsequently became a turning point before the watershed: a victory that was both psychological and political, and that boosted the East German opposition.

News of these events was in the Western media on the evening of the 9th. As they had not been authorized to be there, the journalists were informed mainly via Roland Jahn's clandestine network. The first images of the demonstrations arrived only the next day, broadcast by ARD. They had been taken by a team of activists hiding in one of the city's highrises.[73] Thus the experience of the clandestine filming of video footage, gained over the past two years, served well to compensate for the obstacles encountered by the official media. From then on, the Leipzig demonstrations received extensive media coverage in the West, which the communist authorities were powerless to prevent. Already a ritual in Leipzig, they became so for the entire East Germany, via their media exposure in the West. Too bad if smaller demonstrations in other towns were overlooked. Leipzig became the symbol of the GDR's resistance, just as Gdansk had been in Poland in 1980. On Monday, October 16, between 150,000 and 200,000 people took to the streets of the city. West German, British, French, American and Japanese TV crews were there—which constituted a second victory for those who had demonstrated the previous week. It was a way of crowning their courage but also—who was to know?—of anticipating the drama.

The East German government was nevertheless gradually letting go as mounting international pressure forced it towards reform. Openly or secretly, Bonn, Washington and Moscow were making themselves heard. The day after the 7 and 8 October repression, the FRG accused the GDR of violating the Helsinki agreements because of the police brutality against West German journalists. A declaration on October 11 by the West German president, Richard von Weiszäcker, unambiguously supported the East German opposition.[74] On the same day, US secretary of state James Baker declared on RIAS-TV: "It is time for *Perestroika* and *Glasnost* to come to East Germany." But naturally Moscow's role was the most decisive. The Soviets' strategy to undermine Honecker's position and bring about change in his team was common knowledge. After October 9, internal contradictions in the politburo were intensifying, unknown to the population. On October 18 they led to Honecker's resignation ... "for health reasons."

Egon Krenz's turning point and the awakening of the East German media (October 18 to November 9)

After eighteen years in power, Erich Honecker's fall marked the end of an era. But he was replaced by his successor designate, Egon Krenz, vice-president of the State Council, who necessarily embodied the regime's continuity. Hence, the rebellious irony of the placard carried by a demonstrator when the name of the country's new leader was made known: "Who is Egon Krenz?" From his first speech on television, on October 24, the man was a disappointment. He presented a political program that left little hope for reform. Krenz did nevertheless pronounce a phrase that was to go down in history: "change of direction" (*Wende*): "we will begin a change of direction and in particular regain the political and ideological offensive."[75] But the opposition movements had difficulty believing that this man, so compromised by his participation in the regime, could get real political change underway. On the evening of his speech, several thousand people gathered in Berlin outside the State Council building, chanting: "Egon, your election doesn't count: the people didn't vote for you."

The wish to get to the bottom of the October 7 and 8 repression was still the main preoccupation of the social and political players, who were instrumental in awakening the East German population. The "new" leaders seemed moreover to want to meet their expectations since they announced on October 22 that an official commission of inquiry was to be created. But in spite of this significant victory over a government that was unaccustomed to accounting for its actions, the people were still wary. On October 28 some of East Germany's most renowned writers and artists held a public meeting in an East Berlin church, demanding the elucidation of this repression.[76] On November 3, an independent commission of inquiry into the events of October 7 and 8 was consequently created, consisting of these artists and writers, along with representatives of the churches and of the new political organizations.[77]

There was, however, one area in which the short period of *Wende* did introduce fundamental change: the media. Along with Honecker, two secretaries of the SED had also left the government, one of whom was Joachim Herrmann, former Central Committee Secretary for Agitation and Propaganda which was dissolved. He was replaced by Günter Schabowski, appointed "secretary of the Party's central committee responsible for information and media policy." Almost overnight, the style of the East German media changed and the tone became surprisingly free. As in Hungary at the end of 1956 and Poland in late 1980, we witnessed a restructuring of the official public sphere as a result public pressure.

This transformation of the media was preceded by the creation of new programs designed to appeal to young audiences. In 1986, a radio station for the youth, D.T. 64, had been created to rival RIAS 2, which broadcast almost exclusively popular American music (pop, rock, jazz) from West Berlin and was highly popular among the East German youth. D.T. 64 sought to fill the same niche by providing a platform for young people to express themselves on "hip" topics such as fashion or sex, but never on political issues.[78] In September 1989, East German TV launched a youth program, *Elf 99*, in the same spirit. Such programs, whose success was very relative, copied their Western models in an East German "style." They illustrated the communist regime's incapacity to offer its youth a culture that differed from that of the West, while it sought to limit the influence of that culture by imposing quotas on the Western music broadcast by the media.[79]

The real rebirth of the East German media started on October 9, 1989, in Leipzig, when the local radio station broadcast Kurt Masur's appeal. "From then on," explained Judith Heitkamp, "there was a slow transformation of radio, characteristic of the transformation of the media in the GDR."[80] The youngest members of editorial committees pushed for change. For instance, a D.T. 64 team managed to secure authorization to compile a report on the October 16 demonstration in Leipzig. Changes were perceptible in the press as well: the Party daily, *Neues Deutschland*, started to publish critical letters by readers, while the ban on the magazine *Spoutnik* was lifted. The difference was however most spectacular on television. On Sunday, October 29, the host of *Aktuelle Kamera* read a declaration by journalists: "With extreme consternation we acknowledge our responsibility in the crisis situation that has arisen in the GDR. We allowed intervention from above to take advantage of our television channel. The trust of many TV viewers, starting with that of many employees at the channel, has been broken. We wish to apologize to the citizens of the GDR." This solemn proclamation, expressed on television, brings to mind that of Hungarian journalists at the heart of the 1956 uprising. It was likewise intended to announce the start of a new era: "We want quick news that faithfully reflects reality, on subjects of concern to us all, here and throughout the world. That is our most important duty to you. In the future, nothing will be omitted. News will be commented on and followed by reports, interviews and explanations. Decision-making will be put into context." Although this declaration in the form of a manifesto used the traditional rhetoric of communist self-criticism, it was effectively followed by perceptible changes not only in the content of *Aktuelle Kamera*[81] but also in the general programming. From then on television broadcast political events of prime importance, initially pre-recorded, then live. The near-immediate response to this change was the upsurge of audience ratings, naturally in East Germany but also in West Germany.[82]

From the point of view of communication, the period of *Wende* was characterized by the convergence of historical time and media time. For instance, on October 29, television broadcast excerpts from public debates taking place in the framework of the "Forum for dialogue between the Party and the population," organized in several East German towns. Never before had politicians agreed to answer questions by citizens, in the hope of winning back their confidence. These encounters afforded an extraordinary opportunity for people to speak in public, as in East Berlin where 20,000 people gathered outside the city hall. Even though the organizers dissuaded them from doing so, individuals related their private stories that seriously challenged the officials facing the crowd. Hate could have erupted, but the clergymen who were present endeavored to act as moderators and demanded that each side listen to the other's point of view. Then an incredible scene occurred: after being called several times by the crowd, the East Berlin police chief apologized to the public for the October 7 and 8 repression: "I wish to express my profound regret and my sincere apologies for having intervened violently, thus causing human and spiritual suffering."[83] Another tangible sign of change was the resignation of Karl von Schnitzler, marking the end of the propaganda war that the GDR had still formally been waging against the FRG. The famous host of *Schwarzer Kanal* gave the event a solemn tone by announcing his resignation live and leaving the studio within five minutes, after reading a text in which he reaffirmed his attachment to communism: "This program today will be the shortest of the past thirty years: it will be the last. It is an art to do good, a good that is just, rapid and credible. That is how I will continue my work as a journalist and communist, as an alternative to inhuman capitalism, as a weapon in the class struggle to defend my socialist fatherland."[84]

Another spectacular change was the fact that East German television broadcast live the demonstration organized on Alexanderplatz, East Berlin, on November 4 by writers and artists, with the support of opposition movements and certain members of the SED. This gathering "for the freedom of the press, assembly and expression" was historical for at least three reasons. First, the number of people present: with over 500,000 participants, it was the biggest demonstration of the year in

Central Europe. Second, this gathering was the opposition's first political initiative authorized by the authorities, who thus recognized that they no longer had a monopoly on the occupation of the public sphere. It reflected the transfer of legitimacy, particularly in the many banners re-appropriating the Party's slogans and rituals; for instance a quotation from the writer Christa Wolf: "Suggestion for May 1st: that the leaders march in front of the people."[85] The walls of the State Council were covered in slogans such as "Yes to democracy, no to the Party monarchy" and "Free elections"—something that would have been unthinkable just a few days earlier. The third reason why the gathering was historical pertained to media coverage of the event. At the last minute, Egon Krenz agreed for television to broadcast it live. The entire country could thus experience this historical moment and hear the 27 speeches programmed. This broadcast, which lasted close to five hours, was the climax of the process of convergence between historical time and media time: at that precise moment, the two merged. As public pressure had managed to penetrate the official sphere of the government's communication, the GDR was busy reinventing its own modes of communication. Perhaps it was initiating the reconstruction of its identity. The speakers succeeding one another on the tribune did not reject the socialist system; they pleaded for change: "They must get off the stage," said a famous actress talking about old leaders. She then did so herself after speaking, for she was old as well. They called on all citizens to mobilize themselves, rather than simply following these events on television: "Turn off the TV and walk with us," said Christa Wolf. They argued for a renewed socialism, a "real socialism" as Stephan Heym had always wanted. They certainly were not pleading for the end of the GDR.

The political effects of this gathering and those of Magdeburg (40,000 people) and Jena (10,000) were immediate. On November 7, the whole government resigned and the next day the central committee of the Communist Party elected a new politburo, reduced from 21 to 11 members. Significantly, *Neues Forum* was officially recognized on November 8 as a legal organization, thus enabling it to engage in an official process of dialogue with the government. *Neues Forum* set out to ensure that the other organizations created just after it were recognized as well.

The opening of the Wall and
the victory of public pressure (November 9)
Just as the East German government was seeking a new political balance, it was again destabilized by the unsolved problem of the population drain to West Germany. Coverage of this subject by West German

TV had totally changed since August. Reports showed that the refugee centers in West Germany were overcrowded and that the authorities could no longer cope. This was a way of using the media to warn people who wanted to leave, or even of dissuading them. The East German government was aware that new measures had to be taken to stop the exodus. But how? Pressurized by the events, they acted with urgency, trying to cope with a situation that they could no longer control.

At the politburo meeting on October 24, Egon Krenz had given the order to prepare a "bill on traveling," to be passed by the People's Chamber at Christmas. His intention was to put an end to an absurd situation: East German citizens could emigrate to West Germany, but those who wanted to stay in East Germany were not authorized to travel to the West. The bill, drafted on October 31 and made public on November 7, was deemed to be unrealistic and was criticized, including on television. At the same time a new wave of immigrants arrived in Prague. This time Czechoslovakia took a firmer stand: it informed East Berlin of its intention to close its borders with the GDR if a solution was not found quickly. At Egon Krenz's request, the minister of the interior urgently prepared a "travel decree" to allow East Germans to cross the West German border at certain points, provided they had a permit (readily) issued by their local police station (*Kreis*). This new measure was designed to be provisional, until the new law was passed. The bill was tabled in the early afternoon of November 9 at the central committee session in East Berlin. To be passed, it still had to be endorsed by the government, even though it had resigned. Yet Krenz gave the text to Schabowski just before he went to the press conference at which he was to report on the central committee's work.

It had almost become common for history-in-the-making to be witnessed live, and that was the case with this press conference, broadcast on television. The effects of the news given by the government spokesperson could therefore be immediate. The announcement concerning travel permits was made right at the end, when Schabowski pointed out that new laws were in preparation on freedom of assembly, the media, penal law, the People's Chamber, and traveling. "It is still not in effect," he explained. "A decision was made today, as far as I know. A recommendation from the Politburo was taken up that we take a passage from the [draft of] travel regulation [...] that regulates permanent exit, leaving the Republic. Since we find it unacceptable that this movement is taking place across the territory of an allied state, which is not an easy burden for that country to bear. Therefore, we have decided today to implement a regulation that allows every citizen of the German Democratic Republic to leave the GDR through any of the border crossings."

The journalists immediately pricked up their ears. In the hubbub in the hall, someone asked: "At once?" Schabowski scratched his head and seemed uncomfortable. His speech became hesitant: "You see, comrades, I was informed today, that such an announcement had been distributed earlier today." That meant, basically, you should already know about it. At that point, he started looking for a paper that someone helped him to find,[86] and quickly read the text: "Applications for travel abroad by private individuals can now be made without the previously existing requirements (of demonstrating a need to travel or proving familial relationships). The travel authorizations will be issued within a short time. Grounds for denial will only be applied in particular exceptional cases. [...] Permanent exit [*Ständige Ausreisen*] is possible via all GDR border crossings to the FRG. These changes replace the temporary practice of issuing [travel] authorizations through GDR consulates and permanent exit with a GDR personal identity card via third countries. [...] Until the Volkskammer implements a corresponding law, this transition regulation will be in effect."

When the reading was over, a journalist asked: "When does it come into effect?" The answer: "According to my information, without delay [*ab sofort*]."[87] But what did "without delay" mean? If a permit was necessary, as the text stipulated, then it would be necessary to wait until the next morning for the opening of the competent offices. In his memoirs, Krenz reproached Schabowski for not specifying that the measure was to come into force on the morning of November 10.[88] But Schabowski answered that he had stuck to what was in the text that Krenz had given him and that, according to him, mentioned no date of application.[89] Hence, this "as from now" meant "immediately," that is, 6:57 p.m. The hypothesis seemed extravagant. The camera showed the journalists' faces: some seemed perplexed, others stupefied. There were also some who were moving restlessly, or nodding their heads, or who appeared to be excited. One of them was open-mouthed, as if he had to deal with extraordinary information that he had trouble grasping. A young woman stared wide-eyed and seemed to be overcome by emotion. Did this mini-public of journalists present a spontaneous range of reactions of the broader public of televiewers?

Eventually, a young foreign journalist, who had been waiting to ask a question for a few minutes, raised a particularly relevant point: "Mister Schabowski, what is going to happen to the Wall?" He answered that this was a highly complicated problem ... and launched into an explanation on the meaning of the building of the Wall, which led him on to the problem of disarmament between West and East Germany. In short, he evaded the question. It was 7:10 p.m.

The best West German experts on the GDR had no idea how to interpret the news. For example, Joachim Jauer, editor-in-chief of *Kennzeichen D*, said: "For nearly twenty years I had been working as an East-West correspondent and I didn't know what that meant. I thought that it was necessary to obtain certain documents or a pass. I never imagined that that night thousands of people were going to cross the border freely."[90] The text was indeed open to interpretation, especially due to the notion of *Ständige Ausreisen*.[91]

At 7:30 p.m., the East German TV news *Aktuelle Kamera* broadcast the information without any comments. It was announced flatly, in the same tone as the other measures taken by the central committee that day. But at the same moment, the regional TV news of the SFB (*Sender Freies Berlin*), a West Berlin channel that was part of the ARD network, announced something very different. The journalist presented the "decree on traveling" as headline news and interviewed Walter Momper, mayor of West Berlin. Momper immediately interpreted Schabowski's announcement. His live appearance from 7:45 p.m. proved that he had grasped the importance of the decision and was already anticipating the consequences. Actually, Momper had been secretly informed on October 29 by Schabowski of the forthcoming decision to liberalize traveling conditions, and had immediately decided to set up a task force to prepare the city for that eventuality.[92] Momper started by addressing the West Berliners to prepare them for the historical change: "This is a day of joy, even if we know that many difficulties lie ahead for us. Many citizens of the GDR are going to come to see us in the coming weeks ... I would like to invite and encourage all Berliners at this time to welcome the citizens of the GDR, really with open arms." He then addressed the East Berliners, fearing that their arrival might cause serious traffic problems: "Please, if you come to us, use the subway [...]. I know that many citizens of the GDR would like to come here [...]. Consider it carefully, please, before taking that step. But the decision is yours." He thus gave the news an historical impact: "We are very pleased that our city is no longer separated by the Wall and the border, and that everyone can travel, as we have hoped for twenty-eight years."

Was he not pushing for the event to happen, provoking a *fait accompli*? Even though he had been prepared for the news, Momper could not have known that within a few hours the Wall was to open under pressure from the crowds. The journalist asked him: "When do you think this will come into effect?," to which he replied: "Tomorrow or for next week end. We'd really be happy." The journalist continued: "Does this mean the Wall will be demolished, even though the GDR thinks that other issues have to be addressed first?" And Momper answered: "The Wall lost its function long ago since the citizens of the GDR can leave via Czechoslovakia. Its objective function to keep people in East Germany is already over. Now, it's a vestige [...]. The Wall no longer separates us."

It was nearly 8 p.m.

What was happening in East Berlin? Apparently nothing near the Wall, at least not until 9 p.m. Most of the people did nothing unusual. Yet more and more East Berliners were wondering about the meaning of the news, especially since several Western radio stations had highlighted its importance in their 8 or 9 o'clock evening news. Everything happened as if East Berlin were gradually taken over by a vast conversation on the temporary traveling measure. Although the West Berlin mayor's speech certainly played a part, the East Berliners did their own decoding of the news, either individually, or with friends or family, or over the phone. The first extraordinary phenomenon occurred: East German television interrupted its programs twice to answer the telephone calls that kept coming in from people wanting details on the decree. At 9:26 p.m. the announcer read the main points of the text on "permanent exit permits" over the air, without any comments. This took three minutes. Then at 9:56 p.m. she read the famous decree a second time, but followed the reading with comments: "At the request of many fellow citizens, here are the main points again"—proof that the public's wish to know was intense.

By that stage many people had understood what was happening, but it is one thing to understand information intellectually and quite another to apply it to one's own life. Most of the testimonies show that the prevailing feeling was incredulity: while the news could be true, it still seemed incredible. How could one conceive that this division of the city, entrenched in facts and minds for 28 years, could collapse in a few minutes?

Paradoxically, it was the improbability of the news that gave it meaning in the context, itself improbable, that the GDR had been experiencing for several weeks: "So many extraordinary things are happening today that it may be true." The plausibility of information consequently seemed to require verification and, for that purpose, the simplest means was still to go and see what was happening on the other side of the Wall. More and more people went towards the border posts, just to see, in many cases more as spectators than as actors.

Certain journalists from the West were asking exactly the same question at the same time: "Can people actually get through?" The American radio station RIAS kept receiving phone calls, including from the United States. Western journalists went to find out, and were thus to encounter the people of the East doing likewise. From both sides those who had been the main players in the protests over the preceding months converged on the strategic point that until then they had ignored: the Wall. Soon they were to interact, amplifying a formidable public pressure mounting in both the East and the West.

At about 9 p.m. the East Berliners arrived in small groups at the Bornholmerstrasse bridge crossing. Soon there were a thousand of them. The guards had received no orders and could get nervous. Their first reflex was to drive people back, but the crowd remained and kept growing, though without becoming aggressive. The people stayed there, calmly queuing up ... to get across. The guards seemed to have no precise instructions. On the other side of this passage point there were no journalists yet. After Momper's speech SFB had decided to send a team in a car with a transmitter to prowl around near the Wall. It lacked the technical means however to monitor all the passage points. The journalists were near Invalidenstrasse but there was no one there yet.

The ARD evening news, *Tagesthemen*, very popular in the East, was approaching and these journalists were to appear live. When star host Hans Joachim Friedrich came on the air at 10:42 his tone was solemn: "Brandenburg Gate, as a symbol of the separation of Berlin, has had its day. The same applies to the Wall which, for twenty-eight years, separated East from West [...]. We are using superlatives with great caution. Today, however, we can say that November 9 is an historic day." The journalist at Invalidenstrasse appeared on the screen, surrounded by about ten people. He announced that the situation was still confused and that from where he was it was impossible to have a global view. But he then passed the microphone to a West Berliner who had just arrived from Bornholmer Strasse. This witness attested—for the first time—in front of millions of televiewers that people had indeed started to cross at that point. His testimony served as an incentive. He declared: "At 9:25 a young couple in tears crossed the border. When they reached the white line on the Western side they fell into our arms and we cried together. [...] About a thousand people went to this point. The people had initially been turned away. They were told to wait for 8 o'clock the next morning to receive a police stamp. That proved to be unnecessary. In the end they crossed without any complications. They were also reassured that they could *return* at any time." A second witness, also from Bornholmer Strasse, said that he had also seen people arriving from the East, on foot and in cars. The journalist asked how they had got across. The witness answered that at first they had needed a visa but that in the end their identity card sufficed. Some returned immediately. "Ah, they came over to the other side to see if it really worked?" asked the journalist. The witness agreed. The journalist then turned directly to the TV audience. He had been given a list of border posts that were open and read it out quickly. To conclude, he said, emphasizing every word: "It is almost possible, *without any complication*, to come to West Berlin"—as if he were taking the liberty of inviting everyone. It was around 11 p.m. The late evening news was not over yet and was to last longer than usual: the sign of an exceptional event. Another live interview was shown at the end of the program, but the essential had already been said. The impact of *Tagesthemen* was immediate: "the lights went on in apartment buildings. And the people started to move," recalled Albrecht Hinze.[93] Before 10.30 p.m. there were only a few hundred or maybe thousand people moving towards the Wall to "see," to "test" and perhaps to cross over. From 11 p.m. the entire East Berlin started to walk to the Wall, sure that they *could* cross into the West. The TV program had served as a collective verification. No one wondered anymore about the immediate possibility of getting across; they were sure they could.

That night most West German TV channels reported live from Berlin. East German television was refused authorization to film; it was as if the event did not exit. Yet, ironically, that evening in its program *Kultur Magazin*, East German TV broadcast an interview with Stephan Heym. The writer commented on the huge demonstration of November 4, although his words applied equally to what was happening at the Wall. "For the first time," he said, "the people are becoming active themselves. They have launched the revolution themselves. They carried it and even today they are carrying it. The people have arrived at a degree of political maturity that has hardly ever existed in Germany on such a scale and that is rare in the history of the world." By pure coincidence Heym's words corresponded to the scenes of joy at the Wall, for this interview was prerecorded.

From midnight the movement reached a climax. "Everyone saw the images of these huge crowds that were stopping the traffic on Kurfürstendamm, the corks of bottles of Sekt being popped, and total strangers hugging one another with teary eyes, in short, the biggest street celebration in the history of the world." Timothy Garton Ash found "a magical atmosphere of Pentecost" that he had last known in Poland in 1980. "The Berliners immediately grasped the historical dimensions of the event. A poster proclaimed: 'It's only today that the war has ended.'"[94]

In that exceptional moment, television was the queen of the media. Its reports crowned the population of East Berlin who had precipitated the opening of the Wall. They were also a way of crowning itself, of proving to everyone that at that moment its role was unique: words were futile, because the images spoke for themselves, and because seeing and living seemed to be the same thing. Once again, historical time and media time merged, but this time it was the West that prevailed. From November 9, a profusion of reports, live programs and debates were broadcast and published by the West German (and, more generally, Western) media on the GDR. The country's invasion by the media no longer took place from a distance, as it had in the Cold War years, but on site. Journalists started to travel across East Germany discovering a country that the West hardly knew, except through over-simplified representations. Perhaps this media penetration prefigured the subsequent political penetration by West Germany the following year? The day after the opening of the Wall a West German newspaper, *Die Bild*, anticipated the October 3, 1990, reunification. On the morning of November 10 its main headlines, in black, red and gold, were a huge "Hello Germany."

Towards the destabilization of the Eastern Bloc

Did the opening of the Wall signify the end of the GDR for all that? Other scenarios were probably possible, starting with repression. A desperate reaction by the hardest core of the regime could not be ruled out, judging from recent research that shows that on the morning of November 10, an order to mobilize the army was given by a small group consisting notably of Egon Krenz, General Fritz Streletz, head of the armed forces, and Erich Meilke, head of the Stasi, although all three later denied it.[95] In another, very different scenario, Egon Krenz and his team might have joined the crowds on the night of November 9 to harness the tremendous popular momentum and turn it to their own advantage. In that case, as Krenz reportedly said himself, "they would have celebrated us like those who destroyed the Wall."[96] But the Communist leaders did not have this idea; they were subjected to history rather than controlling its course, and they were not the only ones. Everyone was overwhelmed by the force of events, in East Germany and on the international scene alike.

Everyone, with the exception of one man: Helmut Kohl. On November 28, barely twenty days after the opening of the Wall, Kohl surprised many by proposing the accelerated reunification of Germany. He gambled on developments that were only just emerging in the GDR: on November 21 a new slogan appeared in Leipzig, "*Deutschland*, fatherland united," which soon became "We are one people." The slogan was rapidly adopted in many demonstrations. West German TV channels were then criticized for focusing on these new demonstrators marching with German flags, to the detriment of those who still wanted to believe in a reformed East Germany. Any manipulation that there may have been reinforced an historical process which, with hindsight, seems to have been ineluctable. In the crisis situation that the GDR was experiencing, the FRG was the only stable framework of reference likely to reassure the disoriented East German population aspiring to an economic welfare that it thought it could get from the West. Hence, the German national identity that had never ceased to exist, owing largely to radio and TV bridges, superseded an East German identity that was even more fragile after the opening of the Wall. Many of those who had mobilized since the early 1980s to change the system from within tried to resist this course of events.

Clergymen, writers, politicians: all still wanted to believe in the future of the GDR. They vehemently criticized this march towards reunification, which they interpreted as East Germany's forced integration into the political and legal structures of West Germany, leading to the dissolution of the East German state. But assuming that a future was still possible for the GDR, would it have been able to withstand the earthquake about to occur in the Soviet bloc after the opening of the Berlin Wall? Everyone knew that the strategic partitioning of Europe was so to speak "locked" in Berlin. The former capital of the Reich was the tangible expression of the continent's East-West divide. Once this lock had been broken the door was open, not only to the destabilization of the GDR, but more generally to that of the entire eastern bloc. For the symbolic power of the event was huge: if the Wall contributed to confining people's minds in the East, then its opening contributed to freeing them. The evolution of vocabulary clearly reflected the rapid changes in mental representations: people soon spoke of the "fall of the Wall" and no longer of its "opening." With the word "opening," the Wall still existed, even if it could be crossed. With the word "fall," it had simply ceased to exist.

After November 9, 1989, the entire eastern bloc was deconstructed for psychological as well as strategic reasons, and the media were once again at the heart of the process. Western radio stations (RFE, RL and the BBC in the lead) induced a dynamic of imitation-contagion: "Since the East Germans are 'moving', why not us?" It would take many more pages to write the history of this chain reaction of upheavals in Prague, Bucharest, Sofia and Tallinn.[97] The processes at play were however all fairly similar to those described in this book:

- The pressure of East-West-East communication: the Western media received in the East relayed and amplified the impact of protest demonstrations. In Czechoslovakia and Romania, people throughout the country were informed of the first action in Prague and Timisoara, thanks to the news broadcast by the Western radio stations.
- The extension of West-East-West communication: international "coverage" of these events was rapid, owing to satellite transmissions. The whole world witnessed almost live the events reported by teams of Western journalists everywhere in Central and Eastern Europe (whereas, until 1988, they were concentrated mainly in Warsaw, hardly present in Budapest and Prague, and even less so in Sofia and Bucharest).
- The birth of East-East communication: initiated by the development of a *samizdat* press that developed from the second half of the 1980s. Owing to the political upheavals underway, these titles moved out of their semi-clandestine position and new titles were born. Simultaneously, the opponents made the control of the state media one of their main strategic objectives. Television, in particular, was perceived as the primary means of mobilizing opinion. The Romanian case was the most typical in this respect. The Romanian insurgents used television to get the population on their side, and in the dramatization and manipulation of information that were employed, the international press was itself—unbeknown to it—an accomplice.[98] Television was also at the heart of upheavals in the former Soviet republics. In the Baltic countries in 1990 and in Georgia in 1991, partisans and opponents of change clashed outside the premises of TV channels to take control of them. As if revolutions could be won no longer by storming a Bastille or Winter Palace, but by controlling the small screen.

Can we however still talk of "revolutions," even if they are "velvet"? This is a subject of debate. 1989 brought about no radical change from the former regime, and was characterized rather by a process of "transition" consisting of both continuity and discontinuity.[99] From the point of view of communication, the year marked the decline of Western radio's audiences in the East, begun a few years earlier already.[100] For them too, a period was drawing to a close. The people of the East were no longer seeking their freedom over the airwaves from the West; they wanted freedom to finally be established on the airwaves of their own media. They wanted to join the Europe of democracy and human rights.

But once the euphoria of newfound freedom had worn off, disillusionment set in. Even though the Berlin Wall had fallen, many political, cultural and economic barriers remained. For over 40 years the "two" Europes had hardly spoken to each other. Or, more precisely, the interaction had been one-way only: the East listened to the West. How could authentic two-way communication be restored? There was no lack of topics between European people after this long period of non-dialogue, weighted with misunderstandings and old resentments. How could the West also learn from the East? In addition to the emotion of reunion, the rebirth of communication between the peoples of a Europe delivered from the shackles of its strategic division could but be conflictual. But that is another story.

Notes

1. See: Jacques Lévesque, *1989 La fin d'un empire. L'URSS et la libération de l'Europe de l'Est*, Paris, Presses de la F.N.S.P., 1995; and Hélène Carrère d'Encausse, *La gloire des nations ou la fin de l'empire soviétique*, Paris, Fayard, 1991.

One of the first measures of Glasnost was to put an end to all jamming of Western radio stations, including Radio Liberty, in November 1988.

2. The only case similar to Germany is that of North and South Korea. In Europe, other cases existed in the communist bloc, but between countries with different languages. For instance, a part of Hungary and Czechoslovakia was covered by Austrian TV transmitters, just as the Estonians could receive Finnish TV. On these aspects of "audiovisual overflowing" across borders, the best work is that of George H. Quester, *The International Politics of Television*, Lexington Books, D.C. Heath and Co., 1990.

3. See Part One.

4. Karl von Schnitzler recounted his memoirs and the reasons for his engagement in two books: *Der rote Kanal. Armes Deutschland*, Hamburg, Nautilus Verlag, 1992 and *Meine Schlösser oder Wie Ich mein Vaterland fand*, Hamburg, Nautilus Verlag, 1995.

5. See below.

6. A crucial stage in inter-German relations. On December 21, 1972, the two German states signed a fundamental treaty of mutual recognition.

7. See Isabelle Bourgeois, "Les 20 ans de Kennzeichen D" in CIRAC-Média, n° 8, 1991.

8. Interview with Joachim Jauer, editor-in-chief of *Kennzeichen D* and correspondent in East Berlin from 1968 to 1972. The program had one part on West Germany and another part on strictly "Germano-German" news.

9. Paragraph 4.

10. See Marks D., "Broadcasting across the Wall: the FFI between East and West Germany" in *Journal of Communication*, n° 1, winter 1983, p. 50.
11. Declaration at the 9th Congress of the S.E.D in *Bundesministerium für innerdeutsche Beziehungen*, 1985, p. 386.
12. Günter Gaus, *Wo Deutschland liegt, eine Ortsbestimmung*, Hamburg, Hoffmann und Campe, 1983.
13. These surveys were undertaken at the time by the Leipzig Central Institute for Studies on the Youth.
14. According to Franz Loeser, who used to work for TV news. Interviewed in *Der Spiegel*, n° 33, 1984.
15. ARD correspondent in East Germany from 1970 to 1982.
16. Interview with Fritz Pleitgen in Peter Hall, Fernsehkritik. Revolutionäre Öffentlichkeit. Das Fernsehen und die Demokratisierung im Osten, Mainz, v. Hase und Koehler Verlag, 1990, p. 142.
17. See Anne-Marie Le Gloannec, *La nation orpheline. Les Allemagnes en Europe*, Paris, Calmann-Lévy, 1989, p. 99-100.
18. Kurt Hesse, *Westmedien in der DDR*, 1988. Poll run in 1985 on 100 East-German refugees at the Giessen camp in West Germany.
19. Articles 97 and 99 of this penal code (amended in 1979) stipulated that any "preparation and attempts to spread information to a foreign power or organization" are liable to a prison sentence of 2 to 12 years.
20. The federation of (Lutheran) evangelical churches, combining eight provincial churches, was the country's largest. The Catholic Church was in a minority. A survey in 1990 showed the following statistics: 22.5% of Protestants and 4.7% of Catholics.
21. The largest was the weekly *Die Kirche*, which was supposed to be a basic spiritual reference in the communist world.
22. Sylvie Legrand, "Les Eglises évangéliques de RDA et la 'révolution pacifique' de l'automne 1989" in *Connaissance de la RDA*, January 1991, n° p. 30-31, 19.
23. Interview with Reverend Martin Hofmeister, June 9, 1995.
24. Interview with Reverend Wolfram von Hülsemann, June 9, 1995.
25. Jean-Paul Barbe "Parnasse à céder? Evolution de la vie littéraire en RDA" in *La RDA 1949-1990. Du stalinisme à la liberté*, Publications de l'Institut d'Allemand d'Asnières, 1990, p. 182.
26. In the tradition of Martin Flinker, an Austrian who did a great deal after WWII to make German literature known in France, Nicole Bary opened a bookstore in Paris in 1980 (in the Montparnasse district), where German authors were invited to give public readings. About 100 authors were hosted at the store, 15 of whom were from East Germany and included some of the most famous. Christa Wolf was the first, in December 1982.
27. One exception was Stephan Heym, who had always considered that what he could not say in East Berlin he would say in West Berlin. He could allow himself this freedom of speech because as an antifascist immigrant he had a permanent visa, and could count on Honecker's understanding since they had the same background.
28. We now know that one of the most well-known leaders of these groups, Ibrahim Böhme, founding member of "Peace and Human Rights Initiatives" was a Stasi informer.

29. The "Workshop for Peace," held in East Berlin and various "ecological seminars," the largest of which took place in Wittenberg.

30. Interview with Bernard Dréano, October 15, 1994, former coordinator of *European Nuclear Disarmament* (E.N.D.) and one of the French militants most active in fostering regular contact with independent groups in East Germany during the 1980s.

31. See the collection of all the issues that appeared in East Germany in 1986 and 1987, edited by Ralf Hirsch and Lew Kopelew: *Initiatives Frieden und Menschenrechte : Grenzfall*, Berlin, 1989 (published by the author).

Other titles also appeared during this period: *Das Friedensnetz* (*Peace Network*), *Umweltblätter* (*Leaves of the Environment*) and *Wende* (*The Turningpoint*).

32. On these successive agreements between East and West Germany, see Anne-Marie Le Gloannec, *La nation orpheline*, op. cit., especially the annexes.

33. See Alfred Grosser, *L'Allemagne de notre temps (1945-1978)*, Paris, Fayard, 1978, p. 438.

34. Anne-Marie Le Gloannec, *La nation orpheline*, op. cit. p. 143.

35. For example, the books of Monika Maron published by Fayard.

36. RIAS was nevertheless forced to innovate, due to competition from West German television. In 1986 it launched its own TV program from West Berlin (RIAS television).

37. Friedrich Schorlemmer, *Worte öffnen Fäuste. Die Rückkehr in ein schwieriges Vaterland*. Kindler, München 1992, p. 23 et ss.

38. Demands were made for respect for human rights, freedom of information and opinion, separation between the state and the party, and multi-party elections by secret ballot.

39. Christoph Hein, *Ritter der Tafelrunde*, Dresden, 1989.

40. Interview with Nicole Bary, February 10, 1996.

41. Some were however expelled to the West, including Barbel Bohley, Wolfgang Templin and the protest singer Stephan Krawczyk. Exceptionally, the former was authorized to return to East Germany a few months later, at his own request.

42. In 1989, D. Pollack estimated the membership of these groups at between 10,000 and 15,000 individuals, in *Deutschland Archiv* 8/90, p. 1216-1223.

43. See the articles on him in *Der Spiegel*: N. 45, 1982, n. 25, 1983 and n. 26, 1983, n. 45, 1985.

44. Interview with Roland Jahn, June 10, 1995.

45. Friedrich Schorlemmer, *Worte öffnen Fäuste. Die Rückkehr in ein schwieriges Vaterland*, op. cit. p. 203.

46. Very few researchers developed a specific interest in the GDR before 1989, and the same applies to journalists of the international press (some media even monitored news in this country not from West Berlin but from Bonn!). The journal Connaissance de la RDA, published from 1972 to 1991 (by a research team at the University of Paris VIII) was the only periodical in France that specialized in the GDR. It shared the regime's Marxist orientations. See, in particular, the synthesis articles by Gilbert Badia in the 1979 issue: "Vingt ans après ou comment écrire l'histoire" (p. 66-70) followed by "Clefs pour la RDA" (p. 71-93) in Connaissance de la RDA, n° 9, December 1979.

47. I strongly recommend the book by Jacques Lévesque cited above, and the books and articles by Hélène Carrère d'Encausse, Renatha Fritz-Bournazel and Michel Lesage.

48. Studies by the Historical Research Group on the GDR, coordinated by Laurence Plateau, in the framework of the Marc Bloch Center, are a major contribution in this field.

49. Such an approach can enrich early studies on the general causes of the GDR's collapse. See, for example, the conference organized by the Free University of Berlin in February 1991: Hans Joas and Martin Kohli (eds) *Der Zusammenbruch der DDR*, Francfort, Suhrkamp verlag, 1993.

50. Kurt R. Hesse, "Télévision et révolution," op. cit. p. 165.

51. Dietrich Leder, "Die Tage im Herbst im Westfernsehen" in Peter Christian Hall, *Revolutionäre Öffentlichkeit*, Mainz, Hase und Koehler Verlag, 1990, p. 97-132.

52. *Ibid.* p. 101.

53. *Ibid.* p. 102.

54. Hans Werner Scharze, "DDR und die Medien" in *Journalist*, n° 40, 1988, 11, 8-12.

55. Cited in *Der Spiegel*, April 16, 1990, p. 90.

56. Interview with Mr. Eichhorn, former editor-in-chief of *Radio Aktuell*.

57. *Le Figaro*, October 3, 1989.

58. Bernard Genton, "La reconquête du pluralisme" in *Chronique d'un automne allemand*, texts collected and presented by Nicole Bary, Paris, Jean-Claude Lattès, 1990, p. 190.

59. Cited in *L'opposition démocratique est-allemande par elle-même*, coordinated by Bernard Dréano, December 1989, p. 7.

60. Published against the advice of the chairman of this official institution, this text signed exclusively by women stated the following: "We find it unbearable to see how responsibility for the situation is thrown elsewhere, when the real causes should be sought in the unacknowledged contradictions in our own country. This does not exclude the controversy with the western mass media. This exodus is the accumulation of fundamental problems running through all areas of society. It is not analysis and ideas that are lacking but the possibility to discuss them." Cited in *Le Monde*, September 14, 1989.

61. Interview with Reverend Eppelmann in the West Berlin *Tageszeitung*, October 3, 1989.

62. On these organizations and their programs, see Hubertus Knabe, "L'opposition politique en RDA. Origines, programmes, perspectives" in *La RDA 1949-1990. Du stalinisme à la liberté*, op. cit., p. 69-86.

63. A report dated September 12 mentioned that "RIAS-television has announced the creation of a New Forum and broadcast an interview with Jan Reich, held on September 13, and a telephone interview with Bärbel Bohley." The same report added that "Reverend Eppelmann went to the West on a private trip from September 5 to 14, during which he had contact with *Der Spiegel* and *ZDF*," cited in Armin Mitter and Stefan Wolle, *Ich liebe euch doch alle! Befehle und Lageberichte des Mfs (January-November 1989)*, Basis Druck Verlagsgesellschaft mbH Berlin 1990, p. 155 and 157.

64. *Leipzig. Wir sind das Volk*, Berlin, Ed. Gerhart Rein, 1989, p. 166.

65. Interview with Susanne Rummel, one of the leaders of the prayer evenings at Saint Nicolas church, June 10, 1995.
66. See the article by Irina de Chikoff in *Le Figaro* of October 6.
67. *L'Humanité*, October 10, 1989.
68. These images did not however adequately reflect the police brutality. The inquiry into this police brutality showed that on the night of October 8, the most violent acts were committed out of sight of the cameras, in the Stasi's jail.
69. See Nicole Bary, "Les Six de Leipzig," dans *Chronique d'un automne allemand*, op. cit., p. 56.
70. Interview with Christian Führer, minister at Saint-Nicolas church, June 10, 1995.
71. Interview with Susan Rummel, June 10, 1995.
72. Based on interviews held in Leipzig and on the report by Christoph Links and Hannes Bahrmann, *Wir sind das Volk. Die DDR im Aufbruch eine Chronik*, Berlin, Peter Hammer Verlag, 1990, p. 15-19.
73. During the demonstration, young people had the task of informing Reverend Thurek at the Markos parish as soon as possible on the number of participants. At an agreed time, Roland Jahn called him from West Berlin for this information, which he then passed on to the western media. It was impossible that evening to get video footage out of the country; it was necessary to wait for the next morning, when the police roadblocks were lifted.
74. "We are the witnesses of a profoundly moving conflict. With steadfast courage, with clear-sightedness and with a real desire for nonviolence, forces are mobilized to show the government the ineluctability of reforms. Through their action, these men [and women] are giving their fellow citizens the guarantee of a future in their country. If from here we are able to help them, we must do so and we will do so."
75. *Die Mauer und ihr Fall (1961-1990), Dokumentation Berlin, Service de presse et d'information du Land de Berlin, 1990, p. 49.*
76. For an account of that evening, in which Stephan Heym, Christoph Hein and Stephan Hermlin participated, see Françoise Toraille "Eglise du Rédempteur 28 octobre 1989," in *Chronique d'un automne allemand*, op. cit., p. 77-80.
77. The first demand of this independent commission was for the withdrawal from the official commission of people who were implicated in the events, especially members of the "people's police." When this demand was met, the two commissions merged. See the report: *Und diese verdammte Ohnmacht*, Berlin, BasisDruck, 1991.
78. Deuschland Treffen 64 ("German encounters 64"), because a program of this name had been launched in 1964 to teach the youth socialist values.
79. Since the 1950s this quota had been set at a maximum of 40% western music. It had to be applied not only to the broadcasting media but also in festivities, dance halls, etc.
80. Judith Heitkamp, *Radio im Umbruch*, Münich, Ludwig-Maximilians-Universität, 1993, p. 4.
81. For the first, unfortunately highly incomplete, history of changes at *Aktuelle Kamera* during that period, see Peter Ludes Ed., *D.D.R.-Fernsehen intern. Von der Honecker-Ära bis "Deutschland einig Vaterland,"* Wissenschaftsverlag Volker Spiess, Berlin, 1990, p. 51-78.

82. For instance, in the week of November 6-11, 320,000 West Germans, or 10 times more than usual, watched *Aktuelle Kamera*. See Isabelle Bourgeois in *Le Monde*, February 18-19, 1990.

83. Document made by the O.R.B. (Ostdeutscher Rundfunk Brandenburg) and broadcast by ARTE between November 7 and 10, 1995.

84. O.R.B. document.

85. See Timothy Garton Ash, *The Uses of Adversity*.

86. This gave the impression that someone had slipped into his hand a paper that he did not necessarily know about, and consequently that he had been manipulated—an interpretation that seems totally fanciful.

87. Günter Schabowski (1989) "Günter Schabowski's Press Conference in the GDR International Press Center," available at http://www.wilsoncenter.org /index.cfm?topic_id=1409&fuseaction=va2.document&identifier=5034D7FF -96B6-175C-98E17DFE653CFD6F&sort=Collection&item=End%20of %20the%20Cold%20War (last accessed 17/02/2010)

88. Egon Krentz, "Der 9. November 1989" in Siegfried Prokop, *Die Kurze Zeit der Utopie*, Berlin, Rlefanten Press Verlag, 1994, p. 80.

89. Günter Schabowski, *Der Absturz*, Berlin, Rowohlt Verlag, 1991, p. 307-308.

90. Interview with Joachim Jauer, June 7, 1995.

91. *In this context* the German word "*ständige*," which usually means "permanent" (i.e., lasting in time), meant "definitive."

92. This task force was given a highly technical name: "Preparation for the intensified circulation of visitors and travellers from East Berlin and the GDR" (*Vorbereitung auf einen verstärkten Besucher-und Reiseverkehr aus Ost-Berlin und aus der DDR*).

The group, with the participation of the police, was to work on a variety of topics: public transport, paying welcome money, accommodating lost children and the sick, supplying an information brochure with a map of the city. It was even envisaged to cooperate with the Allies to set up an air bridge to evacuate refugees for whom there was no room in West Berlin and who did not want to return to the East. See the article by Werner Kolhoff (former spokesperson for the Senate of West Berlin) in the *Berliner Zeitung*, n° 263, November 9, 1994.

93. *Berliner Zeitung*, n° 263, November 9, 1994.

94. Timothy Garton Ash, *The Uses of Adversity*. op. cit.

95. This order, lifted on November 11 in the early afternoon, was reportedly met with a formal prohibition by Moscow and refusals to carry it out from within the East German army itself. See the study by Hans-Hermann Ertle in the *Deutschland Archive* of December 1994 and presented in *Der Spiegel*, n° 46, 1994. See also the large survey carried out by the same journal a year later in its 40th issue, 1995.

96. See Günter Schabowski, *Der Absturz*, Berlin, op. cit., p. 310.

97. For a reminder of these facts see François Fejtö and Eva Kulesza-Mietkowski, *La fin des démocraties populaires*, Paris, Le Seuil, 1992 and André Fontaine, *L'un sans l'autre, Paris, Fayard, 1991*.

98. The fake "mass grave" affair at Timisoara triggered self-criticism in the French press. See the conference organized by Reporters Sans Frontières, *Le Nouvel Observateur* et Médecins du Monde: *Roumanie : qui a menti?*, Paris, Editions Reporters sans frontières, 1990.

99. Georges Mink and Jean-Charles Szurek, *Cet étrange post-communisme. Rupture et transitions en Europe centrale et orientale*, Presses du CNRS/La Découverte, Paris, 1992.

100. See Jacques Semelin, "Est-Ouest : naissance d'une nouvelle Europe audiovisuelle ?" in *Médiaspouvoirs*, September 1990, p. 175-183; and "Déclin et renaissance des radios occidentales à l'Est" in *Médiaspouvoirs*, April-May-June 1992, p. 142-149.

CONCLUSION:
The fall of the three walls

The Berlin Wall condensed the existence of three walls. Long before its erection in the former capital of the Reich, two other walls had enclosed Soviet Europe. The wall of fear, first, which existed within every individual, forcing them to wear the mask of their conformity within the norms of the totalitarian system. Irrespective of whether they shared its values, they had to simulate adhesion, under pain of finding themselves in a camp or even disappearing.

This was a psychological wall that set in from the early days of the cold war, under Stalin's terror. The second wall was geopolitical, between East and West. Contrary to a deep-seated belief, it was not erected at the time of the Yalta agreement but in 1956, when the West passively observed the Hungarian tragedy. Even though no international agreement officially sanctioned Soviet domination over Central and Eastern Europe at that point, the West acknowledged de facto that Moscow could do as it pleased in that part of the world. It was only in 1961 that the actual Wall was built, the most unbearable of the three because it could be seen, was immutable and impassable, and some people lost their lives wanting to cross it in spite of all. Erected to seal the separation between the "two" Germanys, the "wall of shame" became the symbol of the tragedy of a Europe divided in two.

The history told in this book is that of the arduous, chaotic and uncertain, yet nevertheless progressive overcoming of these three walls, eventually leading to the collapse of the Soviet system in a little more than 40 years. The fall of the Berlin Wall, that neither Gorbachev nor the other leaders at the time had wanted, thus appeared as the culmination of a process that, visibly or not, had been on-going for years. In brief, the Wall fell because the other two walls, that of fear and that of the East-West divide, were starting to crumble. They had already collapsed to a large degree in several countries, under the weight of the emancipation of civil society, the irrepressible desire to reclaim national identities, and individuals' irresistible yearning for Western modernity. This was exemplified in East Germany, where the economic success of West Germany intensified the population's wish to escape to the West. A centrifugal force was thus at work within the Soviet system, constantly fuelled from the outside by the Western media (both radio and television). The walls, weakened from within, ended up collapsing in the favorable context of *Perestroika*. From this point of view, the upheavals of 1989 were not "revolutions" in the usual sense of the word, but an *implosion of the system*. East-European societies, with their national identities, their cultural and family ties, and the media bridges thrown between East and West, finally prevailed over the strategic partitioning of the continent. In this sense, 1989 was a victory of the people over the order of states.

Yet many experts and politicians had confidently affirmed that the Soviet system was there to stay. As some quipped, theories have never been able to predict great historical events.

Indeed. Let us therefore show humility and attempt to learn something from this triple fall, not only for the sake of history and political science, but also for future struggles for freedom of thought and communication.

1. The first lesson is that the future of East-West relations was all too often judged in terms of military and diplomatic criteria, without adequately taking into account a specific analysis of East-European societies. As a result, we tended to see the countries of the "East" as a whole, which prevented us from perceiving their differences. It is no coincidence that, in the early 1990s, specialists of international relations paid more attention to social changes and non-state players than they had in the past, even though social scientists like Karl Deutsch had been precursors in this domain. The analysis of transnational flows (economic, cultural, human, etc.), in addition to traditional factors relating to the state, is typical today of this change of perspective. This is my approach, as I propose several indicators for observing the evolution of a dictatorship, from the point of view of both its internal transformation and its place in the international system.

2. Among these indicators, the analysis of relations between communication and resistance seems to be one of the best "barometers" of the stability of a non-democratic regime. Even though huge audiences of for-

eign media were not per se an organized sign of resistance in Soviet Europe, they did bear witness to the extreme vulnerability of this type of political system. Braving all sorts of intimidation, individuals gradually managed to impose their right to information that differed from the news distilled by the official media. In addition to international radio, today we have TV programs broadcast by satellite. This phenomenon had already started to develop in certain Eastern countries (primarily Poland) in the late 1980s, and is now spreading in many countries of the South. It is merely a sign of collective defiance of the official media, which has no value as open protest against the regime. Yet it makes the regime seem that much more fragile, for the defiance reflects a serious deficit of legitimacy of the national media and thus of the powers controlling them. The audiences of foreign media therefore seem to be one of the most reliable indicators of the fragility of a regime.

3. It follows that studying the practices of media interference is of particular interest. These practices play a strategic role when it comes to populations that have access only to state-censored media, which is still the case in a majority of the world's countries. The experience gained by radio stations as different as the BBC and RFE, in the context of East-West confrontation is an obvious source of lessons for any defenders of press freedom. For many years, these stations exercised the right to interference, which certain experts like Mario Bettati now defend.[1]

This analysis of the means and objectives of media interference is essential today, as its practices are changing. From a technical point of view, the leading international radio stations now offer their listeners a quality equivalent to that of FM, owing to digitization and satellite broadcasting. From a political point of view, such practices are no longer the doing of states alone, which financed them openly or covertly (via the CIA in the case of RFE) during the cold war. Non-governmental organizations are now starting to do likewise, sometimes with the support of such international institutions as the European Union and the United Nations.

4. In itself, the outside contribution of independent information, even of a high quality, is not however enough to destabilize a regime firmly clinging to the reins of power. A dictatorship is destabilized only if an active process of resistance undermines it from within. It is therefore necessary to study phenomena of civil resistance as well (symbolic demonstrations, strikes, civil disobedience, etc.), for these are often the first forms of nonviolent protest opposing the violence of the state. We sometimes tend to underestimate these types of peaceful protest; yet they evidence a desire for change, defying the iron rule of the powers

that be. Their appearance on the public scene implies that speech is starting to become freer and, consequently, that individuals or groups who wish to protest are learning a subversive use of the media.

5. From this point of view, this history of dissidence is exemplary. It is about the invention of a way of communicating to resist, through the creation of independent publications (*samizdat*) and the indirect use of the Western media broadcasting people's own speech in both the East and the West. While the process of self-publishing had precedents in the 19th century, the use of the media was more recent because it was linked to the generalization of radio. Thanks to the audiovisual media (radio and now also television), individuals and groups who are unable to voice themselves in their own country can nevertheless appear on the international scene. In Soviet Europe, these forms of dissidence were thus a harbinger of an evolution in which political scientists have taken a keen interest since 1989: the emergence of non-state actors in the field of international relations, a field that was formerly almost exclusively the prerogative of princes and governments.[2]

Other technologies now afford new possibilities to defy censorship and abolish borders, by fostering direct interaction between individuals worldwide. In the 1990s, the fax allowed for direct dissemination of written information between private individuals. Then, in the 2000s the development of the Internet profoundly changed modes of communication, making virtually instantaneous interaction possible by eliminating the need for paper. But the optimistic discourse that sees these new tools as the media for global communication is exaggerated, for these technologies require equipment that is available today mainly in the most economically developed countries. No new technology, no matter how revolutionary, has ever replaced a strategy. It can support it, transform and amplify it, but never be a substitute for it.

6. The history of the conquest of free speech in Soviet Europe shows that it depended less on the technical evolution of the media than on the internal dynamics of dissident struggle and any support it received *from outside* the Soviet bloc. In the first 20 years, attempted resistance in the East developed in a climate of general indifference in the West. Its main source of support was from communities of East-European émigrés. On the intellectual front, the role of the Polish magazine *Kultura* was emblematic of success in this respect, for it maintained a minimum of contact with the *intelligentsia* in a country forced to withdraw into itself. One can imagine this taking place today with very different means from those of the 1950s: rather than entering Poland secretly, printed on India paper, articles from a late 2000s *Kultura* would "travel" via the Internet.

But it was during the 1970s, when the West started to change its stance on "real socialism," that the protest struggles in the East benefited from a new complicity outside of immigrant circles. Several factors explain this new receptivity in the West to forms of protest within the Soviet system: the impact in the West of the repression of the Prague Spring; the development of Soviet dissidence; and, of course, Aleksandr Solzhenitsyn's work, starting with *The Gulag Archipelago*.[3] Help first came from certain western journalists who, as Jacques Amalric put it, were no longer prepared to "accept Soviet news standards, which they had done too readily in the past."[4] It also came from political activists or militant organizations who tried to alert western public opinion to the violation of human rights in Eastern bloc countries, demanding that those countries abide by the terms of the Helsinki accords. They thus relayed and amplified the dissidents' combat, creating a sort of lobbying in the West in favor of human rights in the East. As a result, cross-border networks of complicity were formed, through which the international impact of the protest struggles in the East increased, while at home they carried little weight compared to the means of repression of the forces they were fighting. The collapse of the Soviet system was partly the result of the development of these transverse communication networks that brought down states based on centralized and bureaucratic models.

7. Modern states are however adapting to these new developments. When it comes to communication via the Internet and opponents' use thereof, authoritarian regimes have various effective, albeit imperfect, means of surveillance and even of blocking the flow of electronic data. States also know how to fight "on the communication front" to refurbish or improve their own image. That was what *Glasnost* was all about: a policy of communication towards the outside, designed to enhance the USSR's international image. At home, states also have a range of means available. Once again, the history of the Soviet bloc is exemplary: for over 40 years the communist states had a wide range of reactions to the penetration of western media, which were largely representative of those of contemporary dictatorships. From the hunt for satellite dishes in certain countries with Islamic governments, to the creation of more "in" TV programs to counteract the appeal of the western media, the methods remain much the same.

We must therefore be wary of rash optimism, for today's and tomorrow's tyrannies can always, with varying degrees of success, invent new ways of surviving in this modernity that was so lethal to the Soviet system. Since the 1990s we have witnessed the appearance of a new generation of dictatorships that tolerate satellite dishes while keeping individuals under an iron law. Are they destined to the same fate as the communist regimes in 1989, or will they manage to "digest" this modernity and to last?

In 2009, mass protest demonstrations in Iran against the re-election of President Mahmoud Ahmadinejad are clear evidence of the relevance of this question. The events showed once again the importance of the media's role as an ideal means for crystallizing and mobilizing a growing opposition against a particularly authoritarian government. In addition to western radio and television accessible in Iran serving as an amplifier, technologies born with the Internet (like Twitter) provide new resources for escaping state control. In a country relatively well equipped in personal computers, the blogosphere has served as a substitute public sphere, thus defying the censorship of the official media. The use of cell phones has also proved to be highly useful for demonstrators to communicate, to give one another instructions, and so on.

But the opposition's failure to obtain the annulment of Ahmadinejad's election was also a reminder that the decisive balance of political power is effective not in the virtual world of electronic interaction but in the physical world of the streets. Even though young demonstrators braved their fear and state violence—in some cases at the cost of their lives—fierce state repression prevailed over even the most courageous. This immense hope for change turned into tragedy—which goes to say just how relative the "power" of the media is, no matter how modern and sophisticated they may be. The tumultuous history related in the pages of this book tell the same tale, of successive failures of revolt in the East from 1953 up to the victorious scenario of 1989.

Let us not forget, however, the decisive influence of a silent and unpredictable player. The 40 years of East-European crisis show the invisible influence of time, linked to the effects induced by the bloody repression of any quest for freedom. Those who unhesitatingly give orders to shoot at the crowd can strut about, believing in their victory; but who knows whether they are not busy preparing their own downfall? Who knows whether the silent reprobation of their expedient methods does not announce the eventual birth of a new governing elite that will seek first to break with this disastrous heritage? After all, that is exactly what happened in the Soviet bloc, which witnessed the appearance of a figure like Gorbachev.

8. To revert to the fall of the Berlin Wall, it certainly did mark the end of an era, and with it a terminology disappeared. The East-West divide, a reflection of the partitioning of Europe that has been the main theme of this book, became strategically meaningless. The notion of Eastern Europe, inherited from the cold war, is now obsolete. Today we

talk about "the countries of central and eastern Europe" (CCEE), as if refocusing on their geographical position enables us to find our bearings in a world that seems to have lost all direction.

The collapse of this terminology signified another implosion, that of the strategic categories structuring power relations and modes of communication on the international scene. For over 40 years, in the balance of terror between East and West, the war of words replaced war itself, at least in Europe. By destroying the balance of "non-war," the collapse of the Soviet bloc revived the specter of war on the old continent once again. The conflict in former Yugoslavia was its most dramatic expression. Nationalistic passions were unleashed, showing once again that the power of words could prepare, justify and fuel the explosion of the most abject violence. As in the days of Nazism, we rediscovered that in Europe and elsewhere, the media could also spread hatred and trigger wars.[5]

At the same time, the globalization of means of communication can also be a factor of instability, even violence. Who can tell today what the consequences will be? Peace or war? Both alternatives have their partisans, and the media have no inherent virtue: they can serve the cause of peace and that of war alike. Formidable instruments for bringing people together, their effects can also be of the most direful, because they are unpredictable.

As I conclude, I would like to share with the reader a feeling of concern. Although it was a great pleasure for me to recount a history in which the media were used to secure freedom, the knowledge that I gained on these means of mass communication is also a cause of worry. We think we are able to master their use, but that is an illusion. Journalists are far from always being able to verify the veracity of a piece of news. As a result, they sometimes, knowingly or not, convey disinformation or false rumors. In this respect, the journalistic profession's reactions to the major crises of Soviet Europe are enlightening. At one stage or another, the most reliable media all gave credit to false news: Dubcek's death in 1968, the preparation of a Soviet invasion of Poland in 1980, the death of Mazowiecki after martial law was declared in that country in 1981 and, of course, the most recent, still clear in our memories, the false mass graves of Timisoara in 1989.

These difficulties of controlling news at its source are compounded by the unpredictable effects of its dissemination. A multiplicity of publics throughout the world receiving news conveyed by the media has in the past had unexpected consequences. For instance, to many observers' surprise, the events of 1989 facilitated the eruption of political unrest ... in Gabon and Côte d'Ivoire! Do such phenomena not presage the possibility of a crisis on a global scale, triggered by the instantaneous propagation worldwide of an explosive false piece of news? In this light the maneuvers of propaganda and disinformation by a particular power or pressure group appear even more terrifying. Who knows whether, due to a series of unexpected news and uncontrolled events, the media war currently developing throughout the world will spark off the next world war?

Notes

1. Mario Bettati, *Le Droit d'ingérence*, Paris, Odile Jacob, 1996.

2. On this new type of individual international actor, see James N. Rosenau, *Turbulence in World Politics. A Theory of Change and Continuity*, Princeton University Press, 1990; Michel Girard (ed.), *L'individu dans les relations internationals*, Paris, Editions Economica, 1994.

3. In the French case, see Pierre Grémion, *Paris-Prague. La gauche face au renouveau et à la régression tchécoslovaques*, Paris, Julliard, 1985.

4. Interview with Jacques Amalric, September 20, 1995 (Moscow correspondent for the French daily *Le Monde* from 1973 to 1977).

5. See Jacques Semelin, *Purifier et détruire. Usages politiques des massacres et génocides*, Paris, Seuil, 2005.

AFTERWORD

by Howard Barrell

If an adversary's tribute is a particularly strong recommendation, we might be forgiven for thinking that a small group of anti-communist broadcasters won the Cold War for the West. For among their most enthusiastic referees has been Marcus Wolf, communist East Germany's long-serving intelligence chief. In his view, these broadcasters were the "most effective" of any institutions in influencing Eastern Europeans against communism. They provided, he wrote in a memoir in 1997, "excellent counterpropaganda." He added that the three radio stations mainly involved—Radio Free Europe, Radio in the American Sector and Radio Liberty

> were fast on their feet when any sign of instability arose in the Eastern bloc, providing timely and detailed accounts of actions that were invaluable to our opponents in planning a quick response to events that were hushed up or glossed over by the Communist media.[1]

The size of the audiences these stations won for themselves behind the Iron Curtain was impressive. Research during and since the Cold War suggests that in any week from the mid-1960s to 1988, Radio Free Europe reached at least three out of ten adults in Czechoslovakia, and four out of ten in Hungary and Poland—at times a far higher proportion. Moreover, its reach in these countries was complemented by the big Western national broadcasters, such as Voice of America and the BBC.[2] East Germans were the citizenry in Eastern Europe perhaps most intensively targeted by Western radio: by Radio Free Europe, Radio in the American Sector, and by the West German state-owned stations Deutsche

Welle and Deutschlandfunk. Over time, East Germans increasingly gained access to West German television as well. Within the Soviet Union, the combined audience won by Radio Liberty and the major Western national broadcasters exceeded two out of ten adults in any week for most of the Cold War's closing decade.[3]

So Wolf, it seems, was right. He was also very probably wrong. For his implication that cunning outside agencies played a significant role in inducing the collapse of communism in Eastern Europe merely obscures what would have been, for him, almost certainly a more discomfiting explanation and, for the rest of us, a more credible one. The truth is European communism caved in under the weight of its own weaknesses. They were its dysfunctionality, the disillusion of those forced to live under it and, eventually, their growing resistance to it. Western media such as Radio Free Europe had indeed sought to fuel that disillusion and resistance. The primary implosive dynamics, however, were internal to the communist system.

The intricacy of those dynamics, and how the Western media such as Radio Free Europe interacted with them, form Jacques Semelin's focus in this, the English edition of his *La Liberté au bout des ondes: Du coup de Prague à la chute du mur de Berlin*.[4] As Wolf was, in his 1997 memoir, saluting what he saw as the effectiveness of his former clandestine adversaries, Semelin was, that same year, publishing the French first edition of his analysis of the radio stations and anti-communist resistance in Eastern Europe. Semelin set out to answer the question: "What was the role of the media in the main crises of the communist bloc that, from the 1950s, destabilized Moscow's domination of Eastern Europe?" We have seen his detailed answer in his own words. It is a complex picture, in which the role of the Western-based broadcasters was not as singularly decisive as Wolf would have us suppose.

The Western radio stations' coverage of communism's problems was, in almost every respect, some sort of attempt at persuasion. They projected an image of communism as a failing system. They contrasted its difficulties to what eventually became the greater relative prosperity of the West, as well as to the West's more relaxed social attitudes and artistic life. They publicized repressive action against dissenters. And so on. The effects of their many individual attempts to persuade East Europeans are, however, difficult to assess. Causal relationships are seldom clear-cut in the complexities of politics. They are even more opaque when trying to trace the effect of media output on the behaviors of those who consume it. There are, after all, many factors in a political environment autonomous of media output that can and do change people's minds and influence actions. Separating out their various effects is nigh impossible. Isolating the causal effect of media output alone is, as a consequence, almost always conjectural.

So we probably waste our time if we spend time trying to identify those specific points of argument on which these broadcasters managed to persuade people living under communism. Semelin, following the German philosopher Jurgen Habermas, offers an alternative approach. There was, he suggests, probably really only one argument that the stations and local dissidents needed to win in their interactions with the citizens of Eastern Europe, in order to foster broadly based popular resistance to communism. It was the argument that said that these citizens should be allowed to engage in free and open argument and discussion on all issues affecting them, that they should actively assert their rights to a critical public sphere and to participation in it.

How is the media's democratizing effect probably reducible to winning this single argument? Semelin outlines his case in the Preface to the French paperback edition of *La Liberté au bout des ondes*:

> If such a critical public sphere manages to spread, thus reflecting an increasingly broad wish for change within a given society, it becomes more and more probable that individuals and groups will take the risk of physically expressing themselves in public. This will lead them to revert to more traditional forms of public demonstration. Critical expression will be conveyed no longer solely through the dissemination of ideas and images defying all forms of censorship, but also through the presence in the streets and public squares of bodies free of fear and proud to emancipate themselves together, openly.[5]

In other words, in a situation of dictatorship widespread acceptance of the desirability of a critical public sphere has an innate propensity to translate into democratic political force. The radio stations he was studying—along with samizdat and other dissident media published within eastern Europe—had not merely voiced the argument for a critical public sphere; they came, in time, to embody it in their output. Media's role in the development of a critical public sphere is the principal means by which media advance the politics of democratization.

* * *

The broadcasters' role in the development of nascent public spheres in these countries was uneven and sometimes paradoxical. Semelin points out that it took programmers at the Western radio stations some time after the end of World War II to achieve an understanding of whom they were trying to reach, of what their audiences' concerns were, and of how best they might try to communicate with them. Different generations and ethnicities among exiles involved in broadcast programming clashed over what approaches were appropriate. For their part, Europeans living behind the Iron Curtain were, in the early years of the Cold War, often less than receptive to Western stations' messages; many were willing to give Soviet-style "real existing socialism" a chance to succeed. They seemed to become more receptive to Radio Free Europe and its partner stations only as their own experience of communism, and of the Soviet domination on which it relied, worsened. That is to say, Semelin implies that changes in East Europeans' attitudes seemed more often to be a product of their own direct experience than of any innate qualities of the arguments being put to them by the broadcasters.

Likewise, although the Western-based broadcasters would, over succeeding decades, become important secondary contributors to, and popularizers of, spheres of critical debate that were being developed in parts of Eastern Europe, they rarely initiated those developments. Early successes by East European democrats in opening up initially modest spheres of critical debate, in redefining their experience and in (re)discovering their capacity for political agency tended to be home-grown achievements. The broadcasters usually became important partners in these efforts only later—and then their role remained supplemental. The broadcasters' importance came to lie mainly in their ability to amplify the views of dissidents, the activities of the opposition and news of regime repression—the latter sometimes contributing to the swift release of detainees.

Semelin also shows how interactive and multi-directional the media messaging between the Western radio stations and the opponents of communism became. The traffic in information and ideas that eventually defeated communism in Eastern Europe did *not* run solely, or even principally, from West to East. Democratization in the East did not come as a result of people in the West deigning to share their ideas of liberty with their less fortunate kin in the East. Rather, Semelin demonstrates how the democratic impulse that emerged in the East often originated in the East, and how it was often communicated to the West and then was broadcast by Radio Free Europe and others, greatly amplified, back to the East. By the time the Berlin Wall came down in 1989, a significant number of East Europeans had broken down the wall of fear in which communism had once imprisoned their minds. They were also regularly breaching the barrier that had been erected between them and another world of ideas and there, in that other world, they could regularly be found offering their own ideas and sometimes borrowing others'.

The refreshing acknowledgment of the primacy of the struggle waged by people living in the East that Semelin brings to the story can be attributed largely to his political acuity. His grasp of the nonviolent politics of civil resistance that came to shape the tactics of the anti-communist opposition, most notably of Charter 77 in Czechoslovakia and of Solidarity in Poland, resonates through this study.[6] Civil resistance has been a long-time specialty of Semelin's research and writing. Indeed, in 2014 he was awarded the James Lawson Award for Outstanding Achievement in the Study of Nonviolent Conflict. Eight years before writing *La Liberté au bout des ondes*, Semelin had published a study on unarmed resistance to the Nazis—an even more vicious foe than the men in the Kremlin. The product was his *Unarmed Against Hitler*.[7] The immersion of his later analysis of the impact of Western Cold War propaganda in the same politics of civil resistance is the distinguishing feature of *Freedom over the Airwaves*. It accounts for much of the book's originality.

He analyses and compares in a number of contexts—principally East Germany and Poland—the maturation of civil resistance, and its relationship with Radio Free Europe and the other Western broadcasters. A lesser, unique feature of the work is the attention he pays also to the likely political effects of television broadcasts from West to East Germany; he does not limit himself to radio alone. Semelin finds that the airwaves, both radio and television, were important, yes, to the collapse of communism in Eastern Europe. But it was the audience, the way its members came to understand their own direct experience of communism, and what they chose to do about it—that is to say, the mode of organization they chose, the strategies and tactics they evolved—that were sovereign.

***

The role that the Western radio stations were able to play in the struggle against communism in Eastern Europe tends to support a view of news media as dialogue—as a platform for perpetual argument even when only one voice can be heard. This dialogic view of the media, most clearly developed by the Canadian philosopher and argumentation theorist Douglas Walton,[8] offers a useful way of seeing how it is that the media help to construct a critical public sphere. Walton suggests that the argumentative dialogue that occurs in news media can be, though often is not, explicit. It is explicit when, for example, two or more individuals are openly disputing a point in a studio or during a phone-in, or in a newspaper's letters column. But, at other times, the fact that an argument is underway may be less clear. This may be the case when only one individual—let us say he is a presenter—is alone in a studio putting forward his viewpoint on an issue. Here, an argument is underway to the extent that this presenter anticipates—he "simulates" within his own mind—the likely views of his audience/s on the issue at hand. He then articulates his own position on that issue *in a way that takes account of what he understands his listeners' perspectives to be*. Put another way: he responds to the response he would expect from his audience if they were present in the studio arguing directly with him.

Walton suggests that the factor that will largely determine whether our presenter's argument succeeds or fails to persuade his audience is how skillfully he takes account of their "commitments." Their commitments are those deep premises, values, convictions, aspirations and the like that underlie the audience's thinking on the issue being debated. That is important because, according to Walton as well as other argumentation theorists, irrespective of whether an argument is direct or simulative, there are only two ways in which the presenter can persuade his audience to agree with his argument. One way is that he manages to argue from *their* commitments to *his* conclusion, carrying the audience with him each step of the way. This can be rather difficult, though it is not impossible. The other way of persuading the audience is that the presenter—or the audience themselves, or circumstance—brings about a change in the audience's commitments that moves them closer to his commitments. In this eventuality, the presenter can argue from more commonly shared, or even identical, commitments to his conclusion— which is a much easier task.

Walton's portrayal of media output as argumentative dialogue enables a number of other insights. First, his theory of simulation enables us to suggest that, even in the broadcasters' bleakest days—when they had little information about what was happening in the East, and even less direct feedback from people there—they were nonetheless engaged in a form of dialogue with their audiences. Second, the notion of commitments suggests an explanation slightly different from Semelin's as to how east Europeans became, with the passage of time, increasingly receptive to the Western broadcasters' conclusions. It is that east Europeans' disillusion with communism and Soviet domination of Eastern Europe brought about changes in their commitments that shifted them into closer alignment with the broadcasters. And this change at the level of commitments made East Europeans more susceptible to the broadcaster's (often simulative) arguments.

This explanation bears some resemblance to one of the requirements for successful persuasion outlined by the ancient Greeks. As is evident, the notion of commitments includes far more than the relatively narrow set of statements that would qualify as premises in a logical argument. Commitments can include a range of emotionally infused standards and beliefs—some moral, others self-interested, some derived from our sense of identity—that so often inform our political judgments on an issue and drive our political objectives.[9] As such, our commitments bear a strong resemblance to what the Greeks called *ethos*—one of the devices for successful persuasion laid down in the rules of rhetoric. The Greeks would advise someone trying to persuade an audience of something that he should first establish with the audience that he and they shared values, idiom, and/or a point of departure.

* * *

Today the reciprocal relationship between the politics of resistance and the media is a focus of acute interest among scholars and nonviolent action takers. The question organizing much of their new research has been: How do we best understand the role that the various digital and social media have played, and might play in future, in popular or civil resistance struggles? Hence the clamour for an English translation of *La Liberté au bout des ondes*. For Semelin's book implies much about how audiences and media respond to each other politically. And it speaks, by extension (though not of course directly), to a number of the questions that have arisen since it was written about the significance to struggles for democracy of new, digitalized media and communications technologies.

The arrival of these new communications technologies has aroused many claims—a number of them perhaps extravagant. Some people have suggested, for example, that digital technologies have made person-to-person political organization unnecessary. Others have argued that these new media platforms have led to an individualization of news and information flows that will soon render corporate or big media redundant. Yet others have suggested that digital technologies provide a means likely to end the marginalization of those at the periphery of power. And there are those who have argued that digitalization creates opportunities for secure tactical communications between political action takers.

Semelin might be expected to be skeptical of these claims. Digital and social media have, as communicative tools, certainly been tactically important in contemporary struggles for democracy in Arab lands and elsewhere. In the main this is because these technologies have enriched the possibilities for the construction of critical public spheres in nondemocratic societies. But Semelin would likely argue that action takers' focus should remain on politics and on the plausibility and performance of their strategies.

Plus ça change, plus c'est la meme chose, perhaps.

Things can indeed sometimes look very much as they did in the past. Few pieces of writing could provide a better description of the new digital media environment at work in a moment of popular revolt than the following passage:

> Th[e] free expression of inter-individual communication was the strongest and most moving sign that the people had reclaimed the public sphere. The flow of information changed radically, transcending the traditional role attributed to the media. As everyone communicated with everyone else, news was circulated by everyone else, news was circulated by every individual. Multiple communication channels within the population served to convey news from place to place, with the inevitable risk of circulating the most fanciful rumors. The journalist's function as such disappeared, as everyone became the receiver and provider of news on public affairs.

Here is a picture of a mass of individuals at a time of political tumult in control of their own news, of information and of the technologies that spread them. It is a picture that we associate with the uprisings in the Arab world, perhaps most notably Tunisia and Egypt, in 2011.

It may come as a surprise to the reader to learn that this description is Semelin's, published in 1997, of the Prague Spring of 1968.[10] That is to say, it is an account of the moment when Czechs and Slovaks rose to demand democratic freedoms and an end to Soviet domination in the midst of the Cold War. It describes events and modes of political communication 10 years before the first desktop home or personal computer came to be mass-marketed in the West, 16 years before handheld mobile phones reached ordinary consumers, 22 years before communism finally collapsed in Eastern Europe, and about 25 years before the commercialization of the Internet.

So, since the end of the Cold War, just how much has changed in the political uses of media in insurgencies and popular struggles for democracy? A brief outline of some features of the post-Cold War landscape should help us answer the question.

The collapse of Eastern Europe's communist regimes after 1989 created an international environment substantially different from that shaped by superpower rivalry after World War II. One of its defining characteristics was the apparent triumph of the West. The international strategic balance had fundamentally changed. Millions of East Europeans had rejected communism. In China, communism had, since the late 1970s, been mutating into a variant of capitalism overseen by a still dictatorial but only nominally Marxist-Leninist party. The West's market-based economics had proved more resilient and considerably more alluring to others than the socialist alternative. Most countries that had been part of the Warsaw Pact and Soviet Union until those two bodies' dissolution in 1991 now migrated westwards—politically, diplomatically, economically and militarily.

The means by which the Cold War had been lost and won resonated across the new landscape. The desire for political and economic changes had driven events. The strategic use of nonviolent organization and tactics by populations across Eastern Europe had delivered to communism the final *coup de grâce*. Military power had played no active role in the final outcome of the Cold War other than at economic level: the Soviet Union had exhausted its already sclerotic economy with ruinous spending on its war in Afghanistan during the 1980s and on its effort to match US defense capabilities.

The manner of communism's collapse and the new strategic balance began to affect the way in which political disputes were resolved across large parts of the developing world and elsewhere. In the late 1980s and early 1990s, erstwhile member states of the Soviet Union and Warsaw Pact, including a re-emergent Russia, ended support to armed insurgencies involved in class or national liberation struggles around the world. Other, smaller states such as Cuba and Libya that had provided similar military aid also lost the will or means to do so. Armed struggle appeared to many in the developing world no longer to be viable means to realize radical political change. As in the developed world, nonviolent forms of struggle came to seem to many in the developing world to offer more plausible tactics to realize radical objectives. The abandonment of armed insurgencies—by the African National Congress (ANC) in South Africa, the Provisional IRA Northern Ireland and by movements elsewhere were a response, in considerable part, to these developments.

Those non-state actors in the developing world that did not renounce armed struggle in the new global environment belonged mainly to religious, rather than secular, revolutionary traditions.[11] Militant Islam became the principal source of religion-based revolutionary activity. For Islamists, civil resistance had not brought about the collapse of the Soviet Union and European communism. Rather, the cause had been the guerrilla war they had waged against the Soviet Union in Afghanistan. Communism's collapse was thus, in the eyes of Islamists a vindication of armed struggle. And some of them believed it might be within their power to inflict, in future, a similar defeat on the United States and the West—and felt provoked to do so by continuing Western hegemony in the Muslim Middle East that had been most evident in the US-led alliance that had expelled invading Iraqi troops from Kuwait in 1990-91.

In this new environment, rapid advances in communications technologies, developed mainly in the then assertively hegemonic West, spread rapidly across the world. The mass marketing to consumers and companies of computing power, mobile telephony, satellite communications and Internet access through the 1990s radically recast how any one individual could communicate with others—and potentially with humanity as a whole—and the way in which the world transacted business. These advances entailed new possibilities for both reporting on, and participation in, conflict. Scenes of conflict were now being broadcast by news organizations in real time to audiences in distant time zones. Public opinion about a faraway conflict could, as a consequence, be affected in real time, with consequences for countries' foreign and domestic policies. The immediacy and ubiquity of the new forms of coverage of conflict led some scholars to talk of the "mediatization of conflict":[12] they pointed to, among other things, the way that a conflict and its trajectory, as well as the arbitration of its issues, was now sometimes being decided by media coverage.

The Internet extended this trend. Rapidly growing consumer access to the Internet from the mid-1990s, as well as much faster search engines, gave potential global reach to any connected individual who might want to inform the world about a conflict. She could upload a report or images of a particular incident and place it within reach of much of the rest of the connected world a few seconds later. Similarly, widening access to mobile telephony, satellite technologies and the Internet gave any connected individual action taker in a conflict in the early 2000s the potential ability to maintain immediate, flexible digital communication and information exchange with others over long distances. She had the technological means to talk to or message whomever she wished instantaneously while she was on the move. The tactical consequences of these new potentialities for political action takers were (as security concerns were addressed) considerable.

Just how considerable is evident if we step back two decades to the operational constraints on anti-communist dissidents in Eastern Europe or on opponents of apartheid in South Africa in the early 1980s. The experience of a militant South African opponent of apartheid might be informative. He is a member of the domestic underground organization of the ANC in the South Africa's main industrial city of Johannesburg. One of his tasks is to distribute clandestinely to significant individuals in the opposition and strategic sectors of the population information outlining developing ANC positions.

To be able to tap into the thinking of the ANC's exiled leadership regularly, this individual would have bought with cash under a false name a sophisticated shortwave radio receiver in another city and transported it back to Johannesburg. He would also have bought aerial wire and installed it, disguised as a washing line, in his backyard. This would have enabled him to receive very weak, crackly shortwave signals from the ANC's Radio Freedom broadcasting from the Zambian capital, Lusaka, and four other African states. To write the leaflets, he would, again using cash and a false name, have purchased what was, at the time, referred to as a "golf ball electric typewriter." He would also have bought a number of additional "golf balls" (rotund devices, each carrying a typeface) from other suppliers—devices he could relatively easily hide lest they be found in a police raid and be used as forensic evidence against him.

To print the leaflets carrying the information to be distributed, he would have bought a printer—one using old wax-stencil technology in order not to provoke suspicion—in a town 400 miles away, again paying cash and using a false name. He would himself have packaged the printing machine before railing it to Johannesburg for collection, again under a false name. He would have purchased stencils, ink and reams of A4 paper in small quantities from different suppliers—in order not to stand out in their memory as a customer. He would have bought about eight different styles of envelope as well as pens with three or four differently colored inks, and about a thousand stamps—from a variety of different shops and post offices. The radio, typewriter, printer and other supplies would have been hidden in, say, an under-floor chamber reached through a disguised trap door.

On any night on which he went operational, he would have put on a set of rubber gloves and printed about 5,000 leaflets. He would have posted about a thousand of them to individual addressees on a list that he had developed. The addressees would have been leading members of the opposition and, in some cases, members of the government whom he hoped to unnerve. He would have enclosed each leaflet in its own envelope—chosen from the batch of envelopes of different shapes, colors and sizes bought earlier. He would then have addressed each envelope using one of his collection of differently colored pens, while trying to disguise his own handwriting. His attempt to give each envelope a relatively unique appearance would have been intended to increase its chances of reaching its intended recipient. Had the envelopes been identical in appearance, postal or state security authorities would have been able to intercept several hundred of them once they had detected the contents of one. The leafleteer would then have posted the envelopes in batches of about a hundred at different post boxes around the suburbs of Johannesburg and surrounding towns. Finally, he would under cover of predawn darkness have scattered the remainder of the loose leaflets around bus stops and other points of Johannesburg frequented by South Africans from the oppressed black majority.

Using these perhaps obsessive security measures, this ANC action-taker—in fact the writer of this concluding chapter, during his days in the anti-apartheid underground—would have reached probably no more than 300 people with the leaflet. Today, one person with a laptop bought anywhere and equipped with the means to anonymize herself at least temporarily in cyberspace could be considerably more effective. She could hope to send a similar leaflet by email or other means to many thousands, or hundreds of thousands, of people in a few seconds. It is, though, unlikely that she would today be digitally distributing anything quite as prosaic as a leaflet. Nor would she be operating from a single location. More likely, she would be using a smart phone, tablet or other mobile device while on the move to exploit any number of digital platforms and social networking options to communicate her movement's views. Her message would likely include video footage of her movement's activities and an interview with its leader, and so on. She would, moreover, be able to interact with recipients in real time, if it made sense from her perspective to take that additional risk. There would a real danger of her eventual capture—as there had been for the ANC leafleteer (he got away with it!). But she would, even if her skill in covering her tracks defeated the investigative capabilities of the security services seeking her for only a short while, have been a great deal more effective than the young man using wax stencil technology.

* * *

Those who persisted with violent insurgencies after the ANC, PIRA and others had abandoned armed struggle in the late 1980s and early 1990s used the new media technologies to considerable apparent effect. Their use of websites in particular increased rapidly in the early 2000s. US defense department officials disclosed at the time that they were monitoring about 5,000 jihadi Islamist websites, although they focused mainly on fewer than a hundred of the more hostile sites.[13] The output of these sites was largely agitational in tone and designed to aid recruitment and fundraising. The sites' main rhetorical ploy tended to be propaganda of the deed, captured as video. The ploy might take the form of footage of an attack by a suicide bomber and of his earlier justification before the camera of the act that he was about to commit. Or it might take the form of a video of an improvised explosive device destroying a Western vehicle, perhaps even the beheading of a hostage. The ploy offered the viewer entry into a world of revolutionary Muslim macho chic. And many thousands of young Muslims evidently found it convincing.

Some websites occasionally also provided instruction on rudimentary bomb assembly and other operational skills. But, perhaps understandably in view of any website's value as a source of potential intelligence to an adversary, jihadi groups did not, as a rule, use them as a platform for training purposes or planning. Even less did they use websites for command and control purposes. To the extent that jihadis used digital technologies to communicate on operations, they tended to use mobile and satellite telephony. But these technologies, too, would come to cause them considerable security problems.

Still and moving images were no less important a means of persuasion for *non*violent movements seeking optimal outcomes. Arguably, the power of the image was considerably more important to nonviolent action takers, given their reliance on politics by political means alone. One of the most sophisticated and technologically appropriate uses of video imagery to advance a democratic struggle occurred in Myanmar/Burma. It was the work of a group of journalists that had emerged out of the opposition to the country's decades-long military dictatorship. Contrary to the trend that would become prevalent among most nonviolent political movements in the 1990s and early 2000s, these journalists did not focus much effort on using Internet platforms. The reason was simple. Their context differed. The dictatorship they opposed would in future years strictly limit access to the Internet in Myanmar/Burma and closely monitor use of it. As an alternative, these journalists exploited the advances in satellite broadcasting technologies. They set up their own broadcaster, the Democratic Voice of Burma (DVB) in Oslo 1992, a year after the award of the Nobel Peace Prize in the city to the opposition leader Aung San Suu Kyi, whom the dictatorship had refused to allow to attend.

DVB expanded rapidly. It started out broadcasting a weak radio signal over 5,000 miles from the Norwegian capital via a string of relays to Myanmar/Burma. But, by 2005, they were transmitting a few hours of pre-recorded television news each day via satellite into their homeland and planning an upgrade to live broadcasts. Their information on developments inside the country came initially via foreign news agencies, as well as NGOs and private and family sources based there. They gradually expanded their ground cover inside Myanmar/Burma to include a clandestine network of local journalists who occasionally contributed to DVB while working for other, legal news organizations.[14]

DVB's breakthrough came, however, from a different source. It came from a group of young men and women who were trained in secret inside Myanmar/Burma in the basics of reporting and in the use of amateur video cameras, with which they were then equipped. This group of citizen video journalists was up and running when, in 2007, the military junta withdrew fuel subsidies. With Buddhist monks in the lead, tens of thousands of Burmese marched in protest, reflecting a vast reservoir of resentment against the dictatorship. The newly trained citizen journalists, with their video cameras in hand, were on the scene to report the resistance and the brutality with which the dictatorship crushed it. This video footage and other material on the Saffron uprising—as the revolt became known on account of the color of the monks' robes—were smuggled out of Burma. Occasionally this footage was moved abroad via Myanmar/Burma's tightly restricted Internet. More usually, however, it was rushed physically into neighboring states. There, in Thailand and elsewhere, DVB had already developed an intermediate level of organization tasked with linking its Burma-based newsgathering network digitally to its hub in Oslo. The images were then broadcast back into the country within a day or two from Norway via satellite. DVB was thus able to provide Burmese with a version of events in their own country that substituted for the state-approved media's version of, or silence about, those events.

Reliable estimates of DVB's viewership for the period are unavailable. But anecdotal evidence at the time suggested that many thousands of Burmese were able to watch reports about the Saffron protests in which many of them had been personally involved. Private owners of satellite dishes in some cases placed their television sets on pavements outside their homes so that others could watch DVB's footage.[15] Ironic government tribute to the effectiveness of DVB's television channel came in 2008, shortly after the uprising had been contained. The dictatorship increased the license fee for a satellite dish to three times the annual Burmese salary.¹⁶ It was an echo of the communist East German government's attempts three decades earlier to stop its citizens from turning their antennae westwards to watch Western television programs. Semelin tells us that the East German communist party's first secretary at the time, Walter Ulbricht, had referred to the redirected antennae as "the class enemy on the roof," and ordered that they be turned back eastwards.[17] In Burma, according to a BBC estimate, the increase in the price of a licence for a satellite dish affected about 60,000 mainly middle-class citizens, as well as businesses and public video halls that showed mainly foreign football coverage.[18] In 2009, DVB reckoned that one in five of Burma's 50,000,000 people had access of one kind or another to its television channel, and obtained information from it or its sister radio station "a few times every week."[19]

DVB, in addition to broadcasting its own video footage of the uprising in 2007, also sold footage to major international broadcasters whose correspondents had been excluded from Myanmar/Burma.[20] These broadcasters made considerable use of the images. In the process, foreign democratic governments and human rights groups received fresh evidence on which to base demands for a transition to democracy in the country. For ordinary Burmese struggling against the dictatorship, the reports that DVB and international news organizations broadcast back into Myanmar/Burma, particularly over the period of the Saffron uprising, constituted a form of affirmation. Many were encouraged by this feeling of recognition.[21] In the process, the strength of the images that these citizen video reporters provided—often gathered at great personal risk to themselves—gave poignancy to the old journalistic adage, repeated by DVB's executive director in an interview in 2009: "If there is no picture, there is no story." He and others in DVB's leadership well understood that their country's military junta—like all dictators—"fear the camera."[22]

DVB's significance as an instance of civil resistance media is not dependent, however, solely on its success in setting itself up as a transnational broadcaster—remarkable though that achievement was. It derives additional significance from the direction of its leadership's thinking on what professional ethos might best serve their democratic purpose. At its genesis in 1991/92, DVB was merely an amplifier for the opposition. But this approach was soon exposed as inadequate, according to its executive director:

> When we started ... it was just to relay the message to the people inside Burma, mainly about what the opposition organizations working abroad and also within the country [were doing] ... During the process

what we learnt is that the more we [did] propaganda about the opposition movement more and more we lost our credibility. People see you as promoting [the] opposition and [conclude] you are not fair when you criticize the government or what they are doing.[23]

This audience response prompted a rethink that, gradually, caused DVB to broaden its approach. It wanted to become a space in which Burmese could receive information from a number of points of view and engage in open political discussion. Accordingly, it began moving towards a form of broadcasting in which it asserted its independence of all parties, including the opposition, to better serve its audience. Its changing ethos, according to Aye Chan Naing, involved a

delicate balance ... [O]bviously we are not neutral. We want to have a free Burma. We don't want this military government. I mean everybody hates them ... they are basically criminals. They kill people, even Buddhist monks, and lots of political prisoners are in prisons. But, at the same time, as a media organization, when we report the story then we have to be objective. We have to give them a chance to comment or [for] their voice [to be heard] for any kind of accusation or allegations made by opposition groups or even the victims. Whenever we have ... human rights violations that we have been told [about] by victims, we always call the local authorities or police stations or government offices.[24]

In the course of doing so, DVB reporters in Oslo often met incredulous, shocked responses over the phone from government officials in Rangoon.[25] This did not, however, deter them. Aye Chan Naing added in 2009: "Our aim, our dream ... is to become really an independent public service media organization for people inside Burma."[26]

This shift in ethos was a patent attempt by DVB to help develop a critical public sphere in Burmese politics. This was significant in three respects. First, as Semelin has argued in the case of Eastern Europe, success in developing a public sphere has considerable potential to inspire popular action against a nondemocratic state. Second, the approach prefigured a pluralistic future. And third, it was consistent with a strategic imperative in civil resistance strategy to build as broad as possible a democratic movement by, among other things, seeking to gain sympathy among—or at least to lessen the sense of threat felt by— elements aligned to the undemocratic state.

DVB's organized use of the video camera in the hand of the citizen as a persuader in a civil resistance struggle was not the first time this had been done. Semelin relates how, 20 years earlier, at the instigation of Roland Jahn, an East German dissident who had been banished to the west, a group of action takers were provided with smuggled video cameras and trained in their use in 1987. The intention was that they provide video coverage of the realities of life in East Germany and acts of resistance that would be smuggled to the West and, from there, be broadcast back to the East. The goal was to overcome not merely the censorship imposed by the East German authorities but also the self-censorship exercised by some locally based foreign correspondents reporting for Western media. Jahn anticipated that this video coverage and its recycling could help achieve three additional outcomes. It could mobilize Western popular and government opinion behind the opposition in the East. Perhaps more importantly, it could help bring together disparate opposition groups in East Germany that had little knowledge of each other. And, third, it could raise pressures on the communist government in other ways—among others by publicizing both the arrest of opposition figures and the way in which the communists had gerrymandered the political system. Semelin's account suggests the video cameras had the desired effects.[27]

At about the same time as their Burmese counterparts, Egyptian democrats were also discovering the superior persuasive powers of video over voice or print media. They, too, exploited the power of video to considerable effect. In doing so, Egyptian action takers had an advantage over their German and Burmese counterparts. It came courtesy of the arrival and spread of a media platform that enabled them to make the footage their citizen reporters had shot available to potentially millions in their own country and abroad within a few minutes. That new platform was, of course, the Internet. They could make their images available to many more people, and more quickly, than would have been the case had their material been broadcast initially over conventional television channels (assuming the willingness, in the first instance, of these channels to broadcast them).

Within Egypt from about 2005, a new breed of opposition action taker began to emerge. She or he bypassed stringent restrictions on free expression and the largely moribund established Egyptian media by turning the Internet into a space accommodating a freer flow of information and opinion than the regime of President Hosni Mubarak generally allowed. That is to say, they fashioned their corner of the Internet into a sort of proto public sphere. Their mode of operation was cautious. Yet their modest efforts would over time quite evidently accelerate the erosion of the already shallow legitimacy of Mubarak's government. In the process, these action takers—from mainly the liberal intelligentsia and independent worker organizations—temporarily displaced as the center of political opposition to Mubarak both the long-ineffective opposition parties that contended for seats in the parliament in Cairo and the long-suppressed though deeply embedded Muslim Brotherhood.

An exemplar of the kind of operation launched by this new species of Egyptian action taker was a website, Shayfeen.com. It was a website with a difference: the site would help spawn, as well as express the grievances of, what eventually became a mass movement. Its name translated into English as "We-are-watching-you.com." One of Shayfeen's three founders—all of them women—tells how those involved in directing it stumbled across the superior persuasiveness of video in their attempts to bring to the attention of Egyptians important stories that went largely unreported by the cowed conventional media. For tactical reasons, back in 2005 Shayfeen's leadership had chosen

> a very non-confrontational approach. That was monitoring. When we set up the movement, presidential elections—multi-candidate presidential elections—were going to happen in Egypt for the first time ever. And we started monitoring the elections [with] something like five hundred recruits to the movement. We ... wrote some very detailed reports on the electoral fraud as it was happening. And one of our monitors filmed the fraud as it was happening. Rather than write down a report he filmed [it]. We found that film is a much more effective medium than written reports. A couple of months later, we had our parliamentarian elections. For that we ... prepared a number of groups with cameras to follow up and report on elections nationwide. And by then we had three thousand volunteers monitoring for Shayfeen.com. We set up a website where we uploaded our film on the elections. And the website [became] very popular very quickly. Thereafter we became involved in the mobilization and the campaigning for the independence of the judiciary ...[28]

The use by Egyptian opposition action takers of increasingly ubiquitous mobile telephony, the Internet, and various social networking and other digital platforms was innovative and flexible. Media promoting a multiplicity of voices and political ferment seemed to be mutually reinforcing, as Semelin observed it had been in the East European resistance to communism. As fresh sources of opposition to Mubarak broke surface over the six years to the revolution of 2011, more than one radio channel broadcast over the Internet, though no parallel Internet-based television station emerged. In large numbers, Egyptians used text, voice, stills and video to "self-report" Egyptian life, and to monitor and resist the Mubarak government. As self-reporting by ordinary citizens became more prevalent, its output also became a more credible source of news for Egyptians than the established media. "Citizen reporting played a very important role," according to Ghada Shahbender. This alternative media, she adds, came to be "sought by people for the truth."[29] Looking back at the role that these developments played in the 2011 revolution, she took the view that "undoubtedly, the two weapons of Egyptian revolutionaries were the Internet and the camera." We could add to them a third weapon, perhaps still to be acknowledged properly: an explosion of satire.[30] In the climactic days of late January and early February 2011, information flows and media roles in Egypt came to resemble strongly the feverish atmosphere of the Prague Spring in 1968 that Semelin described and that we recounted earlier:

> Th[e] free expression of inter-individual communication was the strongest and most moving sign that the people had reclaimed the public sphere. The flow of information changed radically, transcending the traditional role attributed to the media. As everyone communicated with everyone else, news was circulated by everyone else, news was circulated by every individual ...

During the 18 days of demonstrations that preceded Mubarak's fall, Egyptians used, among other software, Bambuser, a Swedish Internet platform, to live-stream over the Internet video images taken by smartphone or computer. The effect could be electrifying:

> When spirits were down in Alexandria, Internet activists in Cairo sent them live feeds of what was happening in Tahrir Square. This kept up the momentum of the movement in Alexandria. And, when spirits were down in Cairo, we received images from the Suez. It kept us going. So the live images of the demonstrations and the marches in the different cities connected the activists and kept them going. It kept the momentum of the movement rolling and played a very, very important role.[31]

Mobile phones were significant informational, agitational and organizing tools as, too, were blogs and a variety of other Internet platforms. Ironically, the Egyptian government, too, ended up agitating unwittingly on behalf of the opposition. When the government closed down access to Bambuser and Twitter at the height of the uprising, opposition action takers moved to Facebook. When it, too, was closed down, the more technically savvy of them resorted to proxy breakers and a series of other back-door entry points to communicate with each other and the outside world. Then came the closure of text message servers for mobile phones. Over the period of these Internet and communications closures it became clear to opposition action takers that they were not the main losers in the communications shutdown. Rather, the main loser was the Mubarak government itself. The shutdowns backfired. They enraged many apolitical Egyptians; they drove more people onto the streets. According to Shahbender,

> People who had no intention of participation ... went out and took to the streets because they had been deprived of their Internet services and mobile phone services, and because they wanted to know what was happening and had no other means of knowing. That contributed to the success of the Egyptian revolution in a big way.[32]

* * *

The insurrectionary potential of the new digital technologies had become apparent to action takers and scholars well before the uprisings in the Arab world in 2011. It had been foreshadowed particularly clearly in two instances of mass upsurge over the previous 12 years.

The first was a sequence of demonstrations that had disrupted a ministerial meeting of the World Trade Organization in Seattle in the summer of 1999. The Seattle demonstrations had shown how websites, blogs, email and text could be used effectively to mobilize Internet-connected individuals across the world who shared a common interest. The organizers had used digital platforms to marshal tens of thousands of people from many different corners of the globe to a common cause in a single locality. The shape that the protests had taken on the streets of Seattle had also revealed how tactically effective mobile phones could be (certainly at this relatively early stage in the evolution of state countermeasures) as a means to maneuver groups of demonstrators rapidly around a city—in the process confounding security force attempts to assert control.

The second particularly instructive use of digital technologies to advance resistance came during popular protests in Iran in 2009 against alleged election fraud committed by Iran's theocratic state to secure a second term for the country's conservative incumbent president, Mahmoud Ahmajinedad. Here the social networking sites Facebook and Twitter, launched only seven and four years earlier, were significant tactical tools in the early phases of mobilizing for and spreading details of these protests. These sites also provided nigh real-time accounts of the protests on the streets of Tehran to the rest of the world before the government closed down Internet access—though even then the more cyber-savvy among the Iranian protesters found ways to reach the outside world. The most powerful single message to emerge from these protests was, as might have been expected, video footage. It had been digitally dispatched abroad. It showed the bloodied face of a prone 26-year-old philosophy student Neda Agha Soltan who was widely throught to have been shot dead by the *basiji* a pro-government militia, while watching an opposition demonstration.

***

The important communications role that digital technologies played in the two successful unarmed Arab insurrections in 2011—in Tunisia and Egypt—prompted intense debate among action takers and media scholars about the political uses and limitations of the new platforms. The extent to which these technologies had been used in the Arab uprisings and for what tactical purposes—as well as the degree of success or failure of the various attempts at revolution in which they were used—differed among the countries affected. Bahrain, Egypt, Libya, Syria, Tunisia and Yemen each constituted a significantly unique national context. Among the more important of the differences between them were disparities in the maturity and capabilities of the new opposition movements that had arisen—and, hence, in their capacity to exercise effective agency.

Perhaps the most valuable of the studies of media usage during the Arab uprisings has also been among the most restrained in its conclusions. In their examination of the events in 2011, Philip Howard and Muzammil Hussain suggested that, in democratization processes, the new communications technologies were providing a kind of "digital scaffolding for building a modern civil society."[33] They did not argue that the spread within a country of the new media and communications technologies was a sufficient condition for democratization; nor did they say it constituted a necessary condition. What they did conclude, however, was that the presence or absence of these technologies in a particular context was influential in determining the success or failure of democratization. They wrote:

> Weighing multiple political, economic, and cultural conditions, we find that information infrastructure especially mobile phone use—consistently appears as one of the key ingredients in parsimonious models for the conjoined combinations of causes behind regime fragility and social movement success. Internet use is relevant in some solution sets, but by causal logic it is actually the absence of Internet use that explains low levels of success.[34]

Stated more simply, their investigation of the Arab uprisings revealed a complex set of causes and effects. In every country affected, however, "the inciting incidents of the Arab Spring were digitally mediated in some way." Although Arab action takers were roused by many different factors, "information infrastructure, in the form of mobile phones, personal computers and social media, were part of the causal story." The uprisings demonstrated, moreover, "that countries that do not have a civil society equipped with digital scaffolding are much less likely to experience popular movements for democracy than are countries with such an infrastructure."

* * *

We turn now to consider a number of less restrained assumptions and claims that we listed earlier in this chapter about the political role that the new digital technologies can play in achieving radical change. These assumptions are seldom admitted to, even less often are they voiced as claims. Yet they have seemed since the onset of the digital revolution often to inform the conduct of action takers—sometimes at very considerable costs both to themselves and to the achievement of their objectives.

One is that the network building that can be achieved through digital communications can replace direct, person-to-person political organization in civil resistance struggles. This is highly improbable. Certainly these technologies can, and often do, greatly enhance a movement's ability to communicate and amplify among its audience its ideas, objectives, information and propaganda—and to host discussion. As such, these technologies are an important persuasive resource. It is doubtful, however, that these technologies can be used to prepare individuals for the rigors of confrontation with an adversary. Nor does it seem likely that a phone or Skype call, email or tweet can provide adequate evidence for a serious assessment of a movement's or its individual members' *will* to take on an adversary, or likely resilience in the face of an adversary's counter-attack. These are important assessments, particularly when a movement is aiming to achieve an outcome as likely to invite fierce resistance as regime change. Judgments about readiness may be too important to make on the basis of disembodied words alone, however passionately expressed. Words are perhaps nowhere cheaper—yet more costly in their eventual consequences—than in the hothouse bravado of revolutionary politics. The experience of successful revolutionary movements, both armed and unarmed, suggests that there is a distance of effort to be traveled between impalpable words and achieving strong organization. That journey involves moving feet on the ground; it entails mobilizing people in factories and offices, in shops, on farms and in the streets. There is a process of maturation, as Semelin might say, that a democratic movement is likely to have to undergo for it to be able to project decisive political force on a sustained basis. The words with which an oppressed people recasts its experience and frames a strategy to rediscover its agency—whether spoken over shortwave radio or the Internet—form only one part of its interaction on that journey to maturity. The remainder is its organization for, and engagement with, its adversary—and the plausibility of its strategy.

A second assumption is that new media technologies have led to an individualization and disaggregation of news and information flows that will soon render big institutionalized media redundant. This, too, seems unlikely. For sure, the news media industry continues to undergo far-reaching change, particularly in the developed West. As a result, some of its venerable media brands and corporate edifices face collapse. Their possible extinction would result from their failure to adequately exploit new technologies or to service rapidly changing market demand. At the same time, individuals and companies launched in the digital era are increasingly catering to the new market's thirst for more highly differentiated news. Yet there seems every reason to believe that this process of "creative-destruction" in the news media industry will see not only the rise of new media giants but, also, the survival of some of the more adaptable of the big media institutions of yesteryear. The basis for this prediction is that the kind of proliferation in sources of news now underway is likely to make the branding of news *more* important, not less, to many consumers. A race to the bottom—a market in cheap or even free undifferentiated news—will be only partial. Many consumers interested in business, political and cultural specialties will continue to demand what they consider quality information and news. And they will, as in the past, gravitate towards those news brands that they consider most likely to provide that quality—and be willing to pay the price for it. Similarly, those for whom news is a form of entertainment will be drawn to those brands that cater to their taste. The result is that there will in all probability continue to be big news media corporations—quite possibly bigger even than before. The difference will be in their names and their age; there will be new brands among the old. Those political action takers who look forward to the end of big or corporate news media—a source, as they see it, of moribund homogeneity and social control—will almost certainly be disappointed.

The hope that the end of big media is nigh is frequently associated with a third assumption: that the new technologies alone can end the marginalization of those groups and points of view that linger at the periphery of power. This, too, is by no means certain. The Internet has, indeed, emerged as an alternative mass medium of sorts. It has also, along with other digital technologies, greatly reduced the cost to the resource-poor and marginalized of making their views and demands available to the rest of the world. And much space in this chapter has been taken up with how useful these technologies can be, and have been, in enabling movements to cover their own activities. But several reservations are in order. One cause for reserve is the reality that the views and information that marginalized groups put online "will be visited and utilized by those already holding compatible views and ignored by others."[35] Thus the capacity of self-coverage on the Internet to expand a movement's support base may be quite limited. Another cause for pause is that coverage of a movement's activities in cyberspace—an arena in which an almost indeterminate number of organizations are contending for attention—is in no sense guaranteed to thrust that movement towards those political opportunities that could make it a major player. Becoming a major player is likely—as stressed above—to depend upon the strength of a movement's organization, its activities and its actual impact in the political world. A movement's ability to exert political pressure on the structures of power is likely to give credence to the kinds of claims it makes on its own behalf, to draw people to its self-coverage, and give it the means to leverage for itself both recognition in the arena of political opportunity and coverage in the 'big' media. We have seen above how popular action combined with self-coverage helped East German, Burmese and Egyptian action takers to leverage both political opportunity and coverage by the established media. In the words of the Egyptian Shahbender:

> The media will run after your story once you have become a story ... When things are stagnant, no one is interested. When things are happening everyone is interested ... Stop thinking about the media. Think about what you want to happen and what you want to change. And, when that starts happening and that starts changing, the media will be chasing you.[36]

An even less plausible fourth assumption—now restricted perhaps to the most credulous—is that the new technologies provide opportunities for secure tactical communications between political action takers. Exposure in 2013 of the extent of United States global electronic surveillance, and the routinely intense, initially localized monitoring of the internet and other digital platforms by dictatorships in China and elsewhere, should have put paid to this fantasy. Almost all but the poorest and most benevolent of governments now possess the computing power and software enabling them, in real time, to intercept digital communications within their borders in real time; to map the whereabouts of those communicating digitally; and to close down their citizens' access to particular platforms or to the Internet as whole. The ease with which a radical campaign and its main actors can be monitored is apparent from an academic study of the Occupy Wall Street protests in the United States in 2011 in which Twitter was among the most prominent organizing platforms used by action takers.[37] Employing only open source information—that is, without reliance on any covert surveillance of the kind of which most governments are capable—the researchers were able, by means of a simple network analysis, to establish the centrality of particular individuals and groups to the organization of the protests. The high technical precision of digital communications makes possible high precision surveillance. The fumbling ANC propagandist condemned to use wax stencil technology might not have been so disadvantaged after all.

* * *

A strength of the work by Howard and Hussain on the new technologies and democratization is the restraint of its conclusions about the effects of digitalization.[38] In work he has authored alone, Howard has been notable for consistently resisting the blow-hard conclusions of utopians and doomsayers alike on what digital communications and media technologies mean for democracy.[39] Similarly, in the approach he takes, Howard sides neither with those who suggest "that communications tools cause social changes" nor with those arguing that "society causes technological changes." Instead, he argues for what he terms a "soft determinism"

> in which technology designers and policy makers make decisions that provide capacities for and impose constraints on users. And every once in a while, social groups have the opportunity for collective action that allows for a reshaping or undoing of these design capacities and constraints.[40]

He implies that the present is the passing of a 'moment' in history in which a class of people—in his studies on the Middle East, they are mainly young, smart, impatient and Arab—has pushed its use of the capacities of new digital technologies beyond the constraints to which policy makers had wished to be able to restrict them. The results have been evident in uprisings and struggles not only in the Middle East but also elsewhere since the late 1990s, some of them canvassed briefly above. There is little reason to believe the moment has entirely passed.

When, however, we return in years to come to examine the uprisings of 2011 in Arab lands we will likely be asking the same basic questions of those who were involved in them as one tends to ask of any group of would-be revolutionaries: How did those involved read their circumstances in their attempt to exercise agency? How accurate was their reading? And how plausible were the strategy and tactics with which they sought to exercise agency? Few if any group of action takers have read their moment and their circumstances with more wisdom and skill than those who led the democratization of Eastern Europe from the streets and shipyards in the late 1980s. And few, if any, have achieved such considerable revolutionary success at such low cost. Their genius was particularly evident in Poland and Czechoslovakia. Although, in years to come, technologies, their possibilities and constraints will again have changed, the road to understanding radical democratization and the role of media in achieving it is likely still to lead through Gdansk, Prague, Budapest and Berlin—and I doubt there will yet be a map better than the one provided by Jacques Semelin.

Notes

1. Wolf, Marcus. 1997. *Man Without a Face. The Memoirs of a Spymaster*. London: Jonathan Cape.

2. Johnson, A. Ross & Parta, R. Eugene. 2010. "Appendix C: Weekly Listening Rates for Major Western Broadcasters to Poland, Hungary, Czechoslovakia, Romania, Bulgaria and the USSR during the Cold War," in Johnson, A. Ross & Parta, R. Eugene (eds.) *Cold War Broadcasting. Impact on the Soviet Union and Eastern Europe. A Collection of Studies & Documents*. Budapest & New York: Central European University Press, p. 142-144.

3. Johnson, A. Ross & Parta, R. Eugene. 2010. "Appendix C: Weekly Listening Rates for Major Western Broadcasters to Poland, Hungary, Czechoslovakia, Romania, Bulgaria and the USSR during the Cold War" in Johnson, A. Ross & Parta, R. Eugene (eds.) *Cold War Broadcasting. Impact on the Soviet Union and Eastern Europe. A Collection of Studies & Documents*. Budapest & New York: Central European University Press, p. 142-144. See also: Parta, R. Eugene. 2007. *Discovering the Hidden Listener. An Assessment of Radio Liberty and Western Broadcasting to the USSR during the Cold War*. Stanford: Hoover Institution Press.

4. Semelin, Jacques. 1997. *La Liberté au bout des ondes. Du coup de Prague à la chute du mur de Berlin.* Paris: Belfond. A second edition would follow in 2009, published by Nouveau Monde Editions, Paris.

5. p. 15.

6. Civil resistance is sometimes used interchangeably with terms such as "unarmed insurrection" and "people's power revolution." It is generally used to describe a popular challenge mounted mainly outside of constitutional or state-approved institutions that seeks maximal change to a state or social order through the aggressive strategic deployment of a series of nonviolent organizational and agitational tactics. It seeks to secure regime change by organizing an end to popular consent for a regime, raising the cost to a ruler and his allies of his continued rule, and isolating the ruler from his domestic and international supports. There are other kinds of struggle that bear many of the hallmarks of civil resistance but in which mass participation or full and decisive disruption of consent may not be necessary. Such struggles could be those in which the basic dynamic of civil resistance is in play in support of, say, minority or land rights. In such cases, victory may be possible by raising the costs of the existing system, or by destroying the legitimacy of the system domestically and/or among sources of international support for it.

Civil resistance is well described in Peter Ackerman and Christopher Kruegler. 1994. *Strategic nonviolent conflict: The dynamics of people power in the Twentieth Century.* Westport, Connecticut: Praeger. See also: Schock, Kurt. 2005. *Unarmed insurrections: People power movements in Nondemocracies.* Minneapolis: University of Minnesota Press. And see: Chenoweth, Erica, and Maria Stephan. 2011. *Why civil resistance works: The strategic logic of nonviolent conflict.* New York: Columbia University Press.

7. Semelin, Jacques. 1989. *Sans armes face à Hitler: La résistance civile en Europe, 1939-1943.* Paris: Bibliothèque historique Payot. The English edition was published by Praeger in 1993: *Unarmed Against Hitler: Civilian Resistance in Europe, 1939-1943.*

8. Walton, Douglas. 2007. *Media Argumentation. Dialectic, Persuasion, and Rhetoric.* New York: Cambridge University Press.

9. On emotion in politics, see: Westen, Drew. 2007. *The Political Brain. The Role of Emotion in Deciding the Fate of the Nation.* New York: Public Affairs, 2007. See also, Lakoff, George. *Don't Think of an Elephant. Know Your Values and Frame the Debate.* White River Jct, Vermont, USA: Chelsea Green Publishing Co, 1990.

10. The original French can be found at: Semelin, Jacques. 1997. *La Liberté au bout des ondes. Du coup de Prague à la chute du mur de Berlin.* Paris: Belfond. p. 186.

11. A prominent exception to this rule is the Naxalite rebellion in India.

12. See, among others, Cottle, Simon. 2006, *Mediatized Conflicts: Understanding Media and Conflicts in the Contemporary World.* Maidenhead, UK, Open University Press.

13. Cited in Kaplan, Ben. 2009. "Terrorists and the Internet." Backgrounder. Council on Foreign Relations. http://www.cfr.org/terrorism-and-technology/terrorists-internet/p10005 Accessed June 23, 2014.

14. Khin Maung Win, Deputy Director, DVB. 2009. Interview with Howard Barrell. Oslo: unpublished.

15. Aye Chang Naing, Executive Director, DVB. 2009. Interview with Howard Barrell. Oslo: unpublished.
16. BBC. 2/1/2008. "Satellite TV costs soar in Burma" http://news.bbc.co.uk/1/hi/world/asia-pacific/7167911.stm Accessed June 25 2014.
17. p. 258 in the English translation manuscript.
18. BBC. 2/1/2008. "Satellite TV costs soar in Burma" http://news.bbc.co.uk/1/hi/world/asia-pacific/7167911.stm Accessed June 25 2014.
19. Khin Maung Win, Deputy Director, DVB. 2009. Interview with Howard Barrell. Oslo: unpublished.
20. An award-winning television documentary tells the story of how this coverage was organized: Anders Østergaard (Producer). 2008. *Burma VJ. Reporting from a Closed Country*. HBO.
21. The judgment of "Alan," a young Burmese opposition activist, during an unrecorded discussion in Rangoon. He was the clandestine go-between when the author entered Myanmar/Burma to interview Aung San Suu Kyi in early 2011.
22. Aye Chang Naing, Executive Director, DVB. 2009. Interview with Howard Barrell. Oslo: unpublished.
23. Ibid.
24. Ibid.
25. Ibid.
26. Ibid.
27. p. 291 in the English translation manuscript.
28. Shahbender, Ghada. 2011. Interview with Howard Barrell. Medford, Mass.: unpublished.
29. Ibid.
30. See, for example, a short video documentary on the satire of Aalaam Wassef: Berger, Gregory, Joe Rizk & Al Giordano. 2011. *How Egyptians Televised the Revolution When the Media Would Not*. Mexico City: Narco News. Available at https://www.youtube.com/watch?v=WAyZ90XIJgE (Accessed July 4 2014)
31. Shahbender, Ghada. 2011. Interview with Howard Barrell. Medford, Mass.: unpublished.
32. Ibid.
33. Howard, Philip N. & Muzammil M. Hussain. 2013. *Democracy's Fourth Wave? Digital Media and the Arab Spring*. New York: Oxford University Press. p. 123.
34. Howard, Philip N. & Muzammil M. Hussain. 2013. *Democracy's Fourth Wave? Digital Media and the Arab Spring*. New York: Oxford University Press. p. 123. The "parsimonious" model to explain something is a model employing fewer parameters than might be expected.
35. Marmura, Stephen. 2008. "A net advantage? The Internet, grassroots activism and American Middle-Eastern Policy," in *New Media & Society* 2008 10, p. 261.
36. Shahbender, Ghada. 2011. Interview with Howard Barrell. Medford, Mass.: unpublished.
37. Tremayn, Mark. 2013. "Anatomy of Protest in the Digital Era: A Network Analysis of Twitter and Occupy Wall Street," in *Social Media Studies: Journal of Social, Cultural and Protest Politics* 13:1, p. 110-126.

38. Howard, Philip N. & Muzammil M. Hussain. 2013. *Democracy's Fourth Wave? Digital Media and the Arab Spring.* New York: Oxford University Press.

39. See, for example: Howard, Philip N. 2006. *New Media Campaigns and the Managed Citizen.* New York: Cambridge University Press. See also: Howard, Philip N. 2010. *The Digital Origins of Dictatorship and Democracy. Information Technology and Political Islam.* New York: Oxford University Press.

40. Howard, Philip N. 2010. *The Digital Origins of Dictatorship and Democracy. Information Technology and Political Islam.* New York: Oxford University Press. p. 16-17.

Bibliography

This bibliography is not an exhaustive list of all cited works. Instead it offers a selection of references on the following fundamental themes:

- History of Soviet-occupied Europe and East-West relations;
- Key political writings of East European dissidents;
- Civil resistance and nonviolent conflict dynamics and concepts;
- Resistance against the government in communist Eastern Europe;
- Communication and the media;
- Western media whose signals were received in countries in the East;
- Interpretations of the fall of communism and the Soviet empire.

History of Soviet-occupied Europe and East-West relations

Ash, Timothy Garton, *The Magic Lantern: The Revolution of '89 Witnessed in Warsaw, Budapest, Berlin, and Prague*, New York, Vintage Books, A Division of Random House, Inc., 1990.

Berend, Tibor Iván, *Central and Eastern Europe: 1944-1993. Detour from the Periphery to the Periphery*, reprint of 1995 edition, Cambridge, Cambridge University Press, Cambridge Studies in Modern Economic History, 1998.

Duplan, Christian and Vincent Giret, *La Vie en rouge*, 2 volumes, Paris, Le Seuil, 1994.

Fejtö, François, *Histoire des démocraties populaires*, new edition, 2 volumes, Paris, Le Seuil, Collection Points Politique, 1979.

Fejtö, François and Ewa Kulesza-Mietkowski, *La fin des démocraties populaires. Les chemins du post-communisme*, new edition, Paris, Le Seuil, Collection Points Histoire, 1997.

Fontaine, André, *La Guerre froide. 1917-1991*, Paris, Le Seuil, Collection Points Histoire, 2006.

———, *Histoire de la guerre froide*, 2 volumes, Paris, Le Seuil, Collection Points, 1981.

———, *Un seul lit pour deux rêves. Histoire de la détente (1962-1981)*, Paris, Le Seuil, 1982.

———, *L'un sans l'autre*, Paris, Fayard, 1991.

Gaddis, John Lewis, *The Cold War*, London, Allen Lane, 2006.

Hixson, Walter L., *Parting the Curtain. Propaganda, Culture, and the Cold War: 1945-1961*, Basingstoke, Macmillan, 1997.
Mink, Georges, *Vie et mort du bloc soviétique*, [Paris], Casterman; Firenze, Giunti, Collection 20ème Siècle, 1997.
Pearson, Raymond, *The Rise and Fall of the Soviet Empire*, 2nd edition, Basingstoke, Palgrave, Studies in Contemporary History, 2002.
Quétel, Claude (under the direction of), *Dictionnaire de la guerre froide*, Paris, Larousse, Collection À Présent, 2008.
Rothschild, Joseph and Nancy Meriwether Wingfield, *Return to Diversity. A Political History of East Central Europe since World War II*, 4th edition, New York: Oxford, Oxford University Press, 2008.
Rupnik, Jacques, *L'autre Europe. Crise et fin du communisme*, new edition, Paris, O. Jacob, Collection Points, 1993.
Sirinelli, Jean-François and Georges-Henri Soutou (under the direction of), *Culture et guerre froide*, Paris, Presses de l'Université Paris-Sorbonne, Collection Mondes Contemporains, 2008.
Soulet, Jean-François, *Histoire de l'Europe de l'Est. De la Seconde Guerre mondiale à nos jours*, Paris, Armand Colin, Collection U., Histoire Contemporaine Series, 2006.
Soutou, Georges-Henri, *La guerre de cinquante ans. Les relations Est-Ouest, 1943-1990*, Paris, Fayard, 2001.
Swain, Geoff and Nigel Swain, *Eastern Europe since 1945*, 3rd edition, Basingstoke, Palgrave Macmillan, The Making of the Modern World Series, 2003.
Winock, Michel (under the direction of), *Le Temps de la guerre froide*, Paris, Le Seuil, 1994.

Key political writings of East European dissidents
Havel, Vaclav, *The Power of the Powerless: Citizens against the State in Central-Eastern Europe*, edited by John Keane, London, Hutchinson, 1985.
Konrad, George, *Antipolitics*, translated by Richard E. Allen, Harcourt, 1984.
Kuron, Jacek, *Maintenant ou jamais*, Paris, Fayard, 1993.
Michnik, Adam, *Letters from Freedom: Post-Cold War Realities and Perspectives*, translated by Jane Cave, Berkeley, University of California Press, 1998
———, *Letters from Prison and Other Essays*, translated by Maya Latynski, Berkeley, University of California Press, 1986

Civil resistance and nonviolent conflict dynamics and concepts
Ackerman, Peter and Jack DuVall, *A Force More Powerful: A Century of Nonviolent Conflict*, New York, St. Martin's Press, 2000.
Ackerman, Peter and Christopher Kruegler, *Strategic Nonviolent Conflict: The Dynamics of People Power in the Twentieth Century*, Westport, Conn., Praeger Publishers, 1994.
Falcon y Tella, Maria José, *Civil Disobedience*, Leiden; Boston, M. Nijhoff Publishers, The Erik Castrén Institute Monographs on International Law and Human Rights, 2004.
Gros, Dominique and Olivier Camy (under the direction of), *Le droit de résistance à l'oppression*, Paris, Le Seuil, Collection Le Genre Humain, 2005.
Hastings, Tom H., *The Lessons of Nonviolence: Theory and Practice in a World of Conflict*, Jefferson, N.C., McFarland, 2006.

Hiez, David and Bruno Villalba (eds), *La désobéissance civile. Approches politique et juridique*, Villeneuve d'Ascq, Presses universitaires Septentrion, Collection Espaces Politiques, 2008.
Martin, Brian and Wendy Varney, *Nonviolence Speaks: Communicating against Repression*, Cresskill, N.J., Hampton Press, The Hampton Press Communication Series, 2003.
McCarthy, Ronald M., Gene Sharp and Brad Bennett, *Nonviolent Action: A Research Guide*, New York, Garland, 1997.
Mellon, Christian and Jacques Semelin, *La Non-Violence*, Paris, PUF, Collection Que Sais-Je ?, 1994.
Muller, Jean-Marie, *Le courage de la non-violence. Nouveau parcours philosophique*, Gordes (Vaucluse), Le Relié, Collection La Conscience et le Monde, 2001.
Muller, Jean-Marie, *Stratégie de l'action non-violente*, Paris, Le Seuil, 1981.
Powers, Roger S. (ed), *Protest, Power, and Change: An Encyclopedia of Nonviolent Action from ACT-UP to Women's Suffrage*, New York, Garland, Garland Reference Library of the Humanities, 1997.
Randle, Michael, *Civil Resistance*, London, Fontana Press, 1994.
Roberts, Adam (ed.), *Civilian Resistance as a National Defence: Nonviolent Resistance against Aggression*, Harmondsworth, Penguin Books, 1969.
Roberts, Adam and Timothy Garton Ash (eds), *Civil Resistance and Power Politics: The Experience of Non-violent Action from Gandhi to the Present*, Oxford; New York, Oxford University Press, 2009.
Rummel, Rudolph J., *Power Kills: Democracy as a Method of Nonviolence*, New Brunswick, N.J., Transaction, 1997.
Schell, Jonathan, *The Unconquerable World: Power, Non-violence and the Will of the People*, London, Allen Lane, 2003.
Schock, Kurt, *Unarmed Insurrections: People Power Movements in Nondemocracies*, Minneapolis, University of Minnesota Press, Social Movements, Protest, and Contention, 2005.
Semelin, Jacques, *Unarmed Against Hitler: Civilian Resistance in Europe, 1939-1943*, Westport, CT, Praeger Publishers, 1993.
———, « La Notion de résistance civile » in Semelin, Jacques (under the direction of), *Quand les dictatures se fissurent ... Résistances civiles à l'Est et au Sud*, Paris, Desclée de Brouwer, 1995, p. 21-41.
———, « Le Totalitarisme à l'épreuve de la résistance civile (1939-1989) » in *Vingtième Siècle*, July 1993, p. 79-90.
Sharp, Gene, *The Politics of Nonviolent Action: Power and Struggle* (volume I), *The Methods of Nonviolent Action* (volume II), *The Dynamics of Nonviolent Action* (volume III), Boston, Porter Sargent Publisher, 1973.
Stephan, Maria J. and Erica Chenoweth, "Why Civil Resistance Works: The Strategic Logic of Nonviolent Conflict," in *International Security* (33) 1, Summer 2008, p. 7-44. http://belfercenter.ksg.harvard.edu/files/IS3301_pp007-044_Stephan_Chenoweth.pdf
Zunes, Stephen, Lester R. Kurtz and Sarah Beth Asher (eds), *Nonviolent Social Movements: A Geographical Perspective*, Malden, Mass., Blackwell Publisher, 1999.

Resistance against the government in communist Eastern Europe

Bartee, Wayne C., *A Time to Speak Out: The Leipzig Citizen Protests and the Fall of East Germany*, Westport, Conn., Praeger, 2000.

Bispinck, Henrik [et al.], *Aufstände im Ostblock. Zur Krisengeschichte des realen Sozialismus*, Berlin, Ch. Links, Forschungen zur DDR-Gesellschaft, 2004.

Bleiker, Roland, *Popular Dissent, Human Agency and Global Politics*, Cambridge, Cambridge University Press, Cambridge Studies in International Relations, 2000.

Choi, Sung-Wang, *Von der Dissidenz zur Opposition. Die politisch alternativen Gruppen in der DDR von 1978 bis 1989*, Köln, Verlag Wissenschaft und Politik, Bibliothek Wissenschaft und Politik, 1999.

Flam, Helena, *Mosaic of Fear: Poland and East Germany before 1989*, Boulder, Colo., East European Monographs, 1998.

Grix, Jonathan, *The Role of the Masses in the Collapse of the GDR*, Basingstoke, Macmillan; New York, St. Martin's Press, 2000.

Hahn, André, *Der Runde Tisch. Das Volk und die Macht, politische Kultur im letzten Jahr der DDR*, Berlin, Verlag am Park, 1998.

Heydemann, Günther, Gunther Mai and Werner Müller (eds), *Revolution und Transformation in der DDR 1989-90*, Berlin, Duncker und Humblot, Schriftenreihe der Gesellschaft für Deutschlandforschung, 1999.

McDermott, Kevin and Matthew Stibbe (eds), *Revolution and Resistance in Eastern Europe: Challenges to Communist Rule*, New York, Berg, 2006.

Osa, Maryjane, *Solidarity and Contention: Networks of Polish Opposition*, Minneapolis, University of Minnesota Press, Social Movements, Protest, and Contention, 2003.

Pollack, Detlef and Jan Wielgohs (eds), *Dissent and Opposition in Communist Eastern Europe: Origins of Civil Society and Democratic Transition*, Burlington, VT, Ashgate, 2004.

Sharman, Jason Campbell, *Resistance and Repression in Communist Europe*, London: Routledge Curzon, BASEES/Routledge Series on Russian and East European Studies, 2003.

Timmer, Karsten, *Vom Aufbruch zum Umbruch. Die Bürgerbewegung in der DDR 1989*, Göttingen, Vandenhoeck und Ruprecht, Kritische Studien zur Geschichtswissenschaft, 2000.

Trutkowski, Dominik, *Der Sturz der Diktatur. Opposition in Polen und der DDR 1988/89*, Berlin; Münster, Lit, Mittel und Ostmitteleuropastudien, 2007.

Communication and the media

Balle, Francis, *Médias et sociétés. Edition, presse, cinéma, radio, télévision, internet, CD, DVD*, 13th edition, Paris, Montchrestien, Domat Politique Collection, 2007.

Bougnoux, Daniel, *Sciences de l'information et de la communication*, Paris, Larousse, 1993.

Cayrol, Roland, *Les Médias. Presse écrite, radio et télévision*, Paris, PUF, Collection Thémis, 1991.

Debray, Régis, *Cours de médiologie générale*, Paris, Gallimard, 1991.

Flichy, Patrice, *Une histoire de la communication moderne. Espace public et vie privée*, Paris, La Découverte, Collection La Découverte-Poche, Sciences Humaines et Sociales, 2004.

Gerstlé Jacques, *La communication politique*, 2nd edition, Paris, Armand Colin, Collection Cursus, 2008.

Jeanneney, Jean-Noël, *L'écho du siècle. Dictionnaire historique de la radio et de la télévision en France*, in collaboration with Agnès Chauveau, new updated edition, Paris, Hachette littératures; Issy-les-Moulineaux, Arte edition, 5th edition, Collection Pluriel, 2001.

———, *Une histoire des médias. Des origines à nos jours*, reviewed and complete new edition, Paris, Le Seuil, Collection Points. Histoire, 2001.

Mattelart, Armand, *L'invention de la communication*, Paris, La Découverte, Collection La Découverte-Poche. Sciences Humaines et Sociales, 1997-1994.

Mattelart, Tristan, *Le cheval de Troie audiovisuel. Le rideau de fer à l'épreuve des radios et télévisions transfrontières*, Grenoble, Presses Universitaires de Grenoble, Collection Communication, Médias et Sociétés, 1995.

Wolton, Dominique, *Éloge du grand public. Une théorie critique de la télévision*, Paris, Flammarion, 1990.

Wolton, Dominique, *Penser la communication*, Paris, Flammarion, 1997.

Wolton, Dominique et Jean-Louis Missika, *La Folle du logis, la télévision dans les sociétés démocratiques*, Paris, Gallimard, 1983.

Western media whose signals were received in countries in the East

Abshire, David M., *The Washington Papers, International Broadcasting: A New Dimension of Western Diplomacy*, Washington, Sage Publications, 1976.

Browne, Donald R., *International Radio Broadcasting: The Limits of the Limitless Medium*, New York, Praeger Publishers, 1982.

"Cold War Broadcasting Impact." Report on a conference organized by the Hoover Institution and the Cold War International History Project of the Woodrow Wilson International Center for Scholars at Stanford University, October 13-16, 2004, Hoover Institution, Stanford University, 2004. http://media.hoover.org/documents/broadcast_conf_rpt.pdf

Granville, Johanna, "'Caught with Jam on our Fingers': Radio Free Europe and the Hungarian Revolution of 1956," in *Diplomatic History* (29) 5, November 2005, p. 811-839.

Heil, Alan L., *Voice of America: A History*, New York, Columbia University Press, 2003.

Jenks, John, *British Propaganda and News Media in the Cold War*, Edinburgh, Edinburgh University Press, International Communications, 2006.

Johnson, A. Ross. (ed), *Cold War Broadcasting: Goals, Methods and Impact*, Central European Press, 2006.

Johnson, A. Ross, "Setting the Record Straight: The Role of Radio Free Europe in the Hungarian Revolution of 1956," Working Paper, Woodrow Wilson International Center for Scholars, November 2006. http://wilsoncenter.org/topics/pubs/happ.OP-3.pdf

Johnson, A. Ross and R. Eugene Parta, "Briefing on Cold War international Broadcasting: Lessons Learned," in Johnson, A. Ross and George Pratt Shultz (eds), *Communicating with the World of Islam*, Stanford, Calif., Hoover Institution Press, Stanford University, Hoover Institution Press Publication, 2008.

Kasprzak, Michal, "Radio Free Europe and the Catholic Church in Poland during the 1950s and 1960s," in *Canadian Slavonic Papers* (46) 3-4, 2004, p. 315-341.

Krämer, Sonja Isabel, "Westdeutsche Propaganda im Kalten Krieg. Organisationen und Akteure" in Wilke Jürgen (under the direction of), *Pressepolitik und Propaganda. Historische Studien vom Vormärz bis zum Kalten Krieg*, Köln, Böhlau, Medien in Geschichte und Gegenwart, 1997, p. 333-371.

Krugler, David Frederick, *The Voice of America and the Domestic Propaganda Battles: 1945-1953*, Columbia, University of Missouri Press, 2000.

Lepeuple, Anne-Chantal, "Radio Free Europe et Radio Liberty (1950-1994)," in *Vingtième Siècle*, October 1995, p. 31-45.
Lepeuple, Anne-Chantal, "Radio Free Europe-Radio Liberty. La dimension radiophonique de la stratégie américaine de Guerre froide," doctoral thesis, 20th century history, Paris, Institut d'études politiques, under the direction of M. Pierre Milza, 2 volumes, 1996.
Lindenberger, Tomas (ed), *Massenmedien im Kalten Krieg. Akteure, Bilder, Resonanzen, Köln, Böhlau*, Zeithistorische Studien, 2006.
Nelson, Michael, *War of the Black Heavens: The Battles of Western Broadcasting in the Cold War*, London, Brassey's, 1997.
Parta, R. Eugene, *Discovering the Hidden Listener: An Assessment of Radio Liberty and Western Broadcasting to the USSR during the Cold War. A Study Based on Audience Research Findings, 1970-1991*, Stanford, Calif., Hoover Institution Press, Hoover Institution Press, 2007.
Pittaway, Mark, "The Education of Dissent: The Reception of the Voice of Free Hungary: 1951-56," in *Cold War History* (4) 1, October 2003, p. 97-116.
Puddington, Arch, *Broadcasting Freedom: The Cold War Triumph of Radio Free Europe and Radio Liberty*, Lexington, Ky., University Press of Kentucky, 2000.
Rawnsley, Gary D., *Radio Diplomacy and Propaganda: The BBC and VOA in International Politics: 1956-64*, New York, St Martin's Press; Basingstoke, Macmillan, Studies in Diplomacy, 1996.
Semelin, Jacques, « Déclin et renaissance des radios occidentales à l'Est », in *Médiaspouvoirs*, April-June 1992, p. 142-149.
———, « Communication et résistance : les radios occidentales comme vecteur d'ouverture à l'Est » in *Réseaux* (53), May-June 1992, p. 9-24.
———, « Est-Ouest : naissance d'une nouvelle Europe audiovisuelle ? » in *Médiaspouvoirs*, September 1990, p. 175-183.
———, « La Communication Est-Ouest. De la radio sur ondes courtes à la télévision par satellite », in *Études*, April 1989, p. 469-481.
Short, Kenneth M. (ed), *Western Broadcasting over the Iron Curtain*, New York, St. Martin's Press, 1986.
Sosin, Gene, *Sparks of Liberty: An Insider's Memoir of Radio Liberty*, University Park, Pa., Pennsylvania State University Press, 1999.
Street, Nancy Lynch and Marilyn J. Matelski, *Messages from the Underground: Transnational Radio in Resistance and in Solidarity*, Westport, Conn., Praeger, 1997.
Urban, George R., *Radio Free Europe and the Pursuit of Democracy: My War within the Cold War*, New Haven, Conn., Yale University Press, 1997.

Interpretations of the fall of communism and the Soviet empire

Antohi, Sorin and Vladimir Tismaneanu (eds), *Between Past and Future: The Revolutions of 1989 and Their Aftermath*, Budapest, Hungary; New York, Central European University Press, 2000.
Beissinger, Mark R., *Nationalist Mobilization and the Collapse of the Soviet State*, Cambridge, Cambridge University Press, Studies in Comparative Politics, 2002.
Bozóki, András (ed), *The Roundtable Talks of 1989: The Genesis of Hungarian Democracy. Analysis and Documents*, Budapest, Central European University Press, 2002.
Carrère, d'Encausse Hélène, *La Gloire des nations ou la Fin de l'empire soviétique*, Paris, Fayard, 1991.

Cohen, Jean L. and Andrew Arato, *Civil Society and Political Theory*, Cambridge, MIT Press, 1992.
Cox, Michael (ed), *Rethinking the Soviet Collapse: Sovietology, the Death of Communism and the New Russia*, London, Pinter, 1998.
Dahrendorf, Ralf, *Reflections on the Revolution in Europe: In a letter intended to have been sent to a gentleman in Warsaw*, New York, Random House, 1990.
Dale, Gareth, *The East German Revolution of 1989*, Manchester; New York, Manchester University Press, 2006.
De Nevers, Renée, *Comrades No More: The Seeds of Political Change in Eastern Europe*, Cambridge, Mass.; London, MIT Press, Studies in International Security, 2003.
Furet, François, *Le Passé d'une illusion. Essai sur l'idée communiste au XXe siècle*, Paris, Laffont / Calmann-Lévy, 1995.
Hassner, Pierre, *La violence et la paix. De la bombe atomique au nettoyage ethnique*, Paris, Le Seuil, Collection Points Essais, 2000.
———,« Un cadavre encombrant », in *Revue politique et parlementaire*, July 1990.
———, «"Démocrature" et "Révolution" ou la transition bouleversée », in Grémion, Pierre and Pierre Hassner, *Vents d'Est. Vers l'Europe des États de droit ?*, Paris, PUF, 1991.
———, « Les révolutions ne sont plus ce qu'elles étaient », in Semelin, Jacques (under the direction of), *Quand les dictatures se fissurent ... Résistances civiles à l'Est et au Sud*, Paris, Desclée de Brouwer, 1995, p. 241-252.
Hertle, Hans-Hermann, *Der Fall der Mauer. Die unbeabsichtigte Selbstauflösung des SED-Staates*, Opladen, Westdeutscher Verlag, 1999.
Hollander, Paul, *Political Will and Personal Belief: The Decline and Fall of Soviet Communism*, New Haven, Conn., Yale University Press, 1999.
Kende, Pierre et Aleksander Smolar, *La Grande Secousse. Europe de l'Est 1989-1990*, Paris, Presses du CNRS, 1990.
Kumar, Krishan, *1989: Revolutionary Ideas and Ideals*, Minneapolis, University of Minnesota Press, Contradictions of Modernity Series, 2001.
Lévesque, Jacques, *1989, La Fin d'un empire. L'URSS et la libération de l'Europe de l'Est*, Paris, Presses de la FNSP, 1995.
Maier, Charles S., *Dissolution: The Crisis of Communism and the End of East Germany*, Princeton, N.J., Princeton University Press, 1997.
Michel, Patrick, *La Société retrouvée. Politique et religion dans l'Europe soviétisée*, Paris, Albin Michel, 1994.
Mink, Georges and Jean-Charles Szurek (under the direction of), *Cet étrange postcommunisme*, Paris, Presses du CNRS / La Découverte, 1992.
Okey, Robin, *The Demise of Communist East Europe: 1989 in Context*, London, Arnold, Historical Endings Series, 2004.
Pfaff, Steven, *Exit-voice Dynamics and the Collapse of East Germany: The Crisis of Leninism and the Revolution of 1989*, Durham, [N.C.]; London, Duke University Press, 2006.
Pomian, Krzysztof, « L'Après-Communisme : urgences du présent, poids du passé », *Le Débat* (76), 1993.
———, « Totalitarisme », in *Vingtième Siècle* (47), July-September 1995, p. 4-23.
Potel, Jean-Yves, *Quand le soleil se couche à l'Est*, Paris, éditions de l'Aube, 1995.
Revel, Jean-François, *Le Regain démocratique*, Paris, Fayard, 1991.
Richmond, Yale, *Cultural Exchange and the Cold War: Raising the Iron Curtain*, University Park, Pennsylvania State University Press, 2003.

Rupnik, Jacques and Dominique Moïsi, *Le Nouveau Continent : plaidoyer pour une Europe renaissante*, Paris, Calmann-Lévy, 1991.

Saxonberg, Steven, *The Fall: A Comparative Study of the End of Communism in Czechoslovakia, East Germany, Hungary and Poland*, Amsterdam: Harwood Academic Publishers, International Studies in Global Change, 2001.

Schreiber, Thomas and Françoise Barry (under the direction of), « Bouleversements à l'Est 1989-1990 », in *Notes et études documentaires* 4920-21, 1990.

Staniszkis, Jadwiga, *The Dynamics of Breakthrough in Eastern Europe*, Berkeley, University of California Press, 1991.

Tinguy, Anne de (under the direction of), *L'effondrement de l'empire soviétique*, Bruxelles, Bruylant, Collection Organisation Internationale et Relations Internationales, 1998.

Tismaneanu, Vladimir (ed), *The Revolutions of 1989*, London, Routledge, Rewriting Histories Series, 1999.

White, Stephen, *Communism and Its Collapse*, London, Routledge, The Making of the Contemporary World, 2000.

Wydra, Harald, *Communism and the Emergence of Democracy*, Cambridge; New York, Cambridge University Press, 2007.

Index

access to Western broadcasts, 46–54
Adenauer, Konrad, 19, 94
Afghanistan, Russian invasion of, 16
Africa: radio broadcasting targeting, 15–16
African National Congress (ANC), 241, 243–244
Ahmadinejad, Mahmoud, 230
Aktuelle Kamera (television news), 184, 201–202, 206–207
Albania: BBC radio, 14
Alexanderplatz, East Berlin, 207
Alexeieva, Ludmilla, 57
AMCOMLIB (American Committee for Liberation of the People of the USSR), 27
Aneks journal, 175(n12)
antennae hunt (GDR), 183
Antipolitics (Konrad), 57
Arab Spring: comparison to the Central European uprisings, 240–244; role of digital media, 249–254, 256, 258
Arendt, Hannah, 2
armed resistance, 1–2, 241–242; nonviolent action superseding, 4
Aron, Raymond, 16–17, 60
Arzeczunowicz, Andrzej, 176(n26)
audience reception: attacks by communist media, 48–50; communication-resistance relation as barometer of political stability, 226–227; East German ratings of West German television, 184; mail to radio stations, 47–48; number of Eastern radio receivers, 46–47; opinion polls, 50–54; reasons for listening, 60–63; role of Western radio in ending the Cold War, 233–235; West Germany's "television bridge" to the GDR, 182; Western metrics, 46–54; Western radio identifying Eastern audiences, 235–236
Aung San Suu Kyi, 245
Austria: dismantling the Iron Curtain on the Austro-Hungarian border, 195–198; Hungary opening its borders to, 179; international media coverage of the Gdansk agreement, 168; papal visit to Poland, 149–150
Aye Chan Naing, 248
Baker, James, 204
balance of terror, 3, 241–242
Balatonszabadi Radio (Hungary), 110
Balladur, Eduard, 17
Baltic States: Radio Liberty broadcasts, 27–28
Barcikowski, Kazimierz, 162
Barret, Edward, 34
Bary, Nicole, 219(n26)
BBC Radio, 14–16; audience opinion polls, 50–54; audiences between 1982 and 1989, 52(table); credibility in the East, 55–57; death of the Hungarian uprising, 112; immigrants

271

as Western broadcasters, 36; importance to resistance, 3; justifying the expense of, 34; KOR East-West-East communications loop, 145–146; official and popular reception of, 54; papal visit to Poland, 149–150; signal jamming as indicator of East-West tensions, 44–45; West German radio, 20
Behind Enemy Lines (Shanor), 58–59
Bem, Josef, 83
Beria, Lavrenti, 73
Berlin Wall: destabilization of the Eastern Bloc following, 215–218; disrupting information flows, 22; East German literature foreshadowing the fall, 192–193; enigma surrounding, 1; mass exodus from East Germany, 211–214; physical and philosophical changes, 230–231; precursors to the fall of, 180–181; removing psychological barriers for East Germans, 236–237; as symbol of physical and psychological containment, 185–186, 225–226
Biermann, Wolf, 187–188
Board for International Broadcasting (BIB), 29–30, 39(n53)
Bobinski, Christopher, 158
Bohley, Bärbel, 189, 200, 221(n63)
Böhme, Ibrahim, 199, 219(n28)
book smuggling, 143
Borsanyi, Julian, 96
Borusewicz, Bogdan, 152, 157
Brandt, Heinz, 85
Brandt, Willy, 19, 182
Bratkowski, Stefan, 56
Britain: popular musicians' tours, 61; Suez Canal, 97–98. *See also* BBC Radio
Bujak, Zbigniew, 174
Bukovski, Vladimir, 57
Bulgaria: lifting of signal jamming, 45; popular music programs, 61; weekly audience ratings of Western radio, 51(table)
Burma: role of digital media in civil resistance, 245–249, 256
Burnham, James, 24
Campaign of Truth, 12, 24
Carter administration, 13, 30–31

Catholic Church. *See* religion and churches
Caucasus: Radio Liberty broadcasts, 27
censorship: of the arts in the GDR, 187–188; characteristics of dictatorships, 2; communications-resistance connection, 227–228; *Glasnost* policy penetrating East German regime rigidity over, 192–193; papal visit to Poland, 147–150; Poland's *Kultura* journal, 143; as political strategy, 227; discussion circles, 75–76; VOA broadcasting, 11. *See also* jamming signals
Central Asia: Radio Liberty broadcasts, 27
Central Intelligence Agency (CIA): Campaign of Truth, 24–25; NCFE funding for Radio Free Europe, 23; Radio Liberty, 26–27; RFE role in the Hungarian uprising, 94, 98, 102(n53); ties to RFE/RL, 28–30
ceremonial television, 150
China: East German policy of repression and containment, 201–202
churches. *See* religion and churches
citizen reporting: Egyptian activists, 250–251
civil resistance, 2; connection to digital and social media, 239–244; defining and characterizing, 259(n6); Democratic Voice of Burma, 245–249; importance of digital communications, 254–257; undermining a dictatorship from within, 227–228; the study of, 227–228. *See also* public sphere; nonviolent action, methods of
civil society: Gdansk negotiations, 170–174; nonviolent action, 4; social pressure to lift control of Western broadcasts, 54–55. *See also* public sphere
Claye, Lucius, 21, 24
Colin, F., 131–132
collaboration in the communist utopia, 69–70
collaborative government, Czechoslovakia's, 113–114
communism: comparison of contemporary resistance to the post-

Index 273

communist struggles, 240–244; defining totalitarianism under Stalin, 5; Gdansk negotiations, 170–174; immigrants as Western broadcasters, 35–36; Pope John-Paul II's fortification of Polish identity, 147–148; response to the papal visit to Poland, 147; slow disintegration after Stalin, 142–143; social compliance, 69; Western radio's portrayal of the failure of, 234–235
Communist Party (USSR): as audience for Western radio, 53–54; Khrushchev Report on the crimes of, 73. *See also* Soviet Union
Conference on Security and Cooperation in Europe (CSCE), 30, 44
Congress, U.S.: controversy over CIA ties to RFE, 29; VOA funding, 13
Congress for Cultural Freedom (1950), 24
contamination, Western views as, 41–42
Coppens, Simon, 37(n6)
Critchlow, James, 30
critical debate, emergence in the GDR, 185–190, 199
cross-reporting: papal visit to Poland, 149–150
Crusade for Freedom, 24
culture: cultural resistance, 24; Eastern monitoring of Western radio, 61–62; emergence of critical awareness in the GDR, 187–189; West German publications in East Germany, 190–192; West-East cultural link, 10
Czechoslovakia: context of political reform, 77–78; destabilization of the Eastern Bloc, 217; first RFE broadcast, 24; legitimacy of Western news, 59; lifting of signal jamming, 45; mail to Western radio stations, 47–48; mass exodus from East Germany, 201, 209; popular music programs, 60–61; reception of RFE and RL rhetoric, 56; reclaiming the public sphere, 71, 75–76; RFI revival, 18; smuggling books and journals out of Poland, 143; Stalin's death, 72; weekly audience ratings of Western radio, 51(table). *See also* Prague Spring
death: Stalin's death creating a power vacuum, 72–73
decolonization: BBC World Service broadcasts in Africa, 15–16
democracy: dialogic value of news media, 237–239; Eastern source of Eastern democracy, 236–237; free flow of information doctrine, 43; Hungarian protesters' demands, 108–110; impact of digital communications on, 257–258; labor organizing in East Germany calling for elections, 82, 101(n40); role of digital technology in contemporary civil resistance, 239–244, 253–254; Western radio's political missions, 34
democratic opposition, 146
Democratic Voice of Burma (DVB), 245–249
Demokratischer Aufbruch (Democratic Renewal), 199
demonstrations: East Germany, 80–82; 179; 187–189, 193, 200–204; Hungary, 82–83; Iran, 230; Egypt, 251–252; at the World Trade Organization in Seattle, 252
de-semiotization and re-semiotization, 84–85
destabilization: context of political reform in Poland and Czechoslovakia, 77–79; East Germany, 89–93, 180–181; of the Eastern Bloc, 215–218; Western media's contribution to public protest, 89
de-Stalinization: de-semiotization of public places, 84–85; Khrushchev's policy, 72–73; political protest in Poland and Czechoslovakia, 77–79; public debate emerging from, 72–76; public speech and public protest in East Germany, Hungary and Poland, 79–84
détente: communications and media in the GDR, 182–183; East German unrest, 80; effect on representational radio, 16; Gdansk strike negotiations, 162–163; jeopardizing RFE/RL, 29; signal jamming as

indicator of East-West tensions, 44–45; Stalin's death, 73
Deutsche Welle (DW) radio, 18–20, 43, 49, 233–234
Deutschlandfunk, 18–20, 233–234
dialogue, news media as, 237–239
Dienstbier, Jiri, 114–115, 124
digital communications: Arab Spring, 253–254; Burma's DVB broadcast, 245–248; Egyptian activist groups, 249–252; impact on democracy, 257–258; importance in the political sphere, 254–257; individualization and disaggregation of news and information flows, 255–256; Iran's 2009 popular protests, 252–253; role in contemporary civil resistance, 239–244; secure tactical communications by dissidents, 256–257; for violent and nonviolent movements, 244–246; WTO demonstrations, 252
diplomatic pressure blocking Western media, 42–45
disarmament movements, 188–189, 220(n30)
dissidents: CIA control of RFE/RL, 30–31; combining Eastern with Western broadcasting for a larger picture, 58–59; criticism of Western radio, 57; emergence in the 1970s, 4; moving from dissidence to resistance, 2; rise of East German critical awareness, 189; VOA focus and policies, 13
Dizard, Wilson, 34
documentary: Gdansk strike, 162
domestic politics: Western radio as scapegoat for Eastern turmoil, 49–50
D.T. 64 (East German youth radio), 206
Dubcek, Alexander, 75, 77–78, 93, 113, 116, 125
Duras, Marguerite, 140
East European Area Audience and Opinion Research (EEAOR), 50–51
East German Communist Party (SED), 79–80, 193–197, 205, 207
East Germany. *See* German Democratic Republic

East-East communications: Central Europeans' assertion of autonomy from Soviet control, 103–104; cohesion of radio, television, and the press during the Prague Spring, 118–121; collective dissemination of information in Poland, 142–144; destabilization of the Eastern Bloc, 217; developments during the Gdansk strikes, 141–142; East Germany's 1989 crisis, 195; fundamental change in East German media, 205–208; Gdansk negotiations, 155–157; Gdansk strike as speech movement, 152–156; individual communication during the Hungarian and Czechoslovakian resistance, 127–129; journalistic strategy and cohesion during the Prague Spring, 117–118; mass resistance, 71–72; post-Stalin surge in, 3–4; Soviet invasion of Czechoslovakia, 114–115
Eastern media: attacks on Western radio as indicator of audience strength, 48–50; combining with Western broadcasting for a larger picture, 58–59; Czechoslovak resistance, 103; Eastern reception of, 42; Hungarian uprising, 104–113; international coverage of the Gdansk agreement, 168–169; internecine strife in Czechoslovakia, 77–78; Polish entente, 163–164; demonstration in East Berlin and Budapest, 87–88; Stalinist propaganda, 86–87
East-West communications, 175(n11); amateur video footage from East Germany, 193–194; fall of the Berlin Wall, 212–215; internal conflict over exodus from East Germany, 200–201; media coverage of the Prague Spring uprising, 118–121; *samizdat* technique, 28, 39(n48), 144
East-West-East communications: destabilization of the Eastern Bloc, 217; development during the Gdansk uprising, 141–142; East Germany's 1989 crisis, 195; KOR connections

with the West, 144–145; as resistance strategy, 4
ecumenical meetings, global, 192
Egypt: role of digital media in civil resistance, 256; use of video footage by dissidents, 249–252
Eisenhower, Dwight, 12
Eisenhower, Milton, 29
elections: growing mass opposition in East Germany, 193–194; Hungarian rebel radio demands, 108; internal debate over reform in East Germany, 199; the promise of trade elections in Poland, 162–163
Elf 99 (East German youth television), 206
entente (Poland), 162
entertainment: critical awareness in East Germany, 187–188; East German youth radio, 206–207; Eastern audiences for Western radio, 60; Western television in the GDR, 184
environmental pollution, nonviolent action against, 194
Eppelmann, Reiner, 199
Erdei, Ferenc, 108
Erwing, Gordon, 90
Esperanto language, 17
European Broadcasting Union (EBU), 43
expatriates: CIA recruitment for Radio Liberty, 26–27; representation radio stations, 11; RFE/RL, 28–31. *See also* immigrants
Falcke, Heio, 189
Federal Republic of Germany (FRG). *See* West Germany
Fedorowicz, Jace, 56–57
Fejtö, François, 25, 73
Fidelius, Petr, 58
Fifth Plan, 17
Fiszbach, Tadeusz, 142, 155, 163
Flinker, Martin, 219(n26)
France: international coverage of the Gdansk agreement, 168; Poland's liberalization, 143; Radio France Internationale, 16–18, 36, 52(table), 56–57, 173; silence of radio audiences, 32–36; Suez Canal, 97–98; VOA broadcasts, 37(n6)

freedom of information and expression, 2; after the quashing of the Hungarian uprising, 112–113; challenging communist countries' protectionist practices, 43–44; collective dissemination of information as a resistance strategy, 142–146; East German evangelical churches, 186–187; East German media opening, 205–208; East German uprising of 1953, 91–93; emergence of critical debate in the GDR, 185–190, 199; Gdansk strikers' demand for, 161; Hungarian national and rebel radio stations during the uprising, 107–108; Hungary's Petofi Circle, 75; increasing openness, 5; internal dynamics of dissidence, 228–229; international radio stations, 3; mass resistance in the East, 71–72; public debate following Stalin's death, 72–79; reclaiming speech in the public sphere, 86–88; Soviets' attempt at speech emancipation, 3; through literary journals and discussion circles, 74–76
Friedrich, Hans Joachim, 196–197, 213
Führer, Christian, 203–204
Fulbright, J.W., 29
funding for Western radio, 17–18, 29, 31, 45
Garton Ash, Timothy, 2, 215
Gatter, Peter, 158, 169
Gault, François, 178(n72)
Gazette (Hungarian literary magazine), 74
Gdansk uprising (1980): collective information dissemination as resistance strategy, 142–146; declaration of martial law, 42, 47–48, 80–81, 170, 172–173, 255; development of media communications during, 141–142; entente, 162; expansion to a national general strike, 164–165; initial labor strike, 139–140; international media coverage of the conflict, 167–170; media development, 139–141; negotiations, 153–156, 159–161, 163–164, 170–174; resolution of the strikes, 166–167; rise of Solidarity, 161–163; Soviet

threat of intervention, 164–165; stalemate in negotiations, 165–166; the strike as a speech movement, 152–156; verbal pressure against the government, 157–161; working class history, 150–152
Gellert, Andor, 96
Genscher, Hans-Dietrich, 197–198
Geremek, Bronislaw, 25, 159
German Democratic Republic (GDR): collective mobilization against leaving, 179–180; crossing to the West from Hungary, 195–197; emergence of critical debate, 185–190; group appropriation of regime symbols, 84–85; importance of Western radio and television, 233–234; Kohl's push for reunification, 216; lack of journalistic research before 1989, 220(n46); loudspeaker broadcasting in public, 131; mass exodus and destabilization, 180–181, 208–211; mass protest bringing fundamental change to East German media, 205–208; mass resistance, 71–72; modifying radio content, 19; 1953 uprising, 89–93; nonviolent conflict, 202–204; official repression of public protest in Berlin, 201–202; ongoing tension between openness and closure, 190–194; police brutality, 201–202, 222(n68); political opposition and Western amplification, 198–202; political pressure against Western radio, 43; public and popular pressure on the, 194–195; Radio in the American Sector, 21–23; role of digital media in civil resistance, 256; semi-autonomy of evangelical churches, 186–187; social frustration following Stalin's death, 79–82; training video broadcasters, 249; West Germany's "television bridge," 181–185; Western television broadcasts, 10. *See also* Berlin Wall
Germany. *See* German Democratic Republic; West Germany
Gero, Erno, 88, 107
Giedroyc, Jerzy, 143
Gierek, Edward, 143, 147, 159, 162–163

Glasnost policy, 1; demonstrations in East Germany, 204; ending signal jamming, 218(n1); penetration into East Germany, 192–193; Radio Glasnost, 193–194
Glazkov, Nicolai, 39(n48)
Gombrowicz, Witold, 143
Gomulka, Wladyslaw, 25, 75, 77, 79, 93, 143
Gorbachev, Mikhail, 1, 174, 180, 192–193, 198, 201, 226–227
Gorbanevskaia, Natalia, 54
grassroots organizations in East Germany, 191–192
Grenzfall (Borderline cases), 190
Guetta, Bernard, 158, 168–170
The Gulag Archipelago (Solzhenitsyn), 13, 229
Gwiazda, Andrzej, 165–166, 170
Hackley, W. Antony, 48
Hallstein doctrine, 19
ham radio broadcasting, 12
Hankiss, Elémer, 59, 62
Harriman, Averell, 12, 34
Hasek, Jaroslav, 116
Havel, Vaclav, 2, 5, 63, 121, 123–124, 142, 189
Havemann, Robert, 85
Heath, Edward, 16
Hegedus, Andreas, 88
Hein, Christopher, 188, 191–192
Heitkamp, Judith, 206
Hejzlar, Zdenek, 119, 134(n37)
Helsinki Convention, 13, 44, 229
Herrmann, Joachim, 205
Hesse, Kurt, 185
Heym, Stephan, 188, 208, 214, 219(n27)
Hofman, Karel, 114
Holt, Robert, 94–96, 102(n53)
Honecker, Erich, 180, 183, 186–187, 201, 204–205
human rights, 174(n7); GDR dissident groups for, 190; political goals of RFE/RL, 30–31; VOA focus and policies, 13
Hungarian uprising (1956): comparison with the Prague Spring, 126–127; duration, 172; individual communication in the public sphere, 127–129; media role in the insurrection,

104–113; Nagy's radio communication, 104–106; partial success, 104; post-Stalin communication, 3–4; public protest, 82–84; rebel radio stations, 106–108; restructuring of the public sphere, 108–111; RFE programs, 28, 94–99; role of radio, 127–129; Soviet invasion and the end of the Nagy government, 111–113; as unarmed struggle, 1–2; working class history of Gdansk, 151

Hungarian workers socialist party, 109

Hungary: BBC radio, 14; cutting the fence on the Austro-Hungarian border, 195–198; East Germans crossing to the West through, 195–197; group appropriation of regime symbols, 84–86; intellectual revolt, 74; Khrushchev Report on Stalin's crimes, 73–74; lifting of signal jamming, 45; opening its borders to Austria, 179; popular music programs, 60–61; reclaiming the public sphere, 71; weekly audience ratings of Western radio, 51(table)

identity: Gdansk strikes as assertion of, 139–140; GDR's mass exodus and, 181; German reunification, 216; group identity in the public sphere, 84–88; internal resistance to totalitarianism, 70–71; national cohesion against the Soviets during the Prague Spring, 116; Pope John-Paul II's fortification of Polish identity, 147–148; psychological warfare by Western radio, 63; public reclamation of a national identity, 71; rise of Solidarity, 161–162

ideology, 10; emergence of critical debate in the GDR, 185–190; West German television undermining GDR's, 184

immigrants: credibility of Western broadcasting in the East, 55–56; East Germans crossing to the West from Hungary, 195–197; internal controversy over East German exodus, 198–199; language sections of Western radio, 40(n61); mass exodus from East Germany, 208–214; Radio Liberty, 27; as Western broadcasters, 23, 35–36. *See also* expatriates

immobile battle, Gdansk strike as, 141

individualization of news and information flows, 255–256

Indra, Alois, 113, 115–116

industrial sector: East German unrest, 79–80, 89–93; Gdansk labor strike, 139–140

Inkeles, Alex, 49

intellectuals: emergence of critical debate in the GDR, 186–188; foreshadowing the fall of the Berlin Wall, 192–193; Hungary's public protests, 83–84; journals and discussion circles, 74–76; opening public space in East Germany, 219(n26); Polish critique of communist system, 142–143; reclaiming the public sphere, 71, 74; West German publications in East Germany, 190–191

interference, media. *See* censorship; jamming signals

International Labor Organization (ILO), 164

Iran: popular protests in 2009, 230, 252–253

Iraq, 242

Islamists: jihadi websites, 245

Italy: Vatican Radio, 31–32, 46, 52(table)

Jackson, William A., 12

Jackson Report, 12

Jagielski, Miechislas, 159–162, 166, 168

Jahn, Roland, 204, 222(n73), 248–249

jamming signals: diplomatic pressure and, 44–45; *Glasnost* ending, 31, 218(n1); lifting, 41–42; political justification for, 42–43; US countering, 64(n16)

Jaruzelski, Wojciech, 42, 171–173

Jauer, Joachim, 183

jazz, 60

Jdanov, Andrei, 41

Jews, Soviet: immigrants as Western broadcasters, 36, 40(n65)

Jiru, Jaroslav, 56

John-Paul II, 146–150, 175(n18), 176(n24)

Kadar, Janos, 94, 107, 109, 112, 127
Kafarski, Marian, 158
Kaiser, Jakob, 90
Kalugin, Oleg, 64(n23)
Katyn massacre, 13
Kennzeichen D (television program), 183, 194
ketman techniques, 70
Khrushchev, Nikita: de-Stalinization policy, 72–73; Report on Stalin's crimes, 73; VOA broadcasting, 12
The Knights of the Round Table (Hein), 192
Kohl, Helmut, 181, 197, 216
Kolakowski, Leszek, 62, 75, 142
Kolder, Drahomir, 113, 115–116
Konrad, György, 57, 142
KOR (Social Self-Defense Committee; Poland), 175(n12); communication flows, 141–142; disinformation propagation, 163–164; government violence towards, 155; interpreting the Gdansk uprising, 151–152; origins of, 144; Western media connections, 144–145
Kovacs, Bela, 107–108
Krenz, Egon, 180, 205–211, 215
KSS-KOR, 144, 146, 151–152, 155, 158, 163, 174(n7), 198(n7)
Kultura magazine, 61–62, 143, 165, 214, 228–229
Kundera, Milan, 63
Kuron, Jacek, 144–146, 158, 175(nn11,12), 176(n41)
Kuwait, 242
La Liberté au bout des ondes (Semelin), 234–235, 237, 239
labor organizing: de-semiotization of public places, 85–86; East Germany, 79–80, 89–93; East Germany and Hungary, 86–88; Poland, 83, 139–140; rebel radio stations during the Hungarian Uprising, 106–107; representation under Gdansk negotiations, 170–174; working class history of Gdansk, 150–152. *See also* Gdansk uprising; German Democratic Republic. *See also* trade unions, strikes
Lange, Bernd-Lutz, 202

language: analysis of RFE and RL, 56; BBC Radio, 14; cross border media in North and South Korea, 218(n2); educational quality of Western radio, 61; immigrant populations and language sections of Western radio, 40(n61); Poste Colonial Radio, 17; Radio Liberty, 27; representation radio stations, 11; RFE/RL, 31; Vatican Radio, 31; VOA broadcasting, 12; West Germany's "television bridge" to the GDR, 181–182
Lansky, Karel, 114–115*Le Monde* newspaper, 158, 168
Leder, Dietrich, 196
Legal Radio Prague, 131
legitimacy: of East German churches, 186–188; opening of East German media, 208; of radio interference, 33; of Western broadcasting, 30, 58–59
Leipzig, Germany, 200, 202–204
Let the Truth be Told (Mansell), 34
liberalization: Poland, 148–149, 163
liberalization policy (RFE), 98
lighthouse metaphor of Western radio, 62
Lockhart, Bruce, 34
Lodeesen, Jon, 27
longevity of the communist ideology, 69–70
Lukaszewicz, Jerzy, 162
mail: dissemination of information in Gdansk, 156–157; measuring audience reception to Western broadcasts, 47–48
Mansell, Gerard, 34
marches: East Germany, 81, 84–85; Budapest, 85; GDR, 216; Myanmar/Burma, 246; Egypt, 251
Marconi, Guglielmo, 31
Marshall Plan, 9, 17
martial law: Czechoslovakia, 128; East Germany, 93; Hungary, 104–105, 128–129; Poland, 42, 47–48, 80–81, 170, 172–173, 255
Masur, Kurt, 202, 206
Mazowiecki, Tadeusz, 159, 165–166
McCarthyism, 12

media. *See* digital communications; East-East communications; East-West communications; East-West-East communications; press; radio; television; West-East communications; West-East-West communications
media interference, 9, 229–230
Meilke, Erich, 215
messenger, radio as, 128–129
Meyer, Kurt, 202
Michnik, Adam, 2, 142, 158
Mickelson, Sig, 95
micro-resistance, 5–6
Mikes, Imre, 102(n58)
Mikoyan, Anastas, 73, 107
Milosz, Czeslaw, 69–70, 143
Mistiaen, Emmanuel, 31
Mitterrand, François, 18
MKS (Poland), 154–156, 158–162, 164
Mlynar, Zdenek, 78
mobile phones, Egyptian activists' use of, 251–252
Molnar, Miklos, 83, 96
Moscow Agreement, 124–126
Mubarak, Hosni, 249–251
music: Eastern audiences for Western radio, 60–62
Nagy, Imre, 86, 88, 95–96, 104–108, 111–113, 128
National Committee for a Free Europe (NCFE), 23–24
National Security Council (NSC), 39(n53)
National Union of Journalists (France), 18
Natolinians, 77
Nazi Germany: civil resistance through words and symbols, 2–3; criticism of Vatican Radio, 31; East German rise of neo-Nazis, 194; resistance of the Czechoslovakian media, 120; RIAS message against, 21
neo-Nazis, 194
Netherlands: Vatican Radio support, 32
network building, importance of digital communications for, 254–257
Neubert, Erhart, 189
Neues Forum (New Forum; GDR), 199–201, 224, 245(n63)
neutrality, media: BBC Radio, 14–16

New Forum (GDR), 199–201, 224, 245(n63)
new world information and communication order (NWICO), 44
New York Times, 29
Nixon, Richard, 29, 46
noncooperation, collective will towards, 115–116
nonviolent action, methods of. *See* demonstrations, marches, strikes, Gdansk uprising; Hungarian uprising; Prague Spring, protest, resistance
North Korea, 218(n2)
Northern Ireland, 241
Nowak, Jan, 25, 145, 175(nn9,10)
Occupy Wall Street protests, 257
Offenheit (sincerity), 199
Offentlichkeit (public debate), 199
Office of Strategic Services (OSS), 23
Offredo, Jean, 169
openness: signal jamming as barometer of, 45
Operation Ox Head, 183
opinion polls, 50–54
Orwell, George, 143
Osrodek Badania Opinii Publicznej (OBOP), 51, 52(table), 53, 53(table)
Ostpolitik policy, 182
Ox Head, Operation, 183
Palach, Jan, 126
Paloczi-Horvath, Gyorgy, 74
papal visit to Poland, 146–150, 175(n18), 176(n24)
Peace and War: a Theory of International Relations (Aron), 60
Pelikan, Jiri, 120
Perestroika, 204
periphery of power, marginalization of, 256
Petofi, Sandor, 83
Petofi Circle (Hungary), 75–76, 82
Piekarec, Casimir, 56
Pius XI, 31
Po Prostu magazine, 74–75
Poland, 176(n32), 178(n72); audience ratings of Western radio, 51, 51(table); BBC radio, 14; context of political reform, 77–79; credibility

of Western radio in, 55–57; East Germany's 1989 crisis and, 195; immigrants as Western broadcasters, 36; jazz broadcasts, 60; John-Paul II's election and visit to Poland, 146–150, 175(nn18,20), 176(n24); Khrushchev Report on Stalin's crimes, 73–74; KOR's East-West-East communications loop, 144–145; labor strike in Gdansk, 139–141; literary journals preaching political reform, 74–75; mail to Western radio stations, 47–48; mass reception of western stations, 42; Nixon's welcome, 46; origins of the KOR, 144; political goals of RFE/RL, 30–31; political justification for jamming signals, 42–43; popular music programs, 60–61; public speech leading to public protest, 82–83; reclaiming the public sphere, 71; removing signal jamming, 41–42, 45; Stalin's death, 72; Swiatio interview, 25; Western radio as scapegoat for political turmoil, 49–50. *See also* Gdansk uprising; KOR
police brutality: East Germany, 201–202, 222(n68)
Polish October, 82–83
political sphere: Burma's DVB broadcasts, 245–249; CIA control of RFE/RL, 38–31; context of reform in Poland and Czechoslovakia, 77–79; East and West German radio, 19; emergence of critical debate in the GDR, 185–190; fall of the Berlin Wall, 225–226; function of substitution radio stations, 20–21; immigrants as Western broadcasters, 35–36; importance of digital communications, 254–257; obstacle to Poland's solidarity, 171; penetration of Western media into East Germany, 191–192. *See also* Berlin Wall
Poppe, Ulrike, 189, 199
Poste Colonial radio, 16–18, 37(n16). *See also* Radio France Internationale
Potel, Jean-Yves, 170

power: power vacuum after Stalin's death, 73; Soviet grab for power in Czechoslovakia, 113–114
Prague Spring (1968): cohesive roles of radio, television and the press, 118–121; comparison with the Arab Spring, 240–241; comparison with the Hungarian uprising, 113–113–114, 126–127; delocalization of the conflict, 121–123; duration, 172; Eastern reception of Eastern media, 42; increasing flexibility of radio, 127–129; individual communication in the public sphere, 127–129; journalistic strategy and cohesion, 117–118; journalists' political leadership role, 121–123; KOR emerging after, 144; media liberalization and, 78; national cohesion versus collaborationism, 114–116; negotiations, 156; post-Stalin communication, 3–4; public debate and, 75; resumption of signal jamming following, 45; Western complicity, 229
prayers for peace/prayer evenings (GDR), 187, 189, 193, 200
press: arising from the Hungarian protests, 109–110; rebirth of an open East German media, 206–207; role in the Prague Spring uprising, 118–121
programming: culture and music, 60–63; Eastern critiques of Western programs, 43–44; French international radio, 17–18; opening of East German media, 205–208; radio, television, and the press during the Prague Spring, 118–121; Radio Liberty, 28; RFE programming during the Hungarian uprising, 94–99; strident nature of Radio Liberty, 27–28
propaganda: Eastern reception of Western broadcasts, 41–42; international radio stations, 3; USSR's international machine, 43; West German television in the GDR, 182
protest: group identity formation in the public sphere, 84–88; publicists versus revisionists, 74. *See also* resistance

Provisional IRA, 241
psychological battle of resistance, 70–71
public debate: East Germany's opening, 185–190, 199; following Stalin's death, 72–79
public pressure: cutting the fence on the Austro-Hungarian border, 195–198; emigration from East Germany, 195–198; media and popular pressure on the East German regime, 194–195
public sphere: broadcasters' role in the development of, 235–237; cohesion of radio, television, and the press during the Prague Spring, 118–121; context of political reform, 77–79; danger of expressing resistance in, 70–71; death of Hungary's Nagy government, 111–113; delocalization of the Czechoslovakian conflict, 121–123; forms of reclamation, 71; fundamental change in East German media, 205–208; GDR's collective re-appropriation of, 179–180; group identity formation, 84–88; Hungarian uprising, 82–83, 94–99, 108–111; increasing flexibility of radio broadcasting during conflict, 127–129; information flow during the Hungarian uprising, 104, 108–111; journals and discussion circles, 74–76; labor protests in East Germany, 81–82, 89–93; mode of opposition in Gdansk, 139–140; national cohesion during the Prague Spring, 114–115; papal visit to Poland, 146–150; partial success of the Hungarian and Czechoslovak uprisings, 104; public debate following Stalin's death, 72–79; public opinion on Western broadcasts, 46–54; radio as impetus for protest, 128–129; rebel radio stations during the Hungarian Uprising, 106–108; Western media's contribution to public protest, 89. *See also* Gdansk uprising; Hungarian uprising; Prague Spring
publicists, 74
Pyka, Tadeusz, 159–160

quality of programming: BIB criticism of Russian radio, 30; French international radio, 17–18; Vatican Radio, 32
radio: destabilization of the Eastern Bloc, 217; demonstration in East Germany, 203–204; East German youth radio, 206–207; Gdansk strikers' appropriation of, 152–154; Gdansk strikers' demands, 164; international coverage of the Gdansk agreement, 169; KOR East-West-East communications loop, 144–145; multiple functions during conflict, 127–129; papal visit to Poland, 176(n26); Poland's entente, 163; political leadership during the Prague Spring, 123–126; representation stations, 11–20; RFI, 16–18. *See also specific stations*
Radio Berlin International, 18–19
Radio Budapest (Hungary), 110
Radio Canada International (RCI): gauging audience reception to Western broadcasts, 48
Radio France Internationale (RFI), 16–18; audiences between 1982 and 1989, 52(table); credibility in the East, 56–57; immigrants as Western broadcasters, 36; post-Solidarity Polish revival, 173
Radio Free Baranya (Hungary), 129
Radio Free Europe (RFE), 23–26, 175(nn10-11); audience opinion polls, 50–54; audiences between 1982 and 1989, 52(table); credibility in the East, 55–56; death of the Hungarian uprising, 112; Eastern media attacks on, 49; Easterners' familiarity with broadcasters, 55; exclusion from the papal visit to Poland, 149–150; Hungarian uprising, 94–99; importance to resistance, 3; internecine strife in Czechoslovakia, 77–78; Khrushchev Report on Stalin's crimes, 73–74; KOR East-West-East communications loop, 145–146; nationalization, 175(n9); Nixon's visit to Warsaw, 46; papal

visit to Poland, 176(n26); Poland's cessation of signal jamming, 45; role in ending the Cold War, 233–235; Soviet invasion of Budapest, 133(n18); Western controversy, 25–26
Radio Free Europe/Radio Liberty, 28–31, 34
Radio Glasnost, 193–194
Radio Gyor (Hungary), 108, 110, 127
Radio in the American Sector (RIAS), 21–23, 38(n34); amplifying nonviolent protest, 192; East German uprising, 89–93, 153; Hungarian and Czechoslovakian resistance, 130–132; public protest in East Berlin and Budapest, 87–88; Radio Free Europe, 23; role in ending the Cold War, 233–235; television, 220(n36), 221(n63)
Radio Kossuth (Hungary), 104–105, 107, 111–112
Radio Liberty (RL), 26–28; audience opinion polls, 50–54; credibility in the East, 55–56; Eastern dissidents' criticism of, 57; Eastern media attacks on, 49; jamming the signal, 41–42, 45; philosophical conflict with the State Department, 33; role in ending the Cold War, 233–235
Radio Moscow, 43
Radio Petofi (Hungary), 106–107, 110–111
Radio Prague, 114–115
Radio Vatican, 31–32, 46, 52(table)
Radio Vltava, 115
Rajk, Laslo, 83
Ramparts Magazine, 28
Reagan, Ronald, 1, 13–14
real socialism, 4, 208, 229
Reflections on Progress, Peaceful Coexistence, and Intellectual Freedom (Sakharov), 28
refugees. *See* immigrants
Reich, Jens, 200, 221(n63)
religion and churches: Catholic Church moderating the Gdansk strike negotiations, 159–160; East German churches' call for disarmament, 188–189; East German churches' call for public debate, 192–193;
East German nonviolent protest against the regime, 203–204; internal conflict over exodus from East Germany, 200–201; Islamist resistance, 241–242; papal visit to Poland, 146–150, 175(nn18,20), 176(n24); Polish democratic opposition, 146; political semi-autonomy of East German churches, 186–188. *See also* John-Paul II
religious radio stations, 10–11; Vatican Radio, 31–32, 46, 52(table)
representation radio stations, 10–20; BBC, 14–16; Deutsche Welle and Deutschlandfunk, 18–20; political pressure against, 43; Poste Colonial radio, 37(n16); Radio France Internationale, 16–18; Voice of America, 11–14
resistance: communication-resistance relation as barometer of political stability, 226–227; factors in the fall of the Soviet Union, 1–2; internal and individual battle against totalitarianism, 69–72; labor protests in East Germany, 79–82; moving from dissidence to resistance, 2; through literary journals and discussion circles, 74–76. *See also* protest; nonviolent action, methods of
revisionists, 74
Robotnik journal, 146
Rollback policy, 23–24
Romania: cessation of signal jamming, 45; destabilization of the Eastern Bloc, 217; RFI revival, 18; weekly audience ratings of Western radio, 51(table)
roneo, 144
Roosevelt, Franklin, 11–12
Sakharov, Andrei, 28
samizdat technique, 28, 39(n48), 144, 189, 217, 228
Scandinavia, 174(n2)
Schabowski, Günther, 205, 209–211
Scharnowski, Ernst, 90–92
Schnitzler, Karl von, 182
Schönherr, Albrecht, 186
Schorlemmer, Friedrich, 192
Schreiber, Thomas, 131–132, 168

Schwarze, Werner, 183
Schwarzer Kanal (television program), 182, 207
science: Eastern monitoring of Western radio, 61–62
scotomization of the past, 63
secrecy of listening, 54–55
security, 38(n37); secure tactical digital communications by dissidents, 256–257
Selbmann, Fritz, 85
self-reporting by Egyptian activists, 250–251
Semelin, Jacques, 234–237, 239–240
Shahbender, Ghada, 251–252
Shakespeare, Frank, 31
Shanor, Donald, 58–59
Sherwood, Robert, 11–12
shipbuilders. *See* Gdansk uprising
Sigl, Miroslav, 120
silence: of Eastern audiences, 32–36; as form of resistance, 70–71
Sipos, Gyula, 59
skilled labor: migration from East Germany, 198
Slonimski, Antoni, 144
small stabilization, 56
Smolar, Aleksander, 145, 175(n12)
Smolar, Eugenius, 145, 175(n12)
social compliance, 69
Social Democratic Party (SDP; East Germany), 199
social networking, Egyptian activists' use of, 250–252
socialism, GDR's intellectuals advocating, 188
Solidarity (Poland), 141, 161–163, 171, 178(n72)
Soltan, Neda Agha, 253
Solzhenitsyn, Aleksandr, 2, 229
Souslov, Mikhail, 107
South Africa, 241, 243–244
South Korea, 218(n2)
sovereignty as political justification for jamming signals, 42–43
Soviet Union: BIB criticism of Russian radio, 30; control of Czechoslovakian radio during the Prague Spring, 120–121; controlling the number of radio receivers, 47; de-Stalinization policy, 72–73; East German uprising, 93; external pressure for East German liberalization, 204; factors in the fall of, 1–2; Hungarian uprising, 111–113, 133(n18); political pressure against Western radio, 43; potential intervention in Gdansk, 164–165; Prague Spring, 113–114; radio support of public protests in Central Europe, 127–128; reform and liberalization under Gorbachev, 180; response to public demands for reform, 77–78; RFE programming during the Hungarian uprising, 95–98; rise of Poland's Solidarity movement, 172; signal jamming as indicator of East-West tensions, 44–45; suppressing individual communication during the Hungarian and Czechoslovakian resistance, 127–129; VOA revival, 12; weekly audience ratings of Western radio, 51(table). *See also* Gdansk uprising; Hungarian uprising; Prague Spring
The Spectator, 15
speech movement, Gdansk strike as, 152–156
spill-over coverage, 10
Stalin, Joseph: death of, 3; defining totalitarianism under, 5; Khrushchev Report on the crimes of, 73; power vacuum following the death of, 72–73
Ständige Ausreisen (permanent exit permit), 211–212
"Star Wars" program, 1, 9
Stasi (East German secret police), 182–183, 189, 200, 203, 215, 219(n28), 222(n68)
The Strategy of Truth (Dizard), 34
Streletz, Fritz, 215
strikes: East Berlin, 80–93; other strikes throughout Germany, 93; Hungary, 106, 108, 112; Gdansk, 139–142, 152–156, 161–163; Baninka miners' strike, 127–128; "flash strikes," 122, 131. *See also* trade unions and labor organizing
substitution radio stations, 10–11, 20–31; political pressure against, 43;

Radio Free Europe, 23–26; Radio Free Europe/Radio Liberty, 28–31; Radio in American Sector, 21–23; Radio Liberty, 26–28
Suez Canal, 15, 97–98
surveillance, 256–257
Svoboda, 115–116, 125
Swiatio, Jósef, 25
symbolic struggle, Czechoslovak resistance as, 103–104
symbols: de-semiotization of public places, 84–85
Szabad Nep journal, 109
Szabo, Gyorgy, 107
Szczecin, Poland, 158, 162, 166, 176(31)
Szpotanski, Janusz, 2
Tagesthemen (news program), 196–197, 213
tamizdat, 39(n48). *See also* samizdat technique
Tatu, Michel, 168
telephone communications: Egyptian activists' use of mobile phones, 251–252; Gdansk strikers' demands for restoration, 157, 164, 168; penetration of Western media into East Germany, 191–192
television, 178(n72); Burma's DVB broadcasts, 245–246; cutting the fence on the Austro-Hungarian border, 195–198; East German youth radio, 206–207; fall of the Berlin Wall, 213–215; Gdansk coverage, 162, 171; improving media coverage after the Hungarian and Czechoslovakian uprisings, 140–141; increasing availability of, 174(n2); international media coverage of the Gdansk conflict, 167–170; international pressure in support of the Gdansk strikers, 157–161; limited range of, 10; opening of East German media, 205–208; papal visit to Poland, 147, 149–150; public mobilization for East German exodus, 200; RIAS 220(n36), 221(n63); role in the Prague Spring uprising, 118–121; West Germany's "television bridge" to the GDR, 181–185; Westernization of Polish television, 173

Tézenas du Montcel, Henri, 62
TF1 (French television channel), 167–169
"Theses on hope and despair" (Kolakowski), 142
Thibaut, Paul, 61–62
Tigrid, Pavel, 123–124
Tildy, Zoltan, 107–108
totalitarian regimes: defining Stalinism, 5; moving from dissidence to resistance, 2. *See also* communism; *specific countries*
totalitarianism, internal battle of, 69–70
trade unions, 91, 109, 145–146, 152, 162–171. *See also* labor organizing, strikes
transistor set, invention of, 127–129
transnational flows, analysis of, 226–227
Truman, Harry, 12, 24
Truth is our Weapon (Barret), 34
Twitter, 257
Ulbricht, Walter, 79–80, 183
underground telegraph, Western media as, 58–59
UNESCO, 44
United States: US television in the GDR, 184; countering radio jamming, 64(n16); economic and political strategies against the USSR, 9; external pressure for East German liberalization, 204; popular musicians' tours, 61; Radio in American Sector, 21–23; RFE role in the Hungarian uprising, 94–95; RFE's CIA ties, 29; Western controversy over RFE, 25–26. *See also* Radio Liberty; Voice of America; West-East communications
Universal Declaration of Human Rights, 43
Urban, Jerzy, 49–50, 173
U.S. Information Agency (USIA), 12, 39(n53)
USSR. *See* Soviet Union
Vatican Radio, 31–32, 46, 52(table)
veracity of Western news, 58–59
video footage: Burma's DVB broadcasts, 247, 2346; Egyptian activists, 249–252; increasing role in East German opposition, 193–194;

Iran's 2009 popular protests, 252–253; jihadi websites, 245; training East German dissidents, 249
Voice of America (VOA), 11–14; audience opinion polls, 50–53; audiences between 1982 and 1989, 52(table); BIB and, 39(n53); credibility in the East, 55; French hosting of, 37(n6); gauging audience response, 49; importance to resistance, 3; Khrushchev Report on Stalin's crimes, 73–74; papal visit to Poland, 149–150; political pressure against, 43; popular music programming, 61; signal jamming as indicator of East-West tensions, 44–45; US response to jamming, 64(n16)
von Schnitzler, Karl, 200–201, 207
von Weiszächer, Richard, 204

Wagner, Herald, 200
Wajda, Andrzej, 162
Walentynowicz, Anna, 153–154, 170
Walesa, Lech, 152–154, 160–161, 165–167, 170, 178(n72)
Walton, Douglas, 237–239
Washington Post, 29
website use, 245
Wende (change of direction), 205–208
West Germany: Deutsche Welle and Deutschlandfunk, 18–20; East Germany's ongoing tension between openness and closure, 190–194; external pressure for East German liberalization, 204; gauging audience reception to Western broadcasts, 48; international coverage of the Gdansk agreement, 168; mass exodus from East Germany to, 208–211; papal visit to Poland, 149–150; Radio Free Europe/Radio Liberty, 28–31; Radio Liberty, 26–28; reunification with the GDR, 181, 215–216; RIAS, 21–23. *See also* Radio Free Europe; Radio in the American Sector
West-East communications: appeals for help during the Hungarian uprising, 131–132; audience rating metrics, 46–54; Communist Party as audience, 53–54; covering public protest in East Berlin and Budapest, 89–93; diplomatic and technological pressure against, 42–45; international pressure in support of the Gdansk strikers, 157–161; language sections and immigrant populations, 40(n61); number of hours of broadcasting per week, 36(table); official and popular reception of, 54–59; Radio Glasnost, 193–194; Radio Liberty, 26–28; radio station types, 10–11; silence of radio audiences, 32–36; West German publications in East Germany, 190–192; West Germany's "television bridge" to the GDR, 181–185; Western assumptions about Eastern views of, 41–42; Western economic and political strategies, 9–10; Western response to signal jamming, 45. *See also* BBC Radio; Radio Free Europe; Radio Liberty; Voice of America
West-East-West communications: destabilization of the Eastern Bloc, 217; development during the Gdansk uprising, 141–142
Western powers: aid to Eastern resistance, 170–174; appeals for help during the Hungarian uprising, 131–132; complicity with East German reform, 199–200; lack of support in the East German uprising of 1953, 93; television broadcasts, 10
Wilson, Woodrow, 43
Wojtyla, Karol. *See* John-Paul II
Wolf, Christa, 188, 191, 199, 208, 219(n26)
Wolf, Marcus, 233–234
Women for Peace, 189
word of mouth, spreading news by, 58–59
World Trade Organization (WTO) demonstrations, 252
Writers Congress (Czechoslovakia), 75
Wyszynski, Stefan, 148
Yiddish language, 17
young people and youth movements: East German churches, 187; East German entertainment media, 206;

East German nonviolent action, 222(n73); GDR's antennae hunt, 183; Hungary's Petofi Circle, 75; smuggling books and journals out of Poland, 143

Zimmermann, Peter, 202
the zone, 91, 101(n42). *See also* Radio in the American Sector
Zycie Warszawy newspaper, 165